FITTEST OF THE FIT

FITTEST
OF THE FIT

Health and Morale in the Royal Navy, 1939–1945

KEVIN BROWN

Seaforth
PUBLISHING

Copyright © Kevin Brown 2019

First published in Great Britain in 2019 by
Seaforth Publishing,
A division of Pen & Sword Books Ltd,
47 Church Street,
Barnsley S70 2AS

www.seaforthpublishing.com
British Library Cataloguing in Publication Data
A catalogue record for this book is available from the British Library

ISBN 978 1 5267 3427 3 (HARDBACK)
ISBN 978 1 5267 3428 0 (EPUB)
ISBN 978 1 5267 3429 7 (KINDLE)

All rights reserved. No part of this publication may be reproduced or transmitted in any form or by any means, electronic or mechanical, including photocopying, recording, or any information storage and retrieval system, without prior permission in writing of both the copyright owner and the above publisher.

The right of Kevin Brown to be identified as the author of this work has been asserted by him in accordance with the Copyright, Designs and Patents Act 1988.

Pen & Sword Books Limited incorporates the imprints of Atlas, Archaeology, Aviation, Discovery, Family History, Fiction, History, Maritime, Military, Military Classics, Politics, Select, Transport, True Crime, Air World, Frontline Publishing, Leo Cooper, Remember When, Seaforth Publishing, The Praetorian Press, Wharncliffe Local History, Wharncliffe Transport, Wharncliffe True Crime and White Owl

Typeset by Mac Style
Printed and bound in Great Britain by TJ International Ltd, Padstow

Contents

List of Illustrations vi
Preface ix

One   Our Men: Finding the Fittest   1
Two   In Which They Healed   19
Three   Hospitals Under Fire   46
Four   Our Ships at Sea   68
Five   Sea-Room for Change   86
Six   It's in the Air   102
Seven   The Waves Above   119
Eight   Absent Friends: Battle Fatigue   136
Nine   Ourselves: Rest and Recreation   156
Ten   Neither Wives nor Sweethearts   182
Eleven   A Bloody War   196
Twelve   Went the Day Well?   214

Appendices 235
Notes 239
Bibliography 265
Index 271

List of Illustrations

Only the fittest of recruits were selected by the Navy when they were examined at recruitment centres, 1939. (*Camden Local Studies and Archives Centre*)
Surgeon Lieutenant Peter McCrae RNVR. (*Imperial College Healthcare NHS Trust Archives*)
Inoculating men against typhoid. (© IWM A 1218)
For newly-qualified doctors in the Naval Medical Services keeping their links with their medical schools was important since doctors and nurses. (*Artist, Anna Zinkeissen, Imperial College Healthcare NHS Trust Archives*)
Only the toughest of naval surgeons were selected for commando duties. (*TNA, INF3-282*)
Sick bay on HMS *Rodney*, October 1940. (© *IWM, A 1217*)
Sick berth attendants receiving basic instruction from Sisters of Queen Alexandra's Royal Naval Nursing Services. (*J Coulter*)
Occupational therapy for convalescents. (© *IWM, A 11530*)
Rehabilitation of unreliable seamen at HMS *Standard*. (*J Coulter*)
Casualty being received on *Maine*. (*J Coulter*)
Hospital ship ward on *Maine*. (*J Coulter*)
Testing blood on *Maine*. (© *IWM, A 20349*)
Casualties from Courseulles on Hospital Tank Landing Ship *LST 428*. (© *IWM, A 25093*)
All daily life took place on the general mess decks of *Shropshire*, 1942. (© *IWM, A 7598*)
American-style cafeteria messing was introduced on *Dasher*, 1942. (© *IWM, A 13686*)
A lookout on an Arctic Convoy preparing to go on watch on *Sheffield*, December 1941. (© *IWM, A 6896*)

LIST OF ILLUSTRATIONS

Princess Marina, Duchess of Kent, inspecting the Navy Blood Transfusion Service. (*F Henley*)

Penicillin was manufactured in reused gin bottles at the Royal Naval Medical School, Clevedon. (© *IWM, A 25174*)

A naval medical officer spraying DDT for malaria control, Colombo, 1944. (© *IWM, A 28177*)

Recruits were screened with mass radiography for tuberculosis at the Royal Naval Barracks, Chatham 1940. (© *IWM, A 2008*)

Many Fleet Air Arm pilots passed out during high-altitude testing. (© *IWM, A 18253*)

A game of crib on the submarine *Seraph* in November 1944. (© *IWM, A 26391*)

Sunray treatment for light-deprived submariners at depot ship, HMS *Forth*. (© *IWM, A 7778*)

Vaulting on the deck of *Revenge*. (© *IWM, A 1506*)

Evelyn Laye, chairman of ENSA Royal Naval Section.

Davis Apparatus for the rescue of men from submarines. (© *IWM, A 13882*)

Holborn Warships Week, March 1942. (*Camden Local Studies and Archives*)

Raising money for the Overseas League, Empire Day, 1941

Argonaut on Christmas Day 1942. (*F Henley*)

Wearing civilian clothing was considered good for morale but was rarely possible. (© *IWM, A 25868*)

A pint of beer kept up the seaman's spirits and united Allied navies against the Axis. (*TNA, INF3/322*)

The popular wholesome innocent image of the seaman made him irresistible and easy prey to the allurement of feminine wiles. (*TNA, INF 13/217*)

Sailors were warned of the threat to their health and wellbeing from both 'good time girls' and prostitutes. (*National Library of Medicine, USA*)

To Absent Friends

But soon they joke, easy and warm,
As men will who have died once
Yet somehow were able to find their way –
Muttering this was not included in their pay.
(Alan Ross, 'Survivors')

Preface

The inspiration for all book projects comes at the end of a journey of discovery, and marks the beginning of another more intensive journey into the past. This one had its origins on a cold, battleship-grey December day some ten years ago on a visit to the Royal Navy Submarine Museum at Gosport. At the end of a tour of the submarine *Alliance*, built in the later days of the Second World War, the excellent and entertaining volunteer guide, an ex-submariner with post-war experience, asked a rhetorical question about what level of medical care the crew had enjoyed. The answer was very little other than minimal training in first aid for the boatswain at nearby Haslar Hospital. That throwaway remark raised questions in my mind about the whole issue of medical care at sea in a confined environment, far from the medical facilities taken for granted on land. The result was *Poxed and Scurvied*, a survey of the history of sickness and health at sea over many centuries. Naval medicine in the Second World War could only be a small part of that overall story, and submarine medicine, the topic that inspired the book, even less. The Second World War experience, though, seemed to me to be vital for understanding the modern development of healthcare in the Royal Navy.

A truly memorable evening when I was the after-dinner speaker at a mess dinner in 2015 for naval doctors in training at all grades held at the Institute of Naval Medicine in Gosport reinforced my desire to study further naval health and fitness in the Second World War. Many of the enthusiastic young doctors I spoke to in the mess during that evening of naval tradition, carousing and conviviality were interested in the subject of my next book and had a keen interest in the history of their own service. I was warned not to write about the health of 'pongos' again, after being forgiven for having done so in the past, and to confine myself to health at sea as it seemed I understood the naval doctors, which was why they liked me! Medicine in the Second World War was a subject they seemed interested in knowing more about. They were also remarkably open to a historian rather than a naval doctor researching and writing about their service. This was a contrast to the wartime situation when the eminent naval historian Arthur J Marder from Harvard, already an acknowledged authority on the Royal Navy in the approach to the Great War, was not only turned down on medical grounds for service in the Royal Navy in 1944, just as he had been rejected for service in the United States Navy, but was also considered unsuitable for work in the Historical Section of the Admiralty as this 'requires naval experience and technical knowledge which civilian historians unfortunately do not possess'.[1] While not comparing myself at all to Marder, I welcome the more open approach of today's Royal Navy to external expertise.

The naval doctors were not the only ones to encourage me to work on naval health in the Second World War. After I gave a talk on the story of health at sea to a group of senior citizens at an Open Age meeting at Chelsea Football Club, the audience were keen on the subject and urged me to write about it for my next book. Some of the oldest of them had seen naval service in the war so it was of personal relevance to some of them. How could I resist these influences leading me to my next book? It was indeed a subject calling me to examine it in more depth.

Although it has featured in accounts of wartime naval experience as a background issue, the subject of wartime naval health has not been treated at length to any great extent since the publication of Jack Coulter's two volumes on the subject in the official medical history of the Second World War published in 1954 and 1956. As a serving naval medical officer during the war, Coulter was able to bring a wealth of personal experience to his subject and indeed used his own personal records, presented anonymously, in some of the liveliest parts of his narrative. However, he was constrained by being employed by the Royal Navy to write a book that toed the official line. He was not even allowed to write about the important subject of submarine medicine which was still considered to be top secret in the Cold War. More recent studies of military medicine in the Second World War have concentrated on the army side rather than the naval. It is perhaps

PREFACE

timely for the whole subject of keeping the wartime navy healthy and fit to fight to be revisited.

Much of the research has involved solitary delving into archives and libraries, immersing myself in the contemporary record and becoming imaginatively involved in the wartime atmosphere therein invoked. However, the wartime experience was a sociable and communal one and I wish to thank many people for their help, interest and support. Sadly there are few people left now with memories of naval service in the Second World War. I wish to remember in particular Wren Suzanne Willson, Surgeon Lieutenant Felix Eastcott RNVR, and my father's friend and neighbour Joe who served on the Arctic Convoys. I wish to thank again the staff of the archives and libraries I visited in the course of my research which has extended over many years, especially those at The National Archives and the Imperial War Museum. I also wish to express my great thanks to Tudor Allen, Archivist, Camden Local Studies and Archives Centre; Timothy Hall for showing me around the then-abandoned Haslar Royal Naval Hospital; Bob Marchant of the museum at Queen Victoria Hospital East Grinstead; David Hunt for drawing to my attention his father Bernard's experiences as a Second World War naval medical officer; and Robert Gardiner and his colleagues at Seaforth. I also salute the Royal Navy medical and nursing staff, then and now, with that old toast 'To a Bloody War and a Sickly Season!' or perhaps, more appropriately, it should be to 'Absent Friends'.

London
Armistice Day, Sunday, 11 November 2018

Chapter One
Our Men: Finding the Fittest

It should have been easy to get the fittest and healthiest new recruits for the Royal Navy during the Second World War. The general reputation of the British sailor was then at the peak of its popularity. Naval recruitment posters in the 1930s showed handsome, healthy sun-tanned men in exotic locations and urged young men to join the navy to see the world. Films portrayed a positive image of the navy throughout the war and the sailor was depicted as wholesome and resourceful. He was the hero of such popular films as *In Which We Serve*[1] and *We Dive at Dawn*.[2] Even on land, the sailor remained the man of action. In *Went the Day Well?* a sailor home on leave for his wedding, played by Frank Lawton – the real-life husband of the Navy's sweetheart and director of entertainments, Evelyn Laye – saves an almost idyllic English village from a German invasion, giving leadership to patriotic middle-aged villagers and plucky land girls.[3] It was a truism that whatever else might happen, Britain would always have the navy, the most dependable of the armed forces for an island.

The navy indeed prided itself on the superior quality of its recruits 'which was until recently self-selected by expressing a Naval preference at recruitment'.[4] Rather contemptuous of the reliance of the army on conscription for maintaining manpower levels in wartime, the Admiralty commented in 1939 that 'the Navy got through the 1914–18 war without any recourse to conscription entries and probably could do the same in the present war, but in deference to the Government plan for an orderly method of utilizing the manpower of the country was willing to adopt the conscription system'. Even so, it was to consider that 'there is however no reason why, provided that a controlled system of voluntary entry is maintained, the Admiralty could not equally find part of its manpower requirements from volunteers'.[5] The 1939 National Services Act which conscripted men between the ages of 18 and 41 still allowed for a degree of choice by allowing men who were called up to express a preference for the navy or Royal Air Force. The RAF perhaps had the more glamorous and daring image, but the Royal Navy, with its reputation for comradeship and looking after the welfare of its men, was also seen as more attractive than army service and to have its own allure: 'near the coast, the naval uniform is taken for granted, but in an inland pub a sailor has more glamour than the RAF'. At the same time that there was a popular perception that 'everyone from the admiral downwards shares the danger' and adventure at sea, and life afloat was cosier where 'every man has his health and food assured, and is in a settled place'.[6] With so many willing recruits, the navy could choose the best. However, in the early days of the war there were perhaps more men opting for naval service that it could handle. In April 1940, it had the capacity to comfortably cope with about 6,000 new recruits a month, but there were already 16,000 who had passed their medical examinations and another 80,000 waiting for their medicals. Whereas the army had 150 centres for medical examination and the RAF had 60, the navy only had 50.[7]

While the navy had no problems in recruiting men, there remained the problem of selecting the most suitable for sea service. At the recruiting centres, the medical challenge was to determine 'a candidate's likelihood to continue efficient and serviceable in any climate, and under all conditions of service, for a period of not less than twelve years' for regular continuous-service sailors.[8] Such men were to be nurtured as the backbone of the wartime and post-war navy. It was equally important that money and time should not be wasted on training men at risk of becoming unfit for long-term service. Conscript ratings for 'hostilities only' service were not expected to be up to equally high standards, though medical standards for all seamen were higher than those expected by the army or for the ground trades of the RAF.

Before the war, the navy had run its own network of recruiting outstations. The initial decision on the healthiness and suitability of a recruit was made by a naval recruiter who would check height and chest measurements and test the candidate for visual acuity, colour vision, hearing and the condition of his teeth. Questions were also asked about any previous injuries or illnesses that might affect his future performance. This initial health screening ensured the early rejection of any candidates suffering from any obvious defects. The final examination was made by a qualified medical man at the headquarter recruiting stations in London, Birmingham, Bristol, Derby, Glasgow, Liverpool, Manchester, Newcastle and Southampton.[9] All changed on the outbreak of war and with the introduction of conscription. Combined recruitment centres were opened, staffed by representatives of all three services and the Ministry of Labour. Doctors examining recruits were now employed by the Ministry of Labour, not the Royal Navy, although the final medical examinations remained the responsibility of naval surgeons at the naval headquarters recruiting stations.[10] Sometimes the final medical examinations seemed perfunctory. John Somers' experience as a recruit was typical of many:

> A long line of men would file past the doctor, usually seated. A bright light strapped to his forehead, or a torch in his hand. Your turn came. 'Drop 'em'. ie drop your trousers. Down they went. He shines his light on your privates. 'OK!' Takes knackers in the other hand. 'Cough', he says. They bounce. 'You're OK. Next'. You pull up your trousers. You have passed.[11]

Hugh Philip, a surgeon-lieutenant with the Royal Naval Volunteer Reserve (RNVR), was favourably impressed with the recruits he examined while waiting for his own call-up and gratified that 'from a medical point of view it was possible to select only those who were in a state of physical perfection'.[12] The high standards of fitness laid down for men enlisting for continuous and special service laid down in the 1930s were maintained during the war and were higher than those for hostilities-only recruits. The Robinson Committee on Visual Standards had made suggestions in 1932 for new visual standards that were introduced in 1938.[13] Only artificers, sick berth attendants, writers, stewards, cooks and ratings working in the supply branches were allowed to wear glasses. Seamen and stokers required good distant and colour vision. Until July 1941, naval hostilities-only recruits were not tested or graded for colour vision until they reported at a Naval Final Entry Establishment, but so many men then had to be discharged as unfit when found to be colour blind that testing for the condition was introduced. Medical and visual standards were further relaxed in 1943 for candidates for hostilities-only entry. Now 10 per cent of seamen would be accepted with a minimum of visual standard IV for distance vision and grade C colour vision. Stokers required a greater acuity of vision, though now 20 per cent were to be admitted with a minimum vision of standard III and grade C. The visual requirements for telegraphists and Royal Marines were also reduced.[14] Possible recruits were also reminded that a stammer was not necessarily a disqualification for service. In the script treatment for a proposed recruitment film, in a scene set at a recruiting centre the youths waiting interview are nervous: 'Norman is particularly anxious about his stammer. Martyn suggests that when stuck he should whistle. Peter adds that if he does that they are bound to give him a job piping Admirals aboard.'[15]

Dental health was considered important because most naval dentists were employed in shore establishments or on larger ships. While boys were rejected for continuous service if they had five or more missing or irreplaceable teeth, hostilities-only men were permitted to have up to ten missing teeth and were 'not rejected for any dental deficiency or condition capable of being remedied, including a gratuitous supply of dentures'.[16] If dental standards had not been lowered, the poor state of the nation's teeth could have had serious effects on recruitment.

Other conditions which might have caused problems at sea, such as hernias, tuberculous glands, hernias, kidney disease, epilepsy, chronic bronchitis, severe asthma and distortions of the spine, meant instant rejection for the unlucky candidate, though the absence of one testicle, flat feet and knock knees did not mean immediate disqualification from service.[17] All men were also questioned about the state of their mental and nervous health from June 1940, and men with a history of mental instability were rejected. Although medical standards for recruitment were reduced during the war, it was still considered important that certain minimum standards must not be relaxed. In 1943, when special training to bring Grade II recruits up to standard was being considered, it was stressed that no Grade II men should be accepted above the age of 35 nor men who had been rated at standard C in the psychological tests administered at the recruiting stage, since any defects in such recruits would be irremediable. It was also stressed that recruits suffering from varicose veins, skin diseases, obesity and nervous or mental instability should be rejected because 'these disabilities would be a bar to service in the Tropics'.[18] There was concern that, with the relaxation of medical standards, 'a large percentage of men in the lower medical categories were breaking down in conditions of stress, mental or climatic'.[19]

Medical standards were used as the benchmark in the selection of men to the different branches of the service. Signalmen and airman in the Fleet Air Arm obviously needed the highest standards of vision, seamen, stokers and marines still needed good eyesight but at a slightly lower level, while coders might even be selected because their eyesight was weaker and they were less suited for other duties.[20] If a man's eyesight deteriorated, he would be transferred to a role such as submarine detector or air mechanic where good eyesight was less important. If this was not an option for a man who was not considered to have the necessary educational background for such roles, there remained the option of a shore-based job in the boom defence service.[21] The Royal Navy was unwilling to lose any skilled and experienced men.

High standards of hearing were also expected of signalmen, telegraphists, airmen, marines and seamen. However, it was only at the end of 1942 that attention was paid to testing the aural ability of submarine detectors, although certain diseases of the ear already disqualified some candidates for the role. Surgeon Lieutenant Commander Ransome-Wallis investigated the possibility of introducing a special testing procedure using an audiometer to test men's reactions to changes of pitch. Not surprisingly, men with a musical ability and background were found to find it easier to detect changes of pitch. Ransome-Wallis' 'pure tone' tests were used to establish aural standards for detectors and identify men likely to prove themselves to be either good or bad operators since 'aural intelligence plays probably the greatest part in the success or otherwise of an operator'.[22]

The large number of men volunteering for naval service and the stringent medical requirements meant that until 1942 when an expansion programme began only about a third of recruits were accepted. In the first year of the war, 15,386 men from the London area volunteered for naval service, but only 5,132 were accepted; 19.6 per cent had been rejected after the initial medical examination and 24.2 per cent on educational and personality grounds, with a further 19.4 per cent rejected after the final medical examination. In 1941, just over a third of men choosing the Royal Navy were accepted, but in 1942, when new ships laid down before and at the beginning of the war were coming into service, three-quarters of recruits were accepted, anyone who came up to minimum standard.[23] Throughout the war, the main causes of rejection of recruits on medical grounds were defective vision and physical deformity, though dental defects were also a major problem.[24]

With the manning crisis becoming more acute from 1942, the Admiralty had no choice but to accept 'Medical Grade II' recruits and had to consider suitable remedial action to get these men up to the required levels of physical fitness for service at sea. HMS *Bristol*, housed in the former Mullers Orphanage in Bristol, offered remedial physical training to 'recruits from every walk of life, the well-educated, intelligent, the dullard, the professional man, the small trader, the underdeveloped child of 18 years weighing 200 lbs, the policeman with flat feet, the banker with kyphosis'.[25] They were given eight weeks to build up their physique and improve their posture under the guidance of trained PT instructors who instilled them with a competitive spirit lacking in them in civilian life. Each week 100 new recruits arrived for their remedial training and rehabilitation. They were subjected to such agility exercises as boxing, wrestling, pole-vaulting and dribbling with a football, followed by strengthening exercises with wall bars, beams, rope-climbing, leg-swinging and rope-carrying. Marching, running, jumping, cross-country running, obstacle courses and swimming made up their daily activities. They benefitted from a good diet and were forced to adopt a good posture.[26] It was an intensive course, but was not successful for all the young men who passed through its rigours. However, even for those who had failed the training there was still a role in the Royal Navy:

> Men found at the end of the *Bristol* course to be unfit for any form of service at sea and who are below the selection grading required for the Fleet Air Arm and other shore maintenance branches will, if possible, be utilised as seamen and stokers in the patrol service to man the harbour launches which are at present manned by men fit for sea, and as cooks and stewards in Naval Air Stations.[27]

By this stage in the war, even the Royal Navy could not be too choosy, although the last men were sent to *Bristol* for training in October 1943 and medical standards were raised again as soon as possible. Except for that period when demand for recruits to man the new ships of the expanding wartime navy became acute, the Royal Navy justly could claim that it could afford to choose the physically-fittest candidates from those conscripts for whom the navy was their chosen service.

It was perhaps easier for the Naval Recruiter and medical examiner to identify physical disabilities than it was to detect psychological or psychiatric barriers to naval efficiency. The naval recruitment officers at the Combined Recruiting Centres tended to be recalled chief and petty officers who were out of touch with the demands of the modern navy and received little specific training to help them identify suitable recruits. Within a very short period of time, they were expected to assess the moral and intellectual quality of the candidate, find out if he were willing to be inoculated and allocate him to a suitable branch of the service if they decided to accept him. Not surprisingly, mistakes were made that 'a substantial number of men gain entry to the R[oyal] N[avy], who either because of intellectual deficiencies or temperamental instability are incapable of becoming efficient in any form of naval service at present available'.[28] There were repeated complaints about 'the quality of ratings supplied'.[29]

Some of these inferior new ratings were found to lack intelligence, suffer from colour blindness, be too old for training and to show 'an unnecessary ignorance about naval service'. Naval Recruiters were inconsistent in how they assessed the educational level of candidates, often relying too much on simple spelling tests even though their own literacy levels were questionable:

> Some N[aval] R[ecruiter]s clearly placed more reliance upon a candidate's spelling of such words as 'Egypt' and 'necessary' than upon his school or work record. In some cases, failure to spell the only word led to instant rejection. But in one interview a young man who was unable to remember what standard he reached at school and failed dismally to spell 'theatre and bicycle' was 'accepted' for the R[oyal] M[arines] and advised to learn hard words in the newspaper pending his call-up.

Another young man unable to spell 'Egypt' was told that 'your educational standard makes you illegible for the navy'.[30] John Davies, a candidate with an honours degree in English from the University of London was surprised to have his higher education casually and ignorantly dismissed with the gruff comment 'never mind about that. Have you got the School Leaving Certificate?' from an interviewer ignorant of the requirements of university matriculation.[31]

There were also concerns that some of these Naval Recruiters 'did not feel themselves disbarred from taking decisions on purely medical issues'. Two men who had passed their medical examinations by qualified doctors on medical boards and rated Grade I were both rejected because one of them had a history of tuberculosis and the other had once had a mastoid operation. A third candidate was rejected simply on the grounds that 'he looked pale and we must reject some'.[32] Such arrogant and ill-informed decision-making was bound to affect the quality of recruits at a time when men were needed to slot into their allocated roles with little fuss. 'Inefficiency, discontent and inconvenience' were the result.

By 1941 it was recognised that qualified psychologists had a part to play in identifying as early as possible those recruits whose mental disabilities and psychological inadequacies made them unsuitable for naval service. The post of Senior Psychologist to the Royal Navy was established with eight industrial psychologists working for him, later increased to thirteen when demand for their services increased.[33] Coming from industrial backgrounds, they were expected to be 'fully appreciative of the voluntary principle in the recruitment of men for the service' and they were trusted to 'make no attempt to force a man into uncongenial employment'. These specialists were in regular contact with their army and RAF counterparts and prided themselves that 'their relevant experience has lain mainly in the careful selection of young men for technical occupations, and not at all in the use of psycho-analytical techniques'.[34]

Although it was impossible for all new entrants to be examined by such a small number of officers, as the war went on it was becoming obvious that there was a great need for preliminary screening to indicate which men might benefit from a full psychiatric interview. Such screening would even be useful at the most basic level of recruitment since 'in order to judge whether or not John Jones is fit for naval service, the Naval Recruiter must be reasonably well acquainted not only with naval service but also with John Jones'.[35]

It was thought that perhaps the most suitable people to carry out this preliminary work would be sensitive, sympathetic and intelligent women who could interview candidates and assist the Naval Recruiters with sensible advice based on these interviews. In the late summer of 1941, 100 Wrens were appointed to collect information about individual candidates before they were seen by the Naval Recruiters. These women had worked as teachers, social workers and welfare officers in civilian life and were given a very brief course of training at the London School of Economics before being promoted to the rank of petty officer and sent out to do their new job. Numbers were later raised to 300, with fifty of them acting as Personnel Selection Officers. They were supervised by three experienced psychiatric social workers travelling around the country; later the number of supervisors was reduced to two and then to one.[36]

The Wrens collected their information on each candidate in an organised process. When the candidates arrived for interview they would be given a questionnaire to fill in about their schooling, employment record and hobbies. After ten minutes to complete this form, they would be given a twenty-minute intelligence test, referred to as an 'observation test' so as not to alarm the entrants. It was hoped that by using these group intelligence testing methods 'the very dull and backward could be detected with far greater certainty, and the others could be graded, at least roughly, according to their general capacity for absorbing information'.[37] After each man had returned from seeing the medical board, they would have an interview with a Wren, lasting eight minutes, with questions on such subjects as sickness absence from work, headaches, diet and reactions to air raids 'which might help in the detection of men unsuitable for the service'.[38]

Inevitably there was hostility to such screening and scepticism about the value of psychological testing in selecting men suitable for service rather than just in allocating them to particular trades. It was questioned as to 'whether the considerable additional expense and slowing up of the recruiting procedure has been justified by the production of super sailors'.[39] Sir Henry Markham, Secretary to the Admiralty, however, was impressed by the quality of the Wrens involved and after being interviewed by one, commented that 'my fears are completely at rest. I feel that I could tell my life story several times a day to Mrs O'Brien.' Successful candidates would sometimes give presents to the Wrens who had interviewed them and generally the involvement of young women in the selection process was popular among them.[40]

However, the efficacy of psychological testing continued to be questioned. In 1942, 75 per cent of the 214,000 seen by naval and marine recruiters at the Combined Recruiting Centres were accepted for service. Most rejections were for medical reasons or because of unsuitability for the trades for which they had been selected. Only two per cent of men were rejected after the selection test 'and it is probable that the majority of these would in any case have been rejected by the Recruiter without the aid of the test'.[41] The tests were perhaps more useful in years when there was less demand for recruits and it was necessary to be more selective. The Admiralty also distanced itself from its use of psychological testing, stressing that 'the War Cabinet's fear that the services might be making too much use of the psycho-analytical method is not supported by the practice in the Navy. Our psychologists are industrial psychologists and their activities are limited in sphere.'[42]

The German Kriegsmarine also included psychiatrists rather than psychologists on its interviewing boards. Like the Royal Navy, it prided itself on choosing 'the best physical specimens' and, because it was regarded in Germany as a corps d'elite, generally had more applicants than vacancies since men could express a naval preference on call-up. Reports on each applicant were received from both schools and Hitler Youth leaders, performance was assessed in a testing period and sailors were examined for 'a first-class physique and physical condition' in their medicals. Officer selection was even more rigorous, with an emphasis on 'obtaining fine physical specimens, with reasonable scholastic attainments, and who had moreover fitted well into the society in which they had been brought up, and had obtained favourable reports from their schoolmasters, leaders of Hitler Youth organisations and subsequently from their commanding officers'.[43] The idea of a German naval master race did not go down well with British naval medical officers. Ralph Ransome Wallis dismissed captured German sailors as 'arrogant and contemptuous' young men 'who had obviously gone in for sunbathing and the body beautiful in a big way', but was himself very critical of their bad teeth and syphilitic gum infections hidden behind their suntans and superficial good health.[44]

The United States armed forces had flirted with intelligence testing during the First World War but were not convinced of the value of such testing though it was widely adopted in the interwar American school system.[45] During the Second World War recruits and draftees for the United States Navy were put through a series of rigorous physical and psychological tests designed to weed out the undesirable. Most were found fit for service, although sometimes only after remedial work on rotten teeth and poor eyesight. Men were also rejected for neuropsychiatric reasons, including homosexuality. At first African-Americans were not enlisted except for domestic service, but after 1943 the first black naval officers were commissioned. One area in which there was a great difference from the Royal Navy was in the educational background of the American officers who usually had college degrees. When more and more young men were conscripted before they had the opportunity to complete college, a scheme was devised by which suitable young men were enlisted in the navy and trained in universities.[46] These higher educational standards could, however, pose their own problems:

> Our Allies face a difficult problem for their enlisted men are of a higher standard of education than our own; nearly all have been through high school and graduated from there at the age of 17 or 18. They are in general accustomed to a better standard of living and do not admit the existence of class distinctions as we understand them.[47]

Demand for well-integrated and educated officers in the Royal Navy was also high. On the outbreak of war, retired officers on the emergency list were recalled and active list officers of the Royal Naval Reserve (RNR) and Royal Naval Volunteer Reserve (RNVR) were mobilised. A further group of temporary officers came from the Royal Naval Volunteer Supplementary Reserve (RNVSR) which between 1936 and 1939 had enrolled men with seagoing experience, Merchant Navy officers and even private yachtsmen. However, many of these men had received their medical examinations before the outbreak of war either by RNVR medical officers or by civilian general practitioners, who had accepted candidates below the necessary physical standards. In some cases, the physical condition of officers examined as early as 1936 had deteriorated considerably by 1939 and it was found that of the original 1,500 RNVSR officers about 10 per cent were below the acceptable standard when they were given their final medical examination on joining HMS *King Alfred*, the shore-based training depot for wartime temporary officers based at Hove and Lancing College, for training in 1939.[48] It was easier to ensure that direct entries to the RNVR from the universities or ratings selected from the lower deck for training as officers met the required standards. They were given a medical examination before coming in front of the preliminary selection board, then before the interview for final selection and at the beginning of officer training to ensure they met the high standards of health. Ratings selected for officer training, moreover, were already subject to naval medical discipline.

It is surprising that naval psychologists at first showed little interest in officer selection, especially when the selection of men from the lower decks for officer training relied heavily on the identification of officer qualities in ratings with a good educational background. Known as CW candidates because their commanding officers recommended them on form CW 1 issued by the Commission and Warrant Branch, most of these ratings were chosen because they had gone to a good secondary school, yet this did not necessarily mean that they had leadership qualities but these were particularly difficult to identify.[49] The first foray made by the psychologists into the controversial field of officer recruitment was on board HMS *Collingwood*, where the results of psychological tests and interviews were placed in sealed envelopes which were only opened once the commanding officer had decided whether the candidate had passed or failed. At this stage, his envelope was opened and the psychologist's report was compared with the final result, where in most cases 'the psychologist's judgement had been borne out by evidence accumulated later'. A similar trial at HMS *King Alfred* showed comparable results.[50]

The value of intelligence testing in officer selection was linked with it being 'fully recognised that intelligence is far from being the only quality required of officers, and that power of command, for example, is essential'.[51] The psychologists themselves were well aware of the limitations of aptitude tests and the value of previous experience in recruitment, yet they continued to press for improved selection methods involving testing. The War Office Selection Board had already set up courses at a special centre for the selection of army officers, an initiative copied by the navy in March 1943 on HMS *Glendower*, where training was combined with interviews by officers and a psychologist, group discussions, and group and individual tests aimed at identifying officer material and weeding out undesirables.[52]

Psychologists were also advising on the best methods of training recruits. P E Vernon raised questions about whether it was better to train men en masse without regard to individual ability or aptitude, as generally happened with naval courses, or whether it was better to organise classes by ability 'so that the bright are all taught together, and the average and the dull' with the advantage that 'quick learners will not be held up by waiting for slow ones, nor slow ones discouraged by seeing how inferior they are to quick ones', although he recognised that 'in a section containing bright and dull members, the former can assist the latter to some extent in their work at sets and tables; this will be impossible if all members of a section are about equally bright'. He also argued that lectures should last no more than 45 minutes as 'men whose schooldays are not long past cannot concentrate for longer than three quarters of an hour' and suggested that 'non-verbal techniques of imparting information', such as the use of diagrams and pictures, might be more effective than long lectures which were more suitable for the 'verbally-minded minority' than for the 'practically minded majority'.[53] Such professional advice was noted but often ignored by instructors wedded to their long-tested teaching methods.

At HMS *King Alfred*, medical services were not primarily concerned with treating the routine ailments such as minor infections, stress-related physical complaints following the passing-out examinations and accidental injuries. Rather the concern was with the constant observation of the physical and mental character of the candidate in order to assess his suitability to assume the responsibilities of a naval officer at the end of his training. It was recommended that more weight should be given to the psychologist's interview report than to standard intelligence tests at *King Alfred* in assessing borderline candidates.[54] It was found that catarrhal and respiratory infections were common among trainees who had first spent time at sea before beginning their officer training and had lost their immunity when they came ashore 'in the somewhat crowded establishment ... it is evident that they are much healthier at sea than ashore'.[55] One cadet-rating, Peter Scott, ascribed his colds and bronchitis while on *King Alfred* to 'the dampness of the underground garage ... the unaccustomed morning PT or the generally germ-laden atmosphere'.[56] Such minor ailments were no bar to a successful training. What was more important was to be seen to have powers of command. It was an advantage to have the loud voice of the pre-war teacher or the presence of the actor. Alec Guinness puzzled the elderly doctor who gave him his preliminary medical examination with his chest expansion of over 4in when asked to breathe in and out, explaining that 'I'm an actor. It's part of the job to use your lungs.'[57] *King Alfred* was praised both at home and abroad for its success in training officers under pressure and was considered to be an efficiently-run establishment, though it did have a high failure rate.[58]

Candidates for service in submarines and the Fleet Air Arm required special health screening,[59] but there was also now a need to make special provision for the women who were now joining the navy. The Women's Royal Naval Service (WRNS) had been established in 1917 but was disbanded at end of the Great War, only to be revived in April 1939 when it was realised that women could release men from clerical, secretarial, accounting, cooking, waitressing and messenger duties in the shore establishments. Originally, the WRNS was recruited under civilian contracts and it was not considered necessary to bring them under the Naval Discipline Act. They came under the Civil Establishment Branch which tended to regard them as civilians until 1941 when the administration of the WRNS transferred to the Commission and Warrant Branch for officers and to the Naval Branch for ratings, at last treating them in the same way as male naval personnel in most ways. Yet, they were still seen as different. Vera Laughton Mathews, the redoubtable director of the WRNS, universally known as 'Tugboat Annie', accepted that 'there were men in shore bases doing precisely the same work as women and no better, even men precluded by health from going to sea, yet in the main, men in the armed forces were recruited to a life of hardship and danger and sacrifice beyond all comparison of what was demanded of women'.[60]

It was no surprise that the medical procedures at their recruitment differed from those for men. When the WRNS was first set up, aspirant Wrens were expected to be medically examined by their own doctors at their own expense. These doctors had to fill in a form which had been drawn up before anyone had much idea of what was expected of a Wren. In time the form was expanded to include more detailed medical information. Shortly after the outbreak of war, a woman medical officer was appointed as Civilian Admiralty Surgeon and Agent to examine candidates at WRNS Headquarters, while applicants at the home ports or in naval establishments were examined by local naval medical officers. This system continued until 1942 when the responsibility for the examination of all recruits was transferred to the Ministry of Labour. By this time, conscription for women between the ages of 18 and 50 had been introduced and it made more sense for the Ministry of Labour to handle the initial medical inspection of all young women called up. As elsewhere within the navy, the WRNS had its choice of these women as being a Wren was the most popular option open to them. At first there were only seven centres where women could join the WRNS at Portsmouth, Plymouth, Chatham, London, Liverpool, Manchester and Rosyth, though new recruiting centres were later set up in Aberdeen, Belfast, Birmingham, Cardiff, Glasgow, Leeds and Newcastle. Medical facilities for examination of candidates were only available in a few centres and only on certain days each month.[61]

Perhaps less attention was paid to the medical condition than to the fitness of recruits for specialists, officers and male ratings, although the low incidence of sickness among Wrens was ascribed to the 'reasonable care ... taken to exclude candidates who are not Grade I medically fit'.[62] It was thought that the best way of avoiding sickness was to only recruit candidates who were totally medically fit in all respects, and that this would be possible because the supply of potential Wrens always exceeded demand. However, this was more difficult than it seemed, since the medical examinations were so general that they could not be tailored individually to the health requirements of such varied duties as cooks, stewards, writers, messengers, telephone operators, transport drivers and telegraphists, yet it was recognised that 'WRNS candidates are called up for a special type of work and if found not to be medically fit for that work on entry into the training establishments it is not always easy to utilise them in another branch, ie. cooks and stewards cannot, in the majority of cases be transferred to any of the writer categories'.[63] Varicose veins and flat feet immediately disqualified any candidates for domestic duties, while rheumatic and tubercular joint affections, heart disease and menorrhagia or severe dysmenorrhoea were conditions which totally disqualified a woman from service.[64] Surgeon Lieutenant Hugh Philip found it embarrassing to conduct medical examinations of women and 'I am afraid there was no undressing and the stethoscope was put on over the clothes, much to the annoyance of two sisters who assured me later, when I knew them better, that they were really cross because they had washed all over for the occasion'.[65]

So keen were some women to join the Wrens and don the stylish uniform rather than be directed to factories, the Land Army or Auxiliary Territorial Service that they had no scruples about withholding details of their medical histories that may have disqualified them from service.[66] As a result of such misguided patriotism and dedication to join the WRNS in preference to other war service, many young women who had apparently exemplary civilian health records were found unfit for service within a few months of joining. As a result of this there was closer scrutiny of the reports of all medical examinations by an experienced naval medical officer, who also considered whether certain remediable defects noted could be corrected to enable an otherwise suitable candidate to be employed.

At first it was the responsibility of a young woman to remedy at her own expense any defects that may have stopped her from joining up, unlike her male counterparts who were fitted with spectacles and false teeth at public expense. Hearing was expected to be acute, but any candidate below the official visual standard was expected to buy her own glasses until 1943 when spectacles were supplied free of charge to Wrens who required them. With regard to dental health, 'all candidates are required to have a clean healthy mouth with sufficient sound (or readily saveable) teeth in functionable opposition and including some molars for the efficient mastication of food'.[67] Any dental defects had to be attended to at their own expense until 1943, when the women of the navy were afforded the same free dental treatment as men. Only slowly were the women recruits treated the same as men.

When the first new entry depot for the training of WRNS entrants was opened in January 1940, an organised system of medical examination on entry was feasible and it was possible to make a final decision about acceptance or rejection on firmer medical grounds. It was possible to discharge borderline cases as unfit for enrolment after a probationary period of 14 days, but there was concern about the psychological effects on any woman dismissed so quickly after the excitement of being accepted. It was decided that 'recruits found medically unfit on entry must be retained for observation and if necessary formally discharged on medical grounds with 98 days' pay'.[68] Women found medically unfit by the Ministry of Labour civilian medical boards were not to be rejected without the approval of the Admiralty. Such Admiralty approval was also necessary before the dismissal of women found unfit on arrival at the training depot, but 'those who develop disabilities after arrival or whose disabilities are not discovered until one week or more of service are to be brought forward for survey and disposed of in the usual way'.[69]

During their intensive two or three weeks' training at the depot, the emphasis was on 'drill and ceremonial' under the watchful eye of a qualified physical training instructor, together with lectures on the traditions and structure of the Royal Navy. Health matters were covered by 'two very helpful lectures on sex hygiene from a woman doctor from the Central Council for Health Education'.[70] Inoculations and vaccinations were given, and, after 1943, remedial dental work. However, the final medical examination at the end of training still had to be passed.

A Medical Superintendent of the WRNS was appointed to the staff of the Director on 28 November 1939 and on 13 June 1940 she was transferred to the staff of the Medical Director General of the Navy with the rank of surgeon-lieutenant in the Royal Naval Volunteer Reserve. Attracta Genevieve Rewcastle, who had studied medicine at University College Dublin, thus became at the age of 42 the first woman doctor appointed to the Royal Navy.[71] However, the medical care of the Wrens was mainly in the hands of male doctors, usually medical officers of the RNVR who had been general practitioners in civilian life and were experienced in treating gynaecological problems. Any woman needing hospital treatment would be sent to the nearest civilian Emergency Medical Services hospital, though after 1941 most naval establishments had sick bays for Wrens under the supervision of a nursing sister. In 1942 it was decided that there was sufficient demand for the employment of women medical officers for the WRNS and twenty-five were appointed during the war, four of them even serving overseas in Ceylon, India and the Near East.[72]

Generally, the health of the WRNS remained good throughout the war, reflecting the recruitment of healthy young women who were well accommodated and well-fed. There was never any need to harden them up for service nor to provide any remedial schemes for the unfit as was necessary in 1943 with male recruits. Nevertheless, Genevieve Rewcastle stressed that 'women on war service must be regarded from an entirely different standpoint from that applied to men. In temperament, habit of life, personal ambitions … they are diametrically opposed.' She believed that the main challenge to medical officers was to 'protect the Wrens from themselves' and stop them from overworking.[73]

Except during the great expansion of the navy in 1942–3, the Royal Navy was remarkably successful in selecting the fittest recruits for the service. Lord Moran in *Anatomy of Courage* shared the Admiralty's view of the success of its recruitment policies:

> That a boy has set his heart on this tough service goes for something. He has initiative; he is a cut above the ordinary. Long before the Hitler Youth was thought of, the Navy caught him young and soaked him in the pride and joy of a great tradition.[74]

Throughout the war the challenge was to keep these young men healthy and fighting fit.

Chapter Two
In Which They Healed

Naval surgeons were recruited on a false premise in many cases. They were promised adventure and action if they enlisted, but they were not warned of the long periods of tedious routine and boredom that went with the service. In 1943 the *Notes for Medical Officers on Entry into the Royal Navy* given to a surgeon before joining his ship offered an exciting new world:

> You are at the beginning of a fine adventure and of new experiences. No one is 'behind the lines' in a ship nowadays and you will share all the risks and dangers equally with your brother officers and men. This is a great privilege. Strive ever to be worthy of it.[1]

The reality was not so thrilling. A frustrated sense of idle waiting was a common feature of the life of a Second World War naval surgeon, expressed so well and laconically by the elegantly languid ship's doctor played by James Donald in the popular wartime morale-booster *In Which We Serve* in his remark on 'years of expensive medical training resulting in complete atrophy: the doctor wishes he was dead'.[2] Surgeon Lieutenant Commander Bernard Hunt felt guilty on returning home to blitzed London in 1941 that 'Mother and Father had had a far tougher war than their brave son in the Navy, who had been swanning it up and down around the Indian Ocean and the Mediterranean at His Majesty's expense'.[3]

Even before the war, the Royal Naval Medical Branch had not enjoyed a good reputation among ambitious doctors since pay and promotion prospects were poor as a result of government expenditure cuts during the interwar period. By 1930 recruitment of new medical officers had reduced to the point at which 'the shortage of suitable candidates for the Naval Medical Service is at present without exaggeration a very serious menace to the efficiency of the Navy'. A young doctor could enjoy a good standard of living in general practice and 'the income available to the young medical man in civil practice is undoubtedly much higher in proportion to the naval medical officer'.[4]

An advertising campaign was inaugurated aimed at medical schools. Serving medical officers, including the Medical Director General himself, Arthur Gaskell, visited medical schools to talk to students, and articles in medical school journals extolled the merits of medical work at sea. The Fisher Committee in 1933 recommended better training for entrants to the service and greater opportunities for professional development. It found that medical students were deterred from entering the service because 'much of the professional work of a medical officer on a station or a ship is of a minor character; the personnel of the services are almost entirely young men specially selected for their physical fitness, and if they fall ill of anything but the most trivial complaint they are immediately removed to hospital'. Effectively, there was nothing much to do for a doctor and 'the life the services offer is an idle one … the amount of professional work available is slight'. The Committee also recommended cutting the naval medical officer establishment to 355 from 400, considering that 'the reduction effected in the number of medical officers on ships will materially improve the professional opportunities available to the junior officer'.[5]

Nevertheless, despite these efforts to recruit more, as war approached there remained a shortage of naval doctors. It was estimated that 800 would be needed at a time when there were only 370 such men on the active list, 115 on the retired and emergency lists and 190 permanent RNVR medical officers. Of the RNVR medical officers, very few were under the age of 30, yet younger doctors were judged likely to prove the most useful. Meanwhile, additional medical officers were needed for the Fleet Air Arm, training ships and the new ships now under construction. In February 1938, there was already a shortage of twenty officers on account of the end of short service periods and even greater shortfalls were expected in future. There was only one rather unsatisfactory solution to the problem and 'the shortage has been overcome to a certain degree by lowering the standards considered necessary in Naval Medical Officers in the cases of some candidates.'[6]

When war did come in September 1939, conscription ought to have made recruitment easier. However, 'the Medical Branch has been taxed to the uttermost limit to find personnel for the ever increasing units of the Fleet and our new establishments ashore'.[7] By the end of 1939, instead of the anticipated 800 medical officers, there were 1,062, but even this was not considered adequate. It was now necessary to allocate medical officers to full-time passive defence duties in the base hospitals and dockyards. Whereas a single medical officer carried in the flotilla leader was considered adequate provision at sea in peacetime, it was decided that in wartime each destroyer should carry its own surgeon. Similarly, in 1942 new frigates were also allocated a surgeon, again increasing the need for naval medical officers. In the Great War, senior medical students had been employed as surgeon probationers for service in destroyers. This had been promoted as offering them a period of practical experience aboard a ship that would be considered the equivalent of the clinical clerkships and dresserships of a normal medical school course.[8] However, such experience was more limited than it would have been in a teaching hospital and regular officers had dismissed these surgeon probationers as no better than a 'surgical midshipman'.[9] It was no longer seen as an answer and it was considered preferable in the Second World War for medical students to complete their studies before joining the services as qualified medical men.

Throughout the war, the quota of doctors allocated to the navy had continuously fallen, despite the importance for the service of securing 'a proper allocation of medical manpower as between civilian and military services, having regard to the supply of doctors available'. The problem was that there were too many competing demands for doctors from all three services and for maintaining health services on the home front. Civilian health services, in particular, were suffering with the depletion of 20 per cent of registered medical practitioners from civilian practice. In 1941 the Medical Personnel (Priority) Committee recommended that greater use be made of final-year students as house officers in the civil hospitals in an echo of the situation during the Great War, the use of United States and Dominions medical practitioners and the possibility of releasing practitioners from the three services during the winter when the health demands of civilians were greater. It also raised the possibility of a tri-service medical arrangement when the army, air force and navy were in adjacent areas, an idea eventually adopted in the face of late twentieth-century defence cuts.[10] The response of the Admiralty to any idea of reducing medical personnel allocations was to admit that 'there is a serious shortage of medical personnel in the country and further that the proportion of medical officers to total personnel in the Navy is nearly fifty per cent greater that in the Army or Air Force' but to defend this ratio since 'HM ships must carry a medical complement based on the possibility that the vessel may not be able to get back to port for some time after being in action'.[11]

In 1941, there were 380 medical officers with regular commissions in the Royal Navy and 368 with territorial obligations.[12] In 1943, Sheldon Dudley, Medical Director General of the Royal Navy, answered a request to release naval surgeons for work in civilian hospitals in Sheffield with a statement that 'there is already a shortage in the supply of doctors to the Navy and it is regretted that, except on very rare occasions, it is impossible to loan doctors to civilian establishments'. Those 'very rare occasions' had been in Dover and Plymouth where any naval doctors working in a civilian hospital could easily and quickly be recalled to their naval duties. He also noted that 'the Royal Navy is now at a greater disadvantage than civilians in respect of medical manpower'.[13] By 1945, there were 2,535 naval surgeons, but this represented a dangerously low ratio of three medical officers per thousand men of the Royal Navy, and later in the same year, after some of these men had been demobilised, only 1,730 medical officers.[14]

In wartime, military needs took precedence over civilian health services. Dudley argued that it was actually to the benefit of civilian welfare that the naval medical service should be kept 'in the highest state of efficiency, even at the expense of cutting down the number of practitioners of curative medicine available for the civilian workers' since it helped to 'diminish the ever-present risk of epidemic diseases being spread about the civilian population by ships and sailors on leave'.[15] He also argued that giving priority to the Royal Navy would 'be ultimately to the advantage of civilian health by shortening the war',[16] especially 'at a time when we are all told that the U-boat is the only possible obstacle in the way of a complete victory for the Allied Nations'.[17] In this war he contended that 'the Navy, including the Fleet Air Arm, is our first and last line of defence'. As such, it not only needed to recruit more doctors from civil practice, but also needed a greater allocation of medical personnel than both the army and air force because each ship needing a doctor was a small isolated unit and the ships of the Royal Navy were dispersed all over the world involved in continuous fighting at sea, whereas the other armed forces were more concentrated and smaller numbers of doctors were more easily able to care for large numbers of men to whom their services were more accessible.[18] Any reduction in the number of recruits as naval doctors in order to maintain medical provision on the Home Front was condemned as likely to lead to 'a serious deterioration in medical efficiency, loss of naval manpower, deterioration in morale and a falling off in the individual efficiency of individual medical officers in times of emergency and battle'.[19] It was an apocalyptic vision to maintain naval medical efficiency when doctors were everywhere in demand and in constant short supply.

Most of the wartime naval surgeons were indeed recruited from general practice selected by local committees where there was a partner able to carry on the practice. Ralph Ransome Wallis was a 30-year-old country doctor in Rutland when he was called-up in 1940 for service as a surgeon lieutenant in the Royal Naval Volunteer Reserve. He considered his conscription to be fair, 'the dissatisfied party usually being the unfortunate partner who was left behind to do all the work'. Despite having been called-up, the fiction remained that these doctors were volunteers for naval service. When one of Ransome Wallis' friends came to sign the forms to join the RNVR, he crossed out the words 'I hereby volunteer to join the RNVR' and replaced them with 'I do not volunteer, I am being conscripted into the RNVR'. Such honesty was not appreciated and he was told that if he did not volunteer for the RNVR, he would be conscripted but into the seemingly less desirable Royal Army Medical Corps. Ransome Wallis was not too happy with his own interview and medical examination held at the Admiralty in London at the height of the Blitz, especially when it involved 'dancing about in the nude under a glass roof' during an air raid. He was also dismayed during his interview by the grumpiness of the Medical Director General, Sir Percival Nicholls, who later admitted to him that he had been so unfriendly because 'doctors were great individualists; that he thought it was a good thing to be a bit fierce with them when they first joined so that they would realize that they were just cogs in the wheel and not the wheel itself'.[20]

For Bernard Hunt, by contrast, becoming a naval surgeon was almost accidental. In August 1939, he had accepted an appointment as ship's surgeon on a merchant vessel going to India, only to find himself stranded in Calcutta. Faced with the option of returning home on one of 'B[ritish] I[ndia]'s oldest rust buckets' or joining the Royal Navy, he chose 'the more heroic course of action', and 'the more glamorous'. His selection interview was over a gin-fuelled lunch with the Naval Officer in Charge at Calcutta, who offered him a job as surgeon lieutenant commander with two and a half stripes on hearing that Hunt's elder brother was a lieutenant commander in the Fleet Air Arm. Hunt felt pleased with himself to have 'entered the service and received promotion after what must have been the shortest and easiest entrance examination and interview on record'. His fellow surgeon lieutenant when he reported to duty on *Antenor* was less impressed as he had only achieved the two stripes of a surgeon lieutenant after twelve years in the RNVR.[21]

There was also a more orderly call-up of newly-qualified doctors than there had been in the First World War, when young men were encouraged to leave off their medical studies to fight or were enlisted as surgeon probationers. The duty of the medical student was now to qualify as a doctor as soon as possible to meet the country's need for qualified medical practitioners. In Germany, medical students were exempted from military service although their university courses were shortened, offering young men a means of avoiding the call-up. The authorities at the University of Marburg observed that many students 'who earlier would never have thought of becoming a doctor' were now entering medicine.[22] British medical students too were exempted from conscription until they had qualified and served as a house officer for up to a year. However, this exemption was not unlimited and no longer could a medical student take over a decade to qualify, idling his time away with games of rugby, card-playing and heavy drinking so long as his fees were paid. Now if his academic performance was unsatisfactory and he repeatedly failed his examinations, he would be de-registered and be liable for call-up.[23] For some medical students, such as Peter McRae at St Mary's

Hospital, Paddington, hospital life while waiting to join the navy in wartime seemed to be nothing but 'A[ir] R[aid] casualties, bridge, beer, cigarettes'.[24] Visits from men already in uniform only whetted the appetite of students and young doctors to join up for themselves such as when McRae's friend Ivan Jacklin, newly transferred at his own request from a shore job to a destroyer in the Atlantic, visited St Mary's 'with just about three months' pay in his pocket and one idea which is to get me under the table and himself by virtue of his superior Naval gin training, only 99 parts out of 100 there'.[25] When a popular former student such as James Macfarlane serving on the destroyer HMS *Achates*, 'came back at intervals, unexpectedly, as all sailors do, to tell how much he enjoyed the life', this could be a boost to naval medical service recruitment among students at his former hospital.[26]

A doctor entering the navy either straight from his house jobs after medical school or after a number of years in general practice might have considered himself qualified to serve at sea, but the demands on him were to be very different from his previous training and experience. Almost immediately he was expected, whatever other specialisms he may have, to be 'a naval doctor and should be able to deal with the numerous problems of naval hygiene so that he is able to maintain the fighting efficiency of the Navy under conditions which may vary in different classes of ships serving in extremes of climate'.[27] Preventative medicine, hygiene, tropical diseases, medical administration and psychological medicine were not parts of a normal medical school curriculum. Despite requests by the Royal Navy Medical Department and from those of the army and RAF that medical schools should include preliminary training in these subjects to senior medical students before they became eligible for call-up, little was done. The medical schools lacked teaching staff with experience in these areas. The Royal Navy in turn lacked the medical manpower to offer adequate training to new entrants. The best instructors of the pre-war navy were needed elsewhere in the service, while retired medical officers were out of touch with current practice. Instead of the six months' training in naval hygiene which a peacetime entrant could have expected, wartime medical officers were given two weeks, sometimes reduced to one week, before being allocated to duties. For those at shore bases, naval hospitals and on larger ships, there was an opportunity to learn from other medical officers. For the lone naval surgeon on destroyers and frigates, the only learning came from practical experience.[28]

The new naval surgeon was also ignorant of naval tradition and etiquette on joining his first ship and the *Notes for Medical Officers on Entry into the Royal Navy* gave more attention to the all-important topic of protocol than it gave to medical matters. He was reminded that 'naval officers are extraordinarily polite' and instructed on how to address senior officers as 'sir', chief and petty officers by their titles and ratings by their surnames.[29] It was especially important to show due respect to the captain:

> Very shortly after your arrival on board, you will be presented to the Commanding Officer, who, whatever his rank, is referred to as the Captain. Each day, on first sighting him, your 'Good morning, Sir', if in the open air, should be accompanied by a formal salute; thereafter you may pass him without saluting, though naturally you will salute on joining or leaving him on occasions of duty. You rise when he enters the Wardroom and you remove your cap when you enter his cabin.[30]

Equally important was the surgeon's formal relationship with the ratings. It was recognised that 'it is natural to be a little shy of walking into what are, after all, men's homes', but the officer could put the men at ease by carrying his cap under his arm when walking through a mess to show that he required no attention and by ordering the seamen to 'carry on, please'.[31]

Attention to maintaining a smart appearance and wearing correct uniform was also stressed to the new medical officer. He was advised to order two suits of blues, consisting of monkey jacket and trousers, from a good tailor and to complete this Number 5 rig with a pair of black shoes, a uniform cap, raincoat, white shirts, white collars, a black tie and black socks. Tropical rig was also required in the event of a last-minute posting to the Tropics. However, additional items of uniform and underclothing could be bought from naval services more cheaply or on overseas postings from native tailors.[32] With a personal attendant, the naval surgeon of the Second World War should have had no problems with attending to his own uniform and maintaining his sartorial elegance.

Not all new medical officers were as concerned about their uniforms as naval tradition dictated. Bernard Hunt had borrowed a uniform with red and gold stripes around the wrist from a friend who had served as a ship's surgeon in the Merchant Navy for his own engagement on a British India ship in 1939, but after joining up as a naval surgeon in India 'that uniform stayed with me, although the stripes changed, for the next six years'.[33] He also paid a visit to the Army and Navy Stores in Chowringee in order to board the armed merchant cruiser *Antenor* 'resplendent in white shirt and shorts with the gleaming shoulder straps of dark blue, red and gold of a surgeon lieutenant commander RNVR'.[34] Some surgeons, though, began their naval careers less magnificent in their civilian suits and hats with only an armband to show their new status. On arriving at Chatham Barracks with no more uniform than a raincoat and cap, Ralph Ransome Wallis was given an armband with the RNVR surgeon lieutenant's two wavy stripes with a red band between them and was told to wear this 'with civilian clothes and a trilby hat indoors'.[35] Until he received his proper uniform, he found that 'taking off one's hat in reply to salutes from ratings became a bit of a bind'.[36] Even when they had been able to obtain full uniform despite the clothing shortages of the time, some naval medical officers failed to live up to the highest standards of dress and instead of showing 'good cloth, good craftsmanship and good taste' in buying the correct shade of grey flannels appeared in 'that old pair of dashing check plus-fours which you have been so fondly cherishing'.[37]

For pre-war members of the RNVR, having too much uniform could be as great a problem as having difficulty in obtaining it for the wartime recruit. When Hugh Philip signed up in January 1939 he was advised to buy 'everything' in terms of uniform, including frock coat, sword, Mess dress and Undress so that he would be prepared for official functions. Ignorant of correct uniform and even the right shade of blue, he was at the mercy of his tailor and 'nearly sent the samples of cloth back to my tailor with the remark that it was the Navy and not a funeral in which I was interested'.[38] Although he spent over £100 on uniform despite having a uniform allowance of only £50, the only items that were to serve him on war service were a greatcoat, a monkey-jacket suit and a cap. Everything else went into storage in a trunk and prey to moths.

Uniform visibly reflected dissatisfaction about their status among the medical officers who had been in the RNVR before the war because the same uniform with its wavy stripes was also adopted by doctors who had been conscripted and so were technically not volunteers. During the Great War the doctor called up from civilian practice had worn the same uniform with its straight stripes as a permanent Royal Naval medical officer, leaving the RNVR medical officers able to see themselves as an elite of volunteers. In the Second World War, the permanent medical officers themselves were envious of the seniority enjoyed by certain selected specialist RNVR doctors and resented that elitism. In turn pre-war RNVR medical officers feared being confused with conscripts, even if some were of higher status than them in civilian life. As a RNVR officer, though only of a few months' standing and one who had as an undergraduate vowed never to fight for King and Country, Hugh Philip was irritated at seeing a new wartime entrant in RNVR uniform since 'I knew damned well that he was a conscript and an unwilling one at that. Why any differentiation at all, or if you must have it, don't for goodness sake label an unwilling conscript a volunteer.'[39] Yet it was recognised that 'in wartime doctors are an exceptionally favoured class' since 'if they are conscripted, they do their own job as relatively senior commissioned officers, with a living wage; while lawyers, artists, bankers, businessmen and others of the doctors' social class often lose everything and have to serve in the ranks'.[40]

Many conscript doctors initially perhaps took too much luggage to sea with them, although they were warned that 'your journey will be a good deal easier if your luggage is of such a size that you can carry it yourself if necessary'. The new ship's surgeon was also cautioned that if he took his golf clubs, tennis racquet, favourite books or any of his own medical equipment or medical reference books, he was to understand that 'in the event of loss compensation cannot be awarded from Naval funds in respect of the loss of any articles which are not essential to enable you to perform your Naval duties'.[41] It was not always easy to get compensation even for essential kit that had been damaged or lost in action. When Ralph Ransome Wallis' cabin was flooded, his uniforms were badly damaged and the gold braid on them turned green, but his claim for compensation to replace the worst-damaged clothing was rejected since his 'Royal Marine servant and one of the ship's amateur tailoring firms would cope' with any repairs.[42] Since he may also have had to use his cabin as an office, space was at a premium and too much kit an impediment.

The sick berth, serving as consulting room, small hospital and sometimes sleeping accommodation, was usually located in the upper part of the ship where there would good natural light and adequate ventilation. On the largest, best-equipped ships, the medical facilities could rival those of a well-equipped small hospital ashore. The battlecruiser *Hood* had a large sick bay on the upper deck with twelve cots, an examination room, a fully-equipped operating theatre and an isolation ward known as 'Rose Cottage' and reserved for the treatment of venereal diseases. There was also a dispensary, X-ray facilities and bathrooms. On the boat deck was a dental surgery. The surgeon commander was assisted by two surgeon lieutenants and half a dozen sick berth attendants under a chief petty officer.[43] Facilities on such a luxurious scale were rare. On the battleship *Prince of Wales* with a crew of over 1,500, there were 22 swinging cots and space for a further 8 hammocks to be slung.[44] On the 'River'-class frigate *Barle*, the accommodation, with its two swinging cots, folding operating table, folding armchair, wooden drug cabinet and metal instruments cabinet, was well-equipped and 'satisfactory in every way'.[45] However, the sick bay on the aircraft carrier *Indomitable* had very poor accommodation because 'it has not been borne in mind that in the present war ships are operating on the oceans for considerable periods and it is therefore imperative that adequate provision is made for the sick and injured who may have to remain on board for many days'.[46] The surgeon was to spend much of his time in such quarters.

Senior officers were usually treated in their own cabins. When Sub-Lieutenant John Iago, an electrical engineer in civilian life, broke his ankle after slipping on a soapy deck on *Hood* in October 1940, he was happy with the care he received from the medical officers in the officers' sick bay and the luxury of being waited upon:

> I am sitting in front of a radiator waiting for my plaster to dry. I am to have a walking iron, made by the ship's blacksmith, fitted tomorrow

then I shall be completely mobile. In the Officers' Sick Bay, I am at the moment being looked after by Sick Berth Attendants who are really male nurses. The Surgeon Commander is looking after the ankle, ably assisted by the Surgeon Lieutenants, so there is no shortage of medical attention. All my meals are brought to me, I have a large armchair and an electric fire, and so it is all very comfortable.[47]

Ratings in the main sick bay were also made just as comfortable and given plenty of attention. The medical officers were keen to practice medicine whenever they could and pounced upon suitable patients despite the inevitable naval bureaucracy involved in recording each treatment.

The new naval medical officer was rarely accustomed to the amount of paperwork that he was expected to master. Like all naval officers, he was expected to be familiar with King's Regulations and Admiralty Instructions (KR and AI), the Captain's Standing Orders, the Ship's War Orders, Confidential Books (CB on medical matters), Admiralty Fleet Orders (AFO), Confidential Admiralty Fleet Orders (CAFO) and local general orders and temporary memoranda in force in any ports visited, and to understand the multitude of acronyms in use to describe these documents. There were also forms to be filled in for every patient seen, including notifications of infectious diseases, venereal disease, tuberculosis and injuries. Separate vouchers and forms were required if a patient was referred to hospital, sent for dental treatment, prescribed drugs or supplied with a truss. Each patient put on the sick list was to be noted in the daily sick list and reported to the captain, divisional officer and coxswain. The only way of keeping track of which forms were required at each stage of a patient's progress through the sick bay was for the medical officer to display a diagram in a conspicuous position so that he and the sick bay staff would not forget anything.[48]

Even more onerous was the requirement for keeping a meticulously accurate journal in which all treatment was recorded and which became the basis of nosological returns and statistics. Unaccustomed to such a high level of bureaucracy, the new surgeon often failed to meet the required standards especially when subject to other service pressures. On the corvette *Wallflower* in 1942 'there is no medical organisation for war, no training in first aid is given on board, neither the medical records nor medical history sheets are up to date and the men are often overdue for TAB inoculation'.[49] Surgeon Lieutenant Francis Whitwell on the destroyer *Worcester* was reprimanded for not keeping up to date with his paperwork, for 'the untidy and careless way' in which he had compiled his journal and for failing to 'appreciate the importance of the record'.[50] He had joined his ship in 1940 after only a few weeks in naval service, having only qualified as a doctor at St Thomas' Hospital in 1939 and with little knowledge of correct naval procedures and protocol. Almost immediately *Worcester* had been sent to Dunkirk and had evacuated up to 800 troops at a time with 238 casualties alone on one of its six trips. It was little wonder that Whitwell did not have time to attend to his administrative duties of which he was only dimly aware.

On a day-to-day basis, the routine medical work on board a naval vessel was very different from what most of the new surgeons had been accustomed to in their civilian practices. The crew were fit and healthy young men, with none of the health problems a general practitioner could expect from children, old people and expectant mothers. Instead of a large and dispersed practice, he had responsibility for the health of about 140 men in a frigate. Sometimes he might have responsibility for the health of men on other warships or on a convoy under escort. At one time the commanding officer of a ship had regarded his medical officer as his own and exclusive to his own ship, but with the medical manpower shortages facing the wartime navy it was necessary for the medical man's services to be more spread out with motorboats at sea and cars ashore providing the essential transport needed between vessels. This represented a great departure from previous naval practice in medical organisation demanded by wartime exigencies.[51]

Routine medical work on a ship could be monotonous, though it could also demand versatility:

> The greater your skill and the wider your interests the better. Can you put a temporary stopping in a tooth? Can you give a decent anaesthetic in the Tropics with the minimum of apparatus? Can you be sure of spotting malarial parasites in a blood film you have stained yourself? How would you set about disinfecting the water in a large canvas bath? What do you know about the effects of blast,

of the treatment of phosphorous burns, or of immersion foot? An endless list.[52]

How much a surgeon could do was dictated by the size of the ship in which he served and whether he was a lone medical officer or working under the guidance of a principal medical officer with the support of enough sick berth attendants. He was cautioned of 'the need to be a general practitioner in the widest sense and that one lives with one's practice are amongst the earliest difficulties which you will have to adjust yourselves to'.[53] Generally, apart from dealing with minor injuries and illness, the main thrust of a medical officer's work was in the field of preventative medicine. This was one of the greatest differences from general practice where much of the work was concerned with curative medicine, whereas in the navy the priority lay in the field of preventative medicine, especially the avoidance of infectious diseases.[54] Keeping up to date with vaccinations and inoculations was important. Sometimes it seemed that the keenness of a medical officer to vaccinate and inoculate was simply to give him something to do.[55] When men did contract an infection, there were none of the diagnostic tools, such as X-rays and laboratory tests, available in modern hospitals. A microscope, portable diagnostic set and stethoscope were as much as the surgeon could hope to have. He also needed to be careful not to dismiss early signs of an illness as malingering but to be aware that 'it is very much better that a malingerer should get away with it for a day or two than that a serious illness should be missed, and you must take good care that your judgment is not biased by those who have no qualification to give an opinion'. By contrast in the treatment of alcoholism it was 'a mistake to be lenient simply from compassion, for if a semi-intoxicated man, instead of being safely stowed down below until he has recovered, is allowed freedom, he may easily commit another offence such as striking, and then will be in immediate trouble'.[56]

Preparation and planning for action stations was also an important part of the surgeon's duties. He was expected to come up with plans for the location of temporary wards on large mess decks, schemes for how to deal with casualties transferred from other ships or picked up from the sea, and preparations for dealing with a large number of burns.

He needed to check the availability and location of medical stores for use in an emergency. Regular lectures on first aid were given to the ship's companies which could be lifesaving in action at sea. The men were told where they could find first aid containers and Neil Robertson stretchers, warned to wear their identity discs at all times and anti-flash gear in action, and told not to move badly-injured men or apply unnecessary tourniquets though they should stop the bleeding with a first field dressing and cotton wool. The importance of giving sweetened tea to all but men with belly wounds was stressed. There might also be a 'remarkable demonstration of the difference between arterial and venous bleeding with the aid of an ear syringe and a piece of rubber tubing'.[57]

Although 'adaptability, ingenuity, improvisation, self-help and resourcefulness were never more needed by doctors on small ships', the single-handed surgeon on a small ship was not actually responsible for maintaining the fitness and health of the crew.[58] Nor was the principal medical officer on a larger vessel with his junior medical officers under his command. The commanding officer was 'alone responsible for the health of the ship's company'.[59] The medical officer was there to advise him. The captain's permission was needed for any changes to medical policy aboard ship or any changes in practice. The surgeon had to report to him daily on the state of health of the company. The captain was 'the ship', responsible for everything and everyone under his command.

Some medical officers had greater opportunities for more exciting work than the average surgeon lieutenant at sea. They may not have gone to sea in submarines but could be assigned to the submarine depots where they could become involved in research into the particular health problems of that branch.[60] Naval surgeons assigned to the Fleet Air Arm had opportunities to learn about aviation medicine but 'during the war, medical officers are not generally given facilities to obtain their wings' though 'the importance of having a few medical officers qualified as pilots is realised'.[61] There were also rare opportunities for adventure with the Royal Marines. In April 1940, after only three weeks in the navy, Frank Henley, was selected to 'go on this jaunt with the Royal Marines who would be off in less than 48 hours to an unknown destination', enough time for him to buy a complete khaki uniform and camping equipment before setting off with the Mobile Naval Base Defence Organization, a precursor of the later Marine Commandos for the defence of Namsos in Norway. Having landed in Namsos on 28 April, the MBDO, and its medical officer, was withdrawn on 3 May 1940. Henley considered that 'it had been an adventurous, if not a thrilling stay in Namsos, but with the daily rain of bombs and no means of reply, one became a little philosophical'. He was philosophical about his chances of survival and hoped that 'with any luck there will be a next entry in the diary'.[62]

The Royal Marine Commandos were formed in 1942. They were expected to be of a higher fitness standard than other marines and to harden up considerably. Officers surrendered their peacetime wardroom comforts, the services of servants to clean their uniforms and heat up their bath water and instead shared the hardships of their men. Medical officers were specially trained to serve with these units. Bernard Hunt did not know what to expect when he was sent for training with RMNBDO2 to form part of a casualty clearing station for service in Egypt and Italy and reported for duty at a large country house near Alton in his smartest blue uniform only to find that his unit had moved to Newark and that, once there, he would be issued with khaki battledress and tropical kit.[63] Ralph Ransome Wallis received a draft chit in a double-sealed registered envelope in early 1944 appointing him to a Port Repair Party, whose function was to restore the harbour installations when a port had been captured by the army. Training took place on Hampstead Heath where a mock-up of Le Havre allowed the unit to simulate battle conditions, while living in comfort in three large houses recently put into first-class condition by the Royal Marines after having been left bare and shabby as the result of army occupation. Ransome Wallis, taking part in all of these exercises, was given a 'large and very heavy revolver as it was thought that the Germans would be unlikely to pay much attention to any Geneva conventions with regard to any doctors operating with the Commando units'.[64] Ransome Wallis was to serve with this commando unit at Dieppe, Ostend and Antwerp.

Two naval medical surgeons, Dugald Stewart MacPhail and Peter Edward Darrell Sheldon Wilkinson, were recruited to the Special Operations Executive (SOE) for special duties organising medical services for the resistance in occupied territories. MacPhail, inspired by his aunt who had worked as a doctor in Serbia during the Great War, had responded to reports in the press about British officers in Yugoslavia in December 1942 and had 'volunteered to go back in the hope that he can assist from a purely medical point of view'.[65] Despite an unimpressive performance in para-military training at Arisaig in the West Highlands where he proved himself to be 'a serious-minded officer, who is anxious to learn' but was judged 'rather unfit and physically lazy, so he is not really suited for a course of this type',[66] MacPhail's mission was considered potentially to 'have considerable political value'.[67] As well as acting as doctor to the SOE mission to Yugoslavia, this 29-year-old doctor was also to advise General Dragoljub Mihailović on field hospitals, medical supplies and the prevention of such infectious diseases as typhus among the Chetniks; he was promoted to the rank of surgeon lieutenant commander to give him the necessary status and authority in the field.[68] However, he was replaced on the mission by another officer after he injured his back while making a practice parachute descent, which was 'likely to interfere with his future efficiency'.[69] Once recovered, he was parachuted into South Serbia to act as a medical officer with the partisans, including setting up a hospital of brushwood shelters in the woods of Yastrebats, between 7 May and 28 August 1944. He then volunteered for further special duties in the Far East and was sent to organise medical stores for special operations in Malaya with Chinese guerrillas being trained to fight the Japanese. In the jungle he injured his knee escaping from the enemy and went down with amoebic dysentery.[70] Wilkinson, who at the age of 24 was serving on a Greek destroyer *Miaoules* and had a working knowledge of Greek in addition to 'experience of surgery in the field under primitive conditions', was recruited to fill an urgent need for 'duties of a medical nature in the field', setting up medical camps for Greek partisans. Recruited in June 1943, he completed his training course in Palestine that July and was immediately parachuted into Greece where he remained until February 1944.[71] Both MacPhail and Wilkinson, who had a keen interest in classical literature, history and philosophy in addition to social medicine, were quiet, deliberative, calm and studious rather than extrovert and aggressive by nature which made them suitable as

SOE agents on dangerous missions. Most naval medical officers saw much less action and excitement on board ship.

With little to do in terms of medical duties that was not monotonous, the surgeon could easily become bored:

> You may have come to the conclusion that the life of a naval doctor is an exciting and active one but you may in fact ... find that your chief preoccupations are those of mess secretary or sports officer, or much time may pass in censoring letters. But you should remember that out of all this apparent inertia and inactivity may come sudden demands on your skill and judgment which call for a high degree of efficiency as any made on the staff of a large hospital ashore.[72]

It was said that on some ships the surgeons were desperate for 'any surgery they could drum up to keep their hands in as there did not seem to be an awful lot about'.[73] Peter McRae claimed that 'the life is fairly good or as good as it can be when one hasn't got a job to do'[74] but it was also one where 'the staple food, nourishment, business, hobby and relaxation of the officers is gin'.[75] He described his role on the destroyer *Mahratta* in self-deprecating terms:

> The medical department of a destroyer is run by one M.O. ('quack') and one S.B.A. ('doc') – its duties include censoring, cyphering, Captain confidante on the ship's company and crew confidante on the Captain and officers, general welfare and liaison officer between almost everyone and the girlfriends and/or wives and lastly, but miles ahead in importance of all other duties, wardroom wine catering. Most of these duties fall to me while the proper 'Doc', as the S.B.A. is known on the lower deck among the ratings, treats the colds, corns and pimples, occasionally dabbling in a little dispensing work so that the troops can have a pick-me-up on return from a run ashore (canteen leave).[76]

Some naval medical officers objected to such non-medical duties as wine stewarding, messing, acting as recreations officer, substituting as a cipher officer and censoring of mail as a waste of time for a qualified doctor.[77] Others saw a value in these tasks as they meant that 'the doctor ... can make himself very useful and busy in his capacity of being an officer, yet not bound by the same rigid code of his executive colleagues ... responsible for doing all he can for their mental as well as their physical health'.[78]

Censorship of mail was a particularly important duty. Letters from home were both a source of anxiety and of reassurance. The post could be irregular and multiple sacks of letters and parcels could arrive in one go after following the ship from port to port. Many men preferred to open the latest first in case there was bad news. Some correspondents numbered their letters so that they would know if a message had gone astray.[79] The letters were all censored, often by the ship's doctor or chaplain who spent many hours on this chore. Any references to locations, ship movements, casualties or morale were not allowed and there were to be no criticisms of war operations or 'any statement harmful to the reputation of H.M. fighting forces'.[80] This did not stop men from dropping hints in their letters or using pre-arranged coded references to give information that would otherwise be censored.[81] Men who did not write regularly to family and friends were encouraged to do so. Dugald MacPhail did not write to his family after damaging his back as a result of a fall during his parachute training and 'it is not known why he has not kept his family informed but communication has been sent to him suggesting that he does so'.[82] Keeping in touch was seen as key to good mental health.

The battleships did at least have well-appointed sick bays with isolation wards, operating theatres, X-ray apparatus and dispensaries which would have been the envy of less well-equipped hospitals at home.[83] However, on smaller ships there were none of these facilities and nothing to rely upon other than a basic medical training and self-reliance with no fellow doctors to consult. The lone medical officer on a ship found it important to fit in with his fellow officers, sharing in the life of the wardroom and taking on extra duties, but he also felt part of the camaraderie of the wider naval medical world. In many ways it was not an unfamiliar milieu to the product of a medical school. Peter McRae, a Somerset County cricketer, a St Mary's Hospital rugby player and a squash player, found that being an all-round sportsman helped him to be accepted since 'the RN attach as much importance to games as the London hospitals'; his commander when he was first in barracks, 'being an ardent squash player ... likes to have such players around and my path here has been smooth for that reason'.[84] It could be an advantage to be an extrovert, such as Christopher Dent lost on *Hood* in 1941, with 'an amazing capacity for work and an equal capacity for enjoying life',[85] although even a 'quiet spoken, apparently reserved, or even taciturn' doctor, such as Cecil Kirby lost on the cruiser *Cornwall* in 1942, could be equally effective if he could show authority over his patients and could 'condemn some matter of which he disapproved in a very impressive and shatteringly convincing manner'.[86]

Every possible opportunity was also taken to reunite with old friends, especially fellow medical students also serving at sea, although this was not always easy to arrange. In 1942 'during the passage of the most recent convoy to Malta, there were amongst the ships taking part no less than six St Mary's men ... Although the team were not able to effect a complete rendezvous in Gib (which was perhaps just as well for that rocky outpost) many of us did meet at different times, and the event was celebrated needless to say in the traditional manner'.[87] McRae used a minor injury as an excuse for obtaining leave to meet up with his medical school and hospital friends, admitting that 'the jaw remains *intacta* but the zygoma it was that couldn't take the AA fire. However good has come out of it as they decided that a fortnight's sick leave should be given for such grievous bodily harm and this obviously meant a jaunt to town.'[88] It all made the ennui more bearable.

There was a widespread and well-founded fear that when there was no action the sick berth attendants could become as bored as some of the surgeons, and 'it is too easy for the ordinary SBA in these ships to become slovenly in appearance, careless and merely a passenger'. This happened more frequently than was acceptable, whereas the sick berth attendant 'should always be the cleanest man on board, have a pride in his work as well as self-respect, and the officers and men should respect him'. [89] Peter McRae was not impressed by his first sick berth attendant:

> My doc for the first 4 months of the commission was an extraordinary fellow. In civil life he had turned a hand happily to lots of things and had bricklayed, driven lorries, been a steward at sea and finally with the call-up upon him and, having a pal who was a St John's

Ambulance stretcher, bottle and sponge merchant at the football matches, he thought medicine was the job for him. Ten weeks training and here he arrived. And what a scruffy bastard. I have never seen anyone so consistently dirty either in his habits or in his clothes. But he felt everything was alright really because there wasn't much he didn't know about the work. Actually, there was lots he didn't know and then he would give a modest little clearing of the throat as if to get his victim properly attentive and launch into a superb defence of his knowledge, ability and anything that might be in question. It took me four months to get rid of him and now he is replaced by a man who wouldn't say boo to an ordinary seaman. He doesn't know anything either but he's honest and clean too.[90]

Ransome Wallis found his one sick berth attendant, a former schoolmaster, on the destroyer *Martin* to be a likeable man, popular with the crew, but with a tendency to disappear when he was needed only to be found in one of the magazines helping to get up the ammunition or assisting in some other part of the ship rather than carrying out his sick berth duties. This was a contrast with the well-trained team of sick berth attendants on the cruiser *London*, led by a chief and a petty officer, where 'things ran like well-oiled machinery'.[91]

Roger Miles recognised the importance of listening to his sick berth attendant and advised any 'Vandal gaudy with still bright gold on his cuffs' but ignorant of naval medical forms and procedures, to 'just sign on the dotted line'. A good SBA filtered out those patients with constipation, foot-rot, Dhobie Itch or seasickness, as well as those men who were obviously lead-swinging, before they could get the chance to see the ship's surgeon. However, the doctor's life could be more difficult if his SBA was 'the squarest of pegs in the roundest of holes'. Miles had to work with one whose accent he could not understand, especially after the sick berth attendant lost his false teeth at a coaling jetty on a quiet run ashore. This man had been a coal miner before joining the navy at the age of 43. Miles was amused by the man's medical malapropisms, especially when he mentioned 'a case of Anxiety Neuroptics which necessitated a visit to the Phyzziatrist'. There was also room for confusion over his labelling on the bottles on the dispensary shelf with such gems as 'Idine' and 'Mis. Soddy Sally'.[92]

More often than not a new recruit was 'allocated to the Sick Berth Branch merely because he has a physical defect (eg defective vision) which renders him unfit for other employment'.[93] It was not surprising in such cases that 'inefficient nursing is due to the insufficient training of probationers who are conscripts and have no interest in the work, and who are largely old and of low educational standards'.[94] In peacetime, sick berth ratings were engaged for a period of twelve years and given six months' training at one of the naval hospitals in Chatham, Plymouth and Portsmouth. At the end of the training period, those who had passed an examination were often kept on for a few months at the naval hospital to gain further experience before service at sea. This was no longer feasible in wartime and the training period for batches of forty men was reduced to ten weeks, which was later raised to twenty weeks before being reduced back to ten. Most of the academic and theoretical elements of pre-war training were abandoned with emphasis now being placed on practical medical needs and naval procedures. It was longer than the training period for medical officers but was inadequate when most conscripts allocated to the Sick Berth Branch had no prior medical knowledge except for a few men who had been junior medical students, civilian dispensers or hospital porters. Generally, only dental technicians, dispensers, mental nurses and opticians would be qualified in their respective fields.[95]

At the naval hospitals Queen Alexandra's Royal Naval Nursing Service sister tutors were put in charge of sick berth attendant training under the supervision of medical officers. Like the ward sisters and sister tutors of the teaching hospitals, these were formidable women who stood for no nonsense from their students who were in awe of them. At Haslar one sister tutor in 1942 was known as 'Rectum Rosie' because of her fondness for referring to the alimentary canal at the end of every lecture.[96] Another sister tutor at Stonehouse in 1943 was 'the fastest bed-maker I have ever seen'. She told her trainees that they must always raise the end of the bed and lie the patient on his face with a receptacle nearby for him to clear phlegm from his lungs; when she asked a man to repeat what she had told him, he added that to rid the patient of phlegm 'he would slap him on the back and grab his ankles so that he would not slide out of bed'.[97] Luckily even the sister tutor laughed at the absurdity of it all. By the end of his course a trainee was 'normally capable of routine nursing, changing dressings, elementary dispensing, first aid, cookery for the sick, sterilization of instruments and dressings, and elementary diagnosis of injury and sickness, administrative and clerical duties'.[98] Unfortunately practical training was les adequate. In peacetime the new sick berth attendant would have an opportunity to learn from more experienced senior ratings, but in wartime this was not always possible. Not having chosen nursing, many of them had little pride in what they were doing.

Some of the men sent for training as sick berth attendants were 'so illiterate that they have to be returned to the depot the day after they arrive'. Many of the examination papers of those who actually made it through training were not only poorly written but contained great misconceptions which could have had serious consequences for their patients. One man described the lungs as 'two large organs which are on top of the hart [sic]'. Another advised treating a patient rendered insensible by a blow on the head with a warm drink, fresh air, and 'slap his hands and face until he comes round'. Other men believed that syphilis was caused by 'touching something which is infected, spoons, forks and other things', and that the patient should be told 'to wash his hands before passing urine' to avoid infection.[99]

On the destroyer *Foresight* William Stanmore, the sick berth attendant in 1940, had been a butcher's boy before conscription in 1939 when he was 23. He had attended a few lectures on nursing at Haslar but spent most of his time there filling sandbags. Of limited intelligence and suffering badly from seasickness, he distinguished himself by helping the torpedoed survivors of *Eskimo* during the second battle of Narvik with meticulous attention to the instructions of his medical officer.[100] He may have redeemed himself by bravery in action, but perhaps should never have been employed in the sick berth with such hasty and inadequate training.

It was not only at sea that the nursing was considered to be atrocious. There were serious problems at the large Royal Navy hospitals at Haslar, Plymouth, and Chatham, and also at the smaller wartime naval hospitals set up in evacuation areas thought less likely to be attacked as intensively as the naval bases.[101] At Chatham ignorant and poorly-trained staff had attempted to crudely lower a man with a hernia into a bath with a blanket when instructed to give a blanket bath, and had not even noticed when another patient stopped breathing. In the TB ward there were sick berth attendants afraid of catching tuberculosis from their patients and avoiding them. The standard excuse for all of this was 'of course, the war' but 'unless some improvement can be made, disaster is imminent'.[102]

Such ineptness gave a bad name to more experienced and competent sick berth attendants, especially permanent SBAs and men recalled to service from retirement. Such attendants and the more intelligent and competent hostilities-only men could rise to the emergency and were efficient enough so that 'in a very short time the routine achieved by the sick berth staff was comparable with that of a hospital theatre so far as there was no undue delay between cases for want of preparation'.[103] However competent the new sick berth attendant on a ship might be, he still had to undergo the initiation ritual of being hoisted aloft upside down in a Neil Robertson stretcher by his comrades and left suspended until it was obvious that the new man had satisfied them that he was 'physically fit and showed no undue displeasure'.[104] A wise naval surgeon could also learn from the long-service sick berth chief petty officers, including for Bernard Hunt 'the important maxim that an officer should never exercise sarcasm on those below him in rank'.[105] On the best-run ships, attendants would be assigned definite duties such as assisting with the cleanliness of bedding and the general health of the ship's company, the maintenance of first aid gear, the training of seamen in first aid, the routine examination of ratings and keeping records up to date.[106] With the end of the war it was at last possible to raise standards by improving promotion prospects, pay and training so that by 1950 'not only has the status of the nursing profession ashore been raised, but the male nurse now holds a position undreamed of before the war'.[107] So long as the war had lasted, improvement or even a return to pre-war standards had been difficult.

Upholding nursing standards throughout the war were the trained nurses of Queen Alexandra's Royal Naval Nursing Service (QARNS). Founded in 1902, QARNS was still a small service in 1939 with only 85 serving nurses and 168 reserves. A massive expansion was called for and by 1945, there were 1,129 nurses serving in shore establishments, sick quarters and hospital ships at home and abroad. They were engaged in training and supervisory duties, including the instruction of sick berth attendants, the nursing in hospitals and hospital ships and the supervision of partly-trained male sick berth attendants and women Voluntary Aid Detachments (VADs). These VADs, volunteers working as nurses, clerks, cooks and dispensers, were treated as the equivalent of WRNS petty officers in the allocation of accommodation, whereas the nurses of QARNS had their own nursing hierarchy of principal matron, matron, senior sister, sister and nurse under a matron-in-chief. During the war they worked 96 hours each fortnight except during emergencies when they would volunteer for extra duties. None of the women nurses worked in warships, though they did nurse in the hospital ships.[108]

The increased demand for naval nurses came at a time when nurses were also needed by the other armed services, which meant that there were shortages of civilian nurses. At first the three armed forces were 'able to recruit for their nursing services as they pleased and without limit of numbers'.[109] However, by 1943, the situation regarding nursing on the home front had become so critical that it was necessary for the Ministry of Labour and National Service to control the allocation of nurses. The Admiralty accepted this decision but reserved the power of the Medical Director General to select 'professional nurses of integrity and capacity possessing officer-like qualities'.[110] Sir Sheldon Dudley commented that 'our main source has never been the newly qualified nurse. Experience since completion of training is considered essential for a nursing sister post involving the supervision of male sick berth ratings and women VAD members.'[111]

Even in the closing days of the war, there remained a shortage of naval nurses even though the naval nursing services had exceeded their allocation in 1944 by 648 women at a ratio of one nurse to five VADs. It was believed that as the war in Europe came to a close there would be more nurses needed for the war in the Pacific and 'naval estimates for nurses have been based upon the assumption that considerable numbers of nursing sisters and VADs will become available at the end of the war in Europe as a result of the closing of establishments at home. So far nothing of this nature has occurred, in fact there are more patients in hospital at home than previously.'[112]

A different solution had been found to the imbalance between armed service and civilian nursing in the United States with the establishment of a Cadet Nurse Corps by the Bolton Act of Congress in June 1943. Students enrolled in the Cadet Corps received an accelerated training programme and had their fees, textbooks and wages paid for them by the federal government in return for agreeing to serve in the army, navy or vital nursing services for the duration of the war. In many hospitals student nurses in the military style uniforms and berets of the Corps outnumbered those in 'starch and stripes'. Their military bearing complemented the equally visible presence of soldiers and sailors in training. In Chicago, student cadet nurses formed 'dates committees' to request uniformed escorts from the Great Lakes Naval Base to take them to dances.[113]

Not only were doctors and nurses in short supply; so were dentists. They were essential for maintaining the health of the sailor as adequate teeth were vital for coping with the hard foodstuffs in his scran. Only the shore establishments and larger ships carried dentists, who would have men sent to them as necessary and when possible. The Dental Branch in peacetime was made up of men who had trained in a dental hospital or medical school, but wartime shortages meant that it was necessary to consider recruiting dentists without formal qualifications but who were registered to practice under the 1921 Dentists Act which allowed unqualified practitioners to register with the Dental Board of the United Kingdom and practise as dentists if they could prove that they had been practising dentistry for five years before the Act came into force. However, it was feared that academically-qualified dental surgeons in the Royal Navy and RNVR, including consultants and house officers in dental hospitals, would not 'view with equanimity the acceptance on equal terms with them of practitioners having no professional background other than that conferred on them by the 1921 Dentists Act ... and as it is from the younger temporary officers that the post-war Naval Dental Service will be recruited it is considered most unwise to embark on any act which would undoubtedly lower the prestige of the Service'.[114] But there was little option for the navy, army and air force dental services but to take such men for wartime service.

The employment of dental hygienists was also considered as a preventative measure to avoid dental problems becoming serious and to ease the pressures of a shortage of dental surgeons, against the opposition of Sir Norman Bennett, head of the Naval Dental Service who had been in post since 1925 and while 'dentistry has gone a long way since then ... he has not'. The hygienists were praised as 'men and women sufficiently trained in dental matters to look after people's mouths and keep them clean and hygienic and free from tartar, and able to detect anything needing attention from the dental surgeons'.[115] The conservative approach of Bennett and his older colleagues eventually won the day, despite the successful employment of dental hygienists in the RAF, since it was deemed that it would be difficult to introduce a similar scheme in the navy 'not only because of our different methods of entry but also because of the greater dispersal of personnel after entry as compared with the RAF'. It was also declared, with a touch of inter-service rivalry, that 'the dental health of the Navy is quite as good as that of the RAF'.[116]

Elsewhere, particularly acute shortages of qualified medical officers and nurses for the navy were met by the replacement of medical and nursing staff with unqualified people for certain duties. Seaman and other ratings carried out cleaning and unskilled nursing duties. In the Far East Royal Marines were even given instruction in nursing duties, but generally the use of ratings to scrub hospital decks, deliver patients' meals and clean bedpans was not good for naval discipline and efficiency. More successful was the employment of biochemists, physiologists, physicists and engineers to carry out certain hygiene duties that might be better performed by a scientist than a medical officer. A particular success was the employment of twelve entomologists on anti-malarial duties in the Far East who were more knowledgeable than untrained medical officers and could better instruct all ranks in how to avoid and deal with malaria.[117] It may have been a response to manpower shortages but it did provide an effective means of keeping the navy fit, the aim of all the men and women involved in naval health.

Chapter Three
Hospitals Under Fire

For the first time naval hospital establishments at home and abroad came under attack as much as ships at sea, and a greater flexibility was demanded in the approach to providing hospital facilities. Shore-based hospitals, built for an earlier age of naval greatness, were now vulnerable to enemy attack. Eighteenth-century naval hospitals had been built for a time when survivors of a distant battle were brought home for treatment after a sea journey, 'which was the model that the Royal Hospital Haslar was built to serve'.[1] This was no longer as relevant to naval warfare in the twentieth century.

The pre-war pattern of distribution for naval hospitals at home was very much based on the administrative division of the Royal Navy into three Home Commands based at Portsmouth, Plymouth and the Nore, served by the Royal Naval Hospitals of Haslar, Plymouth and Chatham. There were also smaller naval hospitals at Portland and South Queensferry, while Royal Naval Hospital Yarmouth was reserved for psychiatric cases. These hospitals had the primary function of treating the sick and injured but 'there is also the very important ancillary function of training the junior medical officers, nursing sisters and sick berth staff in their duties', functions which had to be maintained with the wartime influx of new staff.[2] Sick quarters with accommodation for emergency and short-term surgical and medical patients were also attached to the permanent shore establishments. There were Royal Marine infirmaries at Deal, Chatham, Portsmouth and Plymouth together with Royal Naval sick quarters attached to Dartmouth Royal Naval College and the Boys' Training Establishment at Shotley. These arrangements worked well in peacetime but were not considered tenable in wartime conditions. Haslar, Chatham, Deal and Shotley were too vulnerable to be earmarked as anything but casualty first aid and clearing stations. Planning in the months before the outbreak of war for medical facilities ashore were based on these assumptions:

> In the event of a war with a European country, the Royal Naval Hospitals at Chatham and Haslar would be untenable as base hospitals, i.e. as hospitals to which sick and wounded from the Fleet could be sent, or in which cases could be kept under treatment for any length of time.[3]

Haslar had been opened in 1754 on the Gosport side of Portsmouth Harbour. Access was by boat to a hospital jetty on the edge of Haslar Creek but the hospital was not so accessible by land. This had been considered an advantage when the hospital was founded and desertion of patients had been a problem but now this was a disadvantage when access by sea and land routes could easily be disrupted.[4] Close to military targets in Portsmouth Harbour, the hospital was vulnerable to attack from both air and sea. It seemed unlikely that it could be maintained as a hospital once Portsmouth came under enemy attack. Its buildings were old and outmoded, but they were separate from each other, spread out over a large site, and were solidly constructed; its cellars offered shelter suitable for a casualty clearing station. Chatham, by contrast, was perhaps even more vulnerable because of its comparatively modern buildings. Opened in 1905, it occupied a modern, compact pavilion on high ground in Gillingham with extensive views over the Medway towns and the surrounding countryside. It was close to the naval dockyard and on the direct flight path of German bombers heading for London and the Thames estuary. Not only could it have been knocked out in one raid with no alternative buildings to which medical facilities could have been dispersed but it was also well lit by large glass windows which could be considered an advantage for staff and patients in peacetime but a major disadvantage in the blackout.[5] In both cases the hospitals were prominent and had been built as prestigious expressions of naval might which made them easy targets in modern war.

It was recommended that patients and staff from Haslar and Chatham should be evacuated to Plymouth immediately on the outbreak of war, although the long-term viability of Plymouth and even Portland to withstand enemy attack was also doubted.[6] Plymouth, originally built in 1758 in an isolated area, was now part of the densely-populated Stonehouse area between Plymouth and Devonport and, although it was always going to be vulnerable to attack because of its proximity to a major naval base, had the advantage of being further from the enemy air force bases at the beginning of the war than Haslar and Chatham.[7]

In 1939 plans were drawn up for the relocation of the main naval hospitals to safer locations, west of a line on the map drawn from Berwick through Nottingham and Reading to Weymouth. Any such base hospital should be easily accessible by rail, remote from military and industrial targets and away from densely-populated areas. Sites in the areas around Newbury, Gloucester, Bath, Hereford, Shrewsbury, Lancaster and Carlisle were all considered. A site was also sought in Devon in case Plymouth proved untenable. It was also important that a base hospital should be provided in Scotland convenient by rail to ships in the Firth of Forth and Firth of Clyde to supplement the existing naval hospital at Port Edgar. Rather than build hospital facilities at Scapa Flow it was decided to rely on a hospital ship and this remained the case throughout the war. At other ports, ships would bring in casualties for reception in either a hospital ship, naval hospital, local sick quarters or a civil hospital before transfer by ambulance train or hospital ship to the nearest main naval base hospital.[8] These plans were made on the assumption that only one of the three main naval hospitals would be available for the reception of the sick and wounded from the fleet and the retention of patients requiring prolonged treatment. At first there was little or no provision for inter-service collaboration, although as the war progressed this made increasing sense.

Auxiliary hospitals were established at a safe distance from the south coast where the older naval hospitals had traditionally been located. Most of them were set up in requisitioned civilian hospitals, although large boarding schools were also considered to be suitable premises. In 1939 auxiliary hospitals were set up in a newly-built mental hospital at Barrow Gurney near Bristol, in the Devon County Council Public Institution at Newton Abbot and in a former mental hospital at Kingseat in Aberdeenshire. The Royal Naval Hospital Great Yarmouth was evacuated to Lancaster for the duration where it continued to specialise in the field of mental health. As the war went on, further auxiliary hospitals were opened, some of them for specialised cases such as the hospitals for neuro-psychiatric cases opened at Cholmondley Castle in Cheshire and at Knowle in Hampshire in 1941. At Kilmacolm near Glasgow, opened in 1942, there was accommodation for venereal diseases cases and sick Wrens. In 1943 the Victoria Hotel at Southport was converted into a hospital for diseases of the chest, especially cases of tuberculosis with the ballroom, dining room and smoking room being turned into wards. There was even an auxiliary hospital opened specifically for officers at Durdham Down, Clifton. Seaforth and Woolton near Liverpool, opened in 1943 in a former mental home and a corporation convalescent home, offered much-needed medical facilities on Merseyside when the Command of the Western Approaches was transferred to Liverpool.[9] Londonderry also obtained its own auxiliary naval hospital in 1944 in a former military camp converted to a hospital by the Royal Army Medical Corps, the naval base having relied upon the United States Naval Hospital at Creevagh since 1942.[10] Only one large hutted hospital was built at Sherborne between July 1941 and February 1942 under the auspices of the Emergency Medical Services (EMS) but allocated to the Royal Navy. It was to specialise in orthopaedic surgery.[11]

Perhaps the largest of the wartime auxiliary hospitals was that at Barrow Gurney, which had 25 medical officers under the command of a surgeon rear admiral, 35 to 45 nursing sisters and up to 165 sick berth attendants. When the Barrow Gurney Mental Hospital was requisitioned by the navy in the autumn of 1939 it was expected that the 500-bedded hospital would have to take in large numbers of casualties for reception, resuscitation and treatment, but the hospital was never fully put to the test. Instead the appointment of consultants in neurology, neuro-surgery and psychological medicine made it a centre for the treatment of mental illness in the navy and for the training of naval medical officers in psychiatric medicine. Psychotherapy, narco-analysis, insulin therapy and electro-convulsive therapy were all used on the patients. The hospital had spacious recreation grounds and gardens enjoyed by both the psychiatric patients and general medical and surgical patients of the hospital.[12] As a reserve establishment, Barrow Gurney was more relaxed with regard to discipline and the observance of regulations than most naval hospitals. The patients would often escape from their wards to a nearby pub for a drink with the connivance of the medical officer on duty doing his rounds so long as they were back when he checked up on them.[13] While the standard of sick berth attendants was considered mediocre or at best 'run of the mill',[14] it was said that the young surgeon captain in charge of the hospital chose the nursing staff 'not only for their ability but also for their pulchritude'.[15] It all helped to maintain good spirits among the patients as well as gladdening the eye of the officer in charge.

In addition to the auxiliary hospitals, Royal Naval sick quarters were established at various shore establishments where there was little access to a hospital. Some of them, such as HMS *Europa* at Lowestoft, had the responsibilities and commitments of a regular hospital but others were little more than glorified sick bays. If a sick berth could be raised to the dignity of sick quarters then sick quarters could just as easily be transformed into a Royal Naval Auxiliary Hospital in 'something of an Alice in Wonderland atmosphere', as Bernard Hunt cynically described it, all to raise the status and salary of the medical officer in charge. If the establishment had 300 beds it would be classed as a Royal Naval Auxiliary Hospital. All that was necessary was for a senior medical officer to order 150 double bunks instead of single beds to transform a 150-bedded sick quarters into a 300-bedded auxiliary hospital. At RN Auxiliary Hospital Seaforth where Hunt was stationed in 1941 to help to 'build up a hospital from scratch as we lacked all the necessary equipment' to serve the sick and wounded from the escort ships on the Western Approaches,[16] there was originally only accommodation for 150 patients in naval sick quarters. Until the hospital buildings could be extended to meet the need for an auxiliary naval hospital in Liverpool, the number of beds was doubled through the use of bunks although this resulted in severe overcrowding for a time in facilities with auxiliary hospital status.[17] The patients were 'exhausted young men who sometimes had no sleep for 48 hours' and for whom hospital services were essential.[18]

Requisitioned hospital buildings, usually mental hospitals such as Seaforth, Barrow Gurney and Kingseat, were easily converted to naval use, but other large buildings such as schools, hotels and country houses were also suitable for conversion into hospitals. Lord Roborough's Georgian country house at Maristow near Plymouth was initially taken over by the Admiralty in 1942 for use as a neuro-psychiatric centre but was instead used as a convalescent facility for patients from the naval hospital at Plymouth.[19] Wraxall Court, a country house between Bristol and Clevedon, was used by the hospital at Barrow Gurney from 1944 as a convalescent home for officers and for the treatment of officers suffering from mild psychiatric disorders. These naval officers enjoyed the use of a drawing room, dining room and billiard room as if they were guests at a pre-war country house party, though they were also expected to attend occupational therapy in a hut in the extensive grounds, whose gardens and greenhouses supplied fruit and vegetables to the hospital and convalescent home.[20] An orthopaedic rehabilitation centre for patients from Chatham was opened at Oakley House near Bromley, with the officers accommodated in the house itself and ratings put up in huts erected in the grounds. However, Oakley House was bombed in June 1944 and the centre was transferred to the less comfortable premises of St Felix School at Southwold, where officers and ratings actually shared the same block.[21] Social and class distinctions were as alive as ever in wartime, whatever the myth of the Blitz spirit may have suggested. The auxiliary hospital at Kilmacolm was housed in the requisitioned Kilmacolm Hydro to the resentment of prosperous local people, who 'seemed to feel that they were suffering some hardship' by losing access to their local spa amenities.[22]

United States Naval Hospitals were, as might be expected, considerably more luxurious than British ones, even though standards in these had also been relaxed by reducing the space between beds from 8ft to 6ft and it was usually necessary to construct temporary ward buildings to deal with wartime demands. In the United Kingdom there were two American naval base hospitals, one at Londonderry, commissioned in 1942, and, from February 1944, another at the Royal Victoria Military Hospital at Netley, Hampshire, supplemented by dispensaries throughout the United Kingdom. Any patients that needed to be returned to the United States for further treatment were evacuated through the US Naval Dispensary at Roseneath in Scotland and the US Naval Advanced Amphibious Base at Plymouth.[23] Convalescent centres were also opened for the first time by the United States Navy in requisitioned hotels, colleges, resorts and sanatoriums to cater for patients who only needed rest, good nutrition, psychotherapy, or physiotherapy rather than medical or surgical treatment. At Blackheath near London there was a 50-bed convalescent home.[24]

Co-operation with other wartime medical services soon became necessary. Where there were insufficient naval hospitals, naval patients had no choice but to be treated in army or civilian hospitals. Any sick and wounded landed on the Tyne would be treated in an army hospital and those landed in Southampton might be sent to an army hospital at Bournemouth or Bath.[25] Naval burns victims requiring plastic surgery were treated by Harold Gillies at Park Prewett, an EMS hospital, where there was a naval medical liaison officer to keep an eye on the progress of naval patients.[26] Other navy burns victims were treated by Gillies' cousin Archibald McIndoe at the RAF unit at the Queen Victoria Hospital at East Grinstead.[27] Neurosurgery cases were sent to the Military Hospital for Head Injuries at Oxford and other injured sailors sent to EMS hospitals at Mount Vernon, Stoke Mandeville and Horton.[28] The Liverpool Radium Institute offered X-ray therapy and the Merseyside Blood Transfusion Services blood supplies to Seaforth.[29] Limbless sailors were sent to Ministry of Pensions hospitals to be fitted with artificial limbs before discharge.[30] The naval hospitals, in turn, liaised closely with army and EMS hospitals and offered their services when needed to soldiers and civilians. Haslar opened its doors to international patients, including British and Empire servicemen, Americans, Free French, Norwegians, Dutch and Poles. Haslar also took in the army wounded following the Normandy landings so that these men would receive the treatment that they needed as soon as possible.[31] Haslar additionally had arrangements with civilian medical services under the 'Mutual Aid Scheme' to offer any necessary help to other local hospitals which may have found it difficult to cope during frequent and damaging air raids. The operating theatre was prepared for the use of the nearby Alverstoke EMS Hospital if it were needed and staff at Haslar guaranteed to deliver the equipment and an operating theatre assistant to Alverstoke within an hour.[32] When a cinema in Portsmouth received a direct hit the charred remains of the victims were brought into Haslar in tarpaulin bundles; it was difficult to differentiate between civilian, soldier and sailor.[33]

Not only were the naval hospitals subject to air raids, but there was also the need to defend them against the threat of invasion as in addition to being hospitals they were also naval facilities at war to be defended against enemy attack. The massive walls built at Haslar and Plymouth to keep eighteenth-century seamen in were now found to be inadequate for keeping the enemy out. Passive defensive measures were essential. At Portsmouth the Commander-in-Chief was rightly concerned that Haslar 'might be a source of embarrassment as regards defence of the port of Portsmouth in the event of an invasion' since it was a weak point in the fortification of the naval base:

> The hospital occupies a considerable proportion of the Gosport peninsula which would be a valuable acquisition to the enemy if captured, and the enemy have long ceased to bother about scraps of paper like the Geneva Convention.[34]

Measures were taken to protect the hospital, including lopping the lower branches of trees in the paddock near the hospital pigsty to clear the line of fire and scything the long grass and undergrowth in the paddock and cemetery to prevent it from being used as cover by any invasion force. Firing platforms were constructed behind loopholes made in the outer walls, the sea walls were topped with barbed wire 'to insure that no landing can be made from the sea under cover of darkness', and sandbagged and camouflaged strongpoints constructed. Roadblocks and barriers were set up on the road and bridge over the creek that made up the already restricted land approach to the hospital.[35]

Invasion did not come, but there was a need for protection against air raids as from the summer of 1940 Portsmouth was within a few minute's flying time of occupied France and the naval base was a prime target. Strict blackout regulations were enforced and the ground-floor wards at Haslar were made blast and splinter-proof on the most exposed sides by the erection of buttressed and traversed brick walls and revetments while the walls facing the inner courtyards were protected by sandbags. The extensive cellars beneath the hospital were used as air-raid shelters equipped with bunks for the patients and ventilated by electric table fans. Two operating theatres, fitted with air-conditioning and a gas filtration unit, were installed.[36] During the heavy air raids on Portsmouth of 1940 and 1941, the hospital museum and library were completely destroyed but the main hospital received only minor damage and no lives were lost, although £80,000 worth of medical stores were destroyed and 'for days afterwards ... feathers from stuffed birds, former resplendent museum exhibits, were flying everywhere'.[37] A resident fire party was also set up from stokers and seamen under the supervision of an executive naval officer, co-operating with nearby naval establishments and the National Fire Service to render assistance where needed. Meanwhile, the hospital remained ready for the reception of casualties at short notice.[38]

At Chatham, there was also a move underground with the proposed construction of an underground operating theatre in 1939, to be followed by similar facilities at Haslar, Plymouth and Portsmouth.[39] Plans for that purpose-built theatre was abandoned when it was realised that it would be too expensive and take too long to construct, but existing basements were quickly converted into four protected, gas-proof and air-conditioned operating theatres, anaesthetic rooms and recovery rooms. A greater challenge was blacking out the 8,000 window panes in the hospital and staff residences, including 2,700 panes of glass in the main corridor alone.[40]

Plymouth was heavily bombed, with 602 raids between 30 June 1940 and 24 April 1944. In March 1941 ten high-explosive bombs and a large number of incendiary bombs fell on the hospital, damaging the mental block, officers' block, officers' mess and the chaplain's residence, and also causing disruption to local water supplies that meant that the only water for the hospital was available from the creek between full and half tides. A dam was then built at the Stonehouse Jetty to ensure that water could always be obtained from the creek regardless of the tide. A ward block was destroyed and other buildings seriously damaged in April and May 1941 with two deaths. When gas supplies to Plymouth were cut off in January 1941, the hospital obtained alternative supplies from Devonport.[41] During his training in 1942, sick berth attendant A J E McCreedy considered himself and his colleagues lucky when the sirens sounded after a bomb fell on the hospital rather than before since 'if the sirens had sounded first, we would have run into the blast and there is no doubt that most of us would have been killed' as they headed for casualty duties in the ward to which they had been assigned.[42] Further damage was done to the fabric of the hospital in a raid on 13 February 1943 when two high-explosive bombs blew out all the doors and windows in the hospital and shattered all the ceilings and roofs. Eight sick berth attendants were injured by the blast and it was necessary to evacuate all patients to the nearest auxiliary hospitals at Maristow, Newton Abbot and Barrow Gurney, yet within five days the hospital was once again functioning as usual. The scale of the air raids and damage to the hospital meant that from 1941 the hospital, whose peacetime bed complement had been raised from 350 to 728 in wartime, was downgraded to a casualty clearing station with accommodation for 150 patients. By the beginning of 1945, with the end of any likelihood of any further air raids, it was possible for the hospital to resume its role as a base hospital despite the destruction of two entire blocks. Throughout the war, teams from the naval hospital would be sent out to assist at local civilian hospitals when necessary, a mobile surgical unit was kept at readiness to assist with air-raid casualties and civilian air-raid casualties were admitted to the naval hospital.[43] So great had been the pressure on the naval hospitals at Plymouth and Newton Abbot that in 1943 consideration was given to the inauguration of a naval hospital at Dartmouth to replace the naval sick quarters there to take some of the strain.[44]

It was not only at home that the traditional organisation and distribution of naval hospitals was disrupted. Abroad there were challenges just as great, if not greater. Bighi Hospital in Malta was the peacetime base hospital for the destroyer and submarine flotillas stationed in Malta and for the Mediterranean Fleet. It was backed up by the hospital ship *Maine* and the use of civil hospitals in Egypt, RAF hospitals in Suez and Palestine and the British Military Hospital in Gibraltar, a forerunner of the wartime co-operation between the medical services of the three armed forces. Even before the outbreak of war it was realised that should Italy enter the conflict, Malta would be vulnerable and that if the Fleet were based at Alexandria there would be a need for more shore medical facilities in Egypt. The only solution would be for army and navy co-operation with the pooling of resources on the basis of mutual need. Such a policy recognised that the trophy naval hospital in Malta would probably have to be abandoned for all practical purposes.[45]

Occupying a prominent and impressive location overlooking the Grand Harbour at Valetta, said to have been chosen by Napoleon as the site for a palace he hoped to build once he had conquered Europe, the Royal Naval Hospital Bighi was an easy target for Italian bombers. The first bombs on Malta fell outside the hospital gates at Bighi on the morning of 11 June 1940, marking the beginning of the second great siege of the island. A leading sick berth attendant was killed outright and a doctor was injured by shrapnel when a bomb fell on a ward.[46] The patients and most of the staff were immediately evacuated inland to the less vulnerable 90th General Hospital at Imtafa, leaving only a skeleton staff at Bighi who at first found it difficult to occupy themselves without their usual patients. Sister Waterman even volunteered for laundry duties although she soon 'blotted my copy book by wielding a heavy flat iron on our rather dandified SBA's long white trousers, forgetting that the creases should have run fore and aft and turning them into bell-bottoms'.[47] She was relieved when she was eventually posted to Imtafa, where 'life was very pleasant in spite of the increasingly heavy air raids, many on the fighter aerodrome of T'Kali just below the hospital complex'. The hospital was a military one but the experience of working with army doctors and nurses proved 'enlivening' for the naval staff from Bighi who established a naval wing.[48] During emergencies such as the influx of casualties after the bombing of *Illustrious* in 1941 'everyone worked flat out that weekend, meals were ignored and even up patients turned to by making tea and toast for any of the staff who could take a break'.[49] Severely damaged by air raids, Bighi still functioned as a casualty clearing station until the attacks on Malta ended and it was possible to repair and modernise the imposing buildings, a symbol of British naval might in the Mediterranean.[50]

The main hospital serving the fleet in the Mediterranean throughout the war was the Naval Wing of 64th General Hospital set up in Victoria College in Alexandria. In this one building the two very different approaches of the Royal Naval Medical Service and the Royal Army Medical Corps were forced to co-exist. As the hospital was under the overall control of the army, the navy had to make compromises. Stores, catering, cooking, dispensing and general administration were under army control, with assistance from naval sick berth attendants, while the bulk of the nursing was carried out by efficient naval staff. Sister Edith MacDonald was praised for her treatment of orthopaedic casualties from the battle of El Alamein and the evacuation of the Greek islands when her 'untiring attention and her unfailing good humour and temper did a very good deal to bring about the recovery of many severely wounded men'.[51] There were differences made in the facilities for sailors, who needed somewhere to stow their bags and hammocks whereas there was no provision for soldiers to store their kit. Crockery and cutlery had to be provided for the naval patients whereas soldiers carried their own with them. Until the closure of the hospital in September 1944 when the army withdrew and an auxiliary naval hospital was set up in the San Stefano Casino to which the students of Victoria College had been evacuated in 1939, the two services managed to work in increasing harmony with each other. In 1941 the Admiralty recognised that 'with the Fleet working from Beirut to Aden it follows that naval patients become somewhat scattered, but there has never been any difficulty in finding the necessary accommodation in army hospitals'.[52] During the battles for Greece and Crete, arrangements were made for army medical treatment of naval casualties.[53] Without army facilities and resources, the Royal Navy would have found it difficult to treat its sick and wounded in the Mediterranean.

Following the successful invasion of North Africa by the Allied forces at Algiers, Oran and Casablanca, victory at El Alamein and the landings in Sicily and Italy, naval liaison with army, air force and other Allied medical services remained vital but changing medical needs led to the establishment of a number of new sick quarters as the advances continued. Many of these were improvised in nature in response to operational requirements. At Tobruk, a sick berth attendant, R Sebbage, was given the task of setting up a sick bay in 1941 with requisitioned beds and linen. Bed linen was in such short supply that Sebbage preferred to leave a merchant seaman with severe diarrhoea seated on the lavatory seat surrounded by pillows where 'he could defecate with impunity – or to put it bluntly – to his backside's content whilst I attended to his dehydration' to stop the linen being dirtied until the toilet was damaged in an air raid and the patient required twenty-seven sutures in his backside after he collapsed on 'the jagged china throne'.[54] Frank Henley was charged with setting up sick quarters at Ferryville in Tunisia in 1943. He requisitioned a school which he converted into a 100-bedded hospital with separate wards for officers and ratings. There were twelve showers which brought many army and navy visitors to the sick quarters not because of ill health but because they craved the luxury of a shower, although another attraction was the four cases of Veuve Cliquot champagne acquired by Henley when shopping for provisions.[55] Tented hospitals for the Mobile Naval Base Defence units of the Royal Marines were looked upon with a measure of suspicion by naval medical officers who considered them to be more suitable for land-based forces and that the medical treatment of casualties on land were better dealt with by the Royal Army Medical Corps, who in many cases had to resupply them from army resources of equipment and medicines.[56] Where such isolated tented hospital units had a place in naval medicine was 'in a static role, where patients can stay in hospital until they are better, and where the need for rapid evacuation does not arise'.[57]

Just as improvised was the Royal Naval Auxiliary Hospital Vaenga established in 1942 in North Russia to care for British casualties from the Arctic convoys since the Russian hospitals were too overcrowded and understaffed to provide adequate treatment for casualties from the Royal Navy and Merchant Navy. The hospital was on the upper floors of a barracks building also occupied by a Russian hospital which made a degree of collaboration inevitable. The British relied on the Russians for ambulance transport, fuel and some food supplies although these were supplemented by supplies sent with the convoy ships. There was no running hot water and surgical instruments had to be sterilised in bowls of heavily chlorinated water heated on a primus stove. Hot water for bathing was provided only once a week and only if adequate coal supplies were available.[58]

With the Japanese attack on the United States at Pearl Harbor and on the British possessions in the Far East, there were new pressures on naval hospitals. The naval hospital at Hong Kong was a serious loss, although it was old-fashioned and in need of replacement even before the war. As soon as the Japanese attack on Hong Kong began on 8 December 1941, all patients fit for duty were discharged and the remaining patients were moved from the top floor to the ground floor of the hospital. All operating and ward drums were packed ready for the receipt of casualties although they were not sterilised. Patients were each given a hand washbowl as head protection and a mattress to cover themselves with during air raids. As the continual air-raid alarms were causing 'too much time to be wasted' and there was indeed 'a very trying shortage of staff during the period of the hostilities', doctors, nursing sisters, sick berth attendants and Auxiliary Nursing Service nurses continued with their work under cover on the ground floor. The Chinese hospital staff, however, were 'petrified' and ran off to the air-raid precautions tunnels under the hospital as soon as the siren sounded and remained there all day. They later threatened to leave unless permission was given for them to join their families in the tunnel shelters at night. This 'trouble with the Chinese' was to come to a head when the Chinese coolies looted the sisters' quarters in the confusion after a bomb hit the ground floor of the hospital on 20 December, a day that 'started badly', shattering the typhoon screen, filling the ward with acrid smoke and fracturing the water and sewage pipes. Already the electricity and water supplies to the hospital from the town had failed. All water had to be collected from underground tanks in front of the hospital. There was only one bowl of water for every twelve patients. Instruments were boiled over a large four-jet primus stove. Laundry was now impossible and clean sheets had to be obtained from the China Fleet Club. Without electricity it was impossible to take X-rays and only after the fall of Hong Kong was it possible to get X-rays taken at the Bowen Road Military Hospital. Operations were carried out in a passage between two wards. Although damaged by air raids and without essential services the hospital did not move to the Aberdeen naval sick quarters as at one time arranged for such an eventuality:

> We had originally planned to evacuate the hospital to Aberdeen should the enemy arrive in Kowloon or should RNH be rendered useless or untenable. In the actual event this seemed to me unnecessary as Aberdeen would have been at least as dangerous and necessarily much less efficient.[59]

As capitulation approached 'the nights were very disturbed now by continuous gunfire and sniping which sounded very close to the hospital'. The wards were dark because the typhoon shutters were closed as protection from gunfire. Miss Franklin, the superintending sister, had a narrow escape from a sniper's bullet. A patient was wounded by fragments from a shell burst as he lay in bed. On Christmas Eve, Surgeon Commander H L Cleave, who was in command of the hospital, 'thinking that the enemy might filter into the hospital', returned all valuables to their owners 'rather than that I should be forced to open my safe and surrender them'. A carol service on Christmas Eve was held with a young sick berth attendant playing the harmonium and leading the singing. The patients were given a good Christmas dinner of roast beef, Christmas pudding, fruit, sweets and a tot of rum paid for by one of the naval chaplains.[60]

After the surrender of Hong Kong on Christmas Day, it was possible to try to restore the badly-damaged hospital to working order, despite visits from the Japanese to steal watches, rings and fountain pens from the staff and patients. Debris was cleared and a RAF ambulance was obtained for the collection of provisions and transfer of patients. As much tinned food was bought as was available and this 'extra tinned milk and fruit undoubtedly helped to save many lives'.[61] In addition to the 120 patients in the hospital at the end of hostilities, a further 18 were admitted from Queen Mary Hospital and 15 from University Hospital to be tended by the 35-strong staff. Most of the patients were 'making a rapid recovery' and the hospital was working efficiently again when on 18 January 1942 the order was given by the Japanese to evacuate to a military hospital set up at St Alban's Convent. In the rush to evacuate the hospital, both Cleave and Franklin lost their attaché cases containing their private papers, receipts, valuables and records. The nurses were only allowed to take one valise each and lost many of their personal possessions.[62] All medical equipment was left behind:

> All hospital equipment and all private and household property was taken over by the Japanese, and only personnel effects, clothing etc. was permitted to be taken with us, with a small amount of hospital food supplies.[63]

What food supplies were brought from the naval hospital were put into a communal store administered by the Royal Army Medical Corps and Cleave admitted that 'it is only fair to say that during our stay at St Albert's we received more from this store than we put into it'.[64]

For the staff and patients from the naval hospital their stay at St Albert's Convent was a short one as they were split up and sent to different camps and hospitals on 25 February 1942. The naval patients were transferred to Bowen Road Military Hospital with Cleave and the naval nursing sisters or were discharged and sent to North Point Camp with the sick berth staff and some of the medical officers. The remaining medical officers were sent to the military hospital set up at St Theresa's Convent in Kowloon. Cleave had expected that the VADs and Auxiliary Nursing Service nurses, many of whom had become nursing volunteers in order to stay with their husbands and families rather than be evacuated from the colony in 1940 with other women and children, would be recognised as civilians and sent to Stanley Camp to join other civilian internees, but instead they were treated as naval personnel and sent to St Theresa's Convent.[65] Cleave's concern for the welfare of the auxiliary nurses was sharpened by his knowledge of the atrocities committed by the invading Japanese at the military hospitals set up at St Stephen's Convent and the Jockey Club, when nurses had been raped and killed after the capitulation. One of the VAD nurses at St Stephen's, Mrs Begg, whose husband was one of the wounded in the hospital, was found with her 'head almost severed from her body'.[66] The naval hospital had been spared such outrages and the carnage experienced at some of the military hospitals, including the bayonetting and shooting of patients and medical staff. After Hong Kong was retaken by the Royal Navy at the end of the war, a new up-to-date naval hospital was built to replace the one that had undergone such a battering during the fall of the colony.

The loss of the only Royal Navy Hospital east of Suez, that at Hong Kong, had removed the lynchpin of the pre-war arrangements for the care of the sick of the China Squadron. Singapore had the Asiatic Hospital at the naval base but that was only for the use of Asian dockyard workers. There were also naval sick quarters at Trincomalee and Diyatalawa. Otherwise the Royal Navy had arrangements with civilian hospitals in Singapore, Johore, Ceylon (Sri Lanka), India, Burma, Aden, Kenya, Tanganyika and Mauritius. Luckily, planning for war in the Far East had arranged that the main centre for naval hospitals in the Far East would be in Ceylon on the assumption that Hong Kong, Singapore and Malaya would fall to the Japanese, as indeed they did. Following that debacle, the severely-depleted East Indies Fleet was withdrawn to East Africa. At Durban and Johannesburg the military hospitals were unable to deal adequately with the demands from naval patients particularly at a time when invalids from India were being evacuated and transported by rounding the Cape at a time when the Mediterranean was closed. A naval hospital was opened at Durban in March 1944 to relieve the pressure.[67] Royal Naval Hospital Simonstown increased its bed complement from 87 beds to 220 in 1941 and was popular with convalescent men.[68]

The increased interest in planning for operations against Japan as the war in Europe came to a close showed the urgent need for new naval hospitals in the Far East. Auxiliary hospitals were established at Sydney and Brisbane. A second auxiliary hospital was opened in Colombo. An auxiliary hospital was commissioned in Bombay and another planned for Mandapam, while facilities at Cochin and Vizagapatam were to be expanded. The Combined Services Hospital at Trincomalee, opened in April 1945, was under naval direction in contrast to other such hospitals in which the army medical services had overall control as at Alexandria. Sick quarters took on the work of small general hospitals. Five new hospital ships were required, but only three old ships were available for conversion and none of them were commissioned before the end of the war.[69] Sheldon Dudley, Medical Director General of the Royal Navy Medical Department, was ever-realistic about what resources could be gained and admitted that 'if one takes risks, and so far in this war casualties have always been overestimated by the General Staff, one may get away with a smaller "bed state" without a medical scandal. In any case the Medical Branch will do its best to avoid one.' He did admit that the American hospital facilities were in his opinion 'so lavish that there is little likelihood of any lack of beds for our men'.[70]

In 1941 there had been nineteen naval hospitals in the United States, three others outside North America, two hospital ships and one mobile hospital, but by the end of the war there were forty-two naval hospitals and twelve naval convalescent hospitals in the United States, with six permanent hospitals, thirty-six mobile, base, or fleet hospitals, twelve hospital ships, three hospital transports, and three military government hospitals overseas for naval needs.[71] Whereas previously inadequacies in naval hospital provision had been compensated for by co-operation with the army, in the Far East the American allies were now relied upon to meet any deficiencies. A new type of hospital, the Special Augmented Hospital, was planned for American use in the onslaught on Japan. It was a cross between a Marine Corps field hospital and the fleet base hospitals that had been used throughout the war in the Pacific. Eight were planned but only two had come into operation on Okinawa before the end of the war. The hospitals were thought to have too many semi-permanent components to be quickly erected during combat but to be too temporary in character to offer much comfort or efficiency once hostilities were over.[72] Nevertheless, there were doubts about whether naval medical resources would have been up to coping with the casualties from a protracted war in the Far East had Japan not capitulated when it did.[73] Had the war continued more hospital ships would have been sorely needed to deal with casualties.

Eleven hospital ships were in use by the Royal Navy during the Second World War, although only *Maine* was in service in 1939. Built in 1902, the ship had originally been built for the South American cattle trade but had been converted into a hospital ship during the First World War and was then purchased by the Admiralty in 1921. It had one main operating theatre, a smaller genito-urinary theatre and a laboratory amidships on the main deck, with a physiotherapy department and mortuary aft on the starboard side of the ship. Patients were brought up from the surgical ward to the main deck by a hand-winched cot lift. The medical ward was aft with the wards for officers above it. The zymotic ward was isolated below the waterline. The ship was coal fired and, when it was necessary to stock up with coal, patients were discharged to their own ships or transferred to shore hospitals, while the crew, sick berth attendants included, unloaded the coal lighters and humped heavy bags of coal, 'the perspiration running in rivulets down their bodies accumulating in rather delicate places'.[74] Attached to the Mediterranean Fleet, *Maine* took part in an emergency mission to rescue under fire refugees from the Spanish Civil War, including women from maternity hospitals, which gave a foretaste of the war to come. Cots were made from fishnets and babies' bottles improvised by fitting condoms over the necks of medicine bottles.[75] As another war became imminent, it was realised that *Maine* was too old and inadequate to be relied upon to provide hospital-ship facilities in a future conflict. The substantial overhaul and refitting necessary to bring her up to standard made a replacement vessel preferable to the high expenditure necessary on *Maine*. In 1937 the Admiralty decided for the first time to commission a purpose-built hospital ship but the preparations for the approach of war meant that there were other shipbuilding priorities and the project was abandoned. Instead, after the outbreak of war, merchant vessels, with their crews, were requisitioned for conversion to hospital ships.[76]

Many of these vessels were unsuitable for use as hospital ships. The conversion of *Vasna* at Bombay was carried out too quickly and was poorly planned. Accommodation for medical and nursing staff was inadequate for tropical service with twenty-two sick berth attendants crammed into a small space next to the engine room and galley. There was a space for storing ice but no refrigeration plant. Wooden deck structures added to the ship for ward accommodation left little deck space for recreation. Unseasoned wood was used and within weeks there were gaping seams and the deck structures were letting in water. The ship was also found to be rat-infested. In view of its many defects as a hospital ship, *Vasna* spent about a third of her commissioned war service in dock for repair and refitting.[77] *Amarapoora* was also ill-equipped for service in the Tropics. A coal-burning ship, she had insufficient power to make any reasonable speed against the monsoon currents and her cooling system broke down when she served as an army hospital carrier in the Bay of Bengal between May and August 1945. Patients had to be embarked and disembarked in torrential rainfall and the heat and humidity on board was considered unbearable at times.[78] Another difficulty found in using European naval hospital ships in Indian waters and the Far East was that they were unsuitable for carrying non-European patients. There were rarely separate galleys for cooking Hindu and Muslim diets, A shortage of rice and lack of separate facilities for their religious and cultural needs on *Oxfordshire* in 1944 resulted in a hunger strike by a number of Sikh patients.[79] *Oxfordshire*, built in 1912, had beds for 505 patients served by ten medical officers under the command of a surgeon captain and nine nursing sisters under a matron. The ship was to treat 22,331 patients during the war compared to the 13,514 received on *Maine* during those six years of war.[80] Wartime needs meant that there was no real alternative to the conversion of unsuitable vessels into hospital ships. American hospital ships, by contrast, were completely air-conditioned and enjoyed all the facilities of a modern hospital unlike their British counterparts.[81]

While a hospital ship for army casualties was primarily seen as a carrier, the Admiralty used its hospital ships as floating hospitals offering full medical and surgical facilities to the Fleet. In planning for D-Day, the decision was made that LSTs should be 'specially fitted to carry wounded on their return trip from the French shore' in the early stages of 'Overlord' before hospital ships could be used.[82]

Painted white with a band of green and with a red cross painted on the hull, hospital ships 'possess special privileges including immunity from capture, which carry with them corresponding obligations in the way of abstention from warlike operations'.[83] Yet these ships were never safe from attack during air raids. The officers' wards, medical officers' cabins, electric circuits and water pipes on *Maine* were badly damaged when it was serving as a base hospital ship at Alexandria in 1941. None of the patients were harmed, but four members of the ship's company, including the principal medical officer, were killed and twelve wounded.[84]

At first the Admiralty was opposed to employing QARNS nurses on board hospital ships because of the difficulties and costs of providing them with living spaces and sanitary facilities when merchant vessels were converted. However, despite the limited accommodation for them, it was soon decided that it would be in the interests of the patients for women nurses to serve on these ships. Nursing sisters found few problems in messing with the naval medical officers or indeed with Merchant Navy officers. Service on a hospital ship was voluntary for nursing sisters and limited to a year, though it was not always possible to enforce this regulation. After serving the Home Fleet in Scapa Flow, *Varna* saw service from 1942 onwards off the coast of West, South and East Africa, off Madagascar, in the Mediterranean, the Indian Ocean, Persian Gulf and the Bay of Bengal, which gave little opportunity for the relief and replacement of nursing sisters although it gave them unrivalled experience of nursing in all climates.[85]

The provision of hospital ships for the war against Japan was affected by a shortage of shipping and the modification of hospital ships to cope with tropical conditions and the long distances to be travelled in the Far East. The original estimates of 500 beds to be provided was reduced to 300. A compromise was reached between military and naval requirements which resulted in the Royal Navy only being allotted three out of the five additional ships originally allocated to it for the war against Japan. Many of the hospital ships, moreover, were in poor condition.[86] The adequacy of this provision was not to be tested. With the surrender of Japan, the hospital ships took on a different role in the repatriation of released prisoners of war and civilian internees as well as continuing to serve the navy.[87] Although not adapted for carrying women and children, the hospital ships found themselves involved with the repatriation of civilians, travelling over long distances. *Oxfordshire* served as a hospital carrying ex-prisoners of war from Hong Kong to Sydney, Singapore and Liverpool, many of them suffering from pellagra, beri-beri, dysentery and malaria. During that voyage seven patients died and one woman was confined.[88] *Amarapoora* carried men, women and children, many of them suffering from malnutrition, from Singapore to Madras then transported a further consignment of patients from Rangoon to Calcutta, including Indian soldiers.[89] *Vasna* transferred invalided prisoners of war to Australia. A further journey took Malayan civilians, Indian and Chinese internees from Rabaul to Singapore.[90] *Tijitjalengka* collected ex-prisoners of war from Yokohama to take to Auckland, New Zealand, then repatriated ex-internees from Shanghai and Singapore, disembarking Asian patients at Madras and the Europeans at Liverpool.[91] For the crew of *Ophir*, requisitioned from the Netherlands Ministry of Shipping and Fisheries, the priority was finding their own wives and children who had been prisoners of the Japanese in Batavia.[92]

The repatriation of sick Japanese prisoners from Batavia, Java, Sumatra and Malaya after the end of the war offered new challenges. These men, suffering from tuberculosis, dysentery and wounds, had expected little or no medical care. On *Amarapoora*, four Japanese medical officers, thirty nursing orderlies and two interpreters assisted the usual medical and nursing officers and sick berth attendants. On arrival in Japan the nursing sisters were presented with bouquets of flowers from the Japanese government.[93]

The hospital services of the Royal Navy on land and sea across the world had come under severe strain under wartime conditions. There had been a need for the expansion of facilities but also a reliance on co-operation with the other armed forces and allies without which the Royal Navy could not have coped with the challenge of global warfare and providing for the health needs of all its seamen wherever they were.

Chapter Four
Our Ships at Sea

Maintaining naval hygiene and a healthy ship was traditionally the duty of the naval surgeon reporting to the captain but in practice it was actually the responsibility of all on board. The ship was the seaman's home and fighting place alike. Conventional thinking had it that, provided that regulations concerning health and sanitation were strictly observed, the ship was a self-contained, hygienically secure unit. The danger came when there was contact with the hostile environment ashore. The army, by contrast, was a constant prey to the unhygienic natural environment by reason of it moving and fighting on land. This illusion that the navy enjoyed a special protection from infection and ill-health while at sea bred a dangerous complacency that the experience of the Second World War was to challenge. Fighting a world war for a long period with overcrowded ships meant that now the Royal Navy had to cope with a greater range of environmental conditions than ever before and adapt its hygiene measures and living conditions to different temperatures and weather conditions from the extremes of the Arctic to the Tropics. This was not an optional matter, though some critics felt that to make ships more comfortable savoured of pampering the modern sailor; rather it was a matter of importance in war:

> Practical steps towards the betterment of living conditions in what are primarily fighting ships tend to be postponed inevitably in times of active service. If it can be shown, however, that such measures would play a part in the promotion of fighting efficiency, the question of relevancy is not in doubt.[1]

The habitability of a ship assumed much more importance than it had enjoyed in peacetime. Controlling the environment to keep men in peak physical condition assumed a significance that had been unknown before the war. The general environment, temperature, overcrowding, diet, clothing and the provision of amenities all affected the welfare of a sailor onboard ship, but what could be done to improve living conditions was limited by the need to maintain the fighting efficiency of the warship. Balancing operational and personnel needs was a problem that was to be addressed not only aboard each ship but also by scientific experts in such fields as physiology, psychology and bacteriology working alongside officers of the Medical Branch of the Royal Navy. The Royal Naval Personnel Research Committee was formed in November 1942 'to advise the Medical Research Council on ... biological, medical and psychological problems affecting the health and fighting efficiency of naval personnel; and to suggest investigations with a view to increasing or improving the health, fighting fitness and environment of naval personnel'.[2]

Although its task was to co-ordinate and direct physiological and psychological research relating to the needs of the navy, the problems of aviation medicine did not come under the remit of the Royal Naval Personnel Research Committee as the Fleet Air Arm was affected by the same medical factors as the Royal Air Force. Problems affecting the habitability of submarines, tropical naval warfare, the needs of the Atlantic and Arctic convoys, the use of Asdic equipment, diving, visual problems, clothing and ventilation were all investigated. Even seasickness was explored since, whilst this was not a major problem, it occasionally did impinge on the efficiency of 'the useful man whose service life is made miserable by the malady'.[3] There was close liaison with the United States Navy and the Royal Canadian Navy,[4] but the most important co-operation was with those departments of the Admiralty concerned with equipment design and production, not only for identifying problems, participating in the research work to solve them and arranging for trials but also in ensuring that the recommendations of the committee were brought into practice as quickly as possible.[5]

In peacetime the problems arising from living in climatic extremes were often overlooked and minimised because of their short duration. The ships were not so crowded as they were to become in wartime nor subject to the same restrictions while long periods of shore leave offered some relief. There had been some improvements in living conditions, including ventilation, between the two world wars, but the impact of war made the environmental problems into a more pressing problem to be resolved if the health and fighting efficiency of the crew was not to be impaired when it should be at its peak.

Ventilation on board ship had been recognised as a problem since the eighteenth century and standards had been laid down as recently as 1937 when a change of air every five minutes was recommended. Air-conditioning had even been used in some magazine spaces and control departments before the war but was not seen as necessary in living spaces. Instead trunking brought fresh air to the mess decks. Air would then be spread around each compartment through 'punkah louvres', directional centrifugal fans. Hammocks, however, restricted air circulation in the mess decks. The efforts made to increase the mechanical fighting strength and firing power of increasingly mechanised ships meant a deterioration in the living standards aboard them. On corvettes of the 'Flower' class, 'the men complain, rightly, that their living spaces get flooded by sea entering the fan inlet'.[6] The introduction of air-conditioning, lagging and insulation to combat solar radiation in the Tropics and maintain heat in the Arctic would also mean reductions in armament, machinery and crew complements. The question was whether a smaller and fitter crew would be more effective in finding and hitting targets than a larger ship's company who, though manning a more heavily-armed vessel, would be fatigued and have their response times impaired through poor living conditions. At the same time it was necessary to balance better conditions with operational safety, such as finding a way 'to ensure efficient ventilation and at the same time to maintain the watertight integrity of the ship'. The best way of doing this was to ensure that 'every effort is made in the design stage to mitigate the difficulties which have arisen from wartime exigencies'.[7]

In the Tropics it was recognised that the 'conditions exist at present which seriously endanger the maintenance of full fighting efficiency' and that it was indisputable that there was 'some falling off in mental and physical efficiency'. These adverse conditions included the separation of men from their families and the inadequacy of mail services, the lack of amenities and overcrowding, domestic worries, and minor illnesses and such discomforts as prickly heat, but 'the greatest cause of deterioration ... is due to environmental, ie climatic, influences proper, namely high temperature with high humidity'.[8] In some ships 'it was just like living in a radiator'.[9] MacDonald Critchley, a neurologist, observed that:

> A common opinion in the Tropics is that after about a year there is a noticeable deterioration in drive, alertness, keenness, memory, the capacity and speed of thought, and power of making decisions. These symptoms may be accompanied by an obvious lassitude, procrastination, irritability, sometimes bibulousness, and slovenliness in personal appearance. The better-educated are conscious of their own declining efficiency, and they note the same change in others.[10]

These symptoms were the result of the tropical climate and 'prolonged exposure to excessive heat ... inevitably reduces the capacity for work, and no matter how determined personnel may be to stick it out and carry on, their efficiency declines – sometimes to a serious extent'.[11]

In peacetime, when most of the ships had been built, conditions afloat in such areas were easier for men to cope with. There were fewer men sharing the same space. On the battleship *Ramillies* there were 1,550 men in 1944 occupying the same living space as 950 before the war. *Ipswich*, built for 66, now accommodated a crew of 101 men. Each man now had to store an increased amount of personal gear, including duffel coats, oilskins, Arctic clothing, tropical rig, respirators, topees, anti-flash gear, steel helmets and mosquito nets so as to be ready for wherever his ship might be sent.[12] The development of specialist functions, such as radar, Asdic and high-frequency direction-finding equipment, all required more space at the expense of personal space for the seaman:

> At the present time HM ships are more heavily manned than ever before in modern history, to fight an unprecedented armament of guns and aircraft, and to operate and maintain an enormous range of new devices concerned with communications and the detection of the enemy. Large increases of ancillary equipment have reduced the already overcrowded living accommodation. Although vigorous

attempts have been made to increase the air supplied to ship's compartments, it is uncertain how far these have reduced the risks due to overcrowding. These risks are greater under conditions of war than in peacetime owing to blackout and other restrictions.[13]

Overcrowding meant that on the cruiser *Emerald*, 'passageways are obstructed by lockers and men asleep for whom there is not sufficient room in the mess decks'.[14]

Part of the problem was that ships had been designed and built for service in different conditions to those in which they found themselves operating. In the early years of the war, warfare in the North Atlantic and the convoy system was the priority and little consideration was given to the different requirements in other environments with the result that 'consideration of Tropical conditions was sacrificed to winning the Battle of the Atlantic'.[15] Standards of ventilation and insulation had also been neglected in those early days of the war in the rush for rapid re-armament, which meant that environmental conditions in ships were not always adequate in the conditions for which they were designed. On the destroyer HMS *Rockingham* in December 1941, Ordinary Seaman K Stott complained about 'the hot, horrid smell of cigarette smoke coming up through the voice pipes when you are queasy and haven't had a cigarette yourself for days'.[16] That was the least of inconveniences on some ships. In the North Atlantic the frigate *Aire* suffered from condensation or 'sweating' caused by the inadequate lining of the bulkheads with cork. The problems were worsened by the 'unhealthy disrespect, that seems to be traditional among seamen, for fresh air on the mess decks'. Punkah louvres were often closed when they should have been open, electrical heaters were used all the time and flaps were closed down over exhaust trunks to stop the 'considerable quantities of ocean water' that 'found their way to the mess decks via these passages'.[17] Ratings tended to accept condensation and the inevitable dampness of blankets and items stowed in lockers as 'a condition inseparable from service in small ships'.[18] The ships being specially built for action in the war against Japan were considered to be of superior standard than the earlier ships built under different climate circumstances.[19]

It was recognised that 'with the increasing extent of naval warfare in the Far East and the imminence of a major campaign at sea against the Japanese, all information bearing upon conditions which affect the general efficiency of personnel is most urgently needed'.[20] Such research was largely focused on the physical labours of ratings, an emphasis which it was 'hoped will not lead to the officer and his different routine being overlooked'.[21] Even without in-depth research, it was widely realised that the solution to the environmental problems on ships in the Tropics lay in improved ventilation, the introduction of air-conditioning, simple dehumidification and the use of table fans.[22] However, dehumidifiers could generate heat and were noisy.[23] On many ships 'the state of ventilation and temperature within the living and working compartments is highly unsatisfactory' and the crew existed in a continual and unremitting state of discomfort, 'which may be aggravated by the occasion of going on watch, to be relieved somewhat only by resting on the weather deck in the shade of awnings'.[24] On some ships, men were encouraged to spend as much time as possible on deck, even being allowed to sleep there. In port, canvas awnings might be used to shade the deck and offer some protection from the sun. In such circumstances, 'it is one thing to spend a week under such conditions, but quite another to spend months on end with little prospect of relief'.[25]

The problem was particularly acute for stokers in the boiler rooms. On the destroyer *Lewes*, boiler room temperatures of 134° Fahrenheit when steaming and 128° in port were so high that at least one stoker was 'on the verge of complete incapacitation'. The commanding officer accepted that temperatures were high in the living spaces but not a cause for complaint and that they could be 'tolerated without excessive loss of efficiency'. However, an investigation concluded that 'the prevailing conditions in the machinery spaces of this ship are not consistent with the maintenance of reasonable efficiency, and can be expected to have such serious effects upon the health of the personnel manning the compartments that it is undesirable that HMS *Lewes* should continue to operate on this station without extensive alterations and additions to the ventilation systems of the machinery spaces and the provision of additional electrical power'.[26]

Suggestions were made as to how conditions on these ships could be improved. It was noted that a 'forced air supply is essential to all enclosed and occupied positions',[27] yet in the blackout supplies of fresh air might be cut off with scuttles being sealed and hatches battened after sunset.[28] Admiralty instructions stated that all air intakes should be kept clear of exhausts and hot air spaces, but this was not always practical. On many ships the intake and exhaust pipes were often side-by-side or facing each other despite the fact that 'at the prevailing temperatures of the Tropics every small increase in temperature and humidity counts heavily and the conditions inside the ship when an intake is receiving foul air is often appalling'.[29] In order to minimise the problems of heat from excessively hot areas affecting living quarters, it was suggested that attempts should be made to group hot compartments next to each other and away from the cooler working and living spaces. It was also necessary that, not only should new ventilation systems be more carefully planned at the design stage, but that more attention should be given to the care, maintenance and adjustment of existing systems.[30]

Wartime conditions on ships serving in the Far East turned on its head the old truism that men in the contained environment of a ship were healthier than those ashore. F P Ellis noted in his report of the 1944 Habitability Mission to the Eastern Fleet that 'the community afloat is less healthy than the community ashore and that the ship's companies of the big ships are less healthy than those of the small ships, while the depot ship's companies are the most unhealthy of all'.[31] Skin diseases, especially boils, impetigo, tinea and prickly heat, accounted for the majority of the infections both in ships and ashore. The incidence of prickly heat was considered to be 'of more than academic or aesthetic importance' since it could 'contribute insidiously to the overall efficiency of a community in addition to the obviously damaging effect of losing men to the sick or attending lists'. Dysentery, minor injuries and the common cold were also problems.[32] Common colds tended not to be reported but 'few will contest that they lower the general efficiency of the ship's company and reduce the general resistance to secondary infections'.[33]

Poor ventilation encouraged the spread of bacterial and viral infection. There tended to be increases in the sick list when a ship first arrived in the Tropics from more temperate waters and a corresponding fall in ill health during visits to cooler waters.[34] Living conditions on ships in the Far East were to improve considerably at the end of the war and with the end of blackout regulations which had worsened the ventilation problems at a time when not showing a light had meant impeding ventilation.[35]

United States ships offered some lessons for the adaptation of British vessels to tropical warfare as they had been specifically designed for service in the Pacific. The Americans themselves were convinced that their way was best and 'there is no doubt in the minds of American officers that in view of the twenty to one wartime expansion in naval personnel, their principle of designing ships' living arrangements on the lines of an overcrowded hotel gave the only satisfactory answer'.[36] The overarching impression gained by Macdonald Critchley of American warships was 'the appearance of great austerity and severity' in which 'all comfort has been ruthlessly sacrificed to the demands of damage control and, in particular, to protection against fire'. All flammable materials were removed from the deck coverings, furniture and fittings leaving all the living spaces, including the cabins and wardrooms, 'bare and comfortless'. Despite this, the ships were 'commodious' with the mess decks containing three tiers of bunks, which could be raised up against the ship's sides by chains when not in use, though this left 'little or no facility for men to sit down and sprawl at their ease unless they are actually turned in'.[37] Each man had his sleeping space, locker for his kit, drinking water, washroom, showers and heads in the same watertight division of the ship in which he fought. However, it was feared that the compartmentalisation of the American system 'destroys mess life but substitutes a team spirit among gun crews and other small bodies of men, who keep watch and fight together'. Water-cooling machines, drinking fountains and even soda fountains prevented men from becoming heat-exhausted and dehydrated. Laundries, barbers, tailors and cobblers all provided onboard services to the sailors 'in order that they will not be distracted from the business of fighting'.[38] British seamen were envious:

> Although it is rather depressing to visit U.S, ships and see the standard of wash places etc., and the laundry facilities installed – even in small ships, it must of course be appreciated that they enjoy both greater resources and less urgency of production, together with possibly a less conservative outlook in ship construction.[39]

Michael Le Fanu, liaison officer between the British Pacific Fleet and the United States Third Fleet, strongly urged that these facilities should become standard for the post-war Royal Navy and would not mollycoddle the British rating nor bring down standards of discipline through more casual attitudes:

> One should not judge the American's discipline by their long-established custom of smoking about their work and the engaging habit whereby a seaman second class will greet one with 'Good morning, Commander, how are you today?'. These words can be as respectful and deferential as the able seaman's 'Morning, Sir'.[40]

However, conditions on British warships remained formal and inferior in contrast to the luxuries enjoyed by their American allies in the Pacific.

The opposite extreme to service in the Tropics was experienced by men serving with the Arctic convoys, though some ship designers thought that while 'Arctic conditions present appreciable problems' these were not 'as severe as those in tropical theatres of operation'.[41] Condensation was just as much of a problem as in the Pacific. Punkah louvres were generally operated at a lower speed in colder conditions and there were steam radiators fitted in mess decks. On the gun turrets, there were 'thick coatings of ice within the walls of the gun house' which were occupied by up to fourteen men for many hours at a time. Foul air, the extreme cold and the moisture from condensation encouraged the spread of infection so that 'the presence of a single member of the gun's crew with an open tubercle would imperil the health of all the others'.[42] The only real solution to this problem was the provision of conditioned air to the gun turrets, but that was an unrealistic aspiration. It was achieved in the newer American ships, but on British ships such as the cruiser *Berwick* the best that could be provided to relieve the coldness was electric radiators or electric blankets.[43]

For the crew of the cruiser *Scylla* in February 1943 there was the problem of adjusting to a swift change from service in the Mediterranean to a return to Tyneside followed by a transfer to escort duties with the Arctic Convoys, changes which 'alone would naturally encourage a lowering of the standard of health but combined with sudden relief from mental anxiety at Tyneside, produced a sudden outbreak of minor ailments'. Even the medical officer, Surgeon Commander Jack Coulter, was 'the worst victim' of an outbreak of conjunctivitis. The skin disease urticaria afflicted one man and there were fifteen cases of pediculosis putis, caused by pubic lice, the 'result of wearing clothing and avoiding baths for a long period'.[44] Ralph Ransome Wallis observed that, apart from cases of frostbite, the health of the men aboard the cruiser *London* and other ship's companies in the Arctic was good. It was too cold for the commonest of pathogenic bacteria to thrive in.[45]

Scylla was well-heated, though not to improve conditions for the crew but rather to prevent the freezing-up of gun mechanisms, machinery and the navigation instruments. Even so, Jack Coulter was able to sleep comfortably with three blankets in the sick bay, heated to 62° Fahrenheit by electric heaters, on a night when the maximum temperature was 32° and the walls and ceilings 'coated in a film of ice'. Conditions in the engine room were comfortable at a minimum of 46° even though at times icicles hung from the supply fans. However, the mess decks could become overheated with average temperatures of 72° if the main steam trunks passed through them. At times Coulter found himself 'sweating profusely, even when not wearing outdoor clothing', when he walked through the mess decks. The ratings complained about the heads being 'overheated' and claimed that 'the only way to defecate in comfort was to strip completely and dress again afterwards'.[46] On the upper deck, sanitary arrangements were equally important because of the long periods at action stations. Sanitary buckets could not be used in the open because of the cold and so had to be lashed in place under cover and emptied and cleaned at least once a day. The contrast between the heat inside and the cold outside was extreme.

Water was in short supply but in great demand on Arctic Convoy ships. The boiler was essential for heat for thawing out and stopping the gun positions from freezing, and for heating the mess decks and sick berth. Fresh water was also needed for drinking and cooking, but it was in short supply for washing and shaving. On the auxiliary anti-aircraft cruiser *Ulster Queen*, ratings were forbidden to have showers or wash clothes while on convoy, and fresh water supplies were cut off for several hours a day. Even the engineers and stokers were unable to enjoy the luxury of an adequate clean-up, though it was pointed out to them that they would not have been able to shower on a submarine either. However, some officers still insisted on a daily shower or bath until it was made a punishable offence to disobey orders about wasting water and it got too cold for them to wish to strip for a bath.[47]

Russian medical services left a lot to be desired for sick or injured Royal Navy or Merchant Navy seamen unlucky enough to be invalided to hospital in North Russia. The hospital at Vaenga was nothing more than improvised sick quarters in the basement and on the ground floor of a block of flats. Ventilation was poor, the air was heavy with the 'constant smoking' of the Russian staff and patients, and stale spittoons and stinking urine bottles cluttered the floor, while the 'odour of septic wounds and suppurating compound fractures in plaster made the foulest atmosphere conceivable'. The hospital at Murmansk was even worse. A British observer said that 'no words of mine can describe the deplorable conditions in which the patients were treated'. He thought that '"bloody awful" in its literal sense' was the closest words he could use to describe what he saw and observed an operating theatre in which 'during these operations, as often as not, someone would be smoking'. He considered the Russian doctors to 'lack the very fundamentals of medical and surgical practice'. This he attributed to 'the fact that they assess the value of human life at a lower value than we do'. At Archangel, the treatment of the British sick and wounded was considered to be 'reasonably good' though 'not coming up to British standards'. However, it was thought that British sailors would feel happier if they were treated by their own naval doctors since 'linguistic difficulties, Russian food … head shaving, their somewhat crude methods and their indifference to alleviating pain all tend to depress patients and to lengthen convalescence'.[48] Negotiations with the Soviet authorities resulted, after an initial refusal, in permission for the Royal Navy to ship in a hospital unit of 100 beds and naval staff to deal with British casualties.[49]

As protection against the cold and wet in the Arctic, warm, water-resistant clothing was essential which should make allowance for the factor that 'men at sea suffer from cold through inadequate protection of the extremities and defective closures, rather than from defective insulation of the trunk'.[50] In line with these principles the Kapok was developed, a wool-padded overall worn under oilskins. However, the Kapok was bulky, and impeded the free movement of men through the passageways. It also made it difficult for stretcher-bearers to 'put a man who is dressed in Arctic clothing into a Neil Robinson stretcher ... In one case it was impossible.'[51] There was also confusion about the function of the Kapok, and 'some officers believe it is sufficiently buoyant to replace the life jacket, others insist on their crews wearing life jackets in addition'.[52] Other forms of protective clothing were no more popular. On *Scylla* there were 40 Bingham Arctic suits and 200 Service Standard weatherproof suits as well as the usual long underpants, jerseys, oilskins and duffel coats the crew preferred and was accustomed to wear as a protection against the cold. The men claimed to feel cold in the Bingham suit, but even more than the freezing conditions they were afraid of ridicule: 'anyway their mates laughed at them, and they felt bloody silly wearing them'.[53]

Consideration was also given to the use of electrically-heated suits specifically for watchkeepers in exposed positions, unable to move about to keep warm and too cramped to wear many layers of clothing, as well as for director crews in control tops and lookouts on bridges. Physiologists considered the correct placing of the heating elements within the suit and whether to warm the trunk, the extremities, or both. It was feared that overheating by the suit might make men somnolent. Such suits had already been adopted by the RAF but were not adapted for use at sea.[54]

For many men on the Arctic Convoys there was no special clothing available and they had to make do with duffel coats, woollen hats, gloves, heavy boots and thick socks. For Jack Neale, navigation officer on the minesweeper *Speedwell*, the most valuable item of clothing was 'long underpants of very fine quality which were so thick they would almost stand up on their own'. Leather boots several sizes too big were also useful in keeping out the cold when worn with three or four pairs of thick socks. Water shortages and the difficulties of washing and shaving gave the captain no option but to suspend the normal rule whereby permission to grow a beard was needed. Neale found that 'a beard did give one's face some protection from the biting winds on watch, but one had to continually "open wide" to prevent one's breath freezing moustache to beard'.[55]

The demands of war also had their effects on tropical uniform. In peacetime, the role of the Royal Navy in the Far East had partly been ceremonial with flag-showing cruises to other countries and the outposts of Empire. Naval clothing had been far more formal than was suitable for service in hot climates. Officers were expected to wear a tropical uniform of a starched white duck uniform tunic with a high collar, long starched white duck trousers, canvas shoes and a white sun helmet. It was not comfortable for working in the heat. Mess undress uniform worn in the evening was equally impractical with its white mess jacket, blue uniform serge trousers, blue uniform waistcoat or cummerbund, stiff fronted evening shirt, wing collar and bow tie. There had been some relaxation of dress codes in the 1930s at the discretion of commanding officers but these were little more than the replacement of the uniform suit by an open-necked tropical shirt and white shorts. Under wartime conditions, when laundering was more difficult on active service and materials were in short supply, a tropical shirt and white shorts became the norm and white uniform tunic and trousers were reserved for formal occasions and shore-going after dark. When evening dress was required, white trousers and a tropical open-necked shirt with a cummerbund were acceptable. The ratings' pre-war tropical uniform of sun helmet, white duck jumper and bell bottoms was also replaced by a more practical uniform that included white shorts.[56]

Shorts were comfortable, clean and healthy in hot weather at sea. Men wearing them were less prone to heat stroke, boils and prickly heat. They were also cheaper to launder. However much of a tonic effect they may have had, they did make a man more vulnerable to sunburn and burns on the exposed flesh from enemy action. Traditionalists also complained that they were unsightly in the wardroom and made it difficult to distinguish officers from ratings. Nevertheless, even they grudgingly admitted that 'whites when clean are smart and when worn ashore do much to enhance prestige and maintain self-respect and pride in appearance'. Even the fact that white uniforms showed up dirt and stains had its advantages as it ensured that they would be washed more, reducing the dangers of infection.[57] Not surprisingly it was disliked on the lower deck for the very reason that 'even with great care tropical clothing requires washing after being worn once'.[58] Ordinary Seaman Wilfred Smith on the monitor *Erebus* in 1942 complained to his mother that at the end of a day's work the 'said infernal shorts are anything but white so once more one repairs to the bathroom (which incidentally is totally inadequate in size), and once more one attempts to produce a clean pair of shorts with the aid of a bucket (if able to borrow someone's) or a bowl if they are not already in use, a bit of Persil and soap and a lot of elbow-grease'.[59] The ratings would have preferred the less attractive but more practical khaki of the Marines and army.

Laundries on board ships were suggested as a way of reducing humidity caused by the laundering of clothes between decks. It was also thought that a constant supply of clean, dry, freshly-laundered clothing would improve health and morale. However, this American innovation was not often welcomed by the ratings it was meant to benefit. Accustomed to dhobying his clothes in a bucket of soapy water, the seaman was reluctant to change his routine and continued with his accustomed practice. Moreover, they were often badly constructed and liable to flooding in rough weather. Where laundries were supplied on new ships, they were rarely used for their intended purpose. In some instances, they were used as additional dressing stations in action.[60]

Increasingly it was seen as important that uniform in the Tropics should be clean, smart, heat-repellent, mosquito-proof and flash-proof in action.[61] Such requirements for safety, smartness and comfort were contradictory. Anti-flash gear was uncomfortable to wear and 'in hot climates the wearing of action clothing and anti-flash gear for any length of time is almost physically impossible'.[62] Both the overall suit and anti-flash gear soon became 'saturated in sweat'. Research was undertaken into the flame-proofing of light fabrics to provide more comfortable protection from flash burns, but such flame protection could only ever be limited.[63] It was also difficult to develop an effective flash burn protective cream that would not have such side effects as rashes and conjunctivitis and which would not soil clothing and optical instruments which would be major drawbacks to its use in hot climates.[64]

Comfort and practicality were very different things. Throughout the war the ratings' messes would have been all too familiar to the Jack Tar of Nelson's navy. Officers were now allocated cabins, but the ratings still had to sling their hammocks wherever they could. In the mess areas hammocks were officially hung 21in (52cm) apart, but on many a crowded wartime ship it was usual for men from different watches to share hammocks, or even sleep on the deck beneath one of the mess tables. J P W Mallalieu described the mess deck as 'the only place where they could eat, sleep, read and write, and stow their gear. It was not very comfortable'.[65]

Vermin remained a problem on all ships and shore establishments. There was a long tradition of rat-catching weeks, but more scientific methods of rodent control were now adopted. Fumigation by hydrocyanic acid gas was costly and not always easy on active service, so poison baits were widely used. On *Belfast* in 1944 'the rat population has been further decreased by systematic hunts in storerooms and by the use of poisons, but it appears impossible to completely clear the ship'.[66] Even had the ship been cleared, more pests would have boarded whenever the ship was in port, such as the rats believed to have boarded *Belfast* when it was alongside at Rosyth. Many of these pests were in search of food stocks.

Food played an important part in establishing a sense of routine on board ship, meals and the rum issue punctuating work routine. What food was available depended very much on local supplies, though 'pot mess', a stew of whatever was available, was perhaps the most common meal served. There was not much variety in diet when ships were on patrol because of the difficulties of obtaining supplies, though on the netlayer *Brittany* it was possible while taking part in Operation 'Husky' in 1943 to obtain lemons, tomatoes, grapes, onions, melons, turnips and nuts locally during the invasion of Sicily.[67] On *Belfast*, during the Normandy landings of 1944, many of the men developed boils from the lack of fresh vegetables, and disliked the dehydrated cabbage and potato they were given instead.[68] Tinned foods were popular at sea and a regular fallback when fresh foodstuffs were unavailable. However, dehydrated foods were less popular though they saved on storage, and trials of dried soups in submarines in 1942 were unsuccessful.[69] Generally, men's tastes were conservative, which meant that in the Tropics it was difficult to cater for the tastes of the ratings who preferred roast meat and considered rice to be 'nigger's food'. On the destroyer *Worcester* in 1940, breakfast consisted of tea, bread, butter and marmalade with a more substantial meal of meat, fried potatoes, over-boiled cabbage and peas followed by a boiled pudding or tinned fruit for lunch. Later there would be tea with bread, butter and jam then a supper of sausages and chips or bacon and eggs.[70] Although stodgy, it was better than rations on the Home Front. Lord Moran, travelling to Cairo with his patient Winston Churchill on the battlecruiser *Renown* in 1943, after the queasiness of his first few days at sea, was impressed by the quality of the jam and biscuits served to guests on the ship and reflected that if ordinary seamen fed as well as the passengers on a warship they would burst.[71] The ordinary seaman, while adequately fed, did not enjoy the luxury and profusion expected by the prime minister's entourage. Although it was boasted that 'naval rations are usually the envy of the Army and RAF', the food was invariably badly cooked and served on dirty, greasy plates with dirty cutlery.[72] On American ships, by contrast, 'the food is rich, very plentiful but perhaps too sweet for the British palate'.[73]

Broadside Messing, a legacy from the past, remained the norm, in which each mess member took his turn as duty cook responsible for collecting rations from the purser, preparing a meal, taking it to the galley for it to be cooked, collecting and serving the meal, and washing up, so that in effect 'each mess is a catering unit in itself'.[74] Such a system, however much it may have sustained the solidarity of the mess and continued a long tradition, often resulted in a poorly-cooked, unbalanced diet. From the late 1920s onwards, galley cooks had taken over the preparation of the food in bigger galleys, and the role of the mess cook had been reduced to merely collecting the cooked food from the galley and serving it to his messmates.[75] Bacteriologists delighted in pointing out that 'the contamination of the atmosphere was greatest when men congregated together at mealtimes, either outside the galley or at the mess tables'.[76]

During the Second World War, General Messing was introduced on ships which had been transferred to the Royal Navy from the United States under the Lend-Lease arrangements. Such ships had canteens, known as Ship's Company Dining Halls, in which the men could eat, rather than at their mess tables, and food was served cafeteria-style. The cruiser *Glasgow* had a self-service service system where the men collected their knives, forks and spoons and a plastic platter before being served with their food from a counter. On the carrier *Implacable* most of the food was pre-plated.[77] The advantage of a General Messing system was that there would be less waste as 'each man would draw only what he wanted, and the food would be kept hot and palatable until the man was ready to eat it'.[78] The commanding officer would also be confident that 'the men will return to their quarters in an emergency without leaving in their messes the remains of a half-eaten meal, mixed up with a litter of mess utensils'.[79]

Meals on such American-built ships as the escort carrier *Tracker* were prepared by cooks in well-equipped galleys containing such labour-saving luxuries as mechanical potato-peelers, ice-cream makers and soda fountains. Unlike British vessels, the American ships were 'dry' but ice-cream soda fountains were intended to compensate for this. Bakers produced fresh bread each day, and specially-trained Marine butchers provided fresh meat. Refrigeration and freezing also improved the range of food available.[80] However, British observers were not so enamoured by the racial segregation in the Unites States Navy which extended even to messing where 'the coloured enlisted men join the same chow-line but they always sit at their own special tables'.[81] Perhaps of greater concern were fears that the American system would destroy the team spirit of the traditional mess.

There were different challenges faced with action messing to ensure that men on duties at their posts received adequate and suitable food and drink. On *Scylla* in the Arctic normal diet was supplemented with extra butter, fats, potatoes and suet puddings, with hot drinks of cocoa, tea and soup available at all times though 'consumed under cover to avoid the possible freezing of lips to the edge of cups'. Every effort was made to release men for meals as opportunities arose since under Arctic conditions it was not practicable 'to bring food out into the open'.[82] While action messing in the Arctic and Atlantic involved a constant supply of hot soup, tea and cocoa as well as hot meat pies that could be eaten with the hand, in tropical waters there was a greater need to ensure adequate supplies of water and the replacement of salt lost through sweating. Salt tablets were issued but often caused stomach pains and nausea, so it was thought preferable to salt the drinking water. Lime juice was also supplied in the Tropics and engine room stokers were supplied with gruel while on duty.[83] For Lieutenant R C G Macnab on HMS *Glasgow* off the Normandy coast following D-Day in 1944 action messing 'entails meals of sandwiches and soup, which palls after a bit', although the monotony of such a diet was enlivened by 'a tot of rum ... issued daily to those who want it (even officers!) and this is as powerful as about four normal drinks'.[84]

For most men the Navy Army and Air Force Institute's (NAAFI's) Naval Canteen Service provided a valuable service in supplementing their limited diet with something slightly more exciting. Since 1921 it had provided little luxuries in terms of food, in addition to selling duty-free tobacco, confectionery known as 'nutty', toothpaste and shoe polish. A percentage of the profits generated from the NAAFI on board ship was put towards a canteen fund for the benefit of the whole crew.[85] Canteen supplies would also be supplemented by gifts from service charities, such as the 50,000 cigarettes sent by the Overseas League and the 1,000lbs of chocolate sent by the Royal Navy War Amenities Fund in 1942 for the men of the Arctic convoys.[86] It all helped to improve the working and living environment of the British sailor.

The Second World War furthered advances in naval hygiene and preventative medicine that were to benefit the post-war navy. Amphibious warfare and the establishment of naval bases and air stations on shore in disease-infested territories meant that the navy could no longer be considered to enjoy a special hygienic immunity. Although research-inspired hygienic measures adopted by the navy reduced the casualties caused by preventable disease during the war, the incidence of sickness caused by environmental conditions still remained high. Wartime experience had demonstrated the importance of modernising facilities, messing and clothing in line with the environment in which ships served. Commander Michael Le Fanu was well aware of the lessons learned for the modern navy and thought that something could be gained from copying American practices:

> For too long our Navy has tended to dismiss the luxuries of American shipboard life as non-essentials. But surely, simply because our men have a lower standard of living, we should not do the bare minimum to ensure the mere existence of our service.[87]

The post-war navy could not afford to return to any pre-war complacency. The modern sailor expected better.

Chapter Five
Sea-Room for Change

The Royal Navy has always prided itself on being an early adopter of new medical innovations, be it in the field of anti-scorbutics or vaccination. In the Second World War new medical advances were implemented if they could be seen to augment the fighting fitness of the fleet. In many areas, such as blood transfusion and plastic surgery, wartime advances were built upon innovations of the Great War. Other new developments like penicillin, mass radiography and anti-malarial therapy were the products of the current war.[1] However, the army was sometimes much faster in implementing medical change than the navy, despite a rivalry between the two services as to which was more forward-thinking in its approach.[2]

With blood transfusion, the Royal Army Medical Corps at first was well ahead of the Royal Navy Medical Branch in setting up a military service to meet wartime needs. Blood banks and blood transfusion facilities were to become some of the main lifesaving developments of the war. What was found to be best for treating secondary wound shock was a transfusion of saline and blood plasma to replace loss of fluids and proteins by the burns victim, a method which had been developed in the 1930s but came into its own during the war.[3] However, at the outbreak of war the use of stored blood and blood banks for the emergency treatment of casualties was still a novel idea and the usual practice remained to draw fresh blood from a donor as needed. There was no recognised technique for blood grouping, although Karl Landsteiner's views on blood typing had been accepted since the Great War and naval medical officers had recognised early in the war that 'the ideal plan would be for every man to be typed and his blood group notation made in his medical history document'.[4] There was also no standardised method for bleeding donors or for giving transfusions.[5]

Towards the end of the First World War citrated blood had been stored before major battles ready for use when needed. In 1938, the Army Blood Transfusion Service was set up, the first such organisation in any military medical service. It was set up by doctors fully confident in the knowledge that refrigerated citrated blood could be kept for several weeks. Under the leadership of Brigadier Lionel Whitby, the Royal Army Medical Corps sct up blood banks, containing stores of blood and dried plasma, which were released and made available as and when needed. Whitby had himself been seriously injured in 1918 and had received a lifesaving blood transfusion before having his leg amputated through the thigh by the surgeon Gordon Taylor, normally a specialist in abdominal surgery, who had then encouraged him to study medicine after the war. Whitby's personal experience of the value of blood transfusion in one war was to inspire him to ensure that it was to be a lifesaver in the next.[6] The army was to take the lead in establishing blood transfusion services in the field, an example to be followed by the navy.

During the Norway campaign and the evacuation of France in 1940, wounded men were often left waiting for a considerable time before they received their necessary transfusion to alleviate their wound shock, a catastrophe that convinced the military doctors that prompt transfusion and resuscitation were essential if lives were to be saved.[7] The organisation was tightened up and by 1941, in North Africa bottled blood was being stored in refrigerators at base transfusion units and distributed by air to mobile blood transfusion teams under the command of Colonel G E Buttle. The surgeon J C Watts, serving with the Eighth Army, observed that whereas 'in 1940 transfusion had involved finding a donor, cross matching his blood to ensure against incompatibility, then withdrawing the blood into a complicated transfusion apparatus', time-consuming tasks performed by the field surgeon himself, now 'thanks to the masterly organization of Colonel Buttle, each group of surgical teams had a field transfusion unit attached, with highly trained personnel and supplied with bottles of blood by air'.[8] The navy, with its different requirements, learned from the army experience.

At first the Royal Navy was dependent upon blood supplies from civilian sources. Just as the army had set up a blood transfusion service so did the Emergency Medical Service. That early Emergency Blood Transfusion Service, the forerunner of the modern National Blood Transfusion Service, was small-scale and merely concerned with maintaining lists of volunteer blood donors, but in July 1938 the Medical Research Council set up four depots in London for the collection, storage and supply of blood. The scheme was extended to the rest of the country in July 1940 with the formation of a regional blood transfusion service with centres in every civil defence region.[9] Although primarily intended 'to meet civilian casualty requirements', there was 'closer liaison with the Fighting Services' as the war progressed.[10] Great demands were made by the armed forces in the aftermath of Dunkirk, but the demand for transfusions for civilians rose considerably once the air raids on London began. Paradoxically though, 'since air raids have become more frequent the response has not been so good' from donors, presumably on account of the difficulties of attending donor sessions in the midst of competing demands on the individual on the home front.[11] The navy urgently needed to ensure its own supplies of donated blood.

After 1940 many of the new medical officers entering the navy had had experience of treating air-raid casualties and saw the importance of blood transfusion. From the beginning of 1941 there was agitation for better transfusion facilities to be made available on ships, such as dried serum and plasma, sterile saline water and blood transfusion apparatus and that 'all ships should carry a transfusion product that is readily available'.[12] A more 'transfusion minded' navy now decided to set up its own naval bleeding units to deal with the shortage of blood products from civilian sources.[13] The first was made up of a surgeon lieutenant, Frank Henley, together with one naval sister and six VADs, who would visit naval establishments and large business firms to bleed volunteers. The nurses were known as the 'Bleeding Beauty Chorus'. In two years Henley bled some 25,000 donors at a rate of about 250 each week.[14] The blood collected was sent to the North-west London Regional Supply Depot at Slough where the collected blood was allowed to clot. Bottles of blood were then forwarded for filtering and freeze drying to the Medical Research Council Experimental Drying Plant at Cambridge.

Although Frank Henley, whose 'enthusiasm and capacity for work appears unending', was praised for organising and building up the service and his petty officer Gallagher was 'an extremely competent laboratory technician ... representative of the best type of senior laboratory man, quiet, business-like and well-trained in laboratory methods', there was criticism of the VADs involved since only one of them, Ann Mumby, was accurate and proficient in serological testing, and if she were away and another VAD took on her duties, there would be errors in the blood-grouping. This seemed to point out the need for 'experience as well as theoretical knowledge' of all scientific procedures and that if the navy were to establish its own transfusion service its staff should be 'adequately trained to the necessary serological standards rather than leave this to any available VAD'.[15]

A second naval bleeding unit based in Leeds, with serum being separated in the laboratories of the University of Leeds School of Medicine, was established in September 1941,[16] but demand continued to exceed supply and a Royal Naval Blood Transfusion Service was finally established at the end of 1941 to organise its own donations and filter all its own serum. Its laboratories were established at the Royal Veterinary College in Camden Town. Burroughs Wellcome offered additional drying space for fifty bottles a week at Beckenham and the ice-cream maker J Lyons loaned to the navy its freezing cabinets, disused since ice-cream production had been prohibited earlier in the war.[17] As a result by the end of 1943 there was enough dried serum available for the entire navy.

Not surprisingly, the superiority of British blood transfusion services in meeting demand was a source of pride to the medical services of the British armed forces which could claim that 'the German doctors themselves envy us our blood transfusion' and that 'what you the donors have done and what the doctors and scientists have done with your gift has been one of the greatest lifesaving measures ever provided for any Army'.[18] For the Normandy landings in 1944 it was estimated that 1,350 pints of blood would be required by the navy on D-Day and then 1,000 pints a week for transfusions. There were fewer casualties than had been expected but during Operation 'Overlord' 15,000 donors were bled and 3,640 pints of the universal blood group 'O' supplied by the Naval Blood Transfusion Service.[19] On *Belfast* casualties from the beaches and other ships were 'rapidly evacuated to the sick bay by first aid parties'. There they were given blood transfusions using the latest in transfusion equipment; which 'was found extremely useful'.[20] On *Scotsman* during the 1943 invasion of Sicily, by contrast, the civilian Emergency Medical Service 'taking and giving transfusion sets' were found to be easier to use than the standard Schucksmiths apparatus issued by the navy.[21] Wartime experience could also offer valuable lessons for civilian services, as was recognised by W M Butler in 1940, since 'as a national transfusion service for peacetime use of the population is by no means a remote possibility, work done for the army and navy will be a valuable addition to the small groups of voluntary donors already on record'.[22]

Blood plasma transfusion was invaluable for the treatment of burns and the prevention of shock: 'the first consideration in the burnt patient is to combat shock', and all burns cases were seen as 'potential shock cases, the onset of which will depend upon the severity of the burns and the reaction of the individual'.[23] Flame, blast and steam burns could be horrific. During the Great War most burns at sea were the result of cordite ignition and were treated with picric acid which adhered to the burnt area and was painful to remove. Now most of the burns were caused by back flash from incendiary bombs. Electrical and chemical burns were less common. Anti-flash gear was vital to protect exposed parts of the body such as the face and hands.[24] One surgeon involved in the battle of the River Plate was concerned about his 'failure to visualise the burns that a high explosive shell may cause from flash' and that he had 'tannic acid but no solutions prepared for immediate use'.[25] It had been observed that men who had used tannic jellies usually did better than those who had ignored them since the burnt area had usually coagulated under the caked-on black 'cement' caused by the tannin within three to five days and the loss of blood serum had been stopped. Morphia would be injected to deaden the pain.[26] However, there were concerns that the use of tannic acid on the hands, especially on the fingers, could result in 'severe crippling in the case of second and third degree burns'; saline packs or hand baths were considered to be much better for such injuries.[27] It had been noticed that burns casualties evacuated from Dunkirk who had 'been immersed in sea water suffered less from infection than had been expected'.[28] The Medical Research Council accordingly advised against applying tannic acid to facial burns because deep black stains could be left on the skin and instead it recommended the use of gauze impregnated with sterilised Vaseline for the face.[29] John Bunyan, a naval dentist, and William Stannard developed in 1941 the Bunyan-Stannard bag made of oiled silk for the irrigation of burns with hypochlorite. Stannard also developed a glove that could be used as a first-aid dressing for air crew, to be applied immediately on burning to protect the injured hands and to allow the immediate application of sulphanilamide powder.[30] The patient would then be kept warm with hot water bottles or hot blankets and an improvised shock cage with electric light bulbs inside it.[31] A plasma transfusion would be given to deal with the secondary shock.[32] Once the patient reached hospital and his clothing had been removed, the burnt area could be dusted with an antibacterial sulphonamide powder, then a coagulant, made up of silver nitrate and tannic acid or gentian violet, would be applied to all areas other than the face, hands and feet which were not to be tanned and were instead dusted with sulphonamide powder and covered with gauze soaked in paraffin.[33] The bacteriologist Leonard Colebrook doubted that 'we shall ever be able to prevent streptococcus infections of burns altogether as this organism is so ubiquitous and grows so readily in serous fluids'.[34]

Sailors, soldiers and airmen suffering from horrific burns and injuries were by 1940 filling the hospitals and it was realised that it was 'only by the early treatment of these cases that serious deformity and loss of function can be obviated or mitigated'.[35] Reconstructive surgery had been pioneered by Harold Gillies during the First World War, operating on many naval patients, and this new branch of surgery was to come of age during the Second World War. Burns victims from Jutland had been sent in 1916 to the Queen's Military Hospital at Sidcup, including W Vickarage, an able seaman aged twenty, who had suffered severe cordite burns to his face, neck, and hands on board the battleship HMS *Malaya*, and was unable to close his mouth. He was the first patient to be treated with a 'tube pedicule', when Gillies sutured two flaps of skin from his chest together into a tube, which enhanced the blood flow to the reconstructed nose, chosen from an album of photographs of handsome young men. The results were not as aesthetically pleasing as Gillies hoped, and even when he was finally discharged in September 1920, this young sailor remained horribly disfigured by scar tissue.[36] Lessons, though, had been learnt for dealing with similar disfigurements in the next world war.

Many naval patients were sent for reconstructive surgery during the Second World War to Park Prewitt Hospital near Basingstoke where Harold Gillies continued with his plastic surgery work. Most attention, however, was now focused on his cousin Archibald McIndoe who was to build on and, in popular repute, overtake his pioneering work at the Queen Victoria Hospital at East Grinstead. Although the majority of patients at East Grinstead were from the RAF, they did include men from the Fleet Air Arm and Royal Navy. The popular impression, though, is centred on the treatment of the flying heroes of the RAF. One naval patient at East Grinstead was Chief Petty Officer Arthur John Dunnett, whose arms and arms had been burned by a bomb blast on the cruiser *Calcutta* in 1941, who was recommended after skin grafts for light civilian work in an aircraft factory until his arms had healed and his grafts had softened enough for him to return to duty.[37]

McIndoe, a thickset, short-sighted, aggressive New Zealander, firmly believed that 'with efficient and adequate treatment it is possible to push the frontier between the fatal burn and that from which recovery may be expected further and further into the territory of presumptive death' and that 'successful treatment is dependent on close organisation, intelligent medical and nursing co-operation, and adequate equipment'.[38] These principles he put into practice at East Grinstead.[39] All of this required intensive nursing care, though McIndoe, a man driven by his devotion to his work and his patients, was not the easiest of people to work for and often bullied his staff in his pursuit of excellence.[40]

The first stage of treatment for a burns patient in the naval hospitals and at the specialist burns units to which naval patients were referred was for the wound to be cleansed and dressed with Vaseline or saline packs to keep it moist. The patient was regularly bathed in warm saline solutions kept circulating at just above normal blood temperature, which kept the wound flexible and promoted granulation or the creation of a surface suitable for skin grafting. McIndoe subsequently claimed to have pioneered this use of brine, but saline baths had been used earlier for the treatment of mustard gas casualties in the First World War. The baths themselves were specially made of ebonite, an artificial form of ebony with an enamelled finish, so that they would not be corroded by the saline and they had wheels fitted so that they could be moved around easily. The beds too were specially adapted with removable headrests that would permit dressings to be changed from all angles. As they harboured infection, woollen blankets were never used. Special anaesthetic masks were designed to cover the whole face and thereby avoid putting too much pressure on open burn wounds. Skin grafting would be done as soon as possible for third degree burns.[41]

McIndoe prided himself that he had created the environment at East Grinstead, 'with a very strong staff, highly organised, well equipped and practically self-contained', in which he could reconstruct faces.[42] There were limits to what the surgeon could achieve without the determination of these young men to live as normal a life as possible despite their disfigurements. McIndoe told the press that 'this is the happiest hospital I've ever had … the patients are so cheerful that they do as much to heal themselves as I do for them'.[43] Most of the patients wore their own civilian clothes when they were able to get out of bed and dress themselves. Officers and other ranks shared the same ward and mixed socially without regard to rank. Crates of beer were secreted under the beds and the anaesthetist John Hunter jovially made wagers with the men that he would buy them a drink if they were sick after he administered the anaesthetic. Popular entertainers such as Flanagan and Allen, Joyce Grenfell, Tommy Trinder, Douglas Byng, Frances Day and even the Hollywood film star Clark Gable regularly performed for the men. Most important of all, the men were encouraged to visit the many pubs, restaurants and cinemas in the nearby town of East Grinstead and it was their ready acceptance by the local people despite their disfigurements that helped to reintegrate them into the wider world after their discharge.[44] McIndoe laid great stress on 'the psychological importance of encouraging the patients to have confidence in the ability of the surgeon to return him to complete normality and claims that the patient's attitude of mind has a great deal to do with the success of his treatment'.[45] For the navy too, treatment did not end with a successful skin graft or reconstructive surgery, and 'as burns form one of the commonest casualties in the Royal Navy it is important that each naval hospital should have a follow up system whereby the late results of war burns may be assessed in their proper light'.[46]

It was important that people with horrible disfigurements only partly rectified by reconstructive surgery should be accepted by the public. In 1941, a film was made about plastic surgery in wartime to highlight what was being done for the victims of air raids as well as for military casualties. The tone was relentlessly upbeat as the surgeon calmly reassured the audience that one young seaman who had been burned badly during an air raid while on leave would recover: 'he has taken a good long time to heal and we expect now to make him a very satisfactory repair of the upper lip and the cheek from his forehead'. Such techniques as skin grafting, the making of a new thumb by joining up the second fingers and the forging of a new nose from a flap of skin from the forehead were patiently explained to the cinema audience in the hope that anyone seeing the results would be more understanding and sympathetic.[47]

The general public was already well aware of the dangers of tuberculosis from experience and from pre-war public health campaigns. It had also 'long been realised that tuberculosis is a menace of the first order to the naval service'.[48] The incidence of pulmonary tuberculosis had always been high in the navy, with two per thousand men invalided out of the service since 1906. While improved living standards ashore resulted in a fall in the prevalence of tuberculosis, it remained a problem for the navy as 'the direct result of that crowded community life which is inseparable from a warship's environment'.[49]

In combatting the spread of tuberculosis, it was essential to identify sufferers from the disease as soon as possible and then segregate then from healthy men. This could be done through regular chest examinations, the recording of a man's weight and frequent X-rays. In 1938 a trial of multi X-ray photography of chests was carried out at the Chatham barracks. Batches of new recruits were to be X-rayed at six-monthly intervals for up to two or three years after entry. The results were encouraging and it was decided to install similar equipment at the naval barracks at Portsmouth and Devonport although preparations for the coming war delayed the introduction of the scheme.[50] The preliminary investigations were successful and of the 8,493 men examined, 52 were discharged to hospital suffering from TB.[51] Compulsory chest X-rays at yearly intervals were soon introduced. This policy of conducting regular chest examinations and weighings of ship's companies for the early detection of tuberculosis, with suspected cases and their contacts being referred for radiological investigation, together with the maximum use of all available means of ventilation in ships and shore establishments, was considered to be successful in reducing incidences of TB in the Western Approaches Command in 1943.[52]

Any officer or rating found to be suffering from open and active pulmonary tuberculosis would be withdrawn from service at sea immediately and even when cured of the disease would only be allowed to serve ashore provided he was unlikely to infect others.[53] In 1942 regulations on the dismissal of permanent officers on the active list who were found to be tubercular were revised at a time when all available manpower was needed. Now an officer who had contracted TB need no longer be invalided out when there was a reasonable chance that he would recover.[54]

The introduction of mass miniature radiography was 'the cheapest and most efficient method of detecting possible cases of pulmonary tuberculosis' in officers and ratings.[55] It was perhaps the most significant wartime development in preventative medicine. It allowed the early diagnosis of tuberculosis but could not eliminate the risk of infection, yet it was an innovation using modern technology to contain a problem that was considered particularly serious for the efficiency of the navy.

Modern science was also used to combat malaria. There was still a feeling among many naval officers that 'malaria concerns more the army and RAF than the RN but it needs emphasis that the RN is faced with the problem to an ever-increasing extent by virtue of its greater and greater shore-based personnel'. Medical officers even dismissed it as an 'executive problem' and saw their role as merely being to advise.[56] As an executive problem, malaria control was sometimes not given its due importance. In hot climates men preferred the comfort of shorts to wearing longer trousers which gave them protection against mosquito bites which could transmit malaria. In India the Royal Navy even 'undermines the anti-malarial campaigns of the army and RAF by not being strict enough in prohibiting ratings ashore after sundown in shorts'. However, for Royal Marines 'shorts were an impossible rig in the jungle, long trousers were essential' which gave them an advantage in avoiding mosquito bites.[57]

Ships were advised to lie as far offshore as possible in malarial areas and that there should be as little communication with the shore as possible between dusk and dawn. Portholes, doors and ventilators were to be mosquito-proofed and, where possible, incense sticks used to keep mosquitos away. Men were forbidden to sleep on deck without suitable mosquito nets to protect them and were advised to bathe during daylight. Long sleeves, long trousers and two pairs of socks were also advised, though covering the whole body could be uncomfortable in the heat.[58]

There was now a strong insecticide available that was effective against mosquitoes, flies and body lice, all of which spread disease. DDT (dichlorodiphenyl-trichloroethane) had first been synthesised in 1874 but it was not until 1939 that its potential as a powerful insecticide had been discovered by Paul Müller, managing chemist of the Swiss Geigy Corporation. Its first large-scale deployment came in early 1944 when a typhus epidemic broke out in Naples. The city was declared out of bounds to Allied troops, who were inoculated against the infection and had their kit regularly disinfected. Medical teams were sent into Naples with supplies of DDT to disinfect the civil population. Crowded air-raid shelters were suspected of being breeding grounds for the epidemic. Mass delousing of the people sheltering there, many of them refugees or people made homeless by the bombings, was made compulsory.[59] The insecticide was also used to control malaria in Italy and other theatres of war. In Italy many men wearing shorts were bitten by mosquitoes and failed to take the drugs Mepacrine or quinine or use anti-mosquito creams. Indeed 'men who had been in Sicily swore that anti-mosquito cream actually attracted mosquitoes'.[60] With the introduction of DDT, it was possible to disinfect kit and buildings with it and to spray malarial areas to control dangerous mosquito breeding.[61] It was boasted that 'power sprays, DDT, aerosol bombs, an effective repellent – these, and the jeep, have made it possible for an Army to protect itself from malaria under the most difficult conditions'.[62] The navy also felt that these measures afforded it protection.

In 1944 the Fleet Air Arm took part in exercises to spray malarial areas in the Pacific and South East Asia with DDT at a time when 'it seemed as if the whole war against Japan would hinge on the question of whether insect-borne disease could be prevented, controlled or at any rate minimised to a degree that was acceptable'.[63] Between September 1943 and February 1944, at a time when there were 5,000 Australian battlefield casualties in New Guinea, 20,000 men were hospitalized from malaria. Air spraying was a success and was later used to disinfect Hong Kong after its liberation at a time when the local medical services were in the course of being reestablished, having proved itself 'a war winning weapon against the Japanese'.[64] On board ships, DDT was also effective for disinfection to control flies, bedbugs and even cockroaches. At that time the dangers of indiscriminate use of DDT were not recognised. The navy also relied on older and safer preventatives.

Quinine, extracted from cinchona bark, had been used as a prophylactic for the prevention of malaria ever since the nineteenth century, but the Japanese occupation of Java had cut off the main source of supplies. Luckily, an alternative was available in the form of the synthetic drug Mepacrine, also known as Hydrochloride Atrebrin. This had been synthesised by German chemists in the early 1930s but the formula had been sold to America. Mass production was got under way soon after America's entry into the war and by 1942 Mepacrine was being made available to front-line units in malarial areas. However, few sailors, unless they went down with malaria, could be bothered to take it regularly and it was believed that it and quinine reduced sexual potency. It was only when decisive commanders insisted on the use of the available preventatives that malaria could be controlled. Even Winston Churchill was inclined to flout the regulations about taking Mepacrine in malarial battle zones. It was the advice of the generals and that of George VI that Winston Churchill was inclined to follow rather than that of his doctors in August 1944 when he refused to take the yellow pills that would save him from malaria, since 'even though he has only to press a bell to bring into the room the greatest malarial experts in the world … he turns his back on science and asks the King whether he ought to take Mepacrine when he visits Italy'. His physician Lord Moran only managed to persuade him to follow the instructions of the doctors by pondering aloud 'if General Alexander's views on medical matters have the same value as mine on military affairs'.[65] The King, with his Great War naval background, probably saw malaria control as an executive matter, if indeed he gave it much more thought than simply agreeing with his articulate prime minister.

More attractive than Mepacrine was the new drug penicillin, perhaps one of the greatest medical achievements of the Second World War and certainly the most lauded. Discovered by the bacteriologist Alexander Fleming at St Mary's Hospital, Paddington, on 3 September 1928, penicillin had been developed by a team of scientists led by the Australian pathologist Howard Florey at the William Dunn School of Pathology at Oxford between 1939 and 1941.[66] Its development and introduction into medical use was accelerated by wartime demand for its benefits in dealing with wound infections and infectious diseases caused by bacteria. If an armed force had a means of getting its sick and wounded back into action more quickly than its enemy, it had a strategic advantage. The Allied armed forces wanted its benefits. Robert Coghill, who headed the fermentation division at the United States Department of Agriculture Northern Regional Research Laboratory at Peoria, Illinois, where modern penicillin production methods were developed, was to truly say that 'Penicillin is a more or less direct ... by-product of the war. It has probably saved more lives and eased much more suffering than the whole war has cost us.'[67]

Penicillin was important enough to the Royal Navy for it to attempt in 1943 to produce its own at the Royal Navy Medical School which had been evacuated to Clevedon in Somerset from the Royal Naval College, Greenwich, where it had been located since its foundation in 1912. In wartime, munitions production takes precedence over pharmaceuticals, which meant that even a drug such as penicillin which was seen as important to the war effort was always going to be scarce. While the armed forces were given priority in the allocation of the lifesaving drug, it remained in short supply for most of the war but was in great demand from all three services. Until 1943 the laboratories of the William Dunn School of Pathology at the University of Oxford remained the largest producer of penicillin in the world. By 1942, ICI had also set up a pilot plant at Trafford Park, Manchester, and Kemball Bishop, based at Bromley-by-Bow in the East End of London, began to cultivate batches of the crude mould to send to Florey at Oxford for processing. Kemball Bishop had sent a biologist, V J Ward, and a young organic chemist, John Gray Barnes, an Oxford athletics blue reckoned to be able to represent the acceptable face of commerce to the university, to Oxford to learn about production techniques.[68] Other small plants followed, dispersed around the country to avoid the risk of the country's penicillin production capacity being destroyed by one air raid. It all pointed to a need for naval action to supply naval demands.

The Royal Navy Medical School had had experience of producing cholera and typhoid vaccines since 1916, both to give the navy some freedom from supply problems that could have arisen from reliance on commercial sources but also to save money. It was even claimed that the money saved for the Admiralty by producing rather than buying such vaccines was more than the salaries and upkeep of the whole of the Naval Medical School.[69] After its evacuation to Clevedon near Bristol, typhoid vaccine continued to be produced and in 1940 it was decided to add a tetanus toxoid to the cholera vaccine so that men would be immunised against both infections concurrently.[70] With such practical manufacturing experience, it was little wonder that, when the possibilities of penicillin for use in naval medicine became apparent, there should be interest in investigating the possibility of producing it at the Royal Navy Medical School.

Surgeon Commander C A Green, an expert on rheumatism, was keen to work on penicillin at Clevedon with mould obtained from Fleming and cogently argued that since penicillin was not yet available from any commercial sources, and that even when it was obtainable, it would be expensive, it would give the navy an advantage if it could 'increase production and offer it for therapeutic purposes'. He recognised that 'the usefulness of penicillin and its full exploitation are handicapped by the technical difficulties involved in producing sufficient material for experimental trial and clinical usage'.[71] However, he believed that at the Royal Navy Medical School in its wartime home at Clevedon there was the expertise and apparatus to begin production. He also, sensibly but in vain, urged that the Royal Naval Medical School should be represented on the Penicillin Committee set up by the Ministry of Supply to encourage production.[72]

Howard Florey, whose team of scientists had brought penicillin into use, was dismissive of the idea, since he believed 'the time is now past for the material to be manufactured on a laboratory scale', even though his own laboratory at Oxford was doing just that and was still at that time the largest penicillin extraction plant in the United Kingdom. In his opinion 'the material is difficult to produce in quality and I assure you that it would take many months to fit up a large scale plant and then you would find the amount of material you produced in the laboratory would be quite inadequate'.[73] Green, however, disagreed with Florey that laboratory-scale production was not worthwhile once commercial firms were involved, believing that the use of new growth media and new techniques such as aeration to increase yields actually made laboratory production more viable. Moreover 'it is obvious that much has to be done on the research side as regards the production and use of penicillin' and he wished to be involved.[74] He persevered with the penicillin project and visited Oxford to see what was being done there to produce penicillin.

Production at Clevedon was got underway using that officer's mess staple the gin bottle as culture vessels for growing the penicillin in. Milk bottles, totalling some 40,000, were also collected locally for use in growing the mould. After sterilisation, the bottles were taken to the culture filling room where they were filled with a culture medium made from the residual washings from beer brewing processes obtained from local breweries. Loaded on to vertical racks, the bottles were then injected with spores of the fungus *Penicillium notatum* with a paint spray gun. A bosun's chair was winched up and down from a steel beam in the ceiling so that the bottles could be easily reached.[75] The racks were then wheeled into one of the four incubator rooms where they were agitated for about ten days before being emptied into a row of crocks from which the extraction process could begin using the methods developed on equally improvised equipment by Florey and his team at Oxford. The penicillin was now extracted in to amyl acetate and then back-extracted into water by use of a counter current system. Impurities were next removed with the newly developed technique of alumina column chromatography. The penicillin was concentrated, at first by vacuum distillation and later by the relatively new technique of freeze-drying. The freeze-dried penicillin was finally placed into phials, capped and labelled. Meanwhile the potency and purity of the batch was checked in the Assay Laboratory.[76] It was a professional organisation to meet an increasing naval demand for penicillin.

Naval production of penicillin was stopped in June 1946 when the pharmaceutical companies were producing sufficient supplies of the wonder drug for widespread civilian and service use much more economically than the Royal Navy Medical School could ever hope to achieve. The commercial stocks of penicillin now available were also purer than anything that could be produced at Clevedon. All commercial companies were now using the new submerged culture methods and fermentation techniques developed during the war at the Northern Regional Research Laboratory at Peoria and pioneered industrially by Pfizer. Reused gin bottles were by now no more than a quaint feature of the days of improvisation, not of modern industrial-scale production. It was with great regret that the Royal Navy decided that it was 'no longer necessary, reasonable nor economical' to manage its own production of penicillin.[77] The Royal Navy Medical School moved from Clevedon to Alverstoke, Hampshire in 1948 rather than back to Greenwich, but the buildings it had occupied during the war were purchased by the pharmaceutical company Distillers for use as a research station. Distillers soon sold the buildings to the Medical Research Council in 1949. Work was done there on the cephalosporin group of antibiotics, continuing until the early 1960s. The Royal Navy Medical School had left behind it at the end of the war a well set-up antibiotic research and small production facility.

However much the navy may have prided itself on being an early adopter of new medical practices and ideas, most of the innovation it had adopted during the war had been developed elsewhere. It had lagged behind in anti-malarial measures, wrongly not considering them to be of great interest for a sea-based armed service. It had followed the lead of the army in developing its blood transfusion service. Even with penicillin production, it had not introduced any new ideas. Perhaps its most successful and most significant wartime innovation was with its mass miniature photo radiography programme where it was indeed a leader. However, an openness to new ideas and developments was necessary to win the war.

Chapter Six
It's in the Air

The Fleet Air Arm had an allure that combined the glamour of the 'Brylcream boys' of the Royal Air Force and the jaunty dash of the Royal Navy. There was a recklessness about its fliers with their *joie de vivre* and youthful high spirits seen earlier on *Furious* in 1917:

> Of the officers, quite a number belonged to the Royal Naval Air Service, being in their early twenties, in fact very little more than boys in habits and manners, although personally I was very pleased to be shipmates with such beings, full of merriment and energy, which tended to alter the usual tone of the wardroom mess and was fortunately not resented by the older members of the mess, although these young members being very little acquainted with Service customs and regulations looked upon it as being rather arbitrary at times. However, it was fully realised that individuals employed on such hazardous work should not allow their minds to think too much of the dangerous side of their calling ... It certainly is very interesting to observe and watch the psychology of such individuals, but youth seems an indispensable qualification for such.[1]

This description of Great War naval fliers could have referred just as well to their successors in the Second World War. With 24 being considered the optimum age for a flier, it was very much a youthful service.[2] The navy was concerned that the influx of young airmen ignorant of tradition should be inculcated in naval culture and not see themselves as aviators rather than sailors. There was also concern about not only the physical but also the psychological welfare of the men and their suitability for such a specialised role. Naval aviation medicine represented a new challenge to ensure that the health of the aviator and his fitness for the role was maintained. Aviation medicine as a discipline was to make major advances during the Second World War.

However, it had been during the First World War that aerial combat had become an important feature of modern warfare, and with it had come recognition of the special medical needs of airmen. The Royal Naval Air Service had merged with the Royal Flying Corps to form the Royal Air Force in April 1918, but in 1924 the Fleet Air Arm was formed from the various RAF units that worked on ships. However, this remained part of the RAF and only in May 1939 was it brought back under the control of the Admiralty and renamed the Air Branch of the Royal Navy. In expanding the service to meet wartime needs, the naval medical services had to meet the special needs of aviation medicine at a time when they were only beginning to realise the nature of those needs and that 'the duty of the medical officer is to keep the flying personnel fit to take to the air at all times and thus prevent accidents'.[3] The achievement of such an aim required co-operation with the Royal Air Force Medical Service from which there was much to be learned.

It was vital that all aircrew should have excellent eyesight and be of a high standard of physical fitness. Whilst these medical standards were basic requirements for all the volunteers putting themselves forward for the Air Branch during the Second World War, this had not always been the situation. In the early days of Great War aviation there had been little acknowledgment that there were minimum physical standards to be met if the airman were to be up to the demands of flying a fighter aircraft, with the result that casualty rates and the loss of planes had been high in the fledgling Royal Naval Air Service and in the Royal Flying Corps. Good eyesight was especially important, yet one airman with poor eyesight, Second Lieutenant Bailey, did not normally wear spectacles but for flying had 'specially made goggles with magnifying glasses in them'; even with these he was unable to see properly for landing his aircraft, a defect that resulted in a fatal crash. Eventually, by 1917, the medical evidence had pointed to the need for much higher standards of vision than those initially laid down for pilots and observers despite 'the many complicated processes and the elaborate physiological and material mechanisms involved in modern Air Flying in War'. As well as the recognition of the importance of good vision came the realisation that 'co-ordination of hand and eye and other neuro-muscular adaptations are necessary' for success in the air. At the same time, it was decided to disqualify any candidates for the air forces suffering from heart disease or syphilis which could be fatal if a sufferer was seized with the symptoms while flying.[4]

Now in the Second World War a stiff day-long medical examination was designed to weed out the unfit before candidates were sent to HMS *St Vincent* at Gosport for their initial navy training before going on for flight training with the RAF. The main considerations taken into account in selecting suitable candidates for duties as pilots and observers were that they should have highly-developed neuromuscular co-ordination, a capacity for physical endurance and show signs of a mental aptitude for flying. The aim was to select only 'those who are alert in body and mind, with good muscle tone and quick reaction time, and who have accurate vision and a good sense of balance'.[5] Eyes, ears, nose, throat and the nervous system were rigorously examined but 'the estimation of mental stability by purely physical means has proved somewhat disappointing'.[6]

It was indeed difficult to assess who would make a good airman simply by looking at his levels of physical fitness. J D Simpson warned against the type of man who would make a poor recruit to the Fleet Air Arm based on his social habits and pulse rate:

> A man who gives a family history of nervous instability and has lived in an atmosphere fraught with anxiety and hypochondria, and who smokes cigarettes rather than a pipe, and drinks cocktails instead of beer (not necessarily in excess) will be found to have a rapid rise in pulse rate when rising from sitting to standing.

Such a raffish man he considered 'unlikely to make a good airman'. At the same time he despised and denigrated 'the cabbage-like individual ... whose reactions are retarded and whose pulse varies but little, who has never wandered more than a few miles from his own home and is perfectly content to follow some dull monotonous job' as equally 'unlikely to make a first class pilot or observer'.[7] It might well be wondered who would be suitable, a question never answered by Simpson whose job it was to weed out the undesirables but who clearly found it difficult to identify the ideal candidate.

Charles McAra, as an ultimately unsuccessful candidate for the Fleet Air Arm, found his own medical examination at Gosport to be particularly challenging:

> The medical itself was very thorough and exhaustive, not to say exhausting. In addition to the usual probing, prodding, cough please, there were tests on vision, hearing, sense of balance, and a test of lung capacity that consisted of blowing up a column of mercury and holding it at a certain level for several seconds. The naval doctors were all brisk, friendly and, in spite of the nature of their work, they remained genial.[8]

Only in 1943 were candidates for the non-flying duties in the Fleet Air Arm allowed to have weaker vision than was required for fliers. Attempts were also made to provide suitable educational courses for healthy and intelligent young men whose level of education would have disqualified them for a role in naval aviation even though they met the fitness requirements.[9] The medicals for naval aviators, though, were and remained perhaps the most thorough of all the medical examinations for recruits to the navy. Medical examinations continued throughout training to ensure that the recruits remained up to standard and a recruit could be 'dipped' and transferred to another branch of the navy if he failed at any stage of training. One of Charles McAra's friends dropped out when he was found to black out at altitudes of 6,000ft.[10]

It was not only the weeding out of unsuitable recruits that had early attracted the attention of medical researchers but also the physiological effects of flying at high altitudes where a lack of oxygen could result in unconsciousness. The physiologists J S Priestley and J G Haldane carried out exhaustive tests during the Great War on acclimatisation to a lack of oxygen. Haldane spent fifty-two hours locked up in a respiration chamber to assess the effects of lack of oxygen on himself, but found that the only effective way of preventing altitude sickness was 'an artificial supply of oxygen' and the use of oxygen masks.[11] Haldane had found it necessary to put the onus on the aviator to keep himself fit to cope with such problems: 'by keeping in good training, and in particular by practising walking, running or rowing, airmen can render themselves less liable to be affected by diminished air pressure'.[12] Second World War aviators were given similar advice. A test devised by Martin Flack during the Great War, the 'Flack Test', to identify men with a large lung volume and slow respiration rate who were less sensitive to the effects of altitude, continued to be used in the selection of flying crew up to the Second World War.[13] The physiological research carried out during and just after the Great War laid the basis of the methods of determining fitness to fly well into the Second World War.

There was little point in selecting the best recruits for naval aviation if care were not taken to keep them healthy and efficient in action. A good working environment was the basis for maintaining health. At first facilities at the Royal Naval Air Stations, established for specialised training such as torpedo bombing and deck landing, maintenance and storage, were inferior to those on RAF airfields. Much of the accommodation was in Nissan huts heated by slow combustion stoves which made them stuffy during the night-time blackout. At some stations, such as *Blackcap* at Stretton in Cheshire, sanitation consisted of latrine buckets.[14] Located close to the wartime fleet bases, many of them were isolated and uncomfortable such as *Landrail* at Macrihanish on the Kintyre peninsula serving ships in the Firth of Clyde which was described as a 'uniquely desolate station' and 'an uneasy, queasy staging point'.[15] Living conditions at *Sparrowhawk* at Hatston near Kirkwall in Orkney were basic when the air station was first established in 1939 to serve the fleet at Scapa Flow. Until accommodation could be built for them, many flying officers were billeted in unsatisfactory lodgings nearby and the officers' mess was temporarily set up in a sleeping hut. At first there was no camp cinema and the terrain was unsuitable for setting up playing fields.[16] There were no facilities for local leave in Orkney and any longer periods of leave were difficult to arrange during times of intense action. The senior medical officer during the Norwegian campaign in 1940, when long sorties were being made to Bergen, Trondheim and Tromso, thought that 'the crews stood up to conditions extremely well, but towards the end of the time they were reaching their limits'.[17] The RAF, by contrast, boasted that its camps with their workshops, barracks, dining halls, kitchens, recreation halls, libraries and sports facilities, were 'the best which could be provided in peace and war'.[18]

The Fleet Air Arm, operating mainly at sea, faced very different stresses and conditions to the RAF. Long-range navigation over the sea was demanding for the observer and deck landing was riskier for the pilot than landing a plane on a runway at an airfield. The planes themselves were often poorly adapted for naval conditions.[19] Living on a ship also offered none of the escape opportunities enjoyed by the RAF who could leave their bases for recreation. All the discomforts of wartime shipboard life were suffered by the aircrew, including overcrowding, noises and the extremes of climate. Norman Hanson remembered that:

> There was no escape from it all. Your Corsair was in the hangar, one deck up. The flight deck, that torrid arena in the grim game of life and death, was two short ladders beyond that. Life was lived, utterly and completely, within a space of about 10,000 yards. Within that area we ate, slept, drank, chatted with our friends, attended church, watched films, took our exercise – and flew, landed or crashed our aircraft.[20]

It may have been a very different experience from that of aircrew based on land, but it was no different from the conditions in which other sailors lived and worked, even the stress caused by feelings of claustrophobia and seasickness.[21] The aircrew, however, saw themselves as having particular needs and working under stresses different from the rest of the ship's company.

The growing awareness of the problems of flying stress made some action necessary. In 1940 H E Whittingham, soon to be Medical Director of the RAF, urged the Fleet Air Arm that 'the physiological efficiency of flying personnel – pilots, observers, air-gunners, photographers and wireless operators – must be maintained and measures to counteract or eliminate factors detrimental to the well-being of aviators must be introduced as required'.[22] A meeting held at the Admiralty in November 1940 to discuss the psychological aspects of this issue laid down the principles of preventative medicine to be followed in the Fleet Air Arm to avoid flight fatigue and to deal with men showing early signs of operational stress.[23] The experience of the RAF offered guidelines for what could be done, but it was recognised that the Fleet Air Arm had to deal with its own special problems and had to find different solutions for aircraft carriers and air stations.

Flying hours posed a major problem, causing many pilots to crack up under the stress in the Fleet Air Arm. During the First World War, the average number of flying hours before a pilot would be permanently grounded was between 1,500 and 3,000 depending on the stamina of the individual and the nature of the operational strains experienced by him.[24] On some carriers, 1,000 hours was as much as some pilots could cope with in the Second World War.[25] It was now thought that pilots at shore training bases should be allowed one full day away from all duties each week to prevent them from becoming stale. For shore-based operational squadrons, 14 days' leave every three months was seen as essential with an additional long weekend between long leaves. To relieve strain after a major operation there should be a 24-hour complete stand-down. This represented leave arrangements comparable with those enjoyed by the RAF but was difficult to implement so long as there was a manpower shortage. It was impossible to offer any guaranteed scale of leave for men on aircraft carriers apart from promising 'to grant leave clear away from the ship when possible'.[26] It was even denied that stress from too many flying hours was a problem since 'no deterioration of morale has been discovered as a result of too many flying hours. Deterioration has in certain cases been evident as a result of too few flying hours and consequent boredom.'[27] The Admiralty, instead of making regulations on flying hours, hoped that commanding officers would try to arrange for private hospitality for aircrew taking recreational leave while overseas and if this proved impossible, such as in Gibraltar whose civilian population had been evacuated except for essential war workers, 'the only remedy is early relief when this can be arranged'.[28]

In a move to alleviate the monotony and boredom of flying duties it was suggested that all flying personnel should be given other jobs such as ships' duties, physical training or games supervision. In the early days of the war it was feasible for Fleet Arm Air officers who had previously been trained as naval officers to take on executive duties on a ship to relieve other officers when they themselves were not needed for flight duties, but later in the war there was more of a gulf between the squadrons and the ship's officers as fewer airmen came from a regular naval training and many had no previous experience of life at sea. Unable to take on other duties and with little opportunity for training from regular officers for those who wished to take on other responsibilities, the younger officers of a squadron had very little to do except when actually flying. For many airmen, stand-by duties and periods of waiting before operational flying could be as stressful as action. It was recommended that such periods should be as brief and made as comfortable as possible, and that flying personnel who had kept the middle or morning watches should not be expected to fly the following afternoon.[29]

There was also a danger that flying personnel were spending too long on one posting. The RAF had found that 'it is unwise to allow flying personnel of a squadron to become too closely welded as under these conditions losses have an unduly adverse effect on the morale of the remainder'.[30] It was suggested that shore-based operational squadrons should be changed every six months and that the maximum period of continuous flying service should be one year. As it was not so easy to interchange aircrew at sea or on foreign naval air stations regularly, this could only be done when there was a spare squadron ashore.

At air stations, there was a need 'to push on with proper recreational facilities' since many of the stations were remote from sources of recreation and entertainment despite the insistence by medical officers that 'the hospitality of local residents is of particular value in providing a complete change of environment'.[31] Instead the need was to provide adequate facilities on the stations. Empty hangars were used for badminton sessions and fields set aside for games. While the men were encouraged to socialise with local people, they were discouraged from having their wives living close to the air station because of the 'acute and recurrent anxieties' that the continuance of normal family life caused. Instead it was urged that 'wives of both flying and non-flying personnel should be banished to "weekend" distance away from stations'.[32]

As well as recreation, rest was essential. This was also easier on shore air stations than on carriers. Aircrew at sea were disturbed by the ordinary life of the ship, orders issued over loudspeakers and the noise of being ready for action. They also found it difficult to sleep just before operational flights. Little could be done about these triggers for stress, but it was easier to ensure that aircrews ashore got adequate sleep and quiet. Men could be billeted away from the aerodrome which would give them a respite from the pressures and noises of an airbase. If that was not possible, there was a suggestion that they be provided with comfortable sleeping quarters in relatively quiet blast-proof shelters since 'there is nothing more disturbing than the knowledge that a rush for cover may be required'.[33]

Where men did show early signs of flying stress, there was often a delay before they were diagnosed and could receive adequate treatment for the condition, time which allowed their symptoms to worsen. Medical officers were advised to spend as much time as possible with the men and to mess with them as 'this would facilitate the detection of the earliest manifestations of incipient flying stress'. A stigma was attached to men diagnosed with a psychiatric disorder, so attempts were made to prevent a man from being labelled as 'neurotic'. Sufferers from stress were granted leave at the discretion of the medical officer but 'this leave should be regarded as ordinary leave and not sick leave since it is important to avoid any suggestion of illness'. Every effort was made to decide whether the problem was likely to be short-term and whether the man could quickly return to his duties or whether his illness was unlikely to be resolved within a couple of weeks and there would be a need to replace him in his unit. Medical officers were also advised to refer cases involving stress or neurosis to neuropsychiatrists rather than try to investigate the roots of the problem themselves, though full reports on 'the conduct, character, morale and efficiency of the patient and any recent changes therein' were to be submitted to help the specialist. An estimation of 'the degree of stress to which the patient had been subjected and his reaction in comparison with other members of his unit' could help the expert to differentiate between 'illness and loss of morale'.[34] 'Waverers', as they were known in the RAF, were considered to be 'lacking in moral fibre' whereas 'true cases of flying stress' or the 'war weary' had cracked and become ill after a spell of arduous operational work, although 'certain phlegmatic and unimaginative men can carry on much longer than their more sensitive fellows'.[35]

It was not until the establishment of the Flying Personnel Research Committee in August 1939 that aviation medicine assumed any great importance in British military planning. Over the next six years much was to be achieved and the War Cabinet Scientific Advisory Committee was in 1944 to endorse the creation of an Institute of Aviation Medicine at Farnborough as 'of first rate importance, not only for the continuation of research in the physiology and medicine of aviation for the Royal Air Force, but also for the Fleet Air Arm, for paratroops, and for civilian aviation'.[36] It had long been realised that 'with the improvement in performance and endurance of machines the problem of improving the endurance and performance of the pilot is becoming an extremely vital one'.[37]

Inevitably one of the major tasks faced by the Royal Air Force physiological laboratories at Farnborough at the beginning of the war was to find a more effective answer to the problems of high-altitude flying.[38] Aircraft flew at even greater altitudes during the Second World War than they had done in the First, yet oxygen equipment barely had advanced in the intervening two decades. Oxygen bottles were still heavy and delivered a continuous flow of oxygen even when it was not needed, with the result that some aircraft could not carry sufficient oxygen supplies for a long sortie. Even where there was an adequate supply of oxygen, the reduced pressure in the cabin at altitudes above 30,000ft could result in the airman suffering symptoms of the bends, including itching, joint pains, visual disturbance and even bleeding of the veins. Waterlogging of the lungs and unconsciousness might follow. The symptoms disappeared when the flier came down to 25,000ft but he would be troubled by blind spots, sick headaches and confusion for several more hours. Blacking-out in high speed flight had first become a problem in the late 1920s when aircraft had developed enough pull to produce centrifugal forces greater than five 'g' (the weight of gravity on the body) when the plane was performing sharp turns. The centrifugal force would drain blood from the pilot's heart and brain causing him to black out once lowered blood pressure starved the central artery in the retina of his eye.[39]

Attempts were made to overcome these problems from the beginning of the war. A research team led by Bryan Matthews, head of the laboratory, within a few months, had devised a new oxygen supply system, the 'Oxygen Economizer' or 'Puffing Billy', which used a rubberised bag and valves to control the flow of oxygen.[40] New, better-fitting oxygen masks were also designed. A very special one was made for the Prime Minister Winston Churchill's flight to Moscow in August 1942 to allow him to smoke his trademark cigars while the oxygen was delivered to his nose through what he called 'this damnable muzzle'.[41]

The services of a Savile Row tailor's cutter, skilled in moulding a suit or uniform to the idiosyncrasies of the body of its wearer, were sought to help develop a pressure suit in 1941 as a possible solution to the problem of decompression sickness or 'the bends'. Improved posture, involving a semi-crouched position with the feet firmly on the upper rudder pedals, was also taught to airmen to stop them from blacking out at increasing 'g' forces. Meanwhile, experiments in a decompression chamber showed that it was lightly-built, fit young men who were less likely to get 'the bends' than older, heavily-built men.[42] Decompression chambers were deemed essential at shore stations to weed out men who would be most susceptible to the effects of high-altitude flying.[43] The new improved portable decompression chambers introduced after 1941were considered by the Fleet Air Arm to be of most use in Fighter School 'where all the pilots will be passed through and there is an adequate supply of oxygen available'.[44] Not only were the men most suitable for flying selected by tests to determine their tolerance of high altitudes in decompression chambers, but they were also taught in them how to prevent and overcome the bends.

In Nazi Germany, research into the problems of aviation medicine was carried out in the concentration camps. At Dachau, high-altitude experiments were conducted by the schizophrenic doctor Sigmund Rascher and his wife on prisoners to investigate the limits of human endurance and existence using low-pressure chambers in which many of the victims died. As a result of these inhuman experiments, Rascher erroneously concluded that an airman could safely leave his aircraft at 68,000ft, but the Luftwaffe prudently ignored these findings and instead developed a parachute which would open automatically when the pilot was more than 10,000ft above the ground, an altitude at which all but Rascher believed the airman abandoning his plane would lose consciousness. In a further series of experiments conducted at Dachau on behalf of the Luftwaffe, victims were left in tanks of freezing water for up to three hours and then revived to investigate the most effective means of treating airmen with hypothermia. Some of them were dressed in their camp rags and others in flying suits. Many prisoners were kept naked outdoors in temperatures below freezing as part of the same experiment; some of 'the victims screamed with pain as parts of their bodies froze'. Hot baths were found to be the most effective means of reheating men though the use of women was one of the most notorious aspects of this work; it was believed that temperatures would rise rapidly during the excitement of sexual intercourse.[45] Whether the data from such unethical experimentation carried out on unwilling victims should ever be used still remains a matter of bitter debate, with some arguing that as the data exists it could benefit mankind however illegitimately obtained and others adamant that it remains unethical to ever use the results of what amounted to torture and murder. The quality of this particular work, however, was scientifically shoddy and its practical value limited.

It was generally thought that German wartime medical research, even allowing for concern about war crimes and the criminality of medical research in the concentration camps, had given a low priority to the needs of the Kriegsmarine in comparison with that carried out for the Wehrmacht and Luftwaffe. Even so, there were few lessons for the Royal Navy to be learnt from German research:

> In general, the amount of valuable new work in Germany (at least that about which the Germans are prepared to talk) in the last seven years is not great. There is no outstanding single contribution comparable with the development of penicillin in England and America, and no immediately obvious opening up of significant new fields of research.[46]

In undertaking research at Farnborough, the physiologist Edgar Pask carried out more ethical experiments on himself and his team of researchers to study the effects of flying at high altitude. His first series of experiments which 'simulated parachute descent', were carried out by five young doctors who described themselves as heavy smokers yet 'in good health but not in good training'. Pask himself volunteered to be the subject of seven of the sixteen experiments, including one which left him hanging in a parachute harness. The team of volunteers were exposed to hypoxic gas mixtures in a decompression chamber, with the mixtures designed to simulate the inspired oxygen concentrations encountered whilst descending. Effectively they were asphyxiated, and then their slow recovery was monitored. Pask also acted as a guinea pig to test out the best methods of artificial resuscitation, having first anaesthetised himself so that he would be unconscious like many of the drowning airmen. He also personally tried out different types of life jackets and immersion suits in a series of experiments that were filmed to demonstrate to aircrew that something was being done for them. After many of his experiments, he had to be admitted to hospital. It was a very different approach to that of the Nazis.[47]

Much-publicised attempts were made to improve the night vision of British pilots using glucose, alcohol, caffeine, quinine, strychnine, nicotine and massive doses of vitamin A but without much success, although popular myths about aircrew being able to see in the dark through eating lots of carrots was to be a good cover for the development of radar.[48] Apparatus was developed to test aircrew for good night vision and measures devised for adapting the eyes of pilots flying at night to the dark by keeping them in a darkened room and wearing dark glasses for half an hour before a flight.[49] Some medical officers saw night blindness as being of psychogenic origin, but solutions to the condition still needed to be sought.[50]

Improvements were made into the clothing of airmen in the RAF which were adopted by the Fleet Air Arm. The naval pilot at the beginning of the war still wore an impractical uniform for flying. His double-breasted uniform jacket was too bulky to be an effective flying suit, its superfine serge material was too easily soiled and its pockets easily torn in the cockpit. A pilot could buy at his own expense his own overall to wear over his uniform suit, with the fur-lined, two-piece Irving suit being especially popular. The RAF devised a marine suit for use by the pilots of Catapult Aircraft Merchant Ships allowing them to be comfortable while flying but also keeping them warm and dry when they landed in the sea. The Royal Navy was perhaps most concerned about keeping the pilot of a small aircraft warm while flying and electrically-heated clothing was devised that would not be too bulky in the cockpit.[51] However, in Arctic conditions this electric heating would be lost in the event of a forced landing. The answer to the problem was the naval immersion suit, introduced in 1943, which extended the life expectation of a naval airman after crashing in the sea from ten minutes to over an hour.[52] Improved flying goggles gave protection against glare, dust, missiles and flash burns, while better flying helmets gave protection against deafness to high tones caused by aircraft noise.[53]

Above all the onus was on the men to keep themselves at a level of fitness equal to their glamorous reputation. Aviation medicine experts such as Harold Whittingham believed that 'the Briton's love of sport, which inures him to excitement and to sudden emergencies, does much to train his nervous system and endocrine glands to react perfectly and not to over-function in emergency' which made British pilots and air crews 'the most physically efficient in the world'.[54]

Although many of the advances in aviation medicine were made by the RAF, progress in this field was of equal benefit to the Fleet Air Arm. Sometimes, it was thought best to refer particular medical cases to RAF doctors with greater expertise, but the men of the Fleet Air Arm were not happy about this and would have preferred to be seen by their own medical officers:

> Aircrews do, undeniably, resent feeling that their problems must be referred to medical officers of another branch of the Services, and not their own, and attribute this, not unnaturally, to a lack of interest. This decreases both liaison and morale.[55]

Continuity of medical care was found to be important as air crews trusted particular medical officers to look after them and be aware of the particular problems of aviation medicine as well as knowing them well enough to detect signs of stress and strain:

> The policy of appointing a medical officer to each squadron and allowing him to remain with the squadron has shown strikingly good results. Much depends on the personality of the medical officer chosen ... he becomes a part of the squadron administration and identifies himself with every side of squadron life. Working as he can, and does, with the squadron C.O. he plays an important part in the upkeep of morale, and is in a unique position to make personal contacts and watch unobtrusively all flying personnel, and not least

the C.O. himself, on whom the greatest responsibility falls including that of operational stress.[56]

A senior medical officer on *Ark Royal* wrote from experience when he described the requirements for an effective naval aviation doctor:

> The Fleet Air Arm medical officer must know all the flying personnel. He must know not only their names but must be able to form a good degree of knowledge of their characters, their professional ability, position in their squadrons, something of their jargon and of the stress to which they are subjected. He must be able to detect quickly a change in their outlook or habits, yet must never have the appearance of spying on them. He must stand in the light of a friend to whom they can turn for sympathy and advice. He must be prepared to listen to their grumbles, without too obviously siding with them or opposing them. He must be able to give friendly warnings without arousing antagonism, and advice without being sententious. Lastly when it falls to his lot to ground a pilot or observer, or send him home for rehabilitation, he must be something of a diplomat, for he must at one and the same time provide hope for the airman's future and rob his enforced treatment of the imputation of being a failure.[57]

It was not an easy task for anyone.

At first there was very little training for naval medical officers in the field of aviation medicine despite it being recognised as being desirable that they should have some special instruction in 'psychological medicine applied to flying'.[58] It was also essential that they should be 'encouraged to familiarise themselves with every aspect of flying'.[59] More conservative officers were against such specialisation as they believed that a naval medical officer should be versatile and able to serve anywhere in the navy. As a result of such attitudes there was merely a short three-week course in aviation. The high light of the first week held at the Royal Naval Barracks at Lee was a practical demonstration in the oxygen tank at Farnborough and a demonstration of the different types of aircraft flown by the Fleet Air Arm. Otherwise there were lectures on the physiology of flying, pilot selection, the care of aircrews and the treatment of flying stress. The second week was devoted to medicine, surgery, neurology and psychiatric medicine at Haslar. For the final week of the course there were lectures and demonstrations at HMS *St Vincent*, lectures on station administration, protection against gas attacks and the administration of medical services for the WRNS back at Lee. The importance of good record-keeping and report-writing was emphasised.[60] It was not the most inspirational of training and was too brief to be more than an introduction.

In 1942, two naval doctors were sent to train in aviation medicine and qualify as pilots at the United States Naval Station Pensacola. The six naval medical officers trained at Pensacola between 1942 and 1944 found the instruction in aviation medicine to be too elementary to be of much value, with only the courses in physiology, flight physical examinations and ophthalmology being of practical use, but they enjoyed the opportunity to learn to fly, only one of them not qualifying as a pilot. Surgeon Lieutenant L G Topham 'personally derived a lot of most valuable information' from his course but felt that it could be shorter by at least two weeks 'as one's interest tends to lag during that last period, when one feels the time is being filled in by padding, with no useful information'.[61]

Many naval medical officers working with the Fleet Air Arm would have welcomed the opportunity to learn to fly, partly so they could better understand the needs of their charges but also for the excitement of becoming aviators. At Pensacola and other American naval airbases, it was common to find doctors who were also fliers. Indeed, by the end of the war most of them had earned their wings and this increased their proficiency and efficiency as naval aviation medical officers. Since these medical officers lived with their squadron, knew the airmen informally and treated whatever the pilot told them confidentially, they were trusted in a way that a non-flier may not have been.[62] In the Royal Navy, there was a recognition that it was important to have a few medical officers who were also qualified pilots as 'it would enable them to get into much closer touch with the flying personnel, who are notoriously apt to form themselves into little cliques and regard non-flying people with suspicion'.[63] In wartime giving medical officers the facilities that they needed to obtain their wings was considered a luxury and it was generally believed that 'if a medical officer does his work conscientiously, the lack of wings is no great handicap'.[64]

Perhaps more important was ensuring that medical officers should be trained more adequately in aviation medicine than they had been at the beginning of the war. On 13 March 1944 the Royal Naval Air Medical School was established at the Royal Naval Air Station Eastleigh to instruct medical officers in the principles and practice of naval aviation medicine and to conduct research into the problems of naval flying. The three-week long course covered the physiology of high-altitude flying and centrifugal force, the psychiatric care of aircrew, oto-rhinology and ophthalmology applied to flying, the medical aspects of safety equipment and the theory of flight. There was even a small element of practical flying experience though it did not involve training as a pilot.[65] Despite advances in aviation medicine remaining the main responsibility of the RAF medical services rather than of the Fleet Air Arm, there was growing recognition that this new discipline was of naval interest and even the generalist naval medical officer must know about the new specialism of flight medicine. Naval aviation medicine specialists had emerged despite the initial opposition to specialism and a new medical specialty was born.

Chapter Seven
The Waves Above

Submarine crews lacked the care of a medical officer taken for granted by most ships' companies and Fleet Air Arm squadrons. Submarines were too small and confined to carry any surplus personnel, yet they offered new medical challenges to keeping their crews healthy in an unnatural environment. Hugh Philip, a medical officer at a submarine base, felt that 'I should be only one more to occupy the hencoop – one more person to share the already precious air supply in case of difficulty, and my value would be very doubtful except that I should learn by experience the difficulties of a submariner's life rather than have to rely on second-hand opinions'.[1] Yet that was what doctors such as Philip had to do if they wanted to contribute to the medical needs of men serving beneath the sea.

Generally, wartime submarines had no more medical treatment on offer to their crews than the training in first aid received by a coxswain in a few hours at Haslar – if that. Illnesses were diagnosed using a 'paper doctor', a medical textbook in which 'you started off with how he looked, and you had to turn to such and such a page, and eventually you hoped to come to what was wrong'.[2] On HMS/M *Thule* the coxswain 'wasn't a doctor, but he was as good as a doctor', who used a hacksaw 'out of the engine room and sawed the leg off above the knee; and it was just like being in a butcher's shop'.[3] The commanding officer of the submarine also had to be not only a sailor 'but an engineer, an electrician, and last but not least the ship's doctor'.[4] Throughout the war there was never any serious discussion of having a medical officer on board a submarine, although consideration was given to following the practice of the United States Navy in having medical ratings on each submarine operating in tropical or Arctic waters. It would have been a sensible move but sick berth attendants were never appointed to submarines during the war.[5]

It was only once they had returned to base that the crew could hope for any medical attention that they might require, including sun lamp treatment to compensate for the deprivation of the health benefits of sunlight they had experienced while on operational duty. Each submarine depot ship carried experienced medical staff. Instead of operating from shore bases, the submarines were serviced by supply ships moored in the major ports which allowed for flexibility; after the fall of France in 1940, depot ships moved westwards from Blyth, Harwich, Rosyth and Dundee to the Firth of Clyde.[6] When in port the submarines would moor alongside the depot ship. Submarine crews did not like these depot ships much and complained that 'they are the biggest disgrace in the Navy':

> I could tell you scores of tales from my own experience. Of submarine crews preferring to go on patrol rather than stay in the depot ships on food fit only for the gash bucket. Of ratings carrying their dinner on deck and ditching it over the side in front of the Commander (who was probably waiting for his six-course lunch). Of crews sleeping in their boats when off patrol, although that was against the rules, because there was no room to sleep in the depot ship.[7]

It was a cause of resentment that the quarters for officers on depot ships were comfortable but messing decks grossly inadequate for the crew.

American submariners were given better facilities on base. There were pre- and post-patrol medical examinations and men deemed in need of rest and recreation were sent to special, rather luxurious facilities such as the Royal Hawaiian Hotel and others on Midway, Majuro, Guam, Saipan, Manus and Milne Bay, where they were entertained with cinema shows, beer gardens, boxing matches, orchestral recitals, plays, sightseeing tours, water sports and even amusement arcades.[8] Germany also believed in the importance of relaxation for its U-boat crews. After their second war patrol from Brest in 1942, the crew of *U-604* were sent to rest and recuperate at a recreation centre set up in a requisitioned chateau at Trevarez near Chateauneuf de Fou in Brittany for ten days, where they enjoyed 'unrestricted use of everything', including fine food, champagne and wines from the owner's cellar and the attentions of the female servants who 'actively welcomed' them.[9]

Life was comfortable for the medical officers attached to the submarine depot ships. It was not always even necessary for them to experience for themselves the conditions on the submarines suffered by the men whose health they looked after. One medical officer indeed lost his life on a submarine but only as a passenger from Gibraltar to Malta.[10] Bernard Hunt, when Principal Medical Officer at the Royal Naval Auxiliary Hospital La Maddalena, Sardinia, which acted as the hospital for the base of the 10th Submarine Flotilla, was invited by the captain of *Undine* to go to sea on a three-week operation off the coast of Italy. He turned down this offer ostensibly because he could not be away from his post for such a length of time but really because he was 'a bit scared'.[11] Hugh Philip was reluctant to go onboard any of the submarines that he saw on his first day when posted to a depot ship because 'they were such hives of industry that I feared I might get in the way'. He was also worried when he saw men 'disappearing down tiny circular hatches which I was sure I should never manage to negotiate if the need arose'.[12] A heavily-built man, he indeed found problems when sent to inspect fresh-water tanks on a submarine and found that he could not get through the necessary hatch and had to content himself with manipulating his body to get his upper end through the opening to make his inspection. He found it 'a strange sensation this first setting foot in one of these monsters of the deep'.[13]

The United States Navy was perhaps better in training its medical officers in submarine medicine, especially in the sanitary and hygienic aspects and the safety problems of life in a submarine. At first the emphasis had been on training them in deep-sea diving, but it soon became apparent that the training courses at the Deep Sea Diving School, Washington, DC, and the Submarine Base, New London, Connecticut should also cover 'tank instruction and escape, inspection and instruction trips on submarines, dark adaptation instruction, and similar matters', as well as 'demonstration of diving equipment, lectures, and demonstrations and participation in the submarine personnel and sound listening personnel selection system'. However, it was not until March 1944 that a qualification in submarine medicine became compulsory for all senior medical officers assigned to submarine bases and squadrons. There was also special training for pharmacists' mates who provided basic first aid aboard American submarines and were 'indoctrinated in special phases of submarine medicine'.[14] What they especially feared was the possibility of a submariner suffering from severe appendicitis and the necessity of an appendectomy having to be performed in the submarine, a rare event but not unknown.

German U-boats also relied on medical care provided by the submarine's commanding officer, other officers or wireless operators with the aid of a medicine chest and a small blue book containing guidance, *Das Blaue Wunder*, since, like the British, they did not have the equivalent of a pharmacist's mate and 'in the ordinary way, a submarine crew goes out against the enemy without a doctor'. During a patrol in St George's Channel, Stoker Second Class Blum on one U-boat reported with a furuncle that was ready for lancing. The officer was about to lance this when the order came to crash dive and a terrific explosion made the boat shudder: 'I think I cut Blum a bit too far into the healthy flesh, but the explosion acted for him as an anaesthetic'. The unfortunate Blum not only had his medical treatment cut short but had to go to his action station still with his furuncle inadequately treated.[15]

In the summer of 1943, medical officers were deployed to U-boats for a short period. This scheme was intended to give commanders the support of a mature confidant and to raise the morale of the crew by reassuring them that there would be medical help on hand. The scheme was soon abandoned, as, lacking experience of submarine warfare, some of the doctors employed were of no practical help at all, if not hindrances to the efficiency of the U-boat. The medical officer attached to *U-230* spent most of the patrol in his bunk suffering from acute seasickness and anxiety.[16] It was realised that the skills of these doctors could be more usefully employed on board a ship on the surface or on land.

Living conditions were primitive and outlandish for all seamen setting off on patrol for the first time, as Able Seaman Sydney Hart found on *Triad*:

> We scrambled down in single file, passed our kits through a small hatch, and so squeezed ourselves into the ship's interior. The

atmosphere was warm and stuffy. The lights seemed dull and listless by contrast with the late autumn sunset outside. So we went through the engine room into the small mess, cramped, as it normally was, and, now with steaming bags all over the place, looking like any London tube at the rush hour. For us this state of affairs would be normal for three weeks duration or thereabouts.[17]

It was a first impression of life on a submarine, but the overcrowding and cramped environment would soon become all too familiar to everyone aboard.

Living and working conditions on submarines were notoriously cramped and uncomfortable. Bunking facilities aboard submarines were designed for peacetime complements. With increased crews and the addition of new equipment, serious overcrowding was inevitable in wartime conditions. On most submarines there were only enough bunks for two-thirds of the men who had to share bunks between different watches. On *Alliance*, laid down in 1945 and designed for war in the Far East, the four messes for ratings, stokers, petty officers and engine room artificers were not big enough for all the sixty crew and some bunks were fitted in the main passageway, while the torpedo crew had to sling their hammocks from the deck head in the torpedo compartments at the bow and stern. The captain had his own small cabin while the four other officers slept in the more comfortable but equally cramped wardroom. The wardroom on older submarines would be no more than 8ft square and surrounded by tiers of bunks for the officers on two sides and a green baize curtain on the others.[18]

Any improvements were slow to be made. Such overcrowding was very little different from the cramped conditions on German U-boats during the First World War, with the head merely separated off from the living space by a curtain. Men 'awoke in the morning with considerable mucous in our heads and frequently with so-called oil-head' from condensation from the steel hull plates. When Johannes Spiess was appointed watch officer on *U-9* in 1912, the officer whom he was replacing 'recommended the use of opium before all cruises lasting over twelve hours'.[19] Even after the Second World War there was little improvement to conditions. Submarine *Andrew* had been built in the late 1940s and later modernised, but by 1966, when a report was made on its operation in tropical waters, living standards on board were old-fashioned and little different from those during the war, and were deteriorating through the age of the submarine. Living spaces remained cramped, and working spaces varied from 'satisfactory' to 'potentially dangerous' with air-conditioning still considered inadequate.[20]

The habitability of submarines was of an even greater concern than it was on warships. It could be affected by the efficiency of the ventilation and air-conditioning plant, the accumulation of carbon dioxide, any increases in pressures and humidity, hot weather, overcrowding, inadequate water supplies, ineffective sanitary tanks and any damage that might be caused by depth-charging and accidental flooding. The dangers of flooding, fire and noxious gasses such as chlorine and carbon tetrachloride were ever present. Whilst these problems were known to impair the efficiency of the crew of a submarine, little attempt was made to correlate poor living conditions with the success of an operation. Instead the effects were merely noted, with conditions in the Indian Ocean having a greater effect on the state of the crew than those on a patrol in the Mediterranean:

> After three weeks patrol, it was quite obvious that the officers had had their physical and mental stuffing knocked out of them. They were not tense, irritable or depressed, but they were tired, lethargic, slow, unwilling to do anything. When they came in from the Mediterranean, they entertained us; this time we had to entertain them.[21]

A high sickness rate amongst submariners was taken for granted, with many suffering from fatigue, prickly heat, poor night vision and respiratory infections. The routine of life on a submarine was considered to be 'topsy-turvy'.[22] It was a nocturnal existence. The submarine surfaced during the night to charge its batteries and could make more speedy progress than it could when submerged. The galley could only operate while on the surface as it would use too much battery power when submerged, so the main meal of the day was often between 1 and 2 in the morning and hot meals were only available at night. Diving at dawn, the submarine would be submerged and those men off duty encouraged to rest in order to save air.

The most common defects in air-conditioning in the early days of the war in those submarines that enjoyed this luxury were caused by the unequal division of air between the forward and after compartments of the submarine and the inadequacies of the cooling capacities of the air-conditioning units. It was such a great problem on one submarine in the Tropics that 'when dived, condensation occurs in the fore end – the torpedo stowage compartments' and that then 'when surfaced again, a great fog arises and lasts for about two minutes'. On another submarine, a member of the crew observed that 'a cooler would be the answer to all our problems. After diving it is too hot to sleep.'[23] On United States Submarine *N* in 1943 high temperatures were such a problem that 'excessive heat and humidity reduced the efficiency of all hands to a marked degree after about two weeks of operation'.[24]

In the Indian Ocean, temperatures could be as high as 85.8° to 90.5° Fahrenheit, well above the normal comfort zone for the submariners. Table fans and dehumidifiers offered some relief but the dehumidifiers themselves were not only noisy but also generated even more heat. Coolers were better, but there was little that could be done to deal with the poor ventilation and stagnant air resulting from the proximity to each other near the deck head of the air intake and air exhaust openings.[25] In such conditions 'the hot atmosphere and sea temperatures' aggravated 'most of the hardships which are attendant upon submarine service generally'. Although dehumidifiers were used three times a day for half an hour a time, the crew of one submarine complained on their return from a three-week patrol of prickly heat, slight constipation, and the lack of ventilation; the cook 'showed a combination of pustular acne and septic prickly heat'. In general, morale was high and 'the chaps are very much on their toes' and more alert after a successful trip, when they were looking forward to rest in port and leave on the upcountry estates of tea planters.[26] Nevertheless, improved air-conditioning could enhance the habitability of submarines in tropical waters and standards of maintenance tended to be higher than on surface ships which ameliorated 'the bad mental and physical effects which the conditions in submarines had on the crews'.[27] On *Storm* better air-conditioning plant in 1944 meant that 'it was frequently more comfortable dived than surfaced'.[28]

Cold-water operations had particular problems of their own. Torpedo room bilges and water pipes frequently froze. Condensation was a major problem with metal fittings. Heaters could only be used at certain times in order to conserve the batteries. The crew slept in the same clothing they worked in and did not change their clothes while on patrol and these soon became very damp when there was high humidity.[29]

However much attention was given to 'making the living conditions of the submariner as satisfactory as is practicable within the limitations imposed by his craft', much also depended on the competence and experience of the commanding officer.[30] When John Roxburgh was appointed as commanding officer of *P.44*, later renamed *United*, at the age of 23 in December 1942, the crew were horrified by how young he looked but were reassured when they discovered that he was married and 'might want to live' unlike his single predecessor who was more interested in glory and had been after a VC.[31] Doctors and scientists were surprised and unfairly criticised the commanding officers, whatever their age or degree of recklessness, because they 'showed a surprising ignorance of the elementary facts of respiratory physiology, a knowledge of which would appear to be an essential part of a submarine officer's equipment'. As a result they rarely used carbon dioxide absorbents, such as soda lime treated with silica gel, or supplies of oxygen and failed to maintain the optimum atmosphere when dived leading to 'physical exhaustion and lack of mental concentration, lack of interest in the surfacing of the boat'.[32] Headaches and sleepiness were frequent and vomiting was common when the men again breathed fresh air.

On his second patrol with *P.44*, John Roxburgh experienced carbon dioxide poisoning for himself when his boat surfaced after having been dived for thirty-six and a half hours. After sinking an Italian destroyer, *P.44* had been depth-charged and hunted through the night with no opportunity to surface to draw in fresh air. Roxburgh was aware of the effect that this could have on his crew and ordered that all activities, such as cooking and the re-loading of torpedoes, should cease and that everyone should sleep. The air pressure in the submarine was high as a result of the torpedoes having been fired, which 'makes breathing carbon dioxide more lethal'. It was only possible to stay on the surface for half an hour but that was enough time to suck in fresh air and recharge the batteries. On board was a young commando who was physically fitter than the crew and was least affected by the carbon monoxide poisoning. Most of the men were quiet and sleepy, though gasping for breath in conditions that were 'bloody uncomfortable'. Roxburgh, when briefly on the bridge during the half hour on the surface, had a splitting headache and was 'as sick as a dog'.[33]

The United States Submarine *P* on operations in northern waters found similar problems with carbon dioxide concentrations:

> The first dive made ... lasted longer than expected with no carbon dioxide absorbents spread. At the end of fourteen hours all hands had difficulty in breathing, carbon dioxide concentration at the time being 2.5 per cent. Eight hundred pounds of oxygen were bled into the boat with slight relief. Upon surfacing two hours later, the concentration in the conning tower was 3.5 per cent.[34]

Such problems were also familiar to the crews of German U-boats. After nine hours of bombardment by a British anti-submarine force, some of the crew of a U-boat operating in St George's Channel were 'obviously short of breath, had bluish lips and were suffering in the sultry, steamy atmosphere'. It was a relief for the men to surface with 'a strong current of air in the ship, reflexive gulping to equalise the pressure on the eardrums, and we suddenly stood in a fog, as the steam, which had become saturated in the excess pressure and heat, became condensed'. For one of those men, 'we were out and I still have a live recollection of those first deep draughts of air'.[35]

Despite the confined environment, smoking was not restricted in any way, and the 'consumption of tobacco was considerable', resulting in high concentrations of carbon monoxide; although it was recognised that the presence of tobacco smoke in the atmosphere could be unpleasant, especially to non-smokers, there was no notion that there might be harmful concentrations of the gas.[36] On Italian submarines the use of both alcohol and tobacco was controlled, with submariners being rationed to fifteen cigarettes a day instead of the twenty issued to other sailors. Italian divers were forbidden to smoke at all.[37]

Supplies of fresh water were scarce and this was a factor limiting the duration of patrols. Even when units capable of producing an adequate supply of fresh water were installed, water supplies could still be contaminated with toxic copper sulphate from the pipes. With drinking water in short supply, there was little to spare for maintaining personal hygiene. Condensation water from the air-conditioning equipment was used for washing. Men had to rinse the worst dirt off themselves in a communal bucket, before using washbasins for a more thorough wash. Shaving was a rare luxury.

It was difficult to keep clothing clean and dry on a submarine. Working dress was little more than dungarees and shirts, often worn with submarine sweaters. In the Tropics, sandals and khaki shorts were worn. Protective clothing was also needed, including anti-flash gear, waterproof Ursula suits and Kapoks, and also regular shore-going uniform which often took up more room than the protective clothing in the very limited stowage space which was 'even more at a premium than in surface ships'. It was also necessary that all protective clothing should not be too bulky or else it would obstruct the men from getting through the hatchways.[38] German naval uniform was considered to be inferior in quality and design to that of the Royal Navy, except for formal mess dress, and its one-piece rubberised protective suit for U-boat crews was 'cumbersome and heavy and less comfortable than a RN destroyer or Ursula suit'.[39] Yet heavy clothing was still needed on all submarines. Although deck watches were shorter than on surface ships, which might have meant that lighter clothing would be sufficient, conditions on the bridge were more exposed and wetter on submarines. Submarine pants were designed to be worn over trousers, but these were too hot to wear below deck and very few submariners sported them. One man had sent the pants issued to him to his girlfriend 'to be unravelled and knitted into sweaters'.[40]

The heads were emptied by blowing their contents into the sea and there was always a danger for a submariner of 'getting his own back' when sea pressure was more than blowing pressure. There was a five-position lever to be operated to discharge waste but the submariner first had to calculate exactly how much air pressure to build up in the system if he wished to avoid any accidents. Once the sewage had been discharged, the tank had to be depressurised before the heads could be used again, which involved the smelly procedure of venting the pressure back into the submarine. There were restrictions on when the heads could be used for fear that the discharge of waste might reveal the presence of the submarine. At night the resulting bubbles would be less visible. Any man wishing to relieve himself had to ask the officer of the watch for permission to 'blow'.[41] There was no privacy at all.

Food on submarines was surprisingly good considering the confined conditions in which the cooks worked, though supplies of fresh meat, bread and vegetables were often exhausted before the end of a patrol and there was a reliance on tinned foodstuffs, with occasional issues of baked beans, tinned sausages, sardines, tinned bacon and tinned fruit as treats. The tins would be double-decked for storage, laid out on the decks and main passageway and covered with layers of hardboard so that the crews could walk over them. Even before the outbreak of war, it was realised that submarines required 'specially favourable treatment in the matter of victualling'. Extra issues of submarine comforts, cocoa essence and soup were essential on patrols lasting more than 48 hours, and some 'special items' not usually available in general naval messing, such as army biscuits, tinned tongue and Marmite, were issued on diving patrols.[42] On American submarines canned luncheon meat and Nescafe were considered to be important in providing variety to enliven an otherwise monotonous diet, and ice cream was considered a great morale-booster.[43] On British submarines a general messing system was adopted and the officers were fed in the same way as the ratings with their messing bills only being payable when they were on the depot ships.[44] However, whereas the men had to draw up rotas for collecting the food from the small galley and finding a way to take it to the messes through narrow spaces and a darkened control room and for washing up, the wardroom steward took care of the officers' messing needs. The officers did not get their daily rum issue but usually their wardroom was well stocked with other spirits.

Effectively constituting a separate service within the Royal Navy, submariners were regarded as an elite enjoying prestige with the public. The Submarine Service, with only 9,090 ratings in September 1944,[45] was small and mainly used for scouting and lookout duties during and after a fleet action and for anti-U-boat action, but its small size made it cohesive and tightly knit. If a submarine was lost, its entire crew was usually lost with it.[46] Living closely together offered support, but could also cause tensions, especially when not all the crew were happy with a submarine posting. Although submarine ratings were all supposed to be volunteers, many were drafted against their will, despite the extra pay of between 9d. and 3s. 9d a day. After men at *Dolphin* in 1941 refused duty because they had not volunteered for submarine service, it was laid down that 'service in the Royal Navy involved a liability for any kind of naval service, and this included service in submarines'.[47]

High medical standards were expected of submariners, who received special screening before being posted. Emphysema and signs of mild lung tuberculosis would disqualify a candidate.[48] A good dental underbite was considered necessary for gripping the mouthpiece of the escape apparatus. Excellent hearing and a high standard of physical fitness were expected. Good night vision was especially important for night lookouts and it was essential to reject anyone suffering from night blindness. In big ships, a lookout could be replaced, but on a submarine 'there are no spares'.[49] Radar operators also required near-vision acuity. The development of night vision dark adaptation tests also allowed for the detection of malingerers wishing to avoid service duties but this was not considered a major problem despite suspected 'bursts of malingering'.[50]

Various measures were adopted to improve night vision. All compartments of the submarine in which men were waiting to go on watch were fitted with dim red lights, and dark goggles were issued to men to be worn when they entered a well-lit compartment within half an hour of going on watch. Night watches were cut down to a maximum of two hours and adequate rest between patrols was advised. Vitamin concentrates were added to the food onboard the submarine. All men were advised to cut down on their consumption of alcohol and tobacco. Five minutes of deep breathing was recommended before going on watch in order to compensate for any oxygen deficiencies.[51] On *Storm* restrictions on smoking by men before going on night duty proved to be particularly effective, though perhaps were not popular with the affected officers and ratings:

> As we are now, most necessarily, 'vision conscious' I would suggest that the last hurried cigarette before lookouts and the officer of the watch go on the bridge at night, is to be condemned and that these

people be not allowed to smoke 15 minutes before they are due to relieve.[52]

Not all navies attached the same importance to night vision as did the British and Americans. Italian submariners were expected to have perfect vision in daylight but no attention was paid to night vision, nor were they subject to psychological testing.[53] In Germany equal if not greater attention as that of the Royal Navy was given to the selection of U-boat personnel, of whom 'the highest possible standard was demanded'. All candidates were questioned about their medical history of nervousness, headaches, sweating and palpitations. The main cause of rejection was perforated eardrums and obstruction of the eustachian tube which could impair hearing and cause tinnitus. There were also some very basic educational and psychological tests, the most usual of which was for a candidate to be asked to write an essay or describe a film that he had seen. Medical examinations were carried out by 'special U-boat medical officers, without any specific psychiatric training, but who had undergone a course covering submarine problems lasting a week or two and who had carried out some patrols'.[54]

Submarine training in the Davis Submerged Escape Apparatus (DSEA) in a mock submarine compartment at the bottom of a tank, could also be used to identify men emotionally unfit for underwater service. Anyone who showed signs of being excessively nervous during this training would be disqualified from submarine duty because if they could not adapt to lung training it was unlikely that they would be able to cope with the stress when depth charges were rolling in action. The effects of immersion for the first time could be traumatic as Arthur Dickison discovered at HMS *Dolphin* at Gosport:

> The experience of the water slowly rising up my body made the hairs stand up on the back of my neck and when it touched my chin I was not far off panicking. One of my fellow trainees did. When the water was at chin height the pressure was equalised and the instructor opened the hatch at the top of the chamber. In turn, we ducked under a canvas tube and floated up to the surface, 100 feet above. On subsequent runs most of us achieved more confidence but sadly there were two of the class who could not get it right.[55]

Twelve per cent of the men selected for training failed the course.[56]

It was important that submarine crews should be well-trained in the use of the DSEA as their survival could depend on it. The apparatus consisted of a breathing bag, a metal canister of soda lime, a rubber mouthpiece, oxygen flasks and a valve connection. Pure oxygen was delivered through the mouthpiece, though it was suggested that at pressures over 150ft the crew might fill their bags partially with expired air and then use the oxygen in their flasks more liberally during the later part of their ascent.[57] If it were necessary to escape from a sunken submarine, the men gathered under one of the hatches which were forward, aft and under the gun. The pressure inside the compartment would then be raised by flooding it with water until it was equal to the outside water pressure. Once the water had risen to the top of the escape door, the hatch would be opened and the men would escape one by one. The senior officer working the valves would be the last to leave.[58] Speed was of the essence.[59] The longer a man was under water, the longer it would take to revive him with artificial respiration.[60] Depot ships had recompression chambers, but on submarines these could be improvised in torpedo compartments, air locks or escape chambers and in airlocks or boilers on warships.[61] Such an escape was not without its physiological dangers, including severe pain in the ears and even burst eardrums, nitrogen poisoning which could lead to the greater danger of irrational behaviour, headaches from carbon dioxide, asphyxia and unconsciousness from lack of oxygen, lung injuries from the excessive air pressure, the bends and gas embolisms in the blood vessels.[62]

Avoiding these dangers demanded some awareness of submarine medicine as 'it cannot be too strongly emphasised that there is no reasonable prospect of saving an acceptable proportion of the complement of a sunken submarine unless the methods adopted are founded upon physiological principles'.[63] Nevertheless, some men ignored them and still survived. Edward Young did not bother using the DSEA when he escaped from *Umpire* in 1941 because he was worried that it would be too restrictive in an already very tight environment. He was lucky to survive but most of his fellow survivors did use the apparatus, 'coming up at fairly regular intervals, strange Martian creatures with their DSEA goggles and oxygen bags and

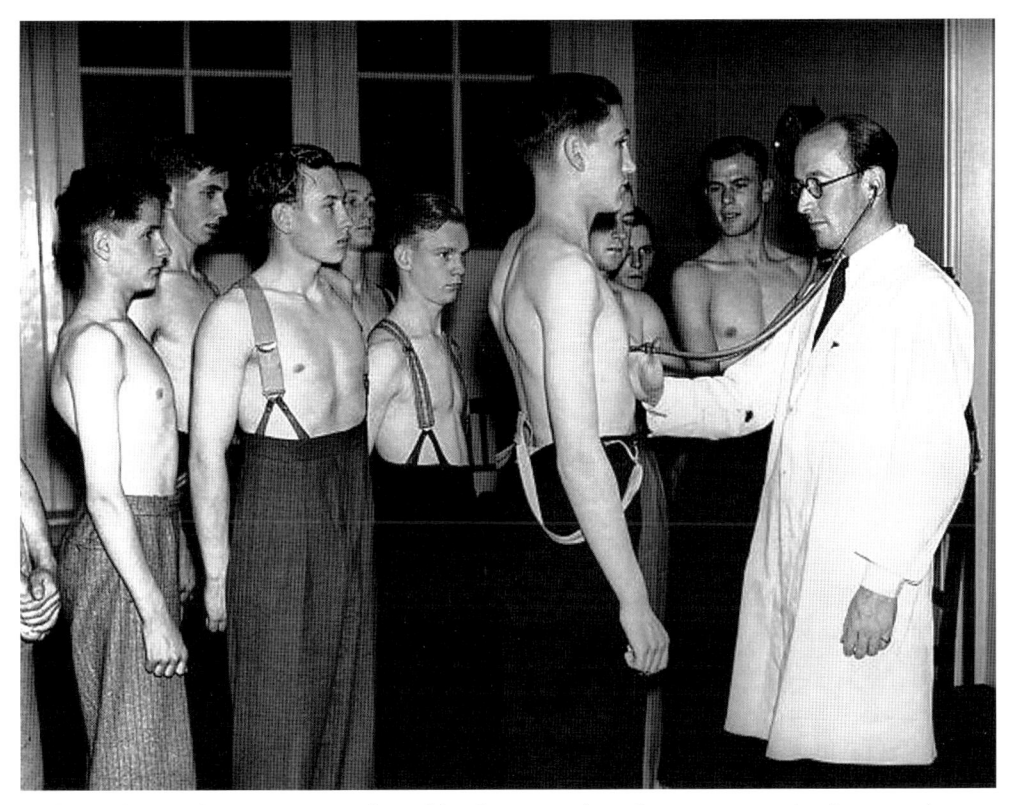

Only the fittest of recruits were selected by the navy when they were examined at recruitment centres, 1939. (*Camden Local Studies and Archives Centre*)

Peter McCrae disliked being photographed, but was happy to be seen in his uniform as a RNVR surgeon lieutenant before his heroic death on HMS *Mahratta*. (*Imperial College Healthcare NHS Trust Archives*)

Inoculating men against typhoid was an essential if routine job for the naval surgeon lieutenant and sick berth attendant, and gave them something useful to do.
(© *IWM A 1218*)

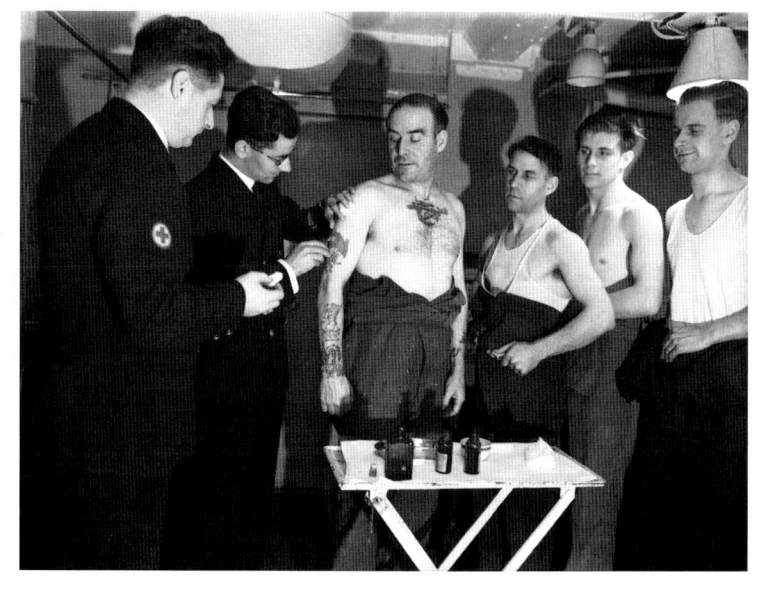

For newly-qualified doctors in the Naval Medical Services keeping their links with their medical schools was important since doctors and nurses, whatever their uniform, were all in the front line and part of the same community. (*Artist, Anna Zinkeissen, Imperial College Healthcare NHS Trust Archives*)

Only the toughest of naval surgeons were selected for commando duties. Recruitment poster by Abram Games. (*TNA, INF3-282*)

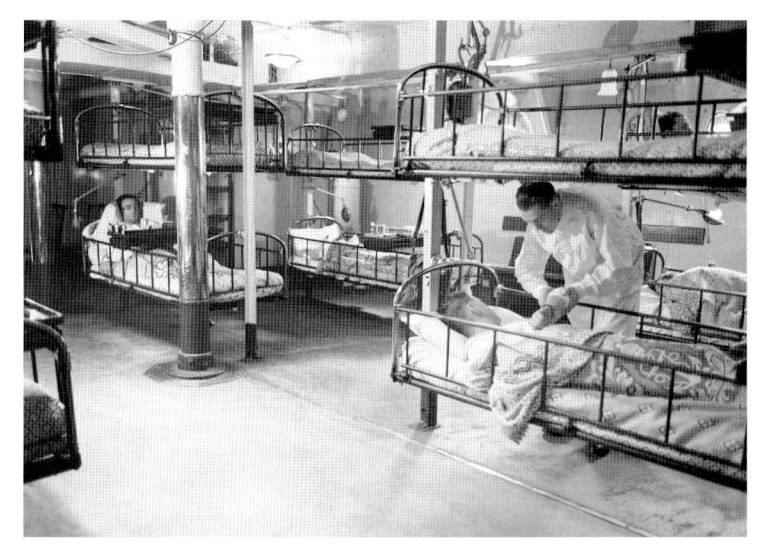

Sick bays on larger ships such as HMS *Rodney*, October 1940, were well equipped but not so commodious on smaller vessels. (© *IWM, A 1217*)

Sick berth attendants received basic instruction from Sisters of Queen Alexandra's Royal Naval Nursing Services in the naval hospitals (*J. Coulter*)

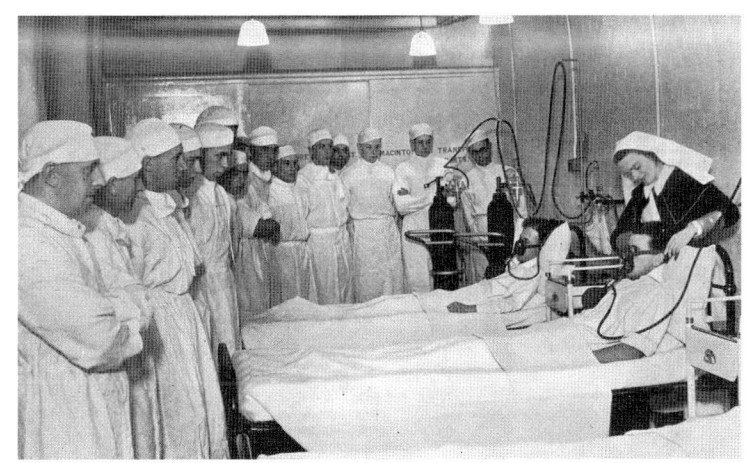

Occupational therapy for convalescents to get them back to peak mental and physical condition at Royal Naval Auxiliary Hospital Cholmondley Castle, July 1942 (© *IWM, A 11530*)

Hard labour and strict discipline for the rehabilitation of unreliable seamen at HMS *Standard* in Kielder Forest. (*J Coulter*)

Casualty being received on hospital ship RFA *Maine*. (*J Coulter*)

Hospital ship ward on RFA *Maine*, a vessel considered to be old-fashioned and in need of a replacement even before the war. (*J Coulter*)

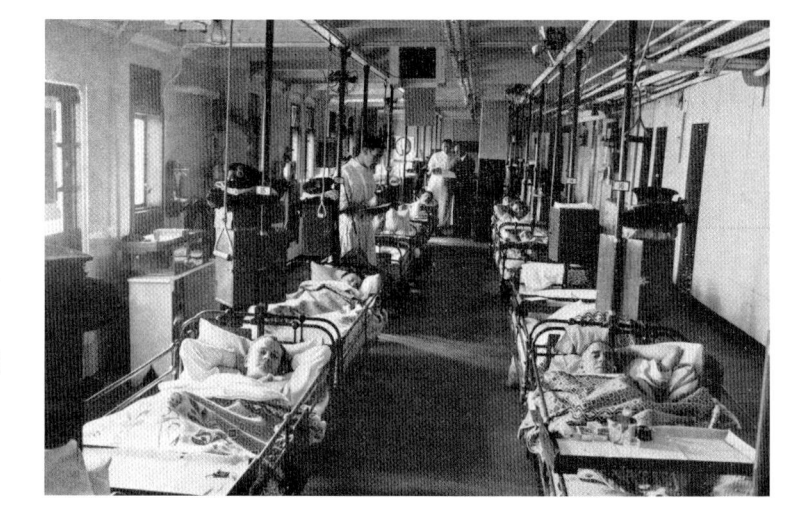

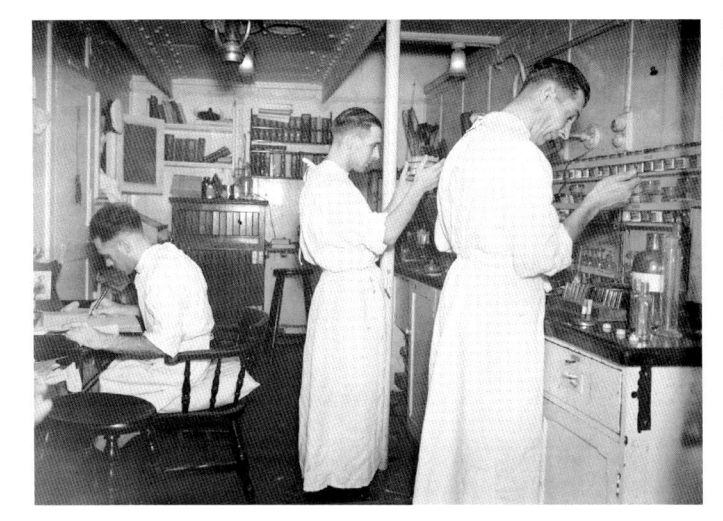

Testing blood on Hospital Ship RFA *Maine*, Suez Canal, July 1942. (© *IWM, A 20349*)

Casualties from Courseulles, France, including enemy wounded, were transported back to the United Kingdom on hospital ship *LST 428*, August 1944. (© *IWM, A 25093*)

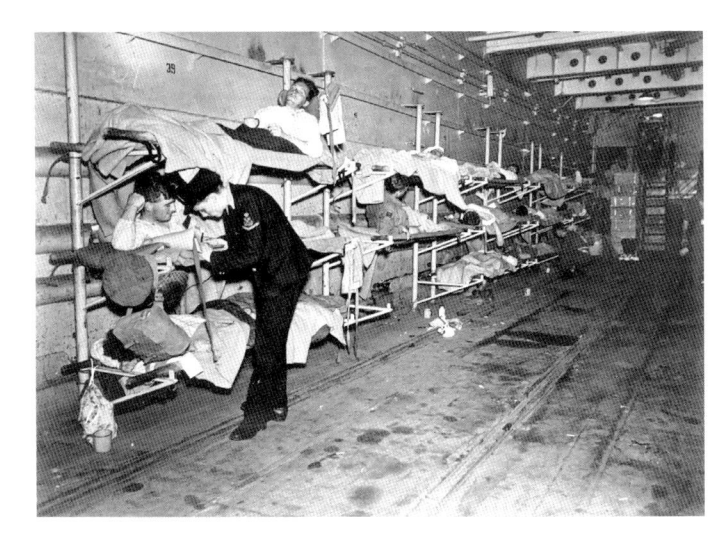

All daily life, including haircuts and letter writing, took place on the general mess decks of HMS *Shropshire*, 1942. (© *IWM, A 7598*)

American-style cafeteria messing was introduced on HMS *Dasher*, 1942. (© *IWM, A 13686*)

A lookout on an Arctic convoy preparing to go on watch on HMS *Sheffield*, December 1941, with his sheepskin greatcoat, sheepskin gloves, two balaclavas, thick woollen pants, two pairs of sea boot stockings and multitude of pullovers. (© *IWM, A 6896*)

Princess Marina, Duchess of Kent, inspected the Navy Blood Transfusion Service and the Bleeding Beauty Chorus at Slough, 1941. (*F Henley*)

Penicillin was manufactured in reused gin bottles at the Royal Naval Medical School, Clevedon, 1944. (© *IWM, A 25174*)

A naval medical officer spraying DDT for malaria control, Colombo, 1944, although his shorts made him vulnerable to mosquito bites. (© *IWM, A 28177*)

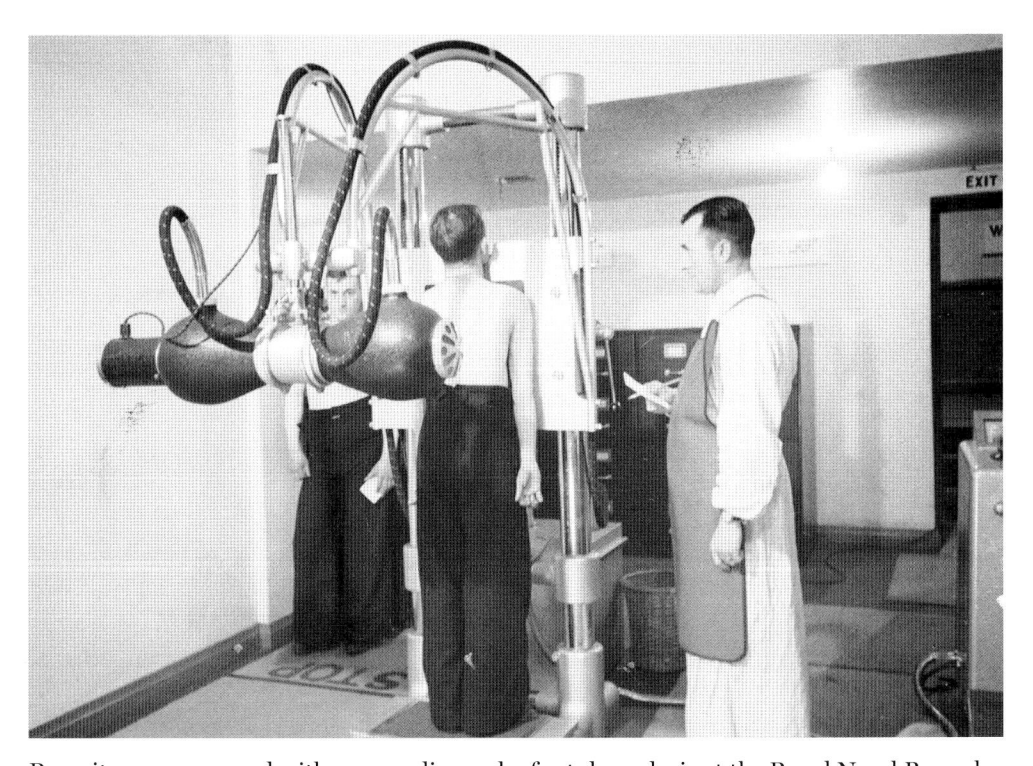

Recruits were screened with mass radiography for tuberculosis at the Royal Naval Barracks, Chatham 1940. (© *IWM, A 2008*)

Many Fleet Air Arm pilots passed out during high altitude testing, July 1943. (© *IWM, A 18253*)

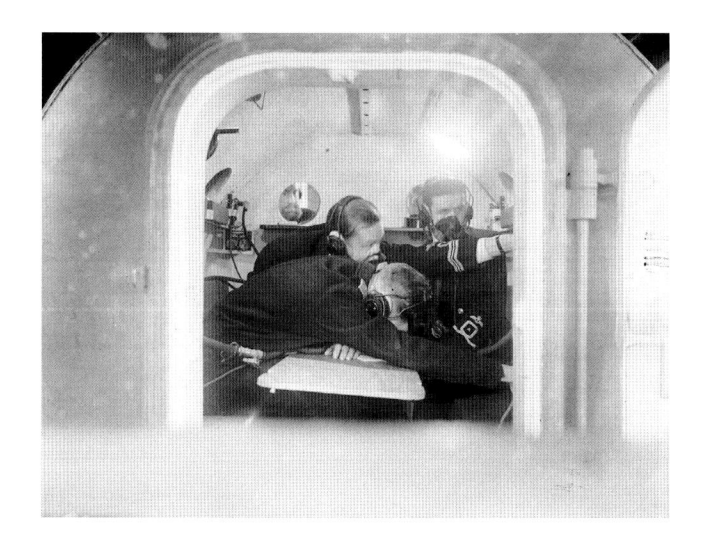

A game of crib on the submarine HMS *Seraph* in November 1944, played while sitting on torpedoes with bread stacked above. (© *IWM, A 26391*)

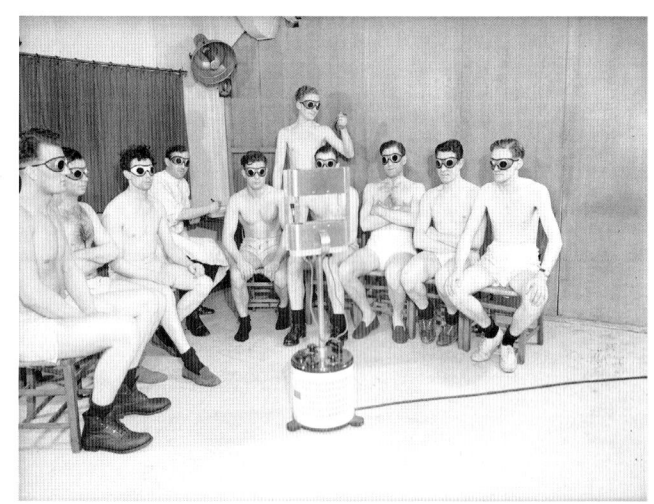

Sunray treatment for light-deprived submariners at depot ship HMS *Forth*, March 1942. (© *IWM, A 7778*)

Vaulting on the deck of HMS *Revenge* kept men fit and entertained, but the guns were never far away. (© *IWM, A 1506*)

Evelyn Laye, chairman of ENSA Royal Naval Section, had a seaman as her dresser who complained to his wife that 'they put me in the navy and now I'm a blooming lady's maid to a film star'.

Davis Apparatus for the rescue of men from submarines was used as part of training at HMS *Dolphin*, Gosport, and to weed out unsuitable candidates for the submarine service, 14 December 1942. (© *IWM, A 13882*)

All the armed services and civil defence organisations supported Holborn Warships Week, March 1942, raising money to sponsor ships and maintain naval links with the home front. (*Camden Local Studies and Archives*)

Raising money for the Overseas League 'to provide comfort and contentment' to sailors and all the fighting forces was a way for civilians to mark Empire Day, 1941.

Formal naval tradition was maintained by officers on HMS *Argonaut* on Christmas Day 1942, even after the ship had been hit and badly damaged by two torpedoes. (*F Henley*)

Wearing civilian clothing was considered good for morale but was rarely possible, though Leading Telegraphist Walter Scott was more than happy to exchange his smart suit for square rig at the Royal Naval Barracks, Portsmouth, October 1944 on his return from France after the sinking of his ship, imprisonment and service with the French Resistance. (© *IWM, A 25868*)

A pint of beer kept up the seaman's spirits and united Allied navies against the Axis. (*TNA, INF3/322*)

Sailors were warned of the threat to their health and wellbeing from good time girls and prostitutes. (*National Library of Medicine, USA*)

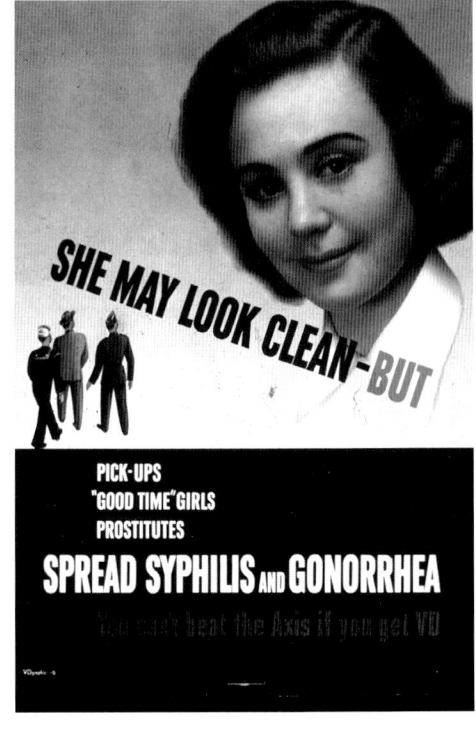

The popular, wholesome and innocent image of the seaman made him irresistible and easy prey to the allurement of feminine wiles, – or so depicted the posters warning against careless talk. (*TNA, INF 13/217*)

rendered almost unrecognisable by black oil which had flooded up from the bilges'.[64]

The length of operations and the environmental conditions in which a submarine operated could affect the health and efficiency of the crew. Monotony could undermine morale, as could a 'zero' run with little action. Heat, pressure, physical effort, confinement in close quarters and mental stress could all result in apathy. One of the crew on a submarine in the Indian Ocean commented that the 'climate is trying and one's memory fails'.[65] After three weeks on patrol, it was common for crews to be tired, lethargic, slow and unwilling to do more than was necessary.[66] Prickly heat, swollen and painful ankles, dimness of vision and heat stroke all took their toll. Yet 'the morale and staying power of the crew struck me as extremely high' even in a submarine such as *Surf*, condemned as unfit for patrols in the Tropics because its living conditions were intolerable and 'over any period quite incompatible with any morale at all'.[67]

Despite these sometimes-intolerable conditions on submarines there was a low rate of breakdown among crews where they had been carefully selected, given regular medical examinations, offered adequate periods of rest and recreation and enjoyed the camaraderie of a close-knit crew that enjoyed high prestige both within and outside the Royal Navy. In the 1943 film *We Dive at Dawn*, the success of a mission exonerates the bad behaviour previously shown by the crew of a submarine on shore leave: their slate at a pub is wiped clean, a jilted bride forgives her groom and a leading seaman is reconciled with his estranged wife and son, giving the boy a model of the German battleship sunk by his submarine to replace the boy's model of his own submarine that had been broken in a domestic dispute.[68] The British submariner's prestige on land and sense of belonging to a close and cohesive company at sea gave him the strength to deal with service stress. It was different in the German U-boats. At the end of operational tours, some of the crew became 'somewhat elated, drank too much and consorted with women', while others would just sleep heavily for several days. There was more pressure on their officers than in the Royal Navy and a high number of breakdowns among U-boat captains especially the older men who were inclined to 'show less dash and to be unduly inclined to weigh the pros and cons which were thought to reduce their effectiveness'.[69] Not only were they under the pressure of a heavy responsibility but they were also expected to be more reckless and keep up a heroic appearance. The captain of a Royal Naval submarine was under less pressure to be a heroic figure, despite bearing an equally heavy burden of responsibility than his German counterpart, and fared better psychologically.

Although it was numerically small, the Submarine Service raised its own unique medical problems that were to preoccupy the doctors and scientists of the Royal Naval Personnel Research Committee of the Medical Research Council during the war and produce a number of reports. Although some research had been done into the problems of submarine habitability and health before 1939, it was really the demands of keeping young men fit in a confined, unnatural underwater environment in order to wage a new type of warfare that stimulated research, as it indeed did in the United States and in Germany. The Naval Medical Research Institute at Bethesda, Maryland, with its teams of physiologists, psychologists, physicists, chemists, bacteriologists, botanists, and entomologists was responsible for naval medical research; much of the submarine medicine research was carried out at the Medical Research Department of the Submarine Base, New London, Connecticut, where work was done on sonar training, selection of personnel, lung training, night vision, lookout training and telephone voice communication.[70] The work on lookout training was inspired by and influenced by British experience in the Battle of the Atlantic.[71] At Carnac in France, the German Kriegsmarine established a Research Institute for U-boat Medicine 'to maintain the health and fighting efficiency of U-boat crews' through clinical and physiological investigations 'with a view to the elimination of physiological hazards to which submarines are exposed'. British observers were disparaging about its achievements as 'not very impressive even though a great deal of effort has clearly been expended'.[72]

The Royal Navy and Medical Research Council had also expended much effort on research into submarine medicine but considered its work to be of greater quality and importance than that of the Kriegsmarine. Significantly, much of the British research was novel and still considered to be of strategic importance after the end of the war. There is a glaring omission in the volumes of the official medical history of the Royal Navy during the Second World War, with nothing about the medical problems facing submariners during the war. As might be expected of a secretive service hidden below the waves, much of the wartime research was still classed as confidential. Jack Coulter, the author of the naval volumes of the official history, as befitted a discrete long-serving naval medical officer since 1931 and a barrister-in-law qualified in 1949 at Gray's Inn, diplomatically commented on this secrecy in 1954 that 'such matters as the health of the Submarine Service would obviously not have been omitted without good reason'.[73] Even a decade after the war, the work done in the early 1940s was considered to be of value in the event of another war and was to be protected. Without any doubt the future of modern underwater medicine had its origins in that Second World War research and remains of importance today.

Chapter Eight
Absent Friends: Battle Fatigue

Perhaps some of the most distressing scenes in the film *In Which We Serve* depict the cowardice of a young stoker, played by an uncredited Richard Attenborough, who deserts his post and lets his colleagues down under the stress of being involved in action for the first time in the Norway Campaign. This is contrasted with the quiet dedication of Shorty Blake, played by John Mills, who returns to work his gun after the gun crew is knocked unconscious by a torpedo strike. Noel Coward's Captain Kinross, based on Lord Louis Mountbatten, later makes one of his many inspirational addresses to the assembled ship's company to congratulate them that during the battle nearly all the crew performed as he would expect of them with the exception of one man. He surprises his men by taking the blame and letting the unfortunate stoker off with a caution as he feels that as captain he has failed to make all his men understand where their duty lay. The younger stoker, wracked with shame and guilt about his cowardice and finding solace in getting drunk, is later seen alone disgracing himself with his boorish behaviour in a pub. When the fictional destroyer *Torrin*, modelled on Mountbatten's *Kelly*, is sunk during the battle of Crete, the young stoker at the end shows courage and dies smiling in the knowledge that Kinross will write and tell his parents that they can be proud that he did his duty at the last.[1]

It was not exactly the message that the Royal Navy wished to project of itself, despite the young stoker redeeming himself by the end of the film. It was claimed that:

> Professional sailors, both officers and men, rarely suffer from nervous troubles, except in cases of very direct and severe physical strain from explosions. Most mental cases are 'hostilities only' enlistments or reservists who, getting on in life, find it difficult to readjust themselves to the Navy after a long period as civilians.[2]

ABSENT FRIENDS: BATTLE FATIGUE

The navy prided itself on its superior recruits and the good psychiatric health of its men, which 'may be attributed to the good material which was until recently self-selected by expressing a Naval preference at recruitment'.[3] Except during the strain on recruitment in 1943, this was perhaps generally true. It was observed that the companies of those ships involved in the Dunkirk evacuation of 1940 were put under severe 'mental strain combined with a lack of sleep and proper meals' but, because there was a vital task to be achieved, the men of a ship such as the destroyer *Icarus* 'bore the strain well and only three cases of mental disturbance were encountered'.[4] The longer the war went on, the greater the strain there was on individuals, and even the toughest could show signs of battle fatigue and stress. Marine Pearson, having seen action on *Exeter* and *Berwick*, was unable to cope with the strain of further combat on the cruiser *Kent* in 1942 and asked to be placed in a quieter station until he could be given a shore job. In the meantime, he suffered from severe depression and was drinking heavily.[5]

Stress-related disorders increased in the hazardous conditions of the Arctic Convoys. The medical officer of the destroyer *Eclipse* noted that 'since our visit to North Russia, with its action with enemy surface craft and the unrest of daily bombing attacks, there has been a marked increase in the sick parade'.[6] His experience was similar to that of another medical officer who recorded that the 'prolonged and repeated stress and strain' led to an 'increase in the numbers attending the sick bay and, collectively, by the development of apathy and listlessness which had previously been quite foreign to the nature of the ship's company'. Even the knowledge that a ship was joining an Arctic Convoy could produce 'a state of nervous tension', as on Rescue Ship *Zaafaran* when 'in spite of our destination being supposedly secret, it was well known to all hands'.[7] The medical officer of the minesweeper HMS *Leda* concluded that because of the mental and physical demands of these convoys no one should sail them for longer than eighteen months.[8] However, it was only after 1943 that the Royal Navy recognised that sailors might be suffering from 'fatigue', a term which avoided the stigma of mental breakdown and thereby encouraged recovery from what had once been dismissed as a 'state of anxiety'.[9]

Courage was an elusive quality and every individual had a different reaction to fear. For Sub-Lieutenant John Carter, the challenge in 1942 was to carry out his duties efficiently despite his fears:

> The nervous strain simply grows and grows until you have to exert all your will-power to stop yourself from appearing jittery or nervous. That is courage – the quality of being able to keep from showing your fear in the face of nervous strain: not able to press a trigger and keep the sights on what appears to be an enormous aircraft diving into your face, bomb hurtling towards you, and the ping and splintering crunches as his bullets tear through the wood and steel around you. Enduring that in the heat of battle, behind a gun of some sort. Courage is behaving calmly and normally during the period before such an attack, during the six long hours which never seem to end, and where time seems to stop, when that sudden deadly attack may develop in a moment.[10]

Such thoughts from a young officer, soon to die of wounds on the destroyer *Kingston* in March 1942 and who used his diary as a safety valve, were reflective of those of Lord Moran, President of the Royal College of Physicians and Winston Churchill's personal doctor, who believed that blank, unimaginative men fared best in wartime while sensitive, imaginative ones were most likely to suffer a breakdown, yet paradoxically it was the imaginative man who made the better leader and whose qualities were most needed in wartime: 'it is not what happens out here but what men think may happen that finds the flaw in them, yet it is the thinking soldier that lasts in modern war'.[11] What Moran said of the soldier, based on his own observations in the Great War, equally applied to the sailor of both wars. However, his views on the navy were that 'every rating is a mechanic, there is a purpose in every day; he is intelligent rather than imaginative, he thinks rather than feels about things'.[12] Naval tradition did not allow for a man to weaken and give in to nervous strain but insisted on the performance of duty.

Jack Coulter, medical officer on *Scylla* on convoy to North Russia in 1942, was struck by the reaction to heavy aerial bombardment of one rating whose job was to telephone orders from the bridge to the gunnery officer and had 'never seen anybody quite so terrified as this sailor'. Although the sailor's head, body and limbs were 'trembling and he transmitted his orders in a high-pitched squeak', the man carried out his duties and 'managed somehow to keep himself from breaking down completely'. Although alert enough to observe and record the behaviour of this sailor, Coulter himself was so disorientated by the air attacks that 'I am not really sure that some of them did not take place yesterday instead of today' and, as a result of the extreme noise and activity raging around him, 'it has been rather a blur'.[13]

On other ships the aftermath of intense aerial bombardment was for the men to retreat into a state of complete apathy and mental torpor. A medical officer with experience of the civilian survivors of earthquakes noted that 'following the explosion many men were found on the upper deck sitting about in an apathetic state'.[14] While they had something to do, they could handle the stress but lethargy set in once that tension was released. In extreme cases the men affected would make no effort to abandon ship and save themselves despite being physically capable of acting. By contrast, there was less evidence of this after the sinking of the cruiser *Bonaventure* in March 1941 in the Mediterranean:

> On the whole these cases do not seem to be badly shaken up and no true psycho-neurotic state was produced. In a few instances, mainly amongst the younger ratings, a mild anxiety state was noticed, evidenced by agitation on hearing air raid sirens etc. and inability to sleep, but these reacted well to sedatives and rest.[15]

Some psychiatrists believed that hysteria might be used by devious ratings as a way of avoiding service and that 'in wartime practice the motive is nearly always the desire to escape from the services' and that 'the mechanism of dissociation is readily available to the hysteric, or, under stress, can become so'.[16] It was a harsh view, but other approaches towards signs of hysteria were more sympathetic and appreciated that 'the most common cause of anxiety is the fear of the individual that he might be a coward'. Rather than to deny that cowardice might have any place in the navy, men were to be told that 'to be afraid is natural – to run away is cowardly' and that 'if you are efficient in your job, you need have no fear of your behaviour in an emergency'. They were also encouraged to talk about their fears and worries 'as admitting your worries to a friend makes it easier' and 'in nine cases out of ten he will be feeling exactly the same'.[17]

The Admiralty still had to stress in 1944 that 'when the medical evidence indicates that a man is genuinely suffering from a mental illness ... he shall be treated as sympathetically as possible', after a rating was tried and sentenced for desertion only to subsequently be found to be suffering from amnesia.[18] Familiar routine, keeping busy with accustomed duties and enjoying the camaraderie of messmates was seen as the solution.

Morale was understandably low among survivors of sinkings when they were picked up, mainly because they had nothing to do and were not used to being 'passengers', which made them critical of the crew of the rescue ship. Even in action there was no role for them despite their experience on their own ships and, as a result of their forcible inaction 'each from master to fireman is criticising the work of his opposite number in the ship'.[19] The men were also 'normally members of a relatively small, highly disciplined and closely organised community' and 'there is in a ship inevitably more comradeship, whether in peace or in wartime, than in any other closed community'.[20] With a sinking, this close and cohesive world of the mess was lost. Unless steps were taken quickly to deal with the trauma of survivors, there was also a serious risk that their discontent would become ingrained. The aim was to minimise 'self-pity' and promote an increased confidence among the survivors. Routine and regular work were recommended after a short period of rest. Officers were advised to assert their authority and make sure that the men were issued with new uniforms and kit as soon as possible to project an illusion of normality. Doctors were warned against asking leading questions about the mental health of any man. After fourteen days' survivors' leave, the men should be re-integrated into a new ship's company. More often than not, the survivors from a number of sunken ships would form a pool and be assigned to a ship's company made up of other survivors. This resulted, as on the battleship *Valiant* in 1942, in anxiety among the ratings, indiscipline and 'an indefinable air of mistrust of officers'.[21]

The role of the officer in keeping morale up after a sinking was crucial. After the loss of the cruiser *Dunedin* in 1942, Commander A

C Watson had to find the best means of maintaining discipline among the survivors from his ship and stop them from indulging in self-pity without causing them to resent him as insensitive to their mood:

> I had to decide on the degree of discipline which I could try to preserve among the men. It did not seem advisable to try to give direct orders unless there was little doubt that they would be obeyed. Generally, it seemed better to suggest things.[22]

Behind Watson's sensitivity to the emotional state of his men was a fear of indiscipline and the possibility of mutiny in the aftermath of disaster, when men might be looking to blame someone and were resentful of authority. It was noticed that the greater discipline of the Royal Navy helped to hold men together better than the looser attention to authority among merchant seamen when their ships were lost at sea:

> The difference between the naval gunners aboard, who were keen and well-disciplined, and the merchant crew became well apparent. The former maintained a higher standard of morale as a body of men whereas the latter excelled or degenerated according to their own character rather than that of their leaders.[23]

Sensitive leadership, strong discipline and social cohesion gave men a better chance of maintaining morale and surviving the trauma of a sinking.

The ship's officers on whom the burden of maintaining the morale of the ship's company lay could also suffer from the fatigue that came from extreme exhaustion, especially those on duty with the Atlantic or Arctic convoys. Nicholas Monsarrat recalled:

> Strain and tiredness induce a sort of hysteria: you seem to be moving in a bad dream, pursued not by terrors but by an intolerable routine. You come off watch at midnight, soaked, twitching, your eyes raw with the wind and with staring at shadows; you brew up a cup of tea in the wardroom pantry and strip off the top layer of sodden clothes; you do, say an hour's intricate ciphering, and thereafter snatch a few hours' sleep between wet blankets, with the inflated life-belt in your

ribs reminding you all the time that things happen quickly; and then, every night for seventeen nights on end, you're woken at ten to four by the bosun's mate, and you stare at the deckhead and think: 'My God, I can't go up there again in the dark and filthy rain, and stand another four hours of it'. But you can, of course: it becomes automatic in the end.[24]

The captain had little choice but to carry on regardless of fatigue if he were to offer an example of leadership to his men and ensure the good spirits that made for an efficient ship. During the battle of the River Plate in December 1939, Edward Parry, captain of *Achilles*, was knocked over by a shell, 'luckily only chipping a fragment off my figure' though it broke the chief yeoman's leg. Despite not being able to walk easily with his injury, Parry 'spent hours on a wooden stool at the fore end of the bridge, with the leg up in a chair' while in command of his ship in action. He commented that 'in fact I think my tail wearing through worried me more than the leg!' As they sailed towards Montevideo at the end of the engagement, Parry congratulated himself that 'every available man, including myself, had their first good sleep for some days'.[25]

What made for a happy ship was an elusive quality:

> The medical officer may be impressed by the rarity of neurotic illness in certain 'happy ships' in contrast with the undue number of such cases in other ships where the basic material conditions are the same.[26]

Neurotic illnesses in the navy were often caused by such common service factors as cold, damp, unappealing living and working conditions, vibration and excessive noise, sleeplessness, long periods without shore leave and the boredom that came from lack of recreation and the want of outlets for sexual frustrations. Wartime conditions had exacerbated these problems, with shock being caused by explosions, collisions and immersions when a ship saw action. It was also very difficult for men called up to adjust to 'the hardships of life afloat, especially in small ships' and also to readjust after periods ashore.[27]

Worry over domestic affairs at home also could make men anxious. At home their families were at risk from air raids, especially for those living near such targets as the heavily-bombed naval ports. They had to cope with the hardships of rationing and the dislocation of home life caused by evacuation and war work. When he returned home in 1942 after almost four years away, having been drafted to the Mediterranean soon after his marriage in 1938, A T H Rogers was not only puzzled by the barrage balloons he saw over the dockyards in Portsmouth but sadly accepted that 'my small daughter, three years old, who I saw for the first time during my leave, would have nothing to do with me at first and frequently questioned my wife, "Mummy, who is this man?"'[28] Family Welfare Centres, staffed by trained social workers, in the main base ports and the Soldiers, Sailors and Airmen's Family Association offered support with domestic problems, but men remained worried about the situation at home.[29] Despite the moving toast made in the film *In Which We Serve* by Celia Johnson as Mrs Kinross to her 'most implacable enemy', her husband's ship which 'holds first place in his heart, it comes before wife, home, children, everything', many sailors, especially hostilities-only men, did not leave their domestic worries behind them when they went to sea.[30] It was noticeable that many men reported to the sick berth with minor complaints immediately after receiving a worrying letter from home. On the battlecruiser *Repulse* in 1940 the surgeon reported:

> There is an atmosphere of cheerfulness in the ship, but I do know that everyone feels tired and strained owing to the lack of leave, monotony of surroundings, constant watch keeping and the ever-present anxiety for families and relatives, most of whom live in districts frequently attacked by enemy aircraft ... The burden lies less heavily on the younger members who have fewer responsibilities and greater powers of recuperation.[31]

Not all men reporting for the daily sick parade after receiving bad news were suffering from psychosomatic illnesses nor even swinging the lead. When Roger Miles examined a rating who complained of pain and 'tiredness' in his left leg and knee, not long after being refused compassionate leave to marry his pregnant fiancée, the doctor was inclined to dismiss it as 'a clear case of *Plumbum Pendens*'. Closer examination, however, revealed a small swelling which turned out to be a sarcoma, and the unfortunate thwarted bridegroom had his leg amputated a few weeks later.[32]

If one seaman showed signs of mental unbalance, this could affect the rest of the company. John Harries, a 21-year-old able seaman on *Belfast* in 1944, was 'continually frightened and nervous', and as his state of mind deteriorated, 'tended to lose his self-respect by revealing his fears to his companions'. Although his was not 'a particularly serious case of anxiety neurosis … he was undermining the remainder of his watch, and as the ship was in a continual state of action stations off the Normandy coast, it was not practicable to treat him onboard'.[33]

Morale was not always easy to maintain, even if it was seen as being as important as good physique, but that was the duty of the ship's doctor in the first instance. He was advised to watch out for the symptoms of neurosis in men, most notably unreliability, slipshod work, a slovenly appearance, neglect of kit, truculence, surliness and excessive consumption of alcohol or cigarettes. This would be most obvious if such behaviour formed a contrast with the man's previous personality and conduct. Physical symptoms might also point towards a psychiatric disorder if men were reporting with headaches, indigestion, dizziness, palpitations, tremor, mild diarrhoea or excessive micturition. By watching out for such signs of mental instability, a doctor could avoid having to deal with cases of anxiety states and hysterical reactions, although such symptoms often followed a traumatic event or prolonged stress:

> At the present time all officers and men afloat are exposed to a very great strain. As a general rule it can be said that prolonged stress of a relatively minor intensity, eg. mine sweeping and work on the Northern Patrol, is a greater test than exposure to an acute and dramatic stress that is short-lived, eg. a naval action.[34]

Jack Coulter, reflecting on his time as medical officer on *Scylla*, concluded that 'in the Arctic as elsewhere, the three factors which sustain morale and are almost of greater importance than clothing to a Ship's company are FOOD, RUM, MAILS, the latter being impossible to come by in the North'.[35]

There was little that the medical officer could do to treat men at sea other than try to contain the problem as best he could, although some psychiatrists maintained that 'there is no reason why the ship's medical officer, even if he has no psychiatric training, should not deal effectively with the simpler cases' and that 'he may be the means of preventing a recurrence ... and the loss of a man to the Service'.[36] Harry Balfour realised his own limitations when a rating was brought to the sick berth on the destroyer *Middleton* on Arctic Convoy duties, 'hysterical with fear and cold and could take no more'. Balfour first tried to warm him up in his own cot and sedate him but he remained in a disturbed state and unfit for duty. Balfour then tried to persuade him to overcome his fears even though the doctor's own 'views were not too far removed' from the worries of his patient, although sharing the same feelings would have made him more sympathetic in his approach. After talking through his problems and sleeping, the young rating was 'just about capable of carrying on', but he was transferred to shore duties as soon as the ship returned to Scapa Flow. In the absence of a chaplain, the doctor on a destroyer had 'to learn the great value of listening' and Harry Balfour found that 'sometimes there was positive action I could take to help a problem, but mostly it was allowing them to talk which was of value'. Balfour admitted that his own psychological state while on convoy duty made him less effective as a doctor and that he had 'nearly failed the test' posed by the hardships he faced: 'when conditions were appalling we all, I suppose, buttoned up our personalities inside our duffel coats and I never quite managed to throw mine off even when conditions were reasonable'.[37]

Even if the naval doctor did not feel straitjacketed by his own worries and problems, 'the range of treatment that is practicable on board is limited' though the Admiralty prided itself that 'it can be extremely effective'.[38] The first stage of treatment was to keep the disturbed man on duty but for the doctor to offer reassurance and appropriate medication to keep him calm. The reasoning was that not only would a man be kept too busy to think about his problems but that the work of the ship could be carried on with a full complement of men. Only in advanced cases of neurosis should the man be admitted to the sick bay for treatment or, once the ship was in port, sent to a hospital, barracks or hospital ship, although it was held that 'admission to a hospital is usually best avoided'.[39] Referral to a neuropsychiatrist was only undertaken as a last resort. In most cases shore leave was seen as the solution. Ralph Ransome Wallis recognised that without a psychiatrist readily available, 'it was no good recognising the existence of such conditions as battle fatigue, fear neurosis or being bomb happy' because 'there was nowhere to go to get away from it all so you just had to get on with the job'. He also believed that most people on board *London* displayed psychiatric symptoms but had no choice but to cope with them themselves and carry on with their duties. It was his experience that 'in most cases a few sharp words from the sick berth CPO accompanied by a No. 9 pill containing a powerful purgative worked wonders'.[40]

Another medical officer noticed signs of fatigue in 'a personal friend of mine for whom I had great affection' and found it difficult to report his symptoms in case it harmed his career, though he was eventually to recommend that the other officer should be employed ashore for at least three months to 'avert any breakdown in the near future which might have repercussions on the safety of the ship'. This officer was obsessive about the efficiency of his ship, spent any spare time in working on a book of instructions for newly-joined officers, showed signs of irritability and was unable to sleep even while on leave. He was also plagued by minor illness, including headaches, influenza, gastritis and a recurrent gum infection, taking 'more aspirin habitually than is usual in a young man'. The medical officer was able to observe these symptoms from an early stage in his friend, but that same deep friendship made him more reluctant to do anything that might jeopardise the promotion prospects of his comrade. It is significant that he compared his friend's mental state to a sports car:

> In his present state I would liken him to a highly tuned, supercharged racing car, capable of giving a brilliant performance, but only for a short time. A carefully conserved touring car, with a more phlegmatic and slower performance, would probably last longer and would be more reliable in the long run.[41]

However dashing the officer might be, he was overdue for a period of rest, first in hospital and then in a quiet shore job, that made him fit to return to sea as an efficient officer more able to take the mental stresses and strains aboard a ship in action.

A certain amount of stress and fighting experience could make a sailor more manly, but even the most battle-hardened needed rest and more varied recreation. Lord Moran, wartime physician to Winston Churchill, believed that his own son John Wilson, a 19-year-old rating serving on *Belfast* with the Arctic Convoys, would emerge a better man from combat, noting that 'it's a big experience, a naval action in twilight of Arctic Circle, and I have no doubt if John comes through this war alright it will have an altogether beneficial effect on his character and do much to counter those Max Beerbohm, Noel Coward, film tastes which were so evident'. Even so, he was happy to enable his son to have a memorable period of rest and recreation in North Africa after seeing action in the Arctic when his ship was involved in the sinking of the *Scharnhorst*. Not all able seamen could enjoy the privilege of enjoying leave as a house guest of the prime minister during his stay at Marrakesh in January 1944 that was extended to him when about to begin his officer-training course at *King Alfred*. Moran had wangled an invitation, flights and the opportunity for his son to then travel home as part of the prime minister's entourage. It was important that the young man, educated at Eton, should fit into the house party and instead of his seaman's uniform was expected to bring a tweed jacket and flannels for daytime casual wear on the many picnics Churchill enjoyed during his convalescence from a bout of pneumonia, a lounge suit for more formal occasions and a dinner jacket for the evening, as if a war was not in progress. Resplendent in black tie, he confidently gave Churchill a lower-deck account of the sinking of *Scharnhorst*.[42]

Ships' surgeons were themselves under pressure to keep ships' companies at their duties and were at times discouraged from reporting psychiatric cases. They were told that '"back to duty" as soon as he can do a reasonable day's work must be your constant aim'.[43] This was especially marked in the Fleet Air Arm, where the First Sea Lord Andrew Cunningham was opposed to limits on flying hours to deal with combat stress. William Scott, Surgeon Commander on the aircraft carrier *Ark Royal*, agreed with this approach in so far as 'had we grounded aircrew on the first suspicion of stress this would have severely affected general morale, from the suspicion that all that was needed to secure release from dangerous activities was to produce symptoms for the Medical Department'. However, his own personal experience was that 'in *Ark Royal* I had never cause to doubt the reality of physical complaints produced by any officer or rating and had more difficulty in persuading the manifestly unfit to remain off duty than to return to it those that had recovered'.[44]

Even Desmond Curran, the chief psychiatric consultant to the Royal Navy, was reluctant to admit that 'operational strain' might be the major cause of neurosis and mental breakdown. Instead he emphasised the role played by inherent psychological weaknesses in the men themselves. He argued that 'the great danger for psychiatry is to become a special cult' and that 'the great danger for a specialist psychiatric hospital is to obtain the reputation of a "loony" bin, the entry to which is a prelude to invaliding'.[45] He was also afraid that ships' surgeons with little experience of psychosomatic disorders might actually encourage their development as well as foster hypochondria.[46] He also believed that 'in wartime there is a very real danger of over-emphasizing the dramatic, such as exposure to enemy action, when less dramatic events, such as the regimentation and frustration of service life, separation from home, and domestic difficulties, may really possess more significance'.[47] Yet there were no psychiatric specialists based on ships and men who needed specialist treatment had to wait until they returned to port where the shore-based experts were based in depots and naval hospitals.

There were very few neuropsychiatric specialists in the navy at all. Whereas by 1943, the army had 227 psychiatrists, the navy only had 36 and all but three of these were based in the United Kingdom. The only overseas psychiatric specialists were based at Alexandria, Durban and Colombo.[48] Before the war, the Royal Navy had not seen the need to employ any specialists in psychiatric health. Now there were consultants in neurology, psychiatric medicine and neurology, assisted by specialists in neuropsychiatry and mental diseases. Those specialists based in depots and training establishments were expected to weed out unsuitable recruits or suggest branches of the navy suitable for men with different temperaments, supplementing the work of the psychoanalysts. Special mental hospitals were established at the Royal Naval Auxiliary Hospital at Cholmondley Castle in

Cheshire, HMS *Standard* at Kielder Camp in Northumberland and the Royal Naval Hospital Great Yarmouth, though the services from Great Yarmouth were later moved to Lancaster for the duration of the war.[49] The role of the psychiatrist in such shore establishments was 'to render the maximum number of patients fit for sea in the shortest possible time'.[50] Without experience of service at sea, the work of the psychiatrists was less effective than it might have been if they had had a fuller understanding of the conditions in which the men they treated lived and worked. For the Fleet Air Arm, it was suggested that 'medical officers require some definite training in psychological medicine in order that they may detect latent nervous deficiencies which the stress and strain of flying may sooner or later reveal'.[51]

Despite the insouciance of the naval psychiatrists concerning what they perceived to be the good state of naval mental health, psychiatric casualties in the navy were far from negligible. In 1940 about 5,000 officers and ratings were referred to psychiatrists or psychiatric hospitals from warships. By 1943 numbers had risen to 492 officers and 5,649 ratings, which represented approximately one per cent of all naval personnel. By early 1945 the navy had 736 psychiatric beds in the UK and needed to expand accommodation by a further 140.[52] It was all too easy for men suffering from mental disorders to remain unidentified. When Henry Smith, an engineer on the minesweeping trawler *Negro*, was committed to Broadmoor in 1940 after attempting to murder his girlfriend, it was the first occasion that the Royal Navy was aware of his mental condition and no officer had attended his trial because there had been no notification that a naval rating was being tried.[53] Some medical officers believed that it was better for the men not to be seen by psychiatrists if they suffered from nerves. Jack Coulter on *Scylla* was convinced that 'previous experience had suggested that if such men were seen by a neuropsychiatrist, they would undoubtedly have been regarded as potential "anxiety states" and found unfit for sea service as a routine, in which case it was felt that the "infection" might spread to others'. He preferred to train the ratings 'to take a grip on themselves'.[54]

Every effort was made to render the psychiatric casualty fit again for service, through discipline, training, occupational therapy and psychotherapy. In addition to treatment in hospitals, a labour unit and rehabilitation facility was formed at Kielder Camp in Northumberland for the treatment of men who were physically fit but who had psychiatric problems that were not severe enough for them to be invalided out of the navy but whose delinquency and challenge to discipline was not extreme enough to have them confined in detention quarters. Kielder was chosen because it was isolated in a valley surrounded by hills on three sides and a river on the fourth, remote from the distractions of cinemas and public houses, and offering few possibilities for desertion. It had originally been built as a Ministry of Labour training camp for the unemployed but was derelict when requisitioned by the Admiralty. HMS *Standard* admitted the first trainees, men classed as C/Q because considered unreliable in general service although physically fit, in February 1942. The aim was to instil some sense of self-discipline into them through an ordered routine, starting with lights up at 6.30 in the morning, ward cleaning, working parties, games and lectures filling the day until lights out at 9.30. Originally it was intended that the working parties would find plenty of useful employment in the surrounding Kielder Forest, but forestry work was less common than land drainage projects, farm work and the construction of a reservoir on Admiralty land. Leave was only granted after a probationary period of good conduct for one month. After behaving well on four Saturday afternoons away from the camp, a man would be rewarded with weekend leave at home. On leaving the camp after a successful course of rehabilitation, the sailor would be granted seven days' leave before his drafting to a ship or shore service. Each trainee was interviewed regularly by the commanding officer, schoolmaster, chaplain, medical officer and psychiatrist. Such personal attention was perhaps unprecedented for the Royal Navy, especially once the basic routine was altered to suit individual problems. Physical training, games and manual work were prescribed for men showing aggressive traits and threatening behaviour, while for the more timid and introverted men encouragement was given to exert themselves both physically and mentally.[55]

When *Standard* closed in July 1945, it had treated 842 men, of whom 680 were transferred to useful roles in the navy and a further 271 returned to general service. The others found postings to depot ships, boom defence vessels, small coastal craft or shore bases. Only 162 were discharged as unfit for further service.[56] But not all the rehabilitated ratings stood up to the test of action when they returned to general service. Jack Coulter was concerned about a 'rating on approval from Kielder Camp' who was brought to the main distributing station on *Scylla* in September 1942 in a state of hysterical collapse. Coulter sternly and unsympathetically told the man to 'stand up and take a grip on himself' but the man promptly ran away and hid himself, leaving nobody with the time to look for him.[57] *Standard*, nevertheless, had been generally a successful experiment and in its rigorous training regime 'also played a part in producing a number of good citizens'.[58]

Rehabilitation and occupational therapy were also used to raise the morale and spirits of wounded men by giving them something useful to do and keep them fully occupied. In the naval hospitals it was seen as 'a form of remedial treatment for both bed and ambulant cases'.[59] In naval depots containing 'a collection of men quite unfitted for active service afloat', retraining, physiotherapy and occupational therapy were all offered to rehabilitate men. Light duties would be allocated in the depot according to what work the man had done in civilian life. A clerk would be employed as a writer in the paymaster's office, a mechanic would service transport vehicles and a carpenter would work with the shipwright. The drawback to such a scheme was that the 'men become interested and efficient at their special duties and prefer to remain at it rather than go to sea'.[60]

Rehabilitation for burns victims was considered especially important. After treatment at the Queen Victoria Hospital East Grinstead or Park Prewett Hospital, men would be sent back to the depot with the recommendation that they were fit for light duties until they were due for readmission to their hospital for plastic surgery. Many of these patients complained that they 'hang around the barracks, kicking their heels with nothing to do'.[61] In order to keep up morale among these men, who were not only dealing with their disfigurements but had little to distract them, the Admiralty decided to adopt the rehabilitation scheme used by the RAF 'to prevent deterioration in a patient's mental and physical state due to his long residence in hospital and to facilitate his early return to full duty'.[62] The naval scheme was designed to provide 'suitable and congenial employment outside the Service for naval personnel who are convalescent or under treatment for prolonged periods' which made them unfit for service until their treatment was complete. It was thought that six months' special leave and the opportunity to take on suitable civilian jobs would 'prevent deterioration in the patient's mental and physical state and facilitate rehabilitation, particularly in cases of curative and surgical treatment'.[63] Chief Petty Officer Arthur John Dunnett was successfully treated at East Grinstead for burns on his arms and hands from bomb blast when *Calcutta* sank in June 1941. The scars on his shoulders were treated by deep X-rays at St George's Hospital in London, but at East Grinstead the scar tissue on both his forearms was excised and he was given thick skin grafts, which had not yet softened when his arms had healed after the operation. This meant that he had limited movement in his left elbow, although he was now otherwise fit for duty. It was recommended that he should be found work in aircraft production in which he would not damage his hands until he was fully fit for a return to naval duty.[64] Archibald McIndoe, the pioneering plastic surgeon at East Grinstead, himself recommended that suitable employment be found for his patient Able Seaman J Hart who needed three months' rest after operations on his face: 'he is quite capable of doing a job and I hope he can be fixed up with something well within his capabilities, as well as of sufficient interest to keep him psychologically sound'.[65] Work was found for Hart at Chatham Barracks. Morale and contributing to the war effort went hand-in-hand.

Generally, the mental strain at sea was considered to be greater than in the Great War, especially when possibilities for relaxation were limited.[66] In 1915 Surgeon Lieutenant Thomas Beaton had estimated the incidence of 'mild neurasthenic conditions' at 3 to 4 per cent of the company of a battleship in home waters over a period of five and a half months.[67] Surgeon Captain Meagher found very few signs of 'nervous disorder' among sailors after the battle of Jutland and concluded that the nature of life at sea explained this:

> It is not improbable that the sailor had a psychological advantage compared with the soldier. The life of the sea habituates him to dangers. He fights on board ship, on his own ground as it were. He cannot fail to recognise that the promptings of the instinct to flee from danger are impossible of fulfilment and is therefore freed

from a mental conflict ... and, in addition, he probably has the advantage of having experienced many battle practices and is not the least gun-shy.[68]

The army in the Second World War was able to offer forward-deployed psychiatry to its men in a way which was impossible for the navy with its psychiatrists working ashore and not close to the naval action. They could only treat men suffering from psychiatric disorders when the ship returned to port. The army mental illness specialists could go with the men and treat them as soon as possible. Army psychiatrists were now based in forward areas to deal as swiftly as possible with combat neuroses, manifesting themselves by such symptoms as screaming, tremors, hysterical laughter or tears and even staring cataleptic states. Army Rest Centres were set up close to the battlefields. The most common treatments were rest, reassurance and mild purgatives or strong sedatives. The role of the army psychiatrist, similar to that of his naval counterpart, was to return as many exhausted men as possible to active service by 'debunking battle noise, the tank and the morale-destroying aspects of the dive bomber'.[69] There was a danger that the survivors of armed combat, most of them 'unshaven and unwashed, red-eyed, covered in dust or mud from head to foot, scarcely able to keep their eyes open', would be labelled as simply suffering from 'physical exhaustion' when there was little time available to give them a full assessment, though not labelling a man with a psychiatric diagnosis paradoxically often enabled those suffering from battle stress to recover more quickly.[70] Royal Navy psychiatrists and medical officers shared this belief that ignoring the origins of psychosomatic illnesses and not diagnosing someone with a mental illness could help the patient recover and also avoid the stigma still attached to any one suffering from a mental illness.

The men of the Merchant Navy were considered to be more robust in mental health since they included 'more of the social rebels and rolling stones who have sought and found an independence and brotherhood of their own'.[71] Their psychological resilience was ascribed to this attitude of mind and independence within a group which was seen as giving them the strength to throw off worries and anxieties much more easily than their counterparts in the Royal Navy, who were seen as less independent but more subject to discipline. Nevertheless, the merchant seaman was actually as prone to psychoneuroses as much as anyone despite the stereotypical depictions of their mental stability arising out of pig-headedness. In 1945 doctors discharged 5,113 men as unfit to serve in the Merchant Navy on account of psychiatric illness.[72]

The American armed forces prided themselves on putting their forces through rigorous physical and psychological examinations designed to weed out the unsuitable. Nearly 18 million young men and women were examined throughout the course of the war. Most of them were found fit for service, although sometimes remedial work might be necessary to enable this. In total, two million men were rejected for neuropsychiatric reasons that included homosexuality, while four million were unfit because of rotten teeth, poor eyesight and illiteracy.[73] In 1942 3 or 4 per cent of sailors entering Newport Naval Training Station were identified as being 'mentally deficient' but a large number of these men were found suitable for service by reason of having stable personalities and being receptive to training.[74] Despite this, physically and psychologically the Americans boasted of the superior fitness of their forces.

The German Kriegsmarine was also arrogant about the superiority of its men and displayed a marked complacency about their psychiatric health. There was a pride, 'not perhaps without a certain smug satisfaction as a tribute to the Herrenvolk', in the 'infrequency of hysterical manifestations, such as fits and tremors, compared with the last war'. Even alcohol addiction was rare, partly because as the war progressed spirits were scarce. As in the Royal Navy, the incidence of psychiatric disorders in the Kriegsmarine was lower than that in the army. For any sailor who did develop a mental illness, the treatment in Germany was harsher. Shock therapy, including the use of electricity to stimulate the nerves, a form of treatment deemed by British psychiatrists to be 'foreign to our ideas', was routinely employed. Occupational therapy, popular in Britain and America, was not widely used to treat patients, while the use of prolonged narcosis or deep sleep therapy, widely used in all the United State forces, was 'universally vetoed' in Germany. Nazi ideology promoting racial fitness and Aryan supremacy and with its contempt for weakness, meant that a sailor could not be seen to have a weakness of will and 'proved a certain stiffening in the morale which resisted to some extent the various stresses'.[75]

The Royal Navy was reluctant to admit the possibility of widespread psychiatric disorders among its sailors and was complacent at times in its response. The important thing was to maintain the fighting efficiency of the ship, even if that meant putting the care of machinery before that of men. Even so, there was an admission that neuropsychiatry had 'performed a most valuable function in returning to full or normal duty at the earliest possible date those cases of nervous or mental illness capable of some form of further service and in eliminating those incapable of further useful service'.[76] That was the priority: efficient service at sea that would help to win the war.

Chapter Nine
Ourselves: Rest and Recreation

Physical and psychiatric fitness was fundamental to the creation and maintenance of an efficient navy. The rating was encouraged in the belief that 'I am a British sailor. The British sailor has always been the best seaman and the finest fighter, and the hero of the people. Therefore, I am a hero.'[1] The self-confidence of this creed was reinforced by an emphasis on upholding naval tradition even in wartime, rigid control, a strong sense of discipline, rigorous training, a smart appearance and a feeling of community and cohesion among messmates. Its enemy was the tedium and monotony of life at sea. Opportunities for rest and recreation at sea and to a greater extent ashore were seized upon. Everything was done to ensure that morale was not undermined by boredom through both mental and physical stimulus.

Sport and physical training had been important in the navy since the late nineteenth century to keep men fit and entertained. Although boxing, hockey and cricket were popular aboard ship in the late nineteenth century, most sporting opportunities for the navy were available in port and by 1896 few ships did not have their own football teams. The Royal Navy Football League was formed in 1904 and fixtures were organised between ships and against civilian teams and the army. The *Southern Daily Mail* presented the Navy Cup competed for by naval shore establishments and ships stationed in Home waters or the Channel Fleet. The Naval Rugby Club was formed in 1906 and from 1908 the navy competed at cricket in an annual match against the army.[2] The importance of recreational sport in keeping men healthy and amused was recognised after the First World War when it was felt that a scheme of 'physical, recreational and morale training' would have 'a steadying effect which will be felt far beyond the confines of the Navy itself'.[3] It was argued that sport in the Royal Navy could help to develop discipline, fighting capacity and moral character in the seaman:

> Important as undoubtedly is the development of sports and athletic exercise for the general well-being of the soldier, to the navy, with the unnatural life on board ship and the lack of possibilities of exercise and recreation … the encouragement and development of all forms of physical exercise, games and sports is a vital element in our naval training.[4]

The Royal Navy Physical Training Branch, established in 1902, took these responsibilities seriously, and opportunities for sport were offered on most ships in the interwar period. Individual ships held sports days and there were also squadron and flotilla competitions in a wide range of sports, such as football, swimming, athletics, boxing, cricket, fencing, hockey, shooting, rugby, sailing, rowing and water polo.

Foremost among the ships in which the spirit of athletic competition was especially strong was HMS *Hood*. Her athletes won her many trophies in rowing, sailing, boxing, football, cricket, track and field, swimming, hockey and gunnery, especially between 1933 and 1936 under Commander Rory O'Conor who took particular pride when in 1935 *Hood* overwhelmingly won the Home Fleet Regatta at Rosyth. However, O'Conor, with his focus firmly on recreation at the expense of discipline, was criticised for not giving due attention to the proper upkeep of the ship and to seamanship. Even though there was no longer so much emphasis on promoting sport after O'Connor left the ship, *Hood*'s football team still defeated a team from the German pocket battleship *Deutschland* at Gibraltar in October 1938 and in the same year the boxing team won the Mediterranean Fleet championship, while there was also victory in all five Mediterranean sailing cups. Only the outbreak of war curtailed recreational activities, though they remained of significance in maintaining morale right up to the sinking of the ship on Empire Day – 24 May – 1941.[5]

O'Conor believed that sport offered opportunities for officers to 'prove ability to lead' that were 'too few in times of peace for any to be ignored' and that 'there is no substitute for going all out for your ship whether in work or in play, unless, of course, you are prepared to toddle complacently towards your pension'.[6] It was an attitude that provided a basis for creating an environment that could be of perhaps even greater significance in war than in peace. Admiral the Earl of Cork and Orrery in his preface to O'Conor's 1937 guide to *Running a Big Ship* expressly linked a competitive team spirit in sport and a heightened morale to effort in battle:

> The ship's company that can make a collective effort in one direction can usually make it in others. There are, of course, those who affect to sneer at such successes, saying that the Navy does not exist solely for boat-racing or other competitive drills and recreations. That may be partly true. But the Navy does exist to make great collective efforts under the most difficult conditions. The ship, whose officers and men, of all departments alike, are accustomed to go all out for the honour of their ship, is likely to last out just that fraction of a minute longer than an opponent, which in battle makes all the difference between victory and defeat. Those who 'pull harder than the rest' are likely to 'fight harder' also.[7]

Even in wartime conditions it was important to keep up morale through relaxation and play. Where it was possible to organise games of cricket and hockey when in port, and water polo, swimming and sunbathing at sea, 'it was most pleasing to walk around at Sunday Divisions and observe a well set-up and healthy-looking collection of officers and men'.[8] As the war went on this was not always so easy and there were complaints that where there were few opportunities for sport and recreation 'a man's condition deteriorates under the conditions of service afloat' and also 'the bearing of the average rating (and some officers) ashore compares very unfavourably with that of the average soldier'. As 'an alert bearing is the product of a healthy physical and mental condition' it was essential to offer the sailor more opportunities for healthy exercise and recreation.[9] There was no question that 'recreation means physical and mental refreshment'.[10]

Despite the fact that 'the need for the creation of maintenance of morale is too well recognised to necessitate argument',[11] it was not always possible to offer conditions in which sport could flourish. On many ships, especially those serving in arduous and challenging conditions such as experienced on the Arctic and Atlantic Convoys, there were very few opportunities to play team games. Climate extremes and the need to be ready for action made it impossible. Even on land there could be a shortage of sporting facilities on many bases – there were only six soccer pitches and one rugby ground available for the crews of eighty ships in port at Greenock in January 1945.[12] Many training establishments lacked sufficient gymnasium facilities.[13] As a result, towards the end of the war there were criticisms that

> the majority of men between 19 and 30, who are passing through a period of life where games are not only a normal but extremely necessary part of a man's existence, never play at all. Instead they find relaxation in the cinema, the canteen and the radio, which are soporific rather than tonic recreations.[14]

Such arguments about the inadequacy of recreational opportunities did not impress the Admiralty and its Directorate of Physical Training and Sports which still claimed that 'from the recreational point of view, the welfare of the Royal Navy and Royal Marines can be very favourably compared with the other services in spite of greater difficulties which have to be overcome'.[15]

In encouraging sport on board ship, 'team work is the essence of every naval evolution which concerns more than one man' and this 'is best taught in team games'. Such games could also encourage the development of leadership skills in so far as they taught men 'how to lead and how to be led' as well as boosting quick thinking and rapid action in them. At times when there was a need to identify men for promotion as junior and petty officers and leading seamen, performance in sport could be used to select candidates with the right qualities. Critics of the inadequacy of sporting facilities also argued that improved facilities could also be important in recruitment to attract future sailors since 'the public knowledge that the Admiralty were pursuing an energetic sporting policy in wartime would go far towards encouraging the right type of young man to make the Royal Navy his career in time of peace'.[16]

When it came to the establishment of physical and recreational training schemes for new entrants to the Royal Navy, the role of the PT instructor was essential:

> Physical and recreational training instruction properly carried out is one of the most important means of quickly bringing forward, both physically and mentally, recruits who are undergoing their intensive first entry training course.[17]

It was feared that 'a bad or apathetic instructor will ruin any game'.[18] As large training establishments increased during the war, the need for PT instructors also increased.[19] Many of them were pre-war professional footballers, although most footballers preferred to join the army rather than the navy as there were more opportunities to continue playing the sport if serving on land.[20] Recruits were to be taught how to play the game in the 'proper spirit, fairly without fouling, going all out to win without resorting to cheating' and to 'play for your side and not for yourself'.[21] Instructors were careful to ensure that in any competitive games experienced sportsmen should not be pitted against novices in a competition that could only be unequal, and also that 'neither should a good man be ridiculed in front of a novice'.[22] Sports were also to be treated as more than just mindless exercise for promoting physical strength, but as also having a moral and social dimension:

> Boxing should not be taught as a drill but rather as a form of recreation, the necessary requirements being suppleness of movement, agility, correct hitting, good judgment of distance, perfect timing, a sound defence, in fact doing the right thing at the right moment.[23]

O'Conor similarly believed that 'physical exercises are a valuable help to fitness at sea, when done of the free will and at the right time of day' but that compulsory physical jerks for midshipmen on a wet and slippery deck before breakfast was more likely to be 'an infliction, which is likely to fill him with a lasting dislike' than a way of staying healthy.[24] Physical training was not to become 'an endurance test rather than an enjoyable exercise'.[25] On larger ships, PT was done to music which made it more fun for both ratings and officers.[26]

Many medical officers found themselves taking on duties concerned with the organisation of games and sports. Peter McRae, a Somerset County cricketer, a rugby player at medical school, squash player and all-round sportsman, found that having athletic ability and a sporting reputation was an advantage in smoothing his way when in naval barracks.[27] Jack Coulter's career was not harmed by him being a keen cricketer who had played for the Royal Navy before the war. Such closeness in sport with the men also gave the medical officer an opportunity to observe them and ensure their physical and mental fitness:

> In emergencies in modern warfare the man who is not physically fit and tough is not going to pull his weight during the fighting ... the medical officer, by constant observation of the ship's company and by playing games and taking part in endurance tests with the men, should note those who are below standard.[28]

An interest and record of achievement in sport gave the doctor something in common with his fellow officers and with the ratings. Hugh Philip considered that 'if one mixes in games and on social occasions with those whom one is expected to care for medically, the chances of being able to keep them fit, or catch a disease in its early stages, are greatly increased'.[29] He had being given the job of sports officer at the submarine depot ship on which he was medical officer because of his interest in hockey and cricket, though his more sedentary life as a general practitioner had seen him doing nothing more strenuous than play an occasional round of golf. As there was only one football pitch for 700 men, he had to be creative in order to make the best use of limited facilities. A competition was organised to win a Cup for All-Round Sports, competed for by teams of ten men to play against each other at six-a-side football, deck hockey, deck tennis, darts, billiards and basketball. One particular darts match saw the victory of a team named the Virgins over the Innocents by 'two straight legs', a result which provoked much ribald comment. Later a united services club was formed with local army and air force units, allowing for a higher level of competition, especially when the rugby team at Blyth contained several Rugby Union internationals and international trialists as well as a couple of Northern Union professionals.[30] It was an advantage when the officer in charge of the sports ground working party was keenly interested in games since in many cases this officer was 'specially selected because he was considered too incompetent to keep watch on the quarterdeck' and at a time when there was a 'growing tendency among junior officers to devote the whole of their spare time to pastimes of an individualistic nature, eg golf, shooting'.[31]

In wartime, recreation facilities were always going to be in short supply. The Royal Navy, despite the rigours of rationing, took pains to ensure that ships were supplied with a minimum of kit: fifteen pairs of boxing gloves on capital ships and ten pairs on smaller ships; six dozen jerseys, shorts, pairs of stockings and pairs of boots and six footballs on capital ships; and a dozen jerseys, shorts, stockings and boots, and one football on submarines.[32] There still remained the problem of a shortage of playing fields and other facilities on land. At Scapa Flow, there was no changing hut at the football ground at Flotta and the hockey pitch was in a dangerous condition.[33] There was, however, a good golf course there, popular with the officers rather than the ratings.[34]

Sport could make a difference in the improvement of the general health of a ship's company. The ratings on the cruiser *Bellona* were 'young and newly entered' when the ship was commissioned on the Clyde in September 1943. Many of them 'came from the rather depressing barracks life to the wintry autumn of the Glasgow slums and thence to Scapa Flow to work up'. There they were toughened up and their morale was raised in the process although none of them were in the highest state of physical fitness. At Scapa and later at Plymouth, where deck hockey and whale pulling, football and hockey, physical training, tug of war and swimming were common, over-keenness in sport was preferable to slack discipline and the new ratings were 'very largely integrated with the generally rising morale and fitness of the ship's company'.[35] Even during Operation 'Husky' in 1943 when the recreation facilities on *Brittany* were curtailed, bathing from the ship's side and games of water polo were made available three or four times a week'.[36] On *Belfast*, off the Normandy coast in the weeks after D-Day, as the weather improved, men had to be warned of the dangers of sunbathing, 'as many ratings were exposing themselves for too long, naked, on deck during quiet periods'.[37] Where there were no opportunities for sport and 'there is never any relaxation either at sea or in harbour', as on *Repulse* in 1940, 'the physical and mental strain in this war is greater than it was in the last war'.[38]

Although there was a general consensus within the navy that physical training and exercise were perhaps more important for maintaining morale and mental health than for physical health, there remained some suspicion that sport and physical activities should not be too enjoyable. When it was proposed that sailing boats should be provided at Royal Navy Air Stations to give officers and ratings in the Fleet Air Arm 'some sea sense', a knowledge of boats and their limitations and 'a feeling of self-reliance in matters not directly concerned with their technical knowledge of aircraft', there was opposition on the grounds that the men might 'obtain some pleasure as well as experience' from sailing.[39] Recreation on its own was suspect if meant to be for fun and no other purpose. Sports activity was expected to offer more than just rest and enjoyment.

Football was seen as a way of keeping men active, fit and entertained, especially with the call-up of professional footballers who were now playing for navy teams and raising standards of playing to professional levels. Sport could help to cement inter-service and inter-Allied bonds. *Ark Royal* forged links with the Black Watch, stationed at Gibraltar, by means of 'many a football match and many a party'. After the loss of the ship in November 1941, a match was organised to mark her passing, kicked off by Captain Maund of the torpedoed ship and watched by 5,000 spectators including a thousand survivors from the sinking. The Black Watch won, but the symbolic value of the match was to express the solidarity of the British forces.[40] Army and navy competitions at home also attracted great crowds of spectators.

Although the Football Association had responded to the immediate outbreak of war by suspending the sport, competition was soon reintroduced even if crowds were limited to 8,000 in evacuation areas and 15,000 elsewhere. Competitive inter-service and inter-unit football matches were encouraged and helped to raise funds for service charities. In turn, football clubs feted naval heroes. After their action against the *Graf Spee*, the crew of *Exeter* was invited by Chelsea to a match against Tottenham Hotspur in February 1940.[41] Civilian teams also raised money for naval charities. The final of the Football League War Cup at Stamford Bridge on Saturday, 15 May 1943 between Arsenal and Blackpool, respective winners of the wartime North and South Cups, was attended by 55,195 spectators and raised £7,730 for the benefit of the King George V Fund for Sailors. Blackpool won by four goals to two and was presented with the cup by A V Alexander, First Lord of the Admiralty, who had suggested that naval charities should benefit from the match.[42]

Even boxing competitions could draw big crowds. When the Royal Navy team from Portsmouth, all of them 'tough experienced boxers', played against St Mary's Hospital Boxing Club at Croydon in May 1943 they could draw a crowd of 1,500 spectators. The medical students believed that they had an advantage in their more considered and intellectual approach to boxing than their opponents, one of whom was dismissed as 'a rushing and ferocious opponent' and 'a rather unscientific adversary', but it was the tough naval fighters who won the match by eight bouts to three, despite the naval team being smaller in numbers than that of their opponents.[43] Some of the matches between the navy and other teams could be memorable for more than just the game. When St Mary's Hospital Rugby Club played at Devonport in March 1945 against a team from the Royal Naval Engineering College, Heysham, the visitors were shown over one of the largest capital ships, and 'the Navy's methods of entertainment caused a considerable strain on at least two of the hollow viscera, and somewhere between two cheerful evenings a pleasant game of rugger was played'.[44]

There was pressure to release sportsmen in naval service for sporting events at home. The Admiralty response to requests to release naval footballers to take part in representative international matches between England or Scotland and the Allies to be organised by the Football Association in 1944 or for men to play with Navy, Army and Air Force Combined Services football teams was that there was 'no objection to granting facilities to naval personnel to take part in any of these matches, providing that they can be spared from their duties, but it will of course be understood that this can not be allowed to interfere with normal service requirements for drafting'.[45] A request asking for leave for Petty Officer T Weston, a pre-war jockey, stationed at HMS *Europa* in Lowestoft, to train for a race at Newmarket for two days for 2,000 guineas was initially refused in the run-up to D-Day as all ordinary leave had been suspended.[46] However, Weston's harbour craft was 'broken' and he was duly granted 48 hours leave to race at Newmarket to entertain wartime racegoers despite the impending invasion of Europe.[47]

The United States Navy encouraged sporting prowess much more than the Royal Navy could ever hope to do. There was a different college-dominated sporting tradition in North America, which the war actually encouraged. The emphasis at training stations and in ships at sea was on physical conditioning. Athletic specialists were appointed to carry out the navy's physical training and welfare and recreation program. In April 1941, the Navy Department announced the appointment of Commander James J Tunney, who had won the world heavyweight boxing title from Jack Dempsey in 1926, as Director of the Navy Physical Fitness Program. He encouraged sporting activity on service and in training. With its V-12 programme under which some young naval recruits were trained in colleges, the United States Navy actually encouraged sport in some former liberal arts colleges not previously known for their sporting prowess. At DePauw University, Indiana, the influx of American football from other universities under the V-12 scheme gave it an outstanding team unbeaten by any other colleges in the 1943 season. Basketball at DePauw received a similar boost with championship titles won in the 1943–4 and 1944–5 seasons. Football stars were rumoured to prefer the V-12 Marine units because of their reputation for courage and because they could avoid some of the more demanding mathematics studied by V-12 navy recruits.[48] At the Great Lakes Naval Base, football was actually used encourage enlistment as well as to entertain servicemen and civilians. In 1942, a team played twelve games in Chicago, St Louis and Cleveland as well as the Universities of Michigan, Iowa and Illinois to encourage naval recruitment in landlocked states and to energise recruiting drives.[49] Many of these colleges gave their entire gymnasia and sporting facilities over to the use of the army and navy for physical training but in others these facilities were used as dormitories reducing the opportunities for sport. Butler University, Indianapolis, cancelled its intercollegiate sporting programme for 1943 not for lack of players but rather for lack of facilities as the gymnasium was being used by the navy.[50]

Sporting occasions were seen as major means of encouraging interaction with the wider public both in the United States and in Great Britain, but there were other strategies which the Royal Navy fostered. Warship Weeks organised under the aegis of the National Savings campaign gave opportunities for particular towns to fundraise for the navy and to adopt a ship, the size of the ship allocated to them depending upon how much money a particular community could raise. Parades involving all three armed services were held. In the Borough of Holborn, a large, ungainly model warship made from scraps was proudly exhibited, there was a special film show and a procession past the civic dignitaries was led by the band of the Royal Artillery. A bar of toilet soap was sold for the princely sum of £5 towards the adoption by Holborn of the cruiser *Trinidad*, with other donated lots in the auction including a wireless, watches, books, pictures, chocolate and, above all, the rare luxury of an egg.[51] Even small inland towns, such as the mining town of West Stanley in County Durham, which in 1942 adopted the corvette HMS *Anchusa*, enthusiastically took part and built links with the navy. Parades and exhibitions caught the public imagination and encouraged investment in war savings stamps and certificates. Pupils at Alderman Wood School, the local grammar school, competed to see which forms could raise the most money and beat their targets. Twelve-year-old Roger Simpson, when writing an essay about Wings for Victory Week in June 1943, remembered the excitement of the 'gigantic advertisements and posters, competitions and lotteries or other modern ways of collecting savings money' adopted the previous year for Warship Week.[52] In July 1944 the officers and men of *Anchusa* expressed their gratitude by presenting West Stanley with a photograph of the ship and a commemorative plaque to be hung in the Council Chamber.[53] Aldeburgh timed the presentation of the plaque for its ship with the beginning of Wings for Victory Week to encourage further generosity from local people for the armed forces.[54]

The importance of building such strong local links between individual ships and local communities was highlighted when the Mayor of Darlington asked that another ship be allocated to his borough when he learned that Darlington's original adopted ship *Nizam* had been commissioned as a ship of the Royal Australian Navy and also asked about the possibility of a new ship being named *Darlington*:

It was found in the course of the campaign [Warship Week, 1943] that the adoption of a specific ship gave to the townspeople a feeling of having a specific link with the Royal Navy, and it cannot be doubted that many of them feel a special satisfaction in being responsible for the welfare of a particular ship. That special individual satisfaction would not be engendered by a subscription, however large, to the RN War Amenities Fund, and the money represented by the cheque was collected for the specific object of providing comforts for our ship.[55]

As it was 'a rule not to name HM ships with reference to particular Warship Weeks unless the money saved is made as a gift to the nation', the Mayor's request for a ship to be named after his town was denied and *Barfleur* was adopted in place of *Nizam*.[56]

When South Shields adopted the destroyer *Maori* in 1942 it hoped that 'a lasting association will be established between the ship and the inhabitants of South Shields'.[57] Councils and local people took a pride in their ships and were keen to send comforts and gifts, such as gramophone records, books, clothing and games, to the ships that they had adopted. Some of these gifts would have been very welcome for recreational purposes, but hand-knitted clothing could be of varying standard and utility. One officer received a balaclava with 'a large triangular aperture intended for the face, the apex of which was the point of the chin with the base extending between the nipples'.[58] Ralph Wallis Ransome was amused to find a note in the toe of a stocking he received from a war comforts fund in which the knitter invited him 'if you're single drop a line, if you're married never mind'. He wrote to thank the lady but had to disappoint her romantic hopes by informing her that he already had a wife and children.[59] The people of Halesowen sent a Christmas gift to the company of the destroyer *Achates* in 1942, but the vessel had been lost before the comforts reached the ship. Permission was readily given for the gifts to be transferred to another ship and Halesowen adopted another vessel, *Contest*, in place of *Achates*.[60]

The visibility of the sailor when ashore increased his popularity. A naval uniform was easily recognised and accorded the wearer public admiration and respect. The sailor himself took a pride in his appearance. It was stressed that an 'officer's uniform should automatically make a man look quietly well dressed'.[61] This was all within a naval tradition that prided itself on the smart appearance of its officers at sea and ashore. Naval officer's uniform had closely followed fashion throughout the nineteenth and early twentieth centuries with officers being measured for their civilian suits by the same West End tailors who made their uniforms, with the result that the cut of the smart suit was influenced by the tailoring of a naval officer's uniform.[62] Even in the middle of the Great War, Alexander Scrimgeour, a dashing midshipman fond of 'cocktails and fizz' at the Adelphi, was anxious about the maintenance of his wardrobe including his need for 'two suits of mufti in London' and repairs to his uniform trousers as his 'servant is willing, but unskilled and, being a marine bandsman, wields the piccolo with more skill than a needle'.[63] However, during the Second World War civilian clothes were rarely worn by officers and never by ratings. At a time when invasion was feared and heavy air raids were frequent, it made sense that officers and men should not be caught out of uniform at any time. As the war went on, always wearing uniform became monotonous and it was noted that 'officers and men and members of the WRNS are as proud now as ever of wearing His Majesty's uniform, but there are many, particularly those who have had no opportunity of taking part in games and other sporting opportunities, who have worn uniform all day and every day for three years and more'. This not only meant that opportunities for leisure were less relaxing than they might have been but also that wearing uniform all the time 'leads to an unconscious relaxation in the smartness of their dress and the correctness of their bearing'.[64]

The Admiralty was prepared to relax the requirement for officers and ratings to wear uniform when on leave, although it remained insistent that uniform should be worn in all naval establishments, except during recreational activities, and in 1944 granted permission for plain clothes to be worn by men on leave for more than 48 hours.[65] Officers were also expected to have a jacket and pair of flannels for recreational activities. However, rationed civilian clothing was not so easy to obtain unless a man was lucky enough to have retained his pre-war wardrobe in good condition. Some men had lost their civilian clothing in action and younger officers 'probably have never had time to acquire plain clothes'.[66] Men's clothing was in short supply, with suits, shoes and hats difficult to obtain. When clothes rationing had first been introduced in 1942, a man was allocated enough coupons in one year to replace the suit, shirt, tie, shoes and underwear in which he stood, but after 1942 it would have taken two years to replace these clothes. As the end of the war approached the imminence of demobilisation put increased pressure on the supply of men's clothing.[67] With such stringent rationing, there was no question of issuing special ration coupons for naval men to buy plain clothes just for leave and it was feared that 'there is a danger of a good many naval officers going on leave in a dress that would not bring credit on the Service' if they were encouraged to wear plain clothes.[68]

For Leading Telegraphist Walter Scott, the opportunity to exchange a dapper 7,000-franc double-breasted suit and 3,000-franc shoes and be re-kitted in his more utilitarian square rig uniform at Portsmouth Royal Naval barracks in October 1944 was more welcome than any opportunity to wear plain clothes, however high quality, dashing and expensive they may have been.[69] Scott, whose original name was Marcel Gilles, was a French naval rating who had changed his name and joined the Royal Navy after the fall of France in 1940. He had been captured after the sinking of the cruiser *Manchester* in August 1942 and had been imprisoned at Bizerta once his true nationality had been realised. He had escaped to join the Resistance in Dieppe, where he had been given an expensive suit by the local woman leader of the French Forces of the Interior as part of his cover. The liberation of Dieppe gave him the opportunity to re-join the British navy and be recognised as a warrior in his uniform rather than wage war in the anonymity of civilian clothing.[70] Similarly for many men the wearing of uniform on leave gave them an easily recognisable identity and status. They stood out as sailors when at home and that had just as salutary an effect on individual morale as escaping briefly into civvies could have done.

Entertainment was another way in which links could be made between the sailor and home, making him feel part of the wider community. The Royal Navy was perhaps neglected in terms of live entertainment because its ships were at sea for long periods and it was difficult, if not impossible, to arrange visits from entertainers to ships except when they were in port. Concerts were organised at naval bases and depot ships, but the Royal Navy tended to be forgotten about and was left to organise its own entertainments to a large extent, mainly in the form of film and radio rather than performances by the big stars of the day. In August 1943, the Entertainments National Service Association (ENSA) spent £9,675 in one month on entertainments for the Royal Navy compared with £85,570 for the army and £50,275 for the Royal Air Force.[71] Whilst the army looked on Vera Lynn as its forces' sweetheart and the RAF embraced Anne Shelton, the Royal Navy had the more mature figure of Evelyn Laye and the Merchant Navy had Doris Hare. Gracie Fields made herself popular by indiscriminately entertaining all three services without favouring any one, in addition to raising funds for the Navy League and Spitfire Fund with her overseas tours. In 1941, she undertook an unpaid five-week tour giving eighty-three concerts to a combined audience of 410,000 sailors, soldiers, airmen and munitions workers throughout Great Britain, including the Orkneys, at a total cost of £1,309.[72] Not even the rainfall on an aircraft hangar when she sang to troops of all three forces at Blyth in the early days of the war 'could damp the spirits of the audience nor upset Gracie's appeal'.[73] She had a rare ability to make a smooth transition from a raucous comic song to the solemnity of the Lord's Prayer in a way that could move servicemen to stand in respectful silence after roaring with laughter only a few minutes before.[74] It was even suggested that all that it needed to raise morale and win the war was to 'Give us Gracie and we'll finish the job'.[75] The men of the Royal Navy would have welcomed more of 'Our Gracie' than they ever got.

Although ENSA had been established by the producer and director Basil Dean in June 1939 as an offshoot of the NAAFI to 'mobilise talent in the theatrical, variety, concert and cinema professions' and organise entertainment for the armed forces, the navy did not at first benefit from its services. Although the first ENSA concerts for troops were performed in September 1939, even into the first few months of 1941 'the Royal Navy has had no recent experience of ENSA entertainments' but was 'confident that ENSA will be able to provide the Shore Establishments with the type of show they need'. Only in the week ending 16 February 1941 were ten ENSA concerts organised for the navy, enjoying a combined audience of 2,803.[76] Even so throughout the war, the Senior Service was to remain the Cinderella service in receiving a short supply of entertainment, largely due to a shortage of available artistes.[77] Yet the Royal Navy remained reliant on ENSA because it lacked its own permanent entertainment units.[78]

There was, however, one singer and actress who was determined that the men of the Royal Navy should not be deprived of much-needed entertainment. Evelyn Laye, who had dominated musical theatre in London since the 1920s and had become a film star both in Britain and in Hollywood, made it her mission to bring glamour and gaiety to the Royal Navy. Her first boyfriend had been a young submariner, Jimmy Brierley, with whom she had started a chaste romance when as a seventeen-year-old she was playing 'Goody Two Shoes' in a pantomime at Portsmouth in 1917 and continued during his leaves in London by which time she had become a glamorous Gaiety Girl. He had then disappeared and she had only learned his fate almost two years later when Brierley's best friend had visited her in her dressing room with the news that he had been drowned but that had he survived he would have been blind after being severely wounded in the face.[79] It was thanks to him that the Royal Navy was the service 'closest to her heart'.

The opportunity to do something came in February 1940 when she was asked by Vivian Dunn, conductor of the Royal Marines Band, to sing to men at an embarkation depot in Portsmouth. Afraid that the men would resent being woken up, she had been touched by the way the men, sleeping on benches and on the floor of a huge hall, had responded by humming along to her singing a song 'When I grow too old to dream' that had been written for her by Sigmund Romberg and Oscar Hammerstein II.[80] She had then responded to an invitation from Lord Inverclyde to sing at a concert for the British Sailors' Society with her own counter-request to be allowed to take a concert party to Scapa Flow because Jimmy Brierley had told her 'what a hell on earth' it could be to be stationed there during the Great War with nothing to do when off-duty. It demanded great persistence before Laye, one of whose firmest fans since her early West End success was the King, was allowed her wish. Accompanied by fellow actress Doris Hare, soon to be presenter of the radio programme *Shipmates Ashore* for the men of the Merchant Navy, actor Clifford Mollison, D'Oyly Carte star Martyn Green and her pianist Gordon Whelan, Laye made her first visit to Scapa Flow. Laye and Hare had hoped to bring a touch of glamour to the men stationed there but were both sick on a turbulent flight and arrived without any costumes or make-up only to find themselves performing for 'the greatest audience any of us had known'.[81]

Laye organised many subsequent concert parties to Scapa Flow, encouraging her fellow performers to go there and raising the money needed for this from a series of Sunday concerts in aid of entertainments for the navy until the Admiralty gave her a grant in June 1940 to organise entertainments for the navy, especially at Scapa Flow. The grant coincided not only with her imminent 40th birthday but also came at the time that she organised and presented a special concert broadcast from the Theatre Royal Drury Lane in aid of the navy, in which she appeared with tenor John McCormack and comedians Flanagan and Allen.[82] In the fraught days when Britain faced imminent invasion, there was an emotional charge to her rendition of 'Land of Hope and Glory' at the close of the concert. When ENSA belatedly began to organise entertainment for the men of the Royal Navy, Laye became Chairman of the Naval Section of ENSA, in charge of entertainments for the Senior Service. In 1941 Beatrice Lillie and Evelyn Laye led an ENSA party giving a special concert at the opening of a new canteen at Rosyth by the Commander-in-Chief, Home Fleet, marking greater ENSA involvement with the navy.[83]

The quality of ENSA performances was often poor and many of the jokes were 'near the edge', but 'the smut was no worse than is heard in the average Music Hall, and they generally found that the audience was in no way embarrassed by this sort of thing'.[84] The pianist Ivor Newton observed that 'the troops would have no taste for anything more ambitious than could be provided by comedians who had decided that, as the forces' own language is often luridly obscene, they would make the servicemen feel at home by going one better, as though the use of scandalous language is in itself funny'.[85] The overall feeling within the Royal Navy was that 'although the artistes employed by ENSA did sterling work under difficult conditions and visited every theatre of operations, the entertainment provided often left much to be desired both in quality and quantity'.[86]

Harry Balfour, for one, was not impressed by the only ENSA concert he attended:

OURSELVES: REST AND RECREATION

In fact, I only got to one of these concerts and after months in Arctic waters when one would have expected any form of entertainment – let alone one involving real women – to be exciting, I found it difficult to whip myself into a lather of mild interest in the well-meaning blowsy females and the cretinous comics. I suppose they thought they were doing their bit by entertaining the boys but the bit they were capable of was slight. When I first went ashore in Iceland I saw what the Americans had done for their troops during their brief stay there and compared this with the wooden huts and NAAFI tea provided at Scapa which had been one of our main Naval bases.[87]

ENSA did make attempts to attract American film stars and singers, which became easier to achieve with the entry of the United States into the war and the stationing of American servicemen in Britain. The first star invited was singer and actress Deanna Durbin, whose visit for Christmas 1941 to sing to all three armed services was considered significant because of 'the psychological importance of her providing entertainments for the troops at Christmas' and because if ENSA could 'get a star of the eminence of Miss Durbin to start the scheme it would be easier to persuade other American artistes to come over and give similar concerts subsequently'.[88] Despite the press reporting that Durbin would be singing for the troops that Christmas and say her own personal 'prayer for the boys over there', plans for her visit foundered when ENSA could only obtain a flight for her but not for her producer husband Vaughn Paul nor her chaperone, without whom she could not travel.[89]

A royal visit was seen as a great morale-booster, perhaps even more prestigious than an ENSA concert by a celebrity artiste. Having served as a sub-lieutenant on *Collingwood* at the battle of Jutland, George VI regularly wore naval uniform during the war, whether visiting the bombed-out areas of his kingdom or when presiding over formal investitures. His visits to Scapa Flow were as popular as those of Evelyn Laye, especially if they meant a good ENSA show attended by the King, such as the concert by the comedian Leslie Henson during his four-day visit in March 1943. Hugh Philip looked on a royal visit as 'a great day for us', impressed that the King spoke to everyone on a visit to his depot ship and by the way in which the Queen reassured a nervous officer by asking whether he was married and then telling him to 'speak to me as you would to your wife'.[90] Ransome Wallis was much more impressed by exiled King Peter of Yugoslavia, 'a young man of considerable charm', who arrived on *London* dressed as an admiral but, having 'weighed up the form', appeared in the wardroom in the uniform of a lieutenant-commander in order to fit in with his hosts during his few days on board.[91] The navy valued such traditions as not rising for the loyal toast which made the officers' mess feel a close connection to the monarch. Not everyone was as appreciative of the naval royal connections. Wren Suzanne Willson was threatened with disciplinary action for turning a portrait photograph of Queen Mary, President of Queen Alexandra's Royal Naval Nursing Service, to the wall in the office in which she worked as a writer, because she found it oppressive to look at the stern-faced, austere queen every day as she carried out her duties.[92]

There were no morale-boosting visits for the Arctic Convoys in port in North Russia, nor much to enliven the dull days. Football was played when the weather allowed, such as the scratch match held on 11 May 1943 between a Russian eleven and a team from the British hospital in Vaenga which was won by the Russians and led to one of the British team being hospitalised.[93] Films in English were shown at the Russian Navy Club in Polyarnoe, brought by each new convoy and concert parties were organised. One of the most popular films was *The Great Waltz*, the story of the Strauss family which the Russians came to time after time even though they could not understand the language but enjoyed the music. The cinema itself had swing doors with Stalin's face painted on both sides, which looked impressive when the doors were closed and 'ludicrous' when one of the doors was open.[94]

Among the British films shown was *Dinky-Doo*, the most popular film in Soviet Russia in 1943. It was first shown in Murmansk, but once it was released in Moscow it broke all Russian cinema box-office records in the ten months it ran. The film starred George Formby and was better known to British audiences as *Let George Do It*.[95] In the 1940 film the popular star plays a performer with the Dinky-Doo variety concert party who accidentally boards a ship to Bergen when he intends to go to Blackpool, gets mistaken for a fellow spy by a bandleader who is a Nazi spy, sending coded messages from Norway in his musical arrangements to U-boats preying on Allied shipping, and, after a serious of farcical misadventures, escapes only to find himself aboard a U-boat, from which he is torpedoed to safety and saves the convoy armed only with his ukulele. Perhaps it partly owed its immense popularity with wartime audiences to a fantasy sequence in which the gormless and weedy weakling Formby parachutes into a Nuremberg Rally, takes on Hitler and delivers a knockout blow.[96] Formby was to pay tribute to the navy in his own inimitable slapstick way in *Bell Bottom George*, released in 1944 in which he appears as a steward in a navy club, rejected on medical grounds from naval service, who swaps clothes with a sailor friend and foils the attempt of enemy agents to blow up a British warship.[97] Such films reminded the sailor of home where Formby had been one of the most popular British film stars of the 1930s.

On the larger ships such as *Hood* there was projection equipment for the showing of films. Sailors were proud to see themselves depicted in the cinema, although they could be critical of the way in which the Royal Navy was shown. Even though there were some criticisms of the way the lower deck was represented in the film, sailors tended to like the way that they and their families were portrayed in the film *In Which We Serve* and felt 'a glow of pride' watching it in the cinema with his 'wife, girlfriend or tart wot [*sic*] I picked up'.[98] They were perhaps more critical watching patriotic morale-boosters with their peers than alone or with their families, where they could feel a pride in the Service. On the bigger, more prestigious ships, the music played by the Royal Marines bands was a suitable accompaniment to official ceremony with such rousing marches as 'Heart of Oak', 'Rule Britannia' and 'A Life on the Ocean Wave', but the bands also gave concerts ranging from classical to popular music. In the absence of live music, gramophone records and the wireless, when within range of broadcasting stations, were acceptable substitutes to the live military band.[99]

By and large, though, the men preferred to stick to their traditional onboard pastimes, including tombola or bingo, uckers, a board game similar to Ludo, which had been played by men of the Royal Navy since the early nineteenth century, and the card game euchre, similar to Trumps. John Somers on the cruiser *Dauntless* praised the 'excitement you can have with uckers' and the way in which it 'helps to relieve the tedium'. On *Dauntless* a giant board was painted on the deck and outsize dice were shaken from a bucket in contests in which seamen played against stokers and marines against torpedo men. The players wore fancy dress made out of signal flag bunting. Although playing for money was strictly forbidden, gambling was rife.[100] Concert parties were also held and, in the absence of women, men in drag would take female parts in shows or perform male striptease dances and take part in 'glamour boy' beauty contests.[101] On *Scylla*, morale could be boosted by something as simple as seeing the officers taking a turn at painting the ship in fancy dress, the padre donning a mortar board and the senior medical officer wearing his old opera hat. Jack Coulter admitted that 'we made a poor job of it and felt that the regular ship's painters were very tolerant, considering that they had to do the job again later. Nonetheless, the effect on morale was probably extremely good.'[102]

For the more studious and quiet men there was the ship's library. This would heavily feature the classics of English literature supplied by the Admiralty when the ship was commissioned. but would be supplemented by books donated by the public. Loan libraries included books on technical and scientific subjects as well as relating to hobbies, while there would often also be a drama loan library that could be drawn upon by the ship's drama and writing societies.[103] In the subscription library on *Hood*, for which the men paid one penny per book per week, the most popular books were cowboy tales of the Wild West and detective novels.[104] Lectures were given by officers on a variety of subjects that might entertain and educate their audiences, meeting a hunger for more political topics, since 'men are keenly interested in affairs of the day' demonstrated by the way in which 'crucial announcements by statesmen unfailingly attract attentive crowds to the loudspeakers' of the wireless sets.[105] More forward-thinking officers also organised discussion groups on topical issues and citizenship, such as education, health, state control and nationalisation, press freedom, social services and post-war reconstruction. On one ship in 1944 there was interest in 'the power of the vote' and in schemes of post-war reconstruction but a widespread 'lack of confidence that the proposed schemes will ever be carried out. Mistrust, not of any particular government, but of politicians in general.'[106]

Religion also had a part to play in maintaining morale and routine. Larger ships carried chaplains, usually Anglican, who would conduct a compulsory Sunday prayer service, but even on smaller ships the captain would lead prayers on deck. Many chaplains wore naval officers' uniform without any mark of rank in an attempt to make them seem more accessible to all ranks. In battle they were advised to remain in the casualty distributing station with the medical officer where they could offer comfort to casualties and encourage ratings. Many sailors dismissed them as 'bible thumpers' and 'Holy Joes', but others found consolation in the simplicity of Sunday prayers and a source of pastoral care.[107]

A pet could become important as a ship's mascot and object of affection. A dog picked up by Roger Miles' destroyer gave birth 'rather stormily' a few hours after being picked up from a torpedoed ship. She was adopted by the crew that had rescued her and a year later was still aboard and about to produce another litter, an 'Anglo-French generation'.[108] A fox terrier, Patch, was the mascot on *Martin*, 'highly thought of by all on board and lived up forward in one of the seamen's mess decks except at action stations'. When he heard the alarm bell, Patch would take up his own action station under one of the cots in the sick bay. He was joined by Chocker, 'a rather battered tom cat', who leapt on board *Martin* from his own ship *Musketeer* when the two ships were tied up alongside each other while on convoy duties, who also chose a pile of stretchers fastened to a bulkhead in the sick bay as his own refuge. Both cat and dog soon became friendly with each other, each of them 'accustomed to gun-fire and did not show much anxiety' when under fire, offering an example to the seamen.[109] On *Hood*, the chaplain's bull terrier Bill challenged the position of the two inseparable cats that had hitherto been the mascots of the ship, Ginger and Fishcakes. Ginger's tail had been amputated when it was trapped by the lid of a wash-deck locker. Bill also narrowly escaped injury when he cocked his leg on a length of electric cabling. Having survived near-electrocution, he left the ship with his master before the sinking. Not so lucky were Ginger and Fishcakes, believed to have gone down with the ship and most of her company.[110]

The officers' wardroom remained a bastion of tradition with the atmosphere of a gentleman's club, however cramped and overcrowded it may have been in wartime. Naval rations were supplemented by wardroom funds and meals were served by Royal Marine wardroom attendants acting as waiters. In port there was a lot of entertaining between ships. At Scapa Flow, Ralph Ransome Wallis found 'visiting other ships, either for drinks or for a guest dinner night was both pleasant and interesting'.[111] Jack Coulter enjoyed 'quite a merry evening' on *Scylla* with the senior medical officer of *Curacoa* after a day in July 1942 when he felt 'very tired and fell asleep during the afternoon'.[112] Mess dinners continued to be held even in wartime though with some modifications of protocol but with full etiquette maintained. The traditional toasts, proposed by the youngest officer present immediately after the seated loyal toast, were scrupulously observed: on Sunday, it was to 'Absent Friends', on Monday to 'Our Ships at Sea', Tuesday to 'Our Men', Wednesday to 'Ourselves (For No One Else will Think of Us)', Thursday to 'A Bloody War or a Sickly Season (and a Quick Promotion)', Friday to 'A Willing Foe and Sea Room', ending on Saturday with the humorous toast to 'Our Wives and Sweethearts (May they Never Meet)'. Hugh Philip made the mistake of dressing smartly, even if his bow tie was ready made-up, for his first full-dress mess dinner only to be pelted with oranges, still available in 1939, and vowed 'never again will I go to a mess dinner in a new uniform'.[113]

One tradition in which everyone participated was the Crossing the Line ceremony when ships passed the Equator. For one day normal naval discipline and hierarchies were set aside. Men, irrespective of whether they were officers or ratings, who had not previously crossed the Equator were lined up on deck before a man dressed as Neptune in front of an improvised canvas swimming pool in which they would be ducked in sea water after having been ritually humiliated, daubed with soap suds and shaved by a barber with a large wooden razor.[114] On *London* there were two temporary baths, the first being full of seamen dressed as bears who repeatedly ducked the initiate, who was then almost drowned by Marines in the next bath. For Ransome Wallis, 'the whole thing was made worse by the fact that the sea water in the baths, of which one swallowed copious amounts, was a bit turbid owing to the presence of so many excited and sweaty bodies, quite apart from the First Lieutenant's lather'.[115]

The daily issue of grog was also accompanied by a great deal of ritual which tended to break up the monotony of a day's work. The barrel was brought on deck from the spirit room by a party consisting of the duty gunner regulating petty officer, sergeant of marines, supply petty officer and the ship's butcher, to be opened by the cooper before the hands were called to deck by bosun's pipe. Each rating was given a half-pint of grog, made up of one part of rum diluted by two parts of water. Teetotallers could choose to be given a cash payment in lieu but many ratings would save their rum ration to use as a form of lower-deck currency among themselves to reward favours, act as stakes in card schools and pay debts. This was unofficial and men were supposed to drink their own rum ration when issued with it, though men were occasionally allowed to offer 'sippers' to a messmate celebrating a birthday or 'gulpers' as an award for a special favour. Grog encouraged a hard-drinking culture which could lead to rowdiness ashore.[116]

An attempt had been made during the Great War to deal with the threat to discipline and efficiency from widespread drunkenness. Opening hours of public houses were reduced in port and dock areas, there were local limits on the hours in which women could be served drink, sales of alcohol were forbidden to anyone under eighteen, treating and credit in pubs were banned, and public houses near crucial munitions plants at Enfield Lock, Carlisle and Gretna Green, and the naval bases at Inverness and Cromarty were nationalised.[117] These public houses were still under state-run in the Second World War and provided a form of control over the widespread problem of inebriation among seamen.

Offering an alternative on land to the temptations of drink, missions for seamen had been established since the late nineteenth century. Seamen's Missions and Homes were formed throughout the world to provide rivals to the public house and brothel. On shore the first of Aggie Weston's Sailors' Rests had been opened in 1875. 'Mother Weston' had first started her mission to seamen in 1873 by setting up a tea bar outside the dockyard gates at Plymouth, offering an alternative to the lure of the public house. In 1875 this was extended and became a hostel serving hot meals and providing accommodation at reasonable prices set so as to cover the actual costs rather than make a profit. The Sailor's Rest, intended as a home-from-home for her 'bluejackets', not only had cabins and a dining room, but also a hall that could be used for Bible classes, temperance meetings and social activities.[118] For most sailors it provided cheap and comfortable accommodation in port when they were far from home.

Seamen's homes and institutes in the major British ports offered similar services to seamen. The East London Missions to Seamen, founded in 1897, aimed to 'do all that they can for the pleasure and comfort of the men of the Navy and Merchant Service to whom we owe so much'.[119] The main building containing a concert hall, reading room, billiard room and officers' lounge was extended in 1943 with a new building housing four and six berth cabins, baths, showers and lavatories.[120] A free Christmas dinner was given to over 100 sailors in 1942 at 'a gala which began with an outstanding dinner and ended with a dance'.[121] The British Soldiers' and Sailors' Institute of Colombo, funded by the Government of Ceylon and the Ceylon Chamber of Commerce, provided a library, billiards, darts, chess and even fruit machines, as well as all 'the privileges of club life', to soldiers and sailors visiting Colombo.[122] While many institutes were indiscriminate in providing comforts for all sailors, some did make distinctions between ratings and officers. In Alexandria, there was a separate club for officers only because a mixed club was deemed 'unsatisfactory'.[123]

There was also disagreement within the Royal Navy about the extent to which men of the Merchant Navy should be allowed to use naval and NAAFI canteens. It was not until 1944 that this was officially sanctioned and it became the policy of the Admiralty to bring 'the Merchant Navy into the Naval orbit of welfare as far as was practicable'.[124] When requests were made for ENSA to lay on entertainment for the Merchant Navy in the United States, the immediate response was that 'there is a shortage of artistes for other and more pressing needs' and that the Royal Navy itself would object to 'the diversion of some of the entertainment provided for naval personnel to these Merchant Navy clubs'.[125] There were limits as to how far solidarity extended between the services.

Seamen's Missions also provided an effective social welfare network for the distressed merchant seaman. Barrow Sailors Home Mission, which in 1943–4 offered beds to 10,925 naval ratings and merchant seamen, supplied crews and individual seamen 'destitute through enemy action' with food and clothing.[126] Indeed, the crews of torpedoed merchant ships often had to depend on missions to seamen, charitable clothing depots, charities for the Merchant Navy, such as the Shipwrecked Mariner's Society, and the generosity of individuals for accommodation and clothing, rather than get relief state aid.[127] When the 134 survivors of *Aldegrove* arrived at Gibraltar in 1941, 'some of the men had to walk through the streets in bare feet', but the representative of the Ministry of War Transport had 'no funds at his disposal and could not do anything else for us other than put some of the men up at the Sailors' Home and some in a hotel'. The men had lost all their possessions, and replacement kit and 'clothing was very costly and very scarce'.[128] Public charitable support was all they could count upon.

The maintenance of morale amidst the monotony of naval service was considered vital. Much of that entertainment was provided by the men themselves on board ship where there were few opportunities or facilities for anything else but on land efforts were made to offer diversions, entertainments and sport, however variable in quality it may have been. Even physical training and organised sports were not so much to keep the sailor fit but to offer him amusement and a healthy activity that relieved stress. Some sporting activities and such fundraising initiatives for recreation as Warship Weeks also brought the sailor to the attention of the wider public. Public acclaim also boosted the mental health of the seaman as much as rest and recreation.

Chapter Ten
Neither Wives nor Sweethearts

Late one night in 1943 the quiet of the newly-established Royal Naval Sick Quarters Ferryville in Tunisia was disturbed by a ring on the doorbell. Frank Henley, the medical officer in charge, opened the door to find an abandoned market handcart containing the gore-soaked unconscious body of an American private with blood spurting from his neck. Henley and his sick berth attendants set to work to stem the bleeding and stitch him up without any anaesthetic and without the help of the absent duty surgeon. The next day they discovered that the American soldier had been stabbed when a Frenchman found him in bed with his wife. Henley then found the duty surgeon, John Hill of the Royal Marine Engineers, on a camp bed with his glamorous blonde girlfriend Andrea on the flat roof of the hospital. Henley tipped the camp bed and Hill over onto the concrete roof and told him of the 'most interesting exercise below', ignoring the exercises that had kept Hill preoccupied with Andrea on the roof above.[1] For young men abroad, even for naval surgeons who knew the risks to their health, the sin of sex was irresistible. Once ashore many a seaman sought a remedy for his 'night starvation' in the pleasures of the flesh whatever the consequences may have been.[2]

In wartime sexual recklessness had a distinctive glamour attached to it, and a devil-may-care attitude towards the risks of infection was alluring. Arthur McNalty, the Chief Medical Officer, had declared on the very day that Germany had attacked Poland in September 1939 that 'it is well known that a state of war favours the spread of venereal diseases and is an important cause of the wastage of manpower'.[3] War and syphilis seemed fated to be yoked together in a peculiar marriage of circumstances. Where there are young men away from home and a consequent loosening of morals, venereal disease is rarely far away amid 'a lack of self-control ... favoured by the excitement of war conditions'.[4]

In the Fleet Air Arm, in common with the Royal Air Force, 'the glamour of being a flying man ... appeals so much to the ladies', though even there it was admitted that the most efficient flight crews and units had the lowest incidence of disease and any rises were as much due to the fact that, as the war had gone on, 'the portals of recruiting have been opened wide to all and sundry'.[5] Even the square rig of the naval rating had its own allure. Tristan Jones on his way to the boys' training establishment HMS *Ganges* in 1940 was told by a soldier 'Well, matey, at least you'll be alright where crumpet's concerned. They go for the navy blokes a lot more than the army, see? Can't go wrong in your little old navy-blue suit, can you?'[6]

The offhand and casual attitude of sailors to sex in the Second World War was little different from that of their predecessors during the Great War, seeking pleasure from the immediate moment. Robert Goldrich, a 21-year-old First Lieutenant in charge of the sloop *Poppy*, had prided himself in 1917 that 'the powers of seduction are at a maximum' before embarking on a somewhat disastrous series of sexual encounters while on leave, including a night spent with 'a rather revolting wench' where his father 'tumbled that I had been on the batter', followed by 'a good turn on the beach' in Brighton and further brief encounters with 'very worthy bedfellows' as well as evenings on which he 'got rather canned before the bar closed but had a fair to middling evening'.[7] In the Second World War it was noted that 'alcohol increases desire and impairs judgement, so that a man becomes easy prey in the streets'.[8]

According to Hugh Philip there were two types of men who easily succumbed to sexual temptation and contracted a venereal disease, 'the old salt who is having his fourth or fifth infection' and tended to look upon his infection 'rather as he would a common cold', and the gauche, inexperienced youngster. The 'old salt' was the real danger to his younger messmates who would listen enrapt by tales of sexual prowess and exploits in exotic ports, wishing for nothing more than to emulate them. At the same time as being seduced by the glamour of sexual experience, the younger, virginal rating also felt an inferiority which 'only be allayed by some sexual experience of their own'. Even so it was only with the help of alcohol that 'their inhibitions and their discretion disappear and they are not particular where they satisfy their desires'.[9]

Brothels, often referred to as 'Bag Shanties', were a feature of most ports. When Harry Balfour's destroyer docked in Grimsby, the local vicar came aboard and 'presented me with a list of those houses which had a bad reputation for V.D. and those which were said to be better run' so that Balfour as medical officer could pass the advice on to the ship's company.[10] In Bombay, most of the brothels were officially prohibited except for one establishment for the exclusive use of officers, Madam Andree's, for which even the telephone number was in the official directory. Lieutenant Commander Alex Hughes only regretted that 'it is a pity that there isn't a similar establishment for the men – whose needs are just as great'.[11] In Malta the most notorious establishments in the Gut, 'the low centre of night life at Valletta, a solid row of saloons and brothels and dance halls', were officially prohibited but there was a venereal diseases clinic nearby.[12] Sailors would flock to the area, buy cheap sherry for the girls and 'shoot the rapids' on toboggan races down the steep slope of the Gut. When ships left Malta, 'the girls would miss us no doubt, so would the barman' in that perennial link of prostitution and alcohol.[13] Where prostitution was a problem, the authorities preferred to bring it under control despite not wishing to be seen to condone vice. It was only for political reasons that the notorious Berka brothel in Egypt was placed out of bounds to servicemen in December 1942 following a fight there between British, Australian and New Zealand troops; against a background of rising anti-British sentiment in Egypt, it was vital to stress the moral superiority of the imperial power.[14]

Whereas in Continental Europe there had long been a tradition of licensing brothels and regulating prostitution, the British armed forces were opposed to anything that smacked of licensed prostitution. The Contagious Diseases Acts of the 1860s regulating prostitution in naval ports and garrison towns had been short-lived, though regulation had continued in India and the colonies for a little longer than in Britain. However, toleration was sometimes necessary and during the Italian campaign of 1943–4, the question of regulating or repressing prostitution became a major issue at a time when many British soldiers and sailors were being infected not only in the brothels of the port of Naples but also by casual sexual encounters on 'the doorstep', some of the men being seduced by 'having bottles of wine thrust into their hands in broad daylight by these harpies or their agents'.[15] The American military authorities had accepted the situation and had permitted tolerated brothels to service their troops, but when infection rates soared they put these houses off-limits to their troops and took measures to suppress clandestine prostitution, which reduced the scale of the problem.[16] The British authorities were quick to appreciate this lesson and opposed the use of licensed prostitution for their own troops.[17] They preferred to offer more wholesome alternative attractions though even the singing of Gracie Fields, at that time one of the highest-earning entertainers in the world, at the opera house in Naples was to prove no distraction from the allure of the Neapolitan prostitute.[18]

During the German occupation of Ferryville, Tunisia, prostitution and venereal disease had been kept under tight control to ensure that no German soldier or sailor became infected. One of the three brothels, known familiarly as 'dame houses', was reserved for the exclusive use of the Germans and a second, not so well organised, for the use of the Italians. Disease was prevalent in the third brothel, mainly staffed by Arab prostitutes, for the use of everyone else. The French civil authorities were concerned that the town was now rife with 'amateur women' spreading infection since liberation in June 1943. They wanted two of the houses to be used solely by British and American forces, leaving the third once again for the French and the civilian population, although the brothels at that time were officially out of bounds to all the Allied forces. The American response to the proposal was to close all the brothels since 'President Roosevelt has stated that any man who has extra-marital sexual intercourse is not fit to be in the American forces'. Frank Henley, in charge of the Naval Sick Quarters in Ferryville, reported this decision to the captain superintendent of the Ferryville dockyard with a note that he had only found three of the twenty prostitutes in the dame house to be clean of infection during his medical examination of them. The report was forwarded to Admiral Dickens, who signalled Henley asking for the names of those three girls.[19] Philip Hugh had a similarly relaxed view on licensed houses being 'sure it will be found of value not only in the prevention of disease but also in maintaining the morale of the men'.[20]

For the sailor on leave in the United Kingdom but away from his family there were irresistible temptations. Prostitutes, nicknamed

'Piccadilly Warriors', were to be seen much more in Central London in the blackout than they had been before the war. In Soho two members of the Public Morality Council were shocked to be solicited at midnight by thirty-five women within little more than 100 yards. Even at 4 a.m. there were still seven women peddling their wares. In the darkness of the blackout, the police paid them little attention unless they were involved, as they frequently were, in fights between their customers.[21] Even the worst of the Blitz did not have a serious effect on prostitution and perhaps even added for the customers a certain frisson of risk of death from bombs to the lure of the socially frowned-upon. Even those prostitutes who did leave London for safer areas at the height of the bombing had returned by 1942.[22] In many areas of the capital they were becoming 'more bold', behaviour that was seen as 'an unavoidable consequence of the blackout'.[23] At St Mary's Hospital in the heart of the red-light district near Paddington Station, student nurses would entertain themselves when they had any free moments during the day by observing the rapid turnover of business among the prostitutes in the rooms above the shops opposite the hospital.[24]

It was not only prostitutes who were preying on young sailors on leave and in the ports. Just as dangerous were 'young girls out for a good time'.[25] Taking a break from their arduous war work in munitions factories, as land girls or in one of the women's forces, including the WRNS, these young women, already released from parental control as a result of wartime conditions, wanted a bit of fun with young men. This was a reflection of the situation in the First World War when it was claimed that 'a bad and diseased woman can do more harm than any German fleet of aircraft that has yet passed over London'.[26] Now, again it was most often that the sailor caught an infection from 'the amateur, the prostitute is much less commonly responsible'.[27]

Sailors and other servicemen on leave were warned of the dangers posed by loose women by posters displayed in railway stations and public conveniences, where their warnings might be considered to be most timely.[28] They were humorously alerted 'that's Phyllis' if they were to see a provocatively-dressed siren passing by.[29] Smaller advertisements were placed in the newspapers on such subjects as 'ten plain facts about venereal diseases'.[30] The Ministry of Information also produced a 20-minute documentary, 'Subject for Discussion', which drew attention to the dangers and consequences of syphilis.[31] This public information campaign of 1943 breached the taboo on mentioning such things in the press and on the radio, but propriety ensured that euphemisms and scientific terminology were used in place of the more popularly understood terms such as 'the pox' and 'the clap'.[32]

Legislation was also needed to tackle the problem of venereal diseases. Similar measures had been taken during the Great War when on 22 March 1918 Regulation 40D under the Defence of the Realm Act came into force, decreeing that 'no woman who is suffering from venereal disease in a communicable form shall have sexual intercourse with any member of His Majesty's forces, or solicit or invite any member of His Majesty's forces to have sexual intercourse with her'.[33] The penalty was six months' imprisonment, or a swingeing fine of £100. This had provoked an immediate outcry against a measure that, because it was specifically aimed at women, could be seen as 'making vice safe for men', although the Home Office and War Office both preferred to see it as a regulation 'to keep the realm safe by stamping out centres of infection which injure the fighting capacity of the nation'.[34] As catching a venereal disease was classed under military law as a self-inflicted injury, it could be argued that sailors and soldiers were already liable for punishment and did not need to be brought under Regulation 40D. The Second World War regulations were to be less punitive and less concerned about regulating the conduct of women. Nonetheless, they were to be equally controversial.

Now Regulation 33B under the Defence Regulation Act of November 1943 made it compulsory for all doctors treating any patient with syphilis or gonorrhoea to notify the medical officer of health for the county or county borough, together with details of any sexual contacts from whom the sufferer may have contracted the disease or to whom it may have been passed. If the patient twice refused the treatment offered or declined to name his or her sexual contacts, the medical officer of health could enforce compulsory treatment.[35] Many members of the medical profession deplored this new element of compulsion in the regulation, even if it was 'to bring under medical care those infected persons who have shown themselves unresponsive to education, work or to methods of treatment and who, owing to this refusal to undertake treatment, remain a constant source of danger to the health of the community and a drain on the man-power and woman-power of the nation in its war effort'.[36] Compulsory tracing of contacts proved more difficult than expected, especially when the movements of sailors took them to many ports.

Such a scheme of compulsory notification and treatment had been widely advocated before the war, but compulsion was generally viewed as an unacceptable infringement of individual liberty and notification a threat to the very anonymity upon which the existing system of clinics was based. Most doctors deemed it more effective to have a voluntary system, where treatment was sought at an early stage by the patient and the case could be followed up much more easily. Any compulsory system of notification might deter people from seeking treatment until it was unavoidable, just as servicemen, who had deductions made from their pay if they reported sick with a venereal infection, were likely to cover up their disease or resort to private medical practitioners and be outside the control of the naval medical system.[37]

In the Royal Navy, during the First World War the practice of issuing 'dreadnought packets', containing calomel for syphilis, potassium permanganate for gonorrhoea and cotton wool swabs for applying them to the penis, to sailors going ashore was believed to encourage 'the ignorant class' to 'assume that sexual indulgence is a necessity and plunge in to it dragging other hesitant youths with them'.[38] The much more pragmatic German navy had even introduced vending machines issuing prophylactic packets to those of its sailors not wishing to seek disinfection from a medical officer. How useful such self-disinfection could be was arguable, but disinfection processes continued to be used in the Second World War.

Ashore, a man fearful of having caught an infection could visit, if he could find one as they were well-hidden, a Green Cross Chamber, a disinfection facility set up in the ports and big cities for all servicemen, offering a procedure that was unpleasant, painful, undignified and not particularly effective. Such ablution chambers, at one time known as 'Blue Lamp Depots', on account of the blue lights they used to advertise their location at night, were first set up during the Great War.[39] These places were so uninviting that they were hardly ever used and were no more popular than they had been in the last war. Having urinated in gushes, the unfortunate sailor would then wash his penis, scrotum and lower abdomen, sponging them with potassium permanganate and perchloride of mercury. An orderly next injected another disinfectant into the urethra and a calomel cream was rubbed into the genitals.[40]

Aboard ship the facilities for self-disinfection were perhaps just as unattractive. On HMS *Hood* there was no room for a prophylactic ablution cabinet in the main heads, and the men were very reluctant to use the one attached to the sick bay for prophylactic irrigation because they did not wish to be observed by the medical officer, so instead it was decided to build one next to the night heads on the battery deck, where it 'should be useful, as it is easy of access to all men coming off from shore'.[41]

The arsenical compound salvarsan, first developed by Paul Ehrlich in 1909, continued to be the standard treatment where syphilis had been diagnosed and the infected man confined to the Rose Cottage, the mess deck reserved for them. For sufferers from gonorrhoea, there was a new form of treatment with the sulphonamide drugs developed in the late 1930s. However, during the war gonorrhoea was showing signs of becoming resistant to the sulphonamide drugs.[42] There was also a danger that men could get jaundice if the syringes used to inject them with salvarsan were inadequately sterilised between injections, a problem exacerbated by the rising number of VD patients at a time when new syringes were in short supply and there was too little time to disinfect them between patients. For the navy this represented a severe loss of manpower and also stirred up unrest and discontent among the patients who had expected to be cured of their illness, not to be given another. At first it was thought that the bulk preparation of the neoarsphenamine used in solution for speedy administration onboard ship might be encouraging toxicity as the sterilised water used in the preparation at the Royal Naval Hospital Chatham was found to have a high chlorine content that might react with the arsenical preparation to cause the jaundice. However, abandoning this procedure had little effect. Attention now turned to the syringes and needles being used and there was also a suspicion that storage and refrigeration of the salvarsan might be at fault. The navy also instituted new routines whereby each syringe and needle was carefully cleaned after use and then boiled for 15 minutes before being used again.[43]

More effective than cure was prevention through the issuing of condoms to men going on leave although few bothered to wear them.[44] The medical officer on *Hood* offered free contraceptives and warned the men that failing to take advantage of this would be 'really against your finer judgement and the best interests of the service. It is well known that for protection the soccer player wears shin guards, the cricketer, large pads and gloves'.[45] However, the venereologist Gerard McElligott considered the condom to be 'a two-edged sword' anyway, since it could 'easily engender a false sense of security and, like the schoolboy's half-crown, is apt to burn a hole in the pocket until it is used'.[46] Most careless ordinary sailors just paid for a whore and got drunk without taking any precautions.

Moral persuasion was used to try to make men with venereal diseases feel guilty. Men infected with syphilis were now represented as unpatriotic, bad comrades and as having inadequate personalities. Rather than being the reckless, dashing blade of the past, the sufferer from syphilis was increasingly viewed by doctors and psychiatrists as neurotic, unstable, self-centred and something of a wimp, likely to put personal comfort before his duty to country and comrades.[47] The manly serviceman and civilian was now the one who had the self-control and good sense to take precautions against catching something nasty. It was 'the man to whom reason does not appeal – the rather stupid sensual fellow who indulges most of his appetites' who was most likely to betray his comrades by getting himself infected.[48]

Hugh Philip believed that the venereal diseases lectures of the ship's surgeon could be an effective way of getting such messages across to the company and that 'prevention is, to my mind, fairly simple'. The medical officer should encourage the men to take an interest in other sports and forms of entertainment when ashore to keep them occupied rather than threaten them with the dire consequences of promiscuity: '"Thou shalt not," not only irritates a large proportion of the men, but is a challenge to seek stolen fruit'.[49] Neither must the medical officer preach, but should instead demystify sexual experience and combat ignorance: 'Point out the senselessness of abusing something so fundamentally beautiful and selective, and last but not least remove the bogy of the fear of masturbation. This fear is very prevalent and is not the least of the reasons for the young man's desire for the real thing.'[50]

At sea men were deprived of the company of women. Where abstinence was no longer possible, they needed to find satisfaction for their sexual urges. Peter McCrae had an amusing anecdote about the effects of night starvation on one particular sailor that seems to have done its rounds among many ships:

> The lack of females gets everyone down and there has been a case of an assault on a sheep by some fiery matelot – his excuse was that he thought the thing was a Wren in a duffel coat. The trouble now is that there's a free fight if any sod is foolish enough to go up to the fore of the ship and 'baah' at him.[51]

Masturbation provided an outlet for some men. Others turned to their shipmates. Homosexuality could even be seen as a subject for a joke. When Frank Henley asked his servant to bend down to retrieve a shaving brush that he had dropped between the wall and the bath when he came across the man doing laundry in the shower room, wearing only a towel around his waist, Marine Mason's response was quick-witted: 'He looked at me, smiled, tightened his towel around his waist: 'What sir, after twenty years in the navy? Not bloody likely.'[52]

Other seamen did not see homosexuality as a cause for amusement, though they accepted it as a feature of sea life as much as Marine Mason did. Able Seaman I G Hall on HMS *Glasgow* commented that 'I say nothing of the purely voluntary and clandestine arrangement between two parties, which perhaps harms no one. The attempt at forced compulsion and endeavour to take advantage of a person under the influence of drink is different.'[53] Predatory behaviour rather than the act of sex itself was seen as unacceptable. In the Great War a naval chief petty officer pointed out that 'sodomy in the navy is by no means as rare a practice as is believed. The guilty persons are usually long service petty officers who terrorise new and fair boys into submission.'[54] Nothing was done to stamp out this particular abuse, although homosexuality was illegal and could have been prosecuted under existing laws. It was dealt with severely by court martial. A confidential fleet order of April 1940 reminded medical officers of the penalties for 'unnatural offences', but they continued notwithstanding.[55] Robert Herriman, the surgeon on *Berwick*, had the unsavoury task of examining two men being court-martialled for sodomy, and found 'spermatozoa in specimens from the anal canal and shirt of the passive agent'.[56]

A greater crime than contracting a sexually-transmissible disease was covering it up. But hospital stoppages of 10d a day for men and 4d a day for boys after 30 days in hospital if their 'disease is due to misconduct, carelessness or neglect' were a disincentive to reporting venereal infections to the ship's medical officer.[57] Sheldon Dudley, Medical Director General, was convinced that using 'such stoppages as a penalty has no deterrent influence' and favoured their abolition since 'there is no reliable evidence of any sort that penalties for contracting venereal disease have ever had any result, except to increase the number of men who attempt to conceal their disease'.[58] However, more conservative opinion in the Admiralty was in favour of retaining the stoppages, especially since only a small proportion of venereal diseases cases were actually sent to hospital.[59] Most were treated while on duty. The proposal of the Air Ministry to abolish hospital stoppages because men who went untreated could be a danger to themselves, their aircrew and their aircraft was dismissed on the grounds that such a course of action would 'condone the contraction of this disease'. The opinion of the Admiralty was that 'it seems perfectly reasonable that if a man contracts a disease through his own misconduct, carelessness or neglect, and thus incapacitates himself for naval service, he should not receive, while undergoing the necessary treatment, the same rate of pay as a fit man who is doing his job'.[60]

Penicillin was to revolutionise approaches to venereal disease throughout the world. The great breakthrough in establishing the very remarkable impact that the drug was to have on syphilis came when a young American sailor volunteered to act as a guinea pig to test the new, as-yet experimental and untried drug. The trials were conducted by John Mahoney, director of the United States Marine Hospital and Venereal Disease Research Laboratory at Staten Island, New York. He and his colleagues were studying the effect of penicillin derived from mould grown in their own laboratory on sulphonamide-resistant strains of gonorrhoea. Not really expecting any great results, they had decided to try it out on lesions in rabbits infected with syphilis. In March 1943 Mahoney had already unsuccessfully tested penicillin on the bacteria causing the infection in a test tube. Harry Eagle at Johns Hopkins University School of Medicine had similarly shown that penicillin was useless against the spirochaetes *in vitro*,[61] so it was with no great hope that Mahoney's colleague Richard Arnold now injected a large dose of penicillin into a syphilitic rabbit. Mahoney had insisted that the experiment should go ahead, and a few hours later, Arnold returned to check the condition of the diseased animal and to his surprise found that most of the spirochaetes had disappeared from its ulcers. His chief was equally surprised and later commented that 'we very nearly missed the boat'.[62] At once he and his team repeated the experiment on other rabbits and, over and over again, found that the infection cleared up within some twelve hours. This encouraged them to use properly-manufactured penicillin on a patient, confident that at long last they might have truly found the magic bullet against syphilis that the German scientist Paul Ehrlich had been seeking at the beginning of the twentieth century.

Catching a sexually-transmissible infection could be traumatic for a young sailor and worth volunteering for anything in order to be cured, although volunteering for something new could be just as foolhardy as catching a venereal disease in the first place. The rash young sailor was admitted to the United States Marine Hospital and Venereal Disease Research Laboratory at Staten Island, New York, in June 1943 suffering from syphilis and perhaps foolhardily he answered the call for a volunteer for a clinical trial. Every four hours for the next eight days he had 25,000 units of penicillin intramuscularly injected into him, a total of 1,200,000 units. After only four hours, there was very little trace of the spirochaetes in his blood or ulcer and by the fifteenth day of his treatment Wassermann tests showed him to be free of the disease. The effect was unprecedented and almost miraculous. Within four months of receiving his first injection of penicillin, the young man was found to be completely free from infection and could be declared cured.[63] It was not a fluke. Three other young sailors were treated in exactly the same way and cured just as quickly. Despite such encouraging results, Mahoney necessarily remained cautious in warning that a much longer observation of patients would be needed to make sure that none of them relapsed, since syphilis had a tendency to recur after periods of remission from the symptoms. However, he and his colleagues, as well as other doctors, reported good follow-up results, which confirmed the initial promise of penicillin.[64]

After this initial success in treating the young patient at the Staten Island Marine Hospital, the United States Public Health Service studied the effects of penicillin on patients in the Coast Guard but rejected any massive use on merchant seamen, because 'the study has been largely experimental and in order to evaluate the results the selected cases must be among patients who can be followed'.[65] Naval patients would have been better subjects.

The Royal Navy was quick to seize on the potential of penicillin for treating venereal diseases although insistent on 'proper serological control'.[66] The breakthrough had come during the North African and Italian campaigns of 1943 when more servicemen were out of action as a result of venereal infections than from wounds.[67] Clinical trials of penicillin by Professor Howard Florey of the Sir William Dunn School of Pathology at the University of Oxford and Hugh Cairns, consulting neurosurgeon to the army, in North Africa in August 1943 had shown that penicillin could cure cases of gonorrhoea within twelve hours of treatment.[68] If the scarce drug were to be used on gonorrhoea, the manpower crisis might be solved, whereas if it were used on wounds, there would still be a lengthy period in which healing and rehabilitation took place, even after the infection had cleared, before the troops could return to their units. From a naval and military point of view it made sense to use penicillin on venereal cases, especially once its effect on syphilis was realised, but the political reaction if it ever got out that penicillin was being used to treat sexually-acquired infections rather than the wounds of war heroes could have had serious repercussions. The prime minister Winston Churchill resolved the matter with his decision that that 'this valuable drug must on no account be wasted. It must be used to the best military advantage.'[69] This memo, scrawled in green ink, sounded good, but what did it actually mean? Should it be used on severe battlefield casualties, for more minor wounds and infections, which might heal when the infection had cleared, or to treat cases of VD among the armed forces? It was quickly decided that penicillin should be prioritised for the treatment of venereal infections. Men could be got back into action much more quickly, in more ways than one!

Penicillin quickly became the normal treatment for both syphilis and gonorrhoea. After a fairly painful series of intramuscular injections over a period of twenty-four hours, the discharge from gonorrhoea could be 'turned off like a tap'. Syphilis too could now effectively be treated in about eight days with intramuscular injections of penicillin, compared with the 40–50 days needed with the old treatment with arsenical drugs and bismuth.[70] It was a revolution in the treatment of sexually-transmissible diseases. Sheldon Dudley saw immense advantages for the navy:

> It means that if a man reports in the sick bay at 8 o'clock in the morning, he will be discharged to duty at 4 o'clock on the same afternoon. He is thus treated and cured in his own ship or place of duty within the working hours of one day. Seeing that before the war it took on the average of about 50 days to cure a patient suffering from gonorrhoea, the economy in man hours and sick beds is overwhelming. The special benefits of a course of penicillin injections which does not extend over a night is the avoidance of all hospitalization, a resulting economy in night duty staff, ambulance transport, bedding, paperwork, and delay in starting treatment, besides the often unavoidable delay and difficulty in getting a man in and out of hospital from or to his ship. In future gonorrhoea should cause far less trouble and disability in the Royal Navy than the common cold.[71]

In the treatment of venereal infections and the sphere of sexual health, penicillin had achieved the key naval medical objective of keeping men fit for action.

Chapter Eleven
A Bloody War

Preventative medicine may have been at the heart of naval health and fitness, but many naval doctors were eager to see action rather than the suffer the inertia of their usual life at sea. When they did experience the horrors of modern warfare it was often a shock to them:

> A feeling almost of panic overtakes one, and the question how and where to begin is not easily settled. Lights are out, wounded are crawling about in dark corners, cries from help come from the bottom of ladders, where twisted and torn metal makes investigations terribly difficult and urgent requests for the doctor arrive from several points of the ship at the same time. These are some of the difficulties that make one's medical training a handicap rather than an asset.[1]

However impotent the young inexperienced medical officer may have felt when faced with the reality of battle, there were guidelines he was expected to follow in preparing for action stations. It was also assumed that he would familiarise himself with the construction of the ship, especially the positions of the main bulkheads, hatches and watertight doors, fresh-water tanks and main ventilation trunks.

A failure on the part of a medical officer to understand the layout and working of his ship could endanger everyone. Within a few days of taking up his post on a ship and in his first experience of warfare, a tyro young officer had left his distributing station below the waterline to see for himself what was happening on deck. Stunned by the noise of enemy torpedo bombers and choked by the fumes, he began to grope his way back to the distributing station but could not remember the way. As he travelled the length of the ship, he opened but did not close watertight doors that should have been closed. Completely untrained in naval matters and with minimal medical experience, he only narrowly escaped severe disciplinary measures. His unthinking inexperience could have jeopardised the survival of his ship and the lives of his crewmates.[2]

In the early days of the war, the peacetime regulations for a centralised medical organisation of the ship during action continued to be followed, although its inadequacies were quickly realised. The sick bay was usually in the upper part of the ship to take advantage of natural light and ventilation, but such an exposed position was vulnerable during action and the existing sick would be moved to a more protected location in a distributing station deep in the ship to which casualties would be brought for first aid. On *Exeter*, at the battle of the River Plate a shell 'went clean through the sick bay, through where the heads were, removing all the bedpans and the bath'.[3] The reliance on less-vulnerable distributing stations was an arrangement which had been common during the Great War when 'the fore dressing station is below the main deck and is surrounded by nine inches of armour'.[4] Since 'no part of the ship is immune from damage', it was important that the ratings as well as the medical officer should be on the lookout for suitable places to accommodate the wounded.[5] Then when the action was over, the sick bay would revert to its original function and the wounded would receive treatment. If the sick bay was no longer serviceable, another space would be found on an upper deck where the casualties could be dealt with more methodically. In most cases the wounded would be put to bed and made as comfortable as possible in a situation where 'the cigarette is almost as valuable as the injection – indeed it is sought for before anything else, except in those cases of extreme shock, where all interest and even life have practically gone'.[6] The problem with a centralised distributing station was that it was often inaccessible and inadequately fitted-out.[7]

At Narvik in April 1940 there were a large number of casualties when the destroyer *Hotspur* suffered damage from a heavy concentration of fire. The wounded were removed from the more dangerous positions, collected on deck, laid down in the passages and administered with morphia to relieve the pain. There was nowhere else to leave them because 'the supply of ammunition to the after guns prevented the use of the wardroom or of the captain's cabin'. Once the ship was clear of the enemy, the wounded were transferred to the wardroom but before any operations could be undertaken it was realised that *Hotspur* was so badly damaged as to be in danger of sinking and the casualties were carried back on deck and then transferred by boat to HMS *Hostile*.[8]

By 1942, it was recognised that the traditional centralised arrangements for the reception of casualties was inadequate on larger ships and that it would be better to introduce a more flexible system allowing for a wider dispersal of doctors, sick berth attendants and equipment. Enemy attacks, especially aerial bombardments, could last for several hours and it was not always easy to get the wounded to the distributing station quickly. Haversacks containing field dressings and other first aid supplies were distributed around the ship such as at gun stations and in the engine room where they might be most needed, but it was not always easy in battle for the wounded to receive any attention from their fellow sailors who had their own combat duties to carry out. New regulations turned the distributing station into a satellite sick bay fitted to accommodate the wounded for a considerable time and even to allow for emergency operations. This area was not only to offer more space for treatment but was also to be more accessible with easy access for stretcher cases instead of manhandling these through narrow passages, hatchways and manholes. The Neil Robertson stretcher was invaluable in tight spaces where it was impossible to use a regular stretcher: a semi-rigid canvas cover, supported by bamboo slats and secured with buckled straps, wrapped firmly around the patient and allowed for free movement yet kept the injured man rigid. Auxiliary distributing stations were also to be set up on mess decks, laundries or storerooms at the other end of the ship in case the main one was put out of operation.[9]

First aid posts were also to be established around the ship, usually port, starboard, fore and aft in cruisers, but in more than four locations on larger ships. Suitable areas included crew spaces, the captain's quarters, gun room, bathrooms, recreation areas and even wide lobbies.[10] Each first aid post was to be manned by a medical officer, sick berth attendant or trained first aider assisted by a rating. The senior medical officer was to move from post to post as needed. During lulls in fighting, the wounded were to be taken to the nearest first aid post for treatment, but only once the action was over could stretcher parties remove them to the sick berth or distributing station for more than emergency treatment.[11] On the anti-aircraft ship *Palomares* there were two first aid posts, the forward one in the wardroom and the after one in the stewards' mess. The first aid post in the wardroom was manned by the principal sick berth attendant and four stretcher bearers trained in first aid. Locked away in the wardroom were as many surgical instruments, drugs and dressings as could be spared from the sick bay in case the distributing station was put out of action. The other post in the stewards' mess merely had a box of first aid gear and two Neil Robertson stretchers and was manned by four stretcher bearers.[12] On the battleship *Resolution* a store on the stokers' mess deck was turned into an operating theatre because it was 'sufficiently remote from noises to promote confidence, not only to the team but to the patients'.[13]

On smaller ships, the medical officer was expected to stay at his post unless urgently summoned to another part of the ship to free a casualty pinned down by damage to the structure of the ship or to treat a wounded officer unable to leave his post. His duties were to administer first aid to the injured and 'by his manner of so doing, to reinforce the courage of the seriously wounded and re-establish the morale of those who may be more frightened than hurt'.[14] In such circumstances it was all too easy for mistakes to be made in diagnosis. A small flesh wound in the scalp could easily be overlooked if the patient were feeling fit, but that wound might conceal compound fractures of the skull with retained bomb or ship fragments embedded.[15] In moving around the ship the surgeon himself could become a casualty. It was thought that Surgeon Lieutenant James Macfarlane had been blown over the side of *Achates* as he travelled between the first aid stations he had established at either end of the sinking ship on 31 December 1942.[16] With little more than advanced first aid possible, 'even if there are medical officers left to deal with the situation', it was perhaps complacently considered 'fortunate that at sea we do not experience such gross contamination of the wounds as is the lot of our brethren ashore'.[17]

Generally, during action, whatever the size of the ship, the doctor confined himself to the debridement of wounds, suturing, and life support using blood and plasma. Dale L Groom, an American naval doctor who had recently qualified from the University of Chicago, later reflected on his role on D-Day, and mused that 'I have often been asked how much of my medical education I got to use, and my answer to that is damned little. I didn't have much equipment. I was just doing glorified first aid.'[18] The Royal Naval medical officer's role in providing little more than first aid was shown by the overalls he was advised to wear at action stations with large pockets for field dressings, a bottle of morphine sulphate, a length of rubber tubing to use as a tourniquet and some labels. Pinned to his chest would be a syringe, while a pair of scissors and two artery forceps would be tied to his belt. It was all so that he could easily find the essentials he needed for treatment in the darkness and confusion of battle.[19]

The confusion in battle was no different from that experienced by the medical officer of the Great War, a reflection of how little the doctor's experience of battle had changed in over twenty years. At the battle of Jutland in May 1916, 'all the tiresome awaiting of action had been there but usage had probably dimmed the sense of actuality' for the men on *Warspite*, but when the combat started 'the whole action seemed like an exaggerated battle practice and men were busy with their work and possibly a little curious as to what was happening outside their vision', even as 'the enemy hits could be felt like hammer strikes against the ship's sides'. Stretcher parties brought the men down to the dressing station, the chaplains took charge of first aid on the battery deck, officers had had training in bandaging and the application of tourniquets came from a surgeon who had 'experience in lecturing to railwaymen' on first aid, and once men reached the operating table they were stripped and thoroughly examined for any additional injuries, since often 'only one occupies his whole attention and then he is apt to think he has no other'.[20] Such features of emergency medicine were the same in both wars.

Responsibility for first aid was not just the concern of the medical officer or sick berth attendant. A minimum of 10 per cent of the ship's company was expected be trained in first aid, if indeed not all the officers and men. Ratings too were reminded that they had a role to play and 'it must be rubbed in to each member of the ship's company that he must not be too dependent upon organised first aid parties and that, as the man on the spot, he is responsible for knowing how to cope with his own and his shipmates' wounds'. He should be aware of the haversacks and later metal buckets containing essential first aid kit. The ship's surgeon would also deliver formal lectures and refresher courses on first aid, enlivening them with photos, quizzes and diagrams, with which important features could be 'marked on photographs of attractive female nudes'.[21] How much a rating actually could do when facing the enemy was not considered.

Emergency surgery on board ship often was chaotic and demanding. In the midst of battle, 'the crump of bombs, the rattle of splinters against the ship's side and the noise of our own guns, were not conducive to the steady hand' on the operating table.[22] The official advice was that:

> During action conditions in the operating theatre are such that no serious surgical work can be attempted; the traditional silence is replaced by a confusing medley of sound – the roar of salvoes and shattering detonations as the ship gives and receives punishment, the din of Fire Parties clearing burning debris and Repair Parties shoring up the bulkheads and fixing temporary lighting between decks. There are the added discomfort of fumes, smoke and water, and the ship's evolutions will increase the extent and frequency of her roll and pitch.[23]

During the battle of the River Plate, Surgeon Lieutenant Hunter regretted not carrying out more surgery on the day of the engagement but had expected that there would be further action immediately and 'I did not wish to be doing major surgery if we had to abandon ship'.[24] Sometimes there was no choice but to operate. Jack Coulter recalled:

> The whole operating theatre swaying, shuddering and tilting as the ship zigzags in her course; instruments, doctors and even the patient sliding about; the haze of smoke everywhere; the lights suddenly going out; above all the deafening wall of noise … noise which is so intense that you get punch drunk with it, and then that inward fear, which every normal sailor feels, that at any moment the ship may be hit and start to sink.[25]

HMS *Belfast* had a fairly well-equipped operating theatre and sick berth that was only used for emergencies because of the vibration and movement of the ship. During the Normandy landings, casualties from the beaches and other ships were 'rapidly evacuated to the sick bay by first aid parties'. They were given blood transfusions using the latest in transfusion equipment; which 'was found extremely useful'.[26]

An operation was carried out on a 21-year-old rating, J W Keats, hit in the thigh and buttock by fragments of shell and pieces of iron while in the crow's nest of *Palomares* on convoy from Iceland to Archangel in July 1942. The senior sick berth attendant and a leading seaman had to climb up to the crow's nest in which Keats was jammed to lower him down a line to a Neil Robertson stretcher: 'the patient was conscious and not feeling any pain but at times he fainted on the way down from the crow's nest'. The young man was suffering from shock and was kept warm with blankets and a hot water bottle. His trousers and underpants were cut away to reveal that 'the amount of tissue lost corresponded to about the size of a soccer football'. Surgery was essential, though 'this operation was carried out during action with the lighting and operating table constantly being shaken by our own gunfire'. The surgeon was impressed by the progress made by Keats after this operation and 'with prolonged rehabilitation treatment comprised mostly of physiotherapeutic measures ... I see no reason why his leg should not be restored to normal function in every way'.[27] Had he not been operated on swiftly despite the adverse conditions, Keats may not have had such a successful outcome.

Ransome Wallis, serving on the destroyer *Martin* escorting a convoy to Russia in 1942, found that 'it was nearly impossible to do anything very much in the surgical sense whilst the ship was in action; there was far too much row going on to concentrate'.[28] He found it particularly distressing when he was unable to assist the badly wounded:

> I could not help wondering if I were falling short of what was required. If he lived, the boy with the broken back would end his days in a wheel chair; the deeply unconscious man required brain surgery in the ordered quiet and efficiency of an operating theatre in some great teaching hospital with a team of surgeons, anaesthetists and skilled nursing staff, so different from a stretcher bed on the deck of my cabin in a lurching and heaving destroyer with all the row of gunfire, depth charges and the clanging on the hull as bombs exploded in the sea.[29]

When conditions were more conducive for surgery, Ransome Wallis collected his instruments for sterilizing and boiled an electric kettle. Before getting down to work, he thought that a shave might reinvigorate him for his duties but promptly fell asleep over his shaving basin of hot water.[30] Roger Lancashire felt equally inadequate when dealing with casualties on *Exeter* during the battle of the River Plate in December 1939: 'there were cases where, if I'd had the facilities and an endless supply of blood transfusions, things might have been different, but it wasn't like that'. Instead he was distressed by the death in his arms of 'people who I'd been living with, as it were, for three years'.[31]

Hugh Philip worried about whether or not he should operate on a suspected case of acute appendicitis or wait to get the man to a hospital ship. If the man were only suffering from constipation then it would be dangerous to operate on a healthy abdomen in unhealthy conditions, but if the appendix burst while the ship was in stormy weather and an operation was impossible the consequences could be worse. A makeshift theatre was improvised in the wardroom with a white tablecloth draped over the table; the surgeon wore a clean shirt and his football shorts, while cockroaches crawled on the ceiling. It was Philip's first appendectomy though he did not admit that to the patient, who was found to have an impacted stone and for whom surgery had indeed been essential.[32]

The wounds that the medical officer could be called upon to deal with were often horrendous. One medical officer whose ship had been struck by a magnetic mine was shocked by what he saw:

> A sight of indescribable horror met me. Men were cut in two, scalped, internal viscera strewn about and intestines wrapped around the mast which was visible when I looked up through a large hole in the upper deck. I had three seamen with me when we suddenly noticed a messdeck hatch covered with debris. We worked with frantic haste to uncover the hatch and managed to open it to be greeted by a voice from below. By the aid of a hammock rope I got down with a torch. I landed knee deep in a mixture of oil and water on an insecure deck, which had been torn away from the rest of the ship. I found seven injured stokers and we got them up through the hatch. I then found an eighth. This was a man who had slept with his lifebelt inflated

and had been concussed by the explosion, but otherwise unhurt. His life was probably saved by his head being kept above water and oil by his lifebelt. We got him out. By this time I was up to my hips in the rising oil and water and the ship was lurching. I found the darkness and the silence, broken only by an occasional splash, uncanny and terrifying. I hurriedly looked round for the last time and could only see here and there signs of quivering protoplasm as the only evidences of life in its last throes. I left as quickly as possible and secured the hatch.[33]

Where treatment was possible, the ship's surgeon had to work under difficult conditions. Maurice Hood jumped from his destroyer *Obdurate* in half a gale on to *Northern Gem* to operate on the wounded from *Achates* in December 1942 in the battle of the Barents Sea. Both ships were iced up. Held securely by two ratings he worked for thirty hours probing wounds for shrapnel, shaving heads with a razor to stop infection, setting limbs and treating minor injuries. The skipper of *Northern Gem* was impressed by his endurance, skill and steady hand, commenting that 'I have been going to sea for 17 years and I would never attempt to use a cut-throat razor when a ship is rolling'.[34]

The injuries caused by different forms of attack were distinctive and it was said that a study of the injuries reported would be enough to tell the experienced observer what had happened to that particular ship. On ships hit by magnetic mines, fractures in the lower body were common, especially leg and thigh fractures. The blast of a bomb or shell between decks would kill anyone within 20ft of the hit, often disintegrating the body, but only causing slight injuries or concussion among those sailors further away. Intensive bombing lowered morale and resulted in wounds from bomb splinters and burns. Men were advised to wear anti-flash gear but often failed to obey such instructions and burns were most frequent when men were scantily clad and only wearing shorts. Surgeon Lieutenant Hunter regretted that he had failed 'to visualise the burns that a high explosive shell may cause from flash' and had no solutions of tannic acid prepared for immediate use during the battle of the River Plate.[35] Shellfire caused all too familiar bullet wounds. Penetrating chest wounds would result in air being sucked into the chest and were accompanied by fractured ribs and internal bleeding. Fractures caused by men being thrown down predominated among the victims of torpedo attacks.[36]

Frank Henley was asleep in his bunk on the cruiser *Argonaut* when the ship was torpedoed in December 1942 and woke to find his cabin wrecked with his books and clothes scattered over a flooding deck and to look up to see that 'the dark blue sky of a Mediterranean dawn greeted me through what was once the quarterdeck'. He came across a warrant electrical engineer wearing only his vest and underpants whose last memory was of bending down to put on a sock before being blown from his cabin to the quarterdeck. Henley only realised that he himself was concussed when a marine asked him when he was going to stitch his head and he could not remember having earlier put a dressing on the man's scalp and promising to stitch it up later. Later when he asked people 'what the ship felt like at the time of the impact of the two torpedoes ... they just looked vacant and thought I had gone round the bend'.[37]

Non-swimmers were especially vulnerable when a ship was sunk, yet though 'it seems incredible that non-swimmers should ever go to sea in wartime' it was often the case that such men existed in 'most ships'.[38] There were dangers even in port for non-swimmers, such as 21-year-old Arthur Wood, who fell overboard to his death from *Renown* during the blackout in November 1940.[39] At sea it was even more perilous. When the aircraft carrier *Courageous* was torpedoed in September 1939, three men of the Royal Naval Fleet Reserve remained standing at the rails of the quarterdeck after the order had been given to abandon ship because they were unable to swim. Charles Lamb attempted to take one of them to the safety of a nearby destroyer: 'the man was wearing yellow braces and I clutched him by these, but was unable to prevent him from putting his face into the sea and making burbling noises'. The man was dead by the time they reached the destroyer, causing Lamb to feel 'angry with the Admiralty for dragging these old pensioners back to sea' since the man was 'just too old for the shock of the last twenty minutes'.[40] Even the strongest of swimmers were warned that when it came to abandoning ship they would be 'better off without too much retentive apparatus to drag after' them.[41]

Many men were afraid of the effects of oil fuel in the water when forced to jump ship, which made weak swimmers even more hesitant about leaping into the water. Vomiting, sore eyes and the smell and taste of oil created fear of permanent damage, but the effects were not as terrible as the fearsome appearance suggested by men coated in black viscous oil. When seamen covered with oil were rescued, their wounds were treated before the oil was cleaned off. After *Prince of Wales* was sunk in December 1941 'there were hundreds of men in the oily water swimming towards the rescuing destroyers – as they were hauled aboard their eyes were swabbed to remove oil'.[42] Surgeon Lieutenant T M Adams found that 'in the water things were not too unpleasant' when the cruiser *Juno* was sunk off Crete in February 1942, and that 'there was a thick layer of oil fuel which rather hampered one's style, and it was a bit cold'. What kept him going was that 'the company was cheerful and there was much singing and jocularity', especially when a leading seaman shared his flask of rum with the 'many friends around him to assist him in his thirst'. Adams remained positive, and fortified by the rum, when picked up by *Kandahar*: 'We were stripped and the surface oil wiped off. For this they found the contents of the foam fire extinguisher very useful. A tot of rum and a cigarette put us all in good spirits.'[43]

A bottle of gin and a box of cigarettes helped to maintain spirits among survivors on a raft of the rescue ship *Zaafaran*, sunk on duty with the Russian convoys in July 1942. Chocolate and biscuits were also shared out, while men who had lost most of their clothing were helped out by their fellow survivors. When another rescue ship, the *Zamelek*, was sighted altering course towards the survivors on their raft, 'the mental and physical effects were immediate, and shortly what could only be described as a holiday spirit prevailed and opportunity was taken to promote singing and exercise'.[44]

On most lifeboats and rafts it was a grim struggle for survival with men lost in their own thoughts and fears. Nicholas Monsarrat in his novel *The Cruel Sea* described how men 'swam round and round in the darkness, calling out, cursing their comrades, crying for help, slobbering their prayers. Some of those gripping the ratlines found that they could do so no longer, and drifted away.'[45] Other men suffered from hallucinations of distant ships and battles, dockyards, trees and their own now-vanished ships; one sailor 'felt always in communication with something and that he could not be lost; in short, he had, to a considerable extent, assimilated the ship into his personality'.[46] If a survivor became violent and disruptive the official advice was that 'a difficult individual should be hit over the head rather than be allowed to upset all the others'.[47]

When the cruiser HMS *Gloucester* came under attack off the coast of Crete in May 1941, the medical officer Hugh Singer established an emergency dressing station on the starboard side of the well deck against the bakehouse after the order was given to abandon ship. Here he prepared the wounded for their escape from the ship. Dressings were applied to wounds and fractures were splintered. The most seriously injured were put into Neil Robertson stretchers and passed down to a Carley float moored alongside the port side for casualties. Morphia was administered to the wounded, with the most seriously injured being given at least half a gram as 'their survival seemed highly unlikely and there seemed no point in allowing unnecessary suffering' whereas the most lightly wounded were only given a quarter of a gram of morphia 'in order that they might help themselves as much as possible'.[48] This was in line with advice given to new naval medical officers who were warned against giving morphia as pain relief to men who might soon have to abandon ship as 'if later they have to be left to their own resources, the morphia which has been given to them for purposes of euphoria may well result in euthanasia'.[49]

Singer's 'first impression when I entered the water was that it was agreeably warm but I soon found that water which is pleasant for bathing is not necessarily a suitable medium in which to spend a day and a night'. He also found it 'very lonely in the water after the ship had gone'. Some men in such circumstances quickly gave up the struggle for survival and 'allowed themselves to drown without making any effort at all'. Even on the comparative safety of a Carley float, the slightest 'maldistribution of weight' could lead to the frequent danger of the float overturning. Adrift with ratings, Singer 'acquired a first class knowledge of lower deck slang I had not heard before'. Eventually, he was picked up by a German ship and sent off to a prisoner of war camp. On being landed, the survivors were clothed by Greek civilians. Singer obtained a patched pair of morning suit trousers several sizes too small for him: 'the effect was comic but at least they clothed my nakedness'. All of their own clothing that was left to the survivors was what had been rejected by their German rescuers as of no use to them, such as Singer's badly-damaged reefer jacket.[50]

Although most aspects of naval life were highly regulated, each ship was left to itself to organise the reception of survivors picked up from other ships that had been sunk. The only constant principle was that the men picked up from the sea should be made fit to return to the fight as soon as possible. When survivors from HMS *Zinnia* were picked up by Nicholas Monsarrat's corvette *Campanula* in 1941, the casualties were very mixed in character:

> Survivors in the mess-decks, filling every available space: asleep on the deck, on benches, against bulkheads: sitting at tables with their heads between their hands, talking, shivering, wolfing food, staring at nothing. Some of them half-naked, wrapped in blankets and makeshift shoes, some with pathetic little cardboard suitcases hugged close: puzzled black faces, pinched yellow ones, tired bleary white masks that still muster a grin. Men half-dead, men cocky as bedamned: men suffering from exposure, frost-bite, oil-fuel poisoning, cuts, gashes, broken limbs: men hanging to life by a wet thread.[51]

Such casualties had to occupy whatever space was available because it was important that the crew of the host ship should keep their own mess space and remain at full efficiency. Survivors of the destroyer *Grenville* picked up by *Grenade* in February 1940 were traumatised:

> Those men in the water from twenty minutes to half an hour were mostly suffering from shock, and as far as possible they were made to lie down either in the cabin flats, wrapped in blankets and given hot water bottles, or accommodated on tables in the forward mess decks.

A hypodermic injection of morphia was 'effective in preventing a possible mass hysteria'. Men who were in the water for more than forty minutes were usually unconscious and had to be given artificial respiration followed by a hot bath and a hot drink. Those men who did not survive were usually 'thin or sparsely built' and had been in the water for over forty minutes.[52]

It was not uncommon for a medical officer from a ship that had been sunk to find himself caring for the survivors. When his ship HMS *Cossack* was torpedoed in 1941, Surgeon Lieutenant Walter Scott was picked up after an hour and a half in the water by a corvette, the *Carnation*, which did not carry a doctor, so he 'took charge of the wounded survivors' and, though having lost his instruments, he 'treated them for shock with hot cocoa, warmth and saline compresses to the burnt areas, while awaiting a syringe to be sent from another ship'. When the order had been given to abandon ship, he had filled his pockets with morphia and syringes and put his first aid bag over his shoulder before setting off to search the decks with his torch for the wounded but had lost all his first aid gear in the water. It was not the only loss that he was to suffer. In reporting on his work, he later apologised for the state of his report as 'I much regret the oil on the enclosed form, but my bottle of hair oil was broken during the journey home'.[53]

Acts of heroism by naval medical officers were not enough. Their real function was to save lives and return men to duty. In fulfilling this role they were too valuable to needlessly risk their lives as experienced medical men were in short supply and expensive to train. They could only save the lives of others if they did not recklessly put themselves at risk. Ivan Jacklin was lost on the liner SS *Empress of Canada* when returning to England from South Africa for a shore posting. One witness saw him going below when the boat was settling down to bring up a sick steward and another saw him swim three times from the sinking ship to rafts carrying servicewomen who had been left behind. When the ship went down, he was still to be seen rescuing people in distress and it was 'while doing this work of rescue he disappeared and was seen no more'.[54]

Jacklin's close friend Peter McRae also died a heroic death in February 1944 after the sinking of HMS *Mahratta* on a Russian convoy despite the fact that he 'did not look like a hero. He was tall, thin and delicate-looking. He had suffered from abdominal and chest complaints and had had at least half a dozen operations.' He was a man who had 'few luxuries and spent all his time studying'. One report of his death was that 'he was taking a stretcher case ashore in a small boat, when the boat capsized in a heavy sea. McRae could have saved himself but he supported the wounded man for 20 minutes until help came, in a temperature of something like minus 20 degrees'[55]. Another version had him sacrifice himself for the good of his fellow survivors. The seventeen survivors of *Mahratta* had scrambled on to a Carley float with their medical officer but 'after a while the doctor said "I appear to be in the way here" and before anyone could stop him slipped into the water and was not seen again'.[56] The story of McRae's heroic act of self-sacrifice was never officially confirmed, but arguably he could have been of more service to his shipmates had he stayed with them on the Carley float so that they could benefit from his medical expertise.

The rescue of survivors was never the immediate priority for nearby naval vessels in action. Fighting the enemy, winning the battle, protecting the convoy and ensuring the safety of undamaged vessels came before picking up survivors from the sea. From 1941 onwards, rescue ships were used to pick up shipwrecked crews on convoy service to Russia and Gibraltar. After 1942 no convoy crossed the Atlantic in the summer months unless accompanied by a rescue ship. Sailing under the Blue Ensign but under the direct authority of the Commander-in-Chief, Western Approaches, these ships were manned by merchant seamen and officers, though they carried Royal Navy medical officers, sick berth attendants and gunnery crew. Leased in most cases through the Clyde Shipping Company, these rescue ships had bed accommodation for 100–150 survivors and carried clothing and comforts donated by the Red Cross, Women's Voluntary Service, National Sailors' Society and other naval welfare charities. They were to pick up survivors, act as hospital ships for convoys and maintain the morale of merchant seamen in convoy.[57] The 'mainspring of all rescue work' was the motor lifeboat which picked up men and brought them to the rescue ship.[58] All medical arrangements were the responsibility of the Royal Navy, although the ships were under Merchant Navy control:

> The medical officer in this service has rather a roguish job without many of the amenities and comradeship of a large RN ship, and the customs of the Merchant Navy are not identical with those of the Royal Navy. The medical officer of a rescue ship must fit in.[59]

RS *Rathlin*, formerly used as a cattle ship between the Clyde and Northern Ireland, was manned by fifty merchant seamen from the Hebrides and twenty naval and army gunners. It had one medical officer and one sick berth attendant, with accommodation for 150 survivors. At sea the ship took up a position at the stern of the convoy, but there was nothing to distinguish her from other merchant ships. Without the protection of Red Cross markings, the ship depended upon her own armament for defence. When a ship was bombed, *Rathlin* steamed out of line and closed in as quickly as possible with the sinking ship with its scrambling nets down to pick up survivors from lifeboats and rafts. A search was then made through the wreckage for survivors. In many cases, it was necessary for the rescuers to climb down the rescue netting to try to pass a line around the chest of the oil-covered victim. Sometimes these lines slipped and the survivor fell back into the water. After a search of about two hours and once the rescue ship was satisfied it had picked up everyone still alive, it re-joined the convoy at full speed. The injured were treated in what had been the passengers' saloon, and the other survivors sent below to be allocated a sleeping billet and issued with dry clothing and comforts. The Merchant Navy crew were ingenious when asked to help the medical officer when a piece of equipment was required that was not available, such as welding a piece of iron into the sole of a man's boot for extension of the foot, fashioning a Steinman's pin for pinning a fracture from a length of steel packing metal and making a pair of elevators for 'extracting the buried carious molars of Merchant Navy seamen'.[60]

McBain, the medical officer on *Zaafaran*, was not too popular when he insisted that survivors should not be resuscitated with rum until the men had been dried, warmed and reclothed. He had found that this was the most effective way of stopping them from dawdling and sleeping in the condition in which they had been pulled from the sea. During attacks on the convoy, 'the prospect of early surface action with the enemy meant great mental strain for our crew, which was borne well by everyone'. Even during bombing the needs of the survivors of sunk ships were attended to:

> In spite of the continuous presence of hostile aircraft, a meal was served. To any man showing loss of appetite, infusion of gentian and

a stiff dose of bromide were issued. Though less acceptable than rum, this was found to be more efficacious to those whose morale was wearing thin.[61]

Morale also needed to be maintained when there were dead men aboard a ship. Surgeon Lieutenant Hunter regretted his failure to ask his captain to bury the dead immediately after action in the battle of the River Plate and 'I think had we done so it would have been easier on the feelings of the ship's company'.[62] To leave the dead unattended for even a short time posed health risks in hot climates but also lowered morale among the survivors by reminding them constantly of mortality and the loss of their friends and messmates. For similar reasons, bloodstains were quickly scrubbed from the decks. The hurried burial services in lulls of heavy action or immediately after an engagement were conducted with dignity. Ransome Wallis put on his best uniform jacket and his cap rather than a tin helmet in an attempt to look smart when attending his first funeral at sea. As medical officer on *Martin* he was worried that he might be called upon to conduct the service when he found himself the only officer present with a burial party of ratings. He was relieved when the First Lieutenant appeared to conduct a 'short but dignified' service before the alarm bell rang again for action stations and the burial party was dismissed to return to fighting duties.[63] On *Scylla* on 12 November 1942 the commanding officer and a cook picked up from the torpedoed sloop *Ibis* were both committed to the deep and 'full honours were accorded with firing party, with *Last Post* etc., and photos taken to be forwarded to the next-of kin'.[64] In death there was no distinction made between officer and rating, however strong class divisions and hierarchy may have been in the Royal Navy as a whole.

Combat surgery and medical care may have of necessity been improvised, conservative in nature and carried out under less than ideal conditions but it did save lives and ensured that seamen would be restored to a fit state to continue to fight the war if not that particular battle. The role of the doctor, however, went beyond what little professional expertise he could employ in the heat of battle:

The faith that the lower deck has in their doctors is pathetic, and even though a doctor cannot hope to save many lives in a ship action, yet the effect of the doctor's presence maintains courage and morale before, during and after action to a degree that cannot be ignored.[65]

That faith, far from being pathetic, represented hope, trust and confidence, all needed by men in action.

Chapter Twelve
Went the Day Well?

The purpose of the Royal Navy was to wage war at sea, win battles and protect the British Empire: the Admiralty admitted in 1946 that 'the RN has the training for war as almost its entire object'.[1] In order to achieve this, it needed a healthy and efficient body of men. Just how successful this was in action can be assessed by looking at how well medical organisation and the fitness of men stood up to the test of action at crucial moments of the war and whether or not it learned any lessons from experience in action, in addition to how it maintained fitness in the monotonous lulls between action. The role of the Royal Naval medical services has not always been given full credit compared to the role of the Royal Army Medical Corps in dealing with the medical problems of action in which both were involved, such as the evacuation from Dunkirk in 1940 and the landings which led to the liberation of Europe. In such circumstances when landing to take part in land operations, the medical problems faced by naval medical officers became similar to those of Royal Army Medical Corps doctors. Problems unknown on board ship, such as men suffering from greater degrees of fatigue and the need to maintain hygiene in unhealthy situations, assumed an importance unknown at sea.[2] In preparing for action in the Far East once the war in Europe was over, the Royal Navy was expected to have a greater role than land forces with a corresponding greater importance given to its medical organisation in keeping men in a condition to fight, but thankfully this was not put to the test.

It must have seemed in May 1940 to many of the soldiers waiting for evacuation from Dunkirk, 'the blazing town, which formed a beacon in the sand dunes visible for miles out to sea and … identified by day the pall of black smoke', that Operation 'Dynamo' to save them was 'a feeble effort to tackle the great task'. The speed of the evacuation was slower than hoped because only the smaller ships could enter the channel or lie near the beaches with the result that casualties had to be picked up and transferred to the larger naval vessels.[3] All the destroyers and larger transport ships carried medical officers and sick berth attendants or Royal Army Medical Corps staff ready to administer first aid. The trawlers and smaller craft were not so well organised, even though 'a considerable amount of first aid was necessary before cases were fit for transport'. Neil Robertson stretchers proved their value in enabling the wounded who had been 'stowed for safety in accessible places below deck' to be moved 'without prejudicing their chances of recovery'.[4] *Icarus* carried about eighty wounded from Dunkirk, with the captain's cabin converted into a hospital with camp beds for the most severely wounded while walking cases were received in the officers' cabins. In most cases little more was done than the administration of morphia and the application of field dressings, Severe wounds were excised and shrapnel removed. Two soldiers had advanced gas gangrene and one man had had his ulna nerve severed by a bullet in the forearm.[5]

Casualties could also occur from artillery fire, aerial bombing and intense machine-gun attacks once the soldiers had embarked to the despair of the medical officers attempting to deal with the needs of the evacuated troops, one of whom commented on 29 May 1940:

> For each ship there was this constant menace from the air which was capable of reducing her to a mass of mangled metal. Distributed along the upper decks and throughout the mess decks were soldiers who showed exemplary fortitude. Happily, extreme exhaustion acted somewhat as an anaesthetic. Some had marched long distances, all, including wounded, had waited for long periods on the shelving beaches. Many had had no food for 48 hours and had been on half rations since May 23.[6]

Gunshot wounds, severe burns from the ignition of cordite by incendiary bombs and the rupture of abdominal viscera from depth charge explosions all had to be dealt with.[7] On *Icarus* 'the mental strain combined with a lack of sleep and proper meals was severe, but every man on board bore the strain well and only three cases of mental disturbance were encountered'.[8] This reflected the general experience that:

> Although there were several cases of hysteria and allied nervous syndromes, when the very exhausting conditions of the operation are taken into account, the numbers of these were encouragingly small. We noted that most of these cases occurred in the middle aged, the youngsters stood up to it well.[9]

The main difficulties associated with the receipt of casualties from Operation 'Dynamo' back in Dover were that much of the work was done at night and on two occasions during air raids, with insufficient or delayed information having been received about times and places of arrival. The telephone system was overloaded. The landing stages were often unsuitable and inadequate for the receipt of casualties, especially when there were 18ft rises and falls of tide. The transport of stretcher cases from ships moored in the harbour was hampered by troop movements, refugees and stray dogs. These problems were only overcome by the 'cheerful co-operation' of the ship's companies, who 'though invariably fatigued, were always ready to assist the sick berth staff in disembarking wounded'.[10] Although improvised and responding to the chaos of an unexpected retreat, the Royal Navy coped fairly effectively with the medical demands of the evacuation of troops from Dunkirk.

There was more time for medical planning for Operation 'Husky', the Allied invasion of Sicily in the summer of 1943. The primary function of the naval medical services was to provide medical care for the wounded men of all three services aboard ship and to evacuate casualties from the beaches during the early phases of the operation, with the use of medical sections of naval beach parties, ambulance boats, evacuation ships and hospital facilities on friendly shores. This was to provide a model for medical planning for the Normandy landings the following year, though weaknesses in methods of medical treatment revealed in the Sicily landings were corrected, such as the importance of not closing wounds until the danger of infection had been eliminated and the role of barbiturate sedation in dealing with war neuroses.[11] There was also great concern about the prevention of seasickness among the men on the landing craft. Despite experiments with drugs to cure seasickness by the Royal Army Medical Corps, the most effective methods to prevent it were simply to keep the landing craft clean, the issue of groundsheets to keep the men warm and dry, and the provision of sweets and biscuits. As fewer men were found to suffer from seasickness when seated in the stern of a landing craft with a clear view of the horizon, key personnel for the landing were placed there.[12] On *Brittany*, whose sick bay functioned well as a casualty clearing station which received more serious cases for treatment from the landing beaches, the supply of water for 'bodily hygiene' was identified as the major problem for 'special attention in future operations' since the lack of water had caused septic skin lesions which could easily have been avoided.[13] In choosing sites for camps and field hospitals, it was essential to ensure a clean water supply or purification facilities and guarantee adequate disposal of waste since excremental diseases, such as cholera, dysentery and typhoid, were considered as great a danger as insect-borne diseases but perhaps easier to prevent by good field hygiene practices.[14] However, there was praise for the way in which on many evacuation ships 'in a very short period of time the routine achieved by the sick berth staff was comparable with that of a hospital theatre in so far as there was no undue delay between cases for want of preparation'.[15] All of these lessons were to be learned in time for later landings in Italy and Normandy for the liberation of Europe.

In Operation 'Avalanche', the medical organisation at Salerno in September 1943 did not go as smoothly as planned. Co-operation between the army and navy medical services was essential if casualty stations were to be set up aboard ships. At first delays in stabilising the beachheads made it necessary to evacuate casualties from the beaches under fire. Beach personnel were unfamiliar with the plans for evacuation and moved casualties unnecessarily following the departure of the casualties rather than leaving them in the beach casualty stations until the arrival of hospital ships. There were also misunderstandings about the respective responsibilities of army and navy beach parties for bringing in army wounded to the evacuation stations. The crews of the ambulance boats were considered to have had inadequate training, but the evacuation ships compensated for this with their smooth and efficient handling of casualties. Patients would be taken aboard these ships by the hoisting of boats to the rail or by the hoisting of patients in groups or individually from boats alongside. Unlike the American forces, the British army insisted on the presence of hospital ships to evacuate casualties and refused to accept landing ships tank (LSTs) as evacuation ships, which resulted in 'the US army being willing to accept LSTs but not needing them because better evacuation facilities were provided by the transports and later by the hospital ships, and the British army having six times the LSTs but refusing to accept them and depending entirely upon hospital ships'.[16] Greater co-operation and collaboration between services and allies was necessary if there was to be an adequate medical response to the far greater challenges following D-Day in 1944.

Medical planners had already decided that the majority of casualties from Operation 'Neptune', the initial phase of the Normandy landings in which the Royal Navy played a major role, would be evacuated to the UK for definitive care in the same vessels, the LSTs, from which the troops and tanks were to be landed despite the earlier objections at Salerno of the British army to their use. With expected casualties of 2,600 on the first day alone, it was necessary to evacuate casualties back to the United Kingdom for further treatment as quickly and efficiently as possible.[17] The experience of Dunkirk, when the hospital carriers SS *Worthing* and SS *Paris* had been attacked despite being clearly marked with the Red Cross, was vivid in the minds of the planners and it was decided not to risk using hospital ships in this phase of the operation. It was also realised that in the early stages of the landings it would be impossible for larger vessels to dock and there would be no available quays for the loading of casualties.[18] Forty of the seventy LSTs were manned by the Royal Navy and the others by the Royal Army Medical Corps. Each vessel carried a surgeon, anaesthetist, a medical officer trained in resuscitation and sick berth attendants. Each LST was adapted so that after the tanks had been unloaded on the invasion beaches, they could be used for the evacuation of casualties. They were fitted with resuscitation apparatus, blood transfusion sets, adjustable stretcher racks and supplies of drugs. At the rear of the craft was an emergency operating theatre for any essential surgery necessary during the journey home. As soon as men had been disembarked on the beaches and the tanks unloaded, the tank deck would be prepared to receive the wounded. Up to 320 wounded could be carried in each LST.[19] Over 800 casualties were evacuated from Sword Beach alone on D-Day +1, 7 June 1944.[20]

Until medical first aid posts could be established on shore, the medical officers on the LSTs were responsible for medical care right up to the shoreline under sustained enemy fire.[21] It was pandemonium as Surgeon Lieutenant Graham Airth noted in his diary on D-Day itself:

> This has indeed been D-Day; Dawned-Day, Death-Day, Destruction-Day, Disappointment- and Disillusion-Day. I have seen men die suddenly, horribly. I have twice been near death myself, so near that I desperately wish to forget but probably will never do so.[22]

At first the army medical organisation was not fully functioning, except for the minor dressing stations, which made the role of the naval services even more vital although they too had to adapt to unfamiliar situations. In the opinion of the medical officer of Force 'S' the 'orders for the disposal of casualties were too complicated for young officers already partially dazed. Some to go to the beach when they could see nowhere to take them; some to the LSIs [landing ships infantry] if they could catch them; or to the LSTs when they finally arrived and eventually received them'.[23] There was criticism that many medical officers were appointed for duty in landing craft only a few days before D-Day and there had been no opportunities for training or preparation:

> Some recently qualified medical officers obviously lacked experience in dealing with casualties. This is difficult to remedy, but a few lectures in naval barracks, while newly joined and awaiting first appointments, from persons with actual experience of action stations would have been far more valuable than the handbooks which were provided. It is important for the authorities to realise that active service medicine and surgery is not part of the teaching curriculum in civilian hospitals.[24]

Almost all cases seen by medical staff on LSTs in the first days of the assault were trauma cases. Airth, having got the operating theatre going immediately, recorded that 'there were some ghastly injuries', especially from pieces of shrapnel. In many cases treatment was delayed because 'some of the men had taken 48 hours to reach us; morphia had been plentiful but treatment non-existent'. Airth's most serious case was an amputation of the thigh for gas gangrene, but even several pints of blood could not save the injured man. Blood transfusion was a lifesaver for another casualty who 'sat up after the first pint, came on board the colour of paper'.[25] However, operating on landing craft under the unpredictable conditions at sea could be difficult. Airth was worried about an operation to remove a piece of shrapnel from a man's lower eyelid, and was 'frankly windy of this as the ship has a 20 to 30 degree roll, has been worse, may become worse again, when I'm in the middle of it and can't stop'.[26] Despite the chaos of the landings, for some men, as for those on *Bellona*, D-Day itself and 'the actual invasion came as a sufficiently pleasant surprise after the frightful chaos envisaged to release the tension; and action and bombing, particularly at night, were enough to keep the interest from flagging'.[27]

Once the floating Mulberry harbours had been brought across from England, it was possible to moor the hospital carriers and hospital ships off the beaches and it was no longer necessary to rely upon the LSTs for immediate medical care. However, before they could be taken on board a carrier the wounded first had to be loaded on to Landing Craft Personnel (Small) which would take them to the hospital carrier when tides allowed. Landing Craft Assault (LCAs) were also used as water ambulances and could carry six or seven stretcher cases at a time to the carriers waiting off shore.[28] HMHS *Isle of Jersey* began to load casualties on 9 June and the carrier *Duke of Argyll* docked at Arromanches on 12 August. Hospital carriers were crucial to the successful management of casualties but were not always used to full capacity as they were short of fuel and water so could not remain long off the coast of Normandy to load casualties.[29] The LSTs perhaps played a more important role in the treatment of casualties during the early stages of the landings.

Other ships with medical officers on board also played a part in treating casualties from the beaches of Normandy. HMS *Largs*, the flagship of Force 'S' with responsibility for the landings on Sword Beach, was soon crowded with wounded soldiers brought to the ship by smaller craft starting at 7.30 am on 6 June with the treatment of the crew of a midget submarine suffering from cold and exposure. In one 36-hour period Surgeon Lieutenant MacIver treated forty-seven wounded men, though 'the medical staff of *Largs*, working all-out, was unable to spread itself widely enough to answer all calls for help'. After the shelling of SS *Demetriton* on 21 June, the medical officer of Force 'S' and the medical officer of *Largs* operated on the twenty-nine wounded for eleven-and-a-half hours continuously in the converted dining saloon of *Demetriton*.[30]

HMS *Belfast* also received casualties from landing craft that had been attacked by enemy fire during the landings, though the ship itself suffered no casualties among its own crew from its part in the initial bombardments on D-Day. On 9 June several ratings sustained minor injuries 'in their hurry to take cover' when a stick of German bombs fell near the ship, though no other damage was caused. During its time off the Normandy coast in June and July 1944, *Belfast* remained for twenty days in 'a sustained degree of readiness for action, [men] sleeping in their clothes at or near their action stations; but most nights, little sleep was obtained as sporadic air raids occurred when the ships fired barrages'. All watertight doors and hatches, and all ports were closed for protection against gun blast, restricting ventilation.[31] Despite such discomforts and the constant danger of shelling from the shore, U-boat or midget submarine attacks, human torpedoes and mines, morale remained high now that the long-awaited invasion for the liberation of Europe was a reality.

Most casualties were returned to Southampton and Portsmouth before being transferred to the naval hospitals. Haslar was perhaps the most important hospital for the treatment of casualties evacuated from the invasion beaches, taking in casualties who were too seriously injured to be taken by train to more distant hospitals. For a time Haslar was expected to also receive up to 150 transit cases at a time until a sufficient number of casualties had been collected or a train, but this proved impractical and was soon discontinued.[32] Originally reserved for only naval casualties, with army casualties being intended for treatment in Emergency Medical Service hospitals, when it came to action, Haslar actually made no distinction between navy and army casualties in receiving the most seriously wounded.[33] Problems were caused by the unreliability of information about when the LSTs would arrive with casualties, usually late at night, which 'on many occasions entailed much fruitless waiting for long hours in the night on the part of the staff of the reception station, the majority of whom have a full day's work to perform'.[34]

At Haslar two casualty reception stations capable of holding up to forty cases at a time were established although only one could be fully manned at all times because of a shortage of medical officers. There were fewer gas gangrene and burns cases than expected but a larger number of ophthalmic injuries. Urgent surgery was often necessary on men suffering from severe head trauma and chest wounds. A surgical team was brought in from the Royal Naval Auxiliary Hospital Barrow Gurney in Bristol for the first ten days until the influx of patients began to settle down after 16 June. Of the first 108 patients admitted, most of them moribund on arrival, only 19 of them died. By the end of August 1944. Haslar had accepted 1,347 patients from Normandy.[35] The staff at Haslar felt themselves to be part of the great undertaking for the liberation of occupied Europe and took inspiration from 'the bearing of these very severely wounded and tired men whose fortitude and good humour could not but evoke the best response from those whose duty it was to attend to them'. One American serviceman's response to being reprimanded by the sister after she discovered him swigging the contents of a half-filled medicine bottle he had found marked 'brandy' was to remark that 'well, if that label's wrong, I'm in for one hell of a belly ache'.[36]

Co-operation between all the armed forces was essential for effective treatment of the casualties from the Normandy landings. Co-operation was also necessary with the American military medical services. At Royal Naval Hospital Portland, in theory reserved for casualties from local patrols, shore establishments and air raids, it was necessary to co-operate with the United States services to ensure that temporary accommodation and first aid could be provided to casualties awaiting transport to the auxiliary hospitals at Sherborne and Minterne Magna.[37] In the early stages of the invasion of Europe the role of naval medical services was significant, though the medical care of those taking part in subsequent action on land was the responsibility and achievement of the army medical services. Without the role played by naval medical services, the medical organisation at the launch of the liberation of Europe would have been inadequate to the magnitude of the great task.

As the end of the war in Europe approached, the Royal Navy prepared itself for the part it was to play in the war in the Pacific for the defeat of Japan. Research into the health problems and habitability of ships in the Tropics became more pressing. For those already serving in the Far East, such as Roger Miles on HMS *Quality*, wartime life was already changing:

> Destroyer life is not what it was. The modern vessels are built to stay at sea for too long and if the big ships choose to mill around the ocean indefinitely, the destroyers will follow them round – and like it. Those old Destroyer gatherings in the wardroom which were so good for one's morale and bad for one's health are things of the past, for we only seem to see our colleagues when we come alongside to transfer mail or beef-and-spuds or the big ships paperwork.[38]

There was a new danger to be faced with Kamikaze attacks on ships. Miles found it 'difficult to believe that there is a human being in that machine that speeds on towards its target, though often a ball of flame long before it is anywhere near'. A medical officer on another ship had 'a perfectly preserved Japanese eyeball as a memento' of one such suicide attack.[39] There was a sense of unease about what might happen next.

The Admiralty feared that, while the war in the Far East was 'of greater concern to the Navy than to the other services',[40] such a war was unlikely to be popular with most sailors who 'would almost certainly react unfavourably to the prospect of continuing the struggle against Japan after Germany has been defeated'.[41] However, it was not just a matter of maintaining morale among men facing a new struggle after the end of one and at a time when men in other services would be looking forward to demobilization. Wives and families at home also had to be convinced that the fight against Japan was worthwhile as it was recognised that 'the reactions of personnel to a Far Eastern draft, particularly after the end of the war in Europe, will be largely influenced by the reactions of their wives, mothers and sweethearts, who appear to be profoundly ignorant of the fact that the Japanese war has any direct bearing on their own lives or on the interests of Great Britain'.[42]

However, the war in the Far East ended without the expected heavy naval involvement. The use of the atom bomb ushered in new terrors of war but saved the men of the Royal Navy from the much-anticipated and feared struggle against Japan. Many wartime medical officers looked forward like Roger Miles to 'the day when we can don a white coat and act like human beings again, pushing into the background the memory of these, for most of us, completely wasted and sterile years'.[43] His wife Doris had long considered some of the practical problems demobilization might bring and had a few years earlier worried that 'you won't have a suit to wear' after so long in 'a pretty shiny' uniform; she suggested that he circumvent clothes rationing by getting his brother, a White House Naval Liaison Officer at the British Embassy in Washington, to send him a suit from the United States to replace the grey suit the brother had purloined from his wardrobe to wear in neutral Lisbon when first posted to Washington.[44]

First, though, the Royal Navy had a role to play in the repatriation and care of prisoners of war and civilian internees evacuated from the horrors of the camps.[45] HMHS *Tjitjalengka* acted as a base hospital in the harbour at Yokohama; after a couple of days many of the ex-prisoners of war had recovered sufficiently to be flown out of Japan, but 400 seriously-ill men, many of them suffering from beri-beri, pulmonary tuberculosis and amoebic dysentery, were still on board when the ship sailed in September 1945.[46] In Hong Kong, most British ex-internees were evacuated to Manila but the most severely wounded were sent straight to the United States or Australia in hospital ships or British Pacific Fleet carriers specially converted for that purpose 'at a moment's notice'. The navy also found itself handling stores of food, clothing, medical supplies and Red Cross parcels including unaccustomed items for women and children.[47] From a war footing, it quickly adapted to the new role of providing humanitarian relief to the victims of war.

Naval medicine was always about more than just patching up the casualties of battle. It was about keeping the navy fit and healthy as an effective fighting force. Throughout the Second World War the navy was faced with the problem of maintaining the habitability of ships that might have to sail the Atlantic, face the heat of the Tropics or the bitter cold of the Arctic. It was almost an impossible task since the machine always came before the man and any improvements were secondary to the maintenance of the ship as an effective fighting machine. During the Great War, Admiral Beatty had said with regards to the stresses and strains of war that 'the men can stand it, the machines can't'. The ship and her fighting efficiency was what mattered above, all not her crew.[48] Any air-conditioning plant would have to be installed at the expense of precious space. In wartime conditions ships were already overcrowded with the addition of the equipment needed to fight a modern war and larger crews.[49] Unlike the army and air force, the navy fought and lived in the same confined space. There was no escape from it. This formed a great contrast to conditions aboard modern American naval vessels. Whereas ratings in the Royal Navy slept in hammocks slung wherever they could be fitted into overcrowded mess spaces, the sailor in the United States Navy had his own bunk and expected nothing less. Food was better on the American ships and served cafeteria-style in modern canteens which was a decided improvement on the old-fashioned messing arrangements in the Royal Navy.

Awareness of the superiority of American living arrangements aboard ship offered ideas about how the Royal Navy could make improvements that would help recruitment in the post-war world. In British ships of the Second World War, conditions would have been familiar to nineteenth-century sailors; officers now may have been allocated cabins, but the ratings still had no option other than to sling their hammocks wherever they could. In the mess areas hammocks were still officially hung 21in (52cm) apart, but on many a crowded wartime ship it was common for men from different watches to share hammocks, or even sleep on the deck beneath one of the mess tables. As new ships were built and older ones refitted and modernised in the 1950s bunks replaced hammocks, but the quarters for naval ratings and marines remained cramped with very little storage space – though not as confined as they were on submarines. Cafeterias, laundries, washrooms and showers all represented a great improvement for the post-war rating, and showed him that he was valued.[50]

Preventative health was an area in which the navy was to excel in wartime. The question of habitability in ships became a major preoccupation, centring on ventilation, food and living conditions, protection against diseases (including malaria and venereal diseases) brought aboard from onshore, and the maintenance of physical efficiency and fitness in cramped conditions under every extreme of climate in a truly global war, where adaptations had to be made to cope with extremes of climate. Yet the maintenance of tradition and keeping up a good appearance remained important within the Royal Navy but this could work against maintaining a healthy environment. Uniform was not always practical in modern war conditions. Standards had to be relaxed in extreme environments and at a time of clothes rationing. In the Arctic and on the Russian Convoys, the Kapok was developed to keep the men warm, while in the Tropics dress regulations were relaxed to cope with the heat. Nevertheless, it was in the field of preventative health that the Royal Navy perhaps could claim its greatest wartime success.[51]

Whilst the First World War had perhaps not offered new medical challenges in sea warfare to the extent that trench warfare had raised new problems in military medicine that led to new ways of thinking, there were some trends already apparent that were to loom larger in the Second World War. Burns and facial injuries in Great War naval engagements had offered scope for the innovative work of plastic surgeons and was to continue to do so in the Second World War. New technology and new ways of waging war at sea, such as submarines and naval flight, were in their early days in the First World War, but in the Second these areas demanded new developments in naval aviation and submarine medicine to deal with the new health demands that they raised. When the war began the Fleet Air Arm had only recently returned to naval control from the RAF and medical services needed to be developed. Inevitably the lead would be taken by the RAF in the field of aviation medicine, but the war saw the development of specialists in the medical problems of naval aviation which did differ from flying conditions on land. Submarines did not carry medical officers but posed new problems of maintaining adequate conditions and a healthy crew in difficult circumstances. Research into the problems of submarine health became a priority.

The Royal Navy had always prided itself on being an early adopter of innovations that would improve the health of its men and enhance fighting efficiency. In the Second World War it was very much the adopter rather than the innovator. Blood transfusion, penicillin and mass miniature radiography to screen against pulmonary tuberculosis were three areas in which the navy showed its interest in new methods to keep its men fit. With the development of its own Blood Transfusion Service, the navy followed the lead of the army, while it very much lagged behind in measures to control malaria. With mass radiography, though, the Royal Navy was a trendsetter and its programmes offered models for post-war civilian services. Sometimes there was a need to improvise to get anything done: ice-cream conveyors were used for the transport of blood and its products for the transfusion service, while at the Royal Naval Medical School evacuated to Clevedon near Bristol attempts were made to produce penicillin in reused gin bottles. In the field of innovation, the Royal Navy was very much an early adopter rather than an innovator, even if in some areas such as malaria control it was not as receptive as might have been expected.[52] Collaboration between the naval, army and air force medical services, whether on introducing innovations, manning hospitals or providing care on combined operations, provided an early taster of subsequently greater co-operation culminating in the modern tri-service medical services that are a result of reduced military forces in peacetime austerity rather than wartime shortages of resources.

Medical research now assumed a greater importance for the navy than it had done in the past. In dealing with the problems of maintaining health at sea, research into medical science assumed a greater importance with the work of the Naval Personnel Research Committee of the Medical Research Council which investigated such issues as problems of survival at sea after shipwreck, the physiology of diving and of submarine work, and flash and weather-proof clothing as well as the whole topic of habitability. The RAF inevitably took the lead with new developments and improvements in aviation medicine. With submarine medicine, although the Submarine Service was only a small unit research was undertaken that was still significant enough to be on the secret list in the Cold War. When it became possible in the aftermath of the war to assess similar research undertaken by the enemy, it was considered that little of importance had emerged among the navies of the Axis powers and that Kriegsmarine medical research was inferior to that of the Royal Navy, partly because more emphasis had been given in Germany to the needs of the Luftwaffe and Wehrmacht. In Britain medical research in wartime became entrenched in naval medicine and the foundation for subsequent research was laid down. The modern Institute of Naval Medicine has its origins in that wartime research.[53]

All of this demanded an increase in the number of doctors, sick berth attendants and nurses serving in the Royal Navy. Naval medical services had been run down during the financial cuts of the 1930s and had to be rebuilt. One of the greatest achievements of the Royal Navy was in its expansion of its medical services but this was to represent something of a culture change for the Naval Medical Department.[54] Now the majority of ships' surgeons were civilians in the uniform of the RNVR for the duration. Although specialists in their own fields or general practitioners in their civilian life, they very much felt disoriented in their naval roles, and for much of the time bored with little opportunity to practise their expertise on a generally healthy ship's crew. If they were to help keep up morale, their own self-esteem was in sore need of raising. There was not much time to train them for life at sea or in specialised aspects of naval medicine. The naval doctor was expected to be a generalist and specialism was frowned upon, though such new and very different fields as aviation and underwater medicine called out for specialists and offered new opportunities. Felix Eastcott, who served as a medical officer with the Fleet Air Arm at Yeovilton, later said that 'the Navy gave a new dimension to his life – it was his University'.[55] Nevertheless, the post-war naval surgeon was still expected to be a generalist:

> Although he may be also a specialist in other subjects such as surgery, radiology or ophthalmology, he is essentially a naval doctor and should be able to deal with the numerous problems of naval hygiene so that he is able to maintain the fighting efficiency of the Navy under conditions which vary in different classes of ships serving in extremes of climate.[56]

Yet, despite the official opposition to specialists in the naval medical service, they did emerge out of necessity and the realisation that specialised knowledge was essential to deal with new areas of medicine and new problems. Naval doctors now also had to deal with women patients as medical services were established for the Wrens. Adaptability was essential.

For the lucky doctors there was the opportunity to extend professional knowledge in a new field, but for most ships' surgeons it was more a matter of waiting for action when they would have something to do. Underemployment was a serious problem. Ships were manned by fit and healthy young men whose ailments were usually minor:

> The sailor is usually a fit man. He is a man of picked physique and is well-fed. He is a young man. Many of his operations are done when he is in no sense of the word ill, i.e. hernias, semi-lunar cartilages, interval appendices, tonsils. Added to this, he has become more educated and a more intellectual type, with the result that he has developed a certain amount of fear complex which the old type of beer drinking tough never had.[57]

Only in the heat of battle did the surgeon come into his own in the medical sphere administering what was often little more than first aid. As a result, the 'quack' would often find himself taking on other non-medical duties including censoring letters and cyphering, though that could strip him of his non-combatant status if he were captured by the enemy. This also gave the doctor the opportunity to get to know the men under his care better and so identify barriers to good physical and mental health and fitness from developing at an early stage.

The rapid wartime expansion of the navy reached its peak in 1943 when new ships were coming into use and manpower was at a premium. Health and fitness standards for new recruits had to be lowered and means found to improve the physique of men who would once have been rejected. The Royal Navy rose to this challenge by setting up facilities for training men to reach the required fitness levels. Once the personnel crisis had passed and it was possible to take the pick of conscripts again from men who had chosen naval service over any of the other armed services, such boot camps were abandoned and the navy reverted to its previous insouciance regarding the quality of its recruits. The year 1943 had also been a time when the navy had had to denude civilian medical services to recruit enough doctors. The quality of sick berth attendants was to fall during the war with the fittest and most able men being needed in other branches of the navy.[58]

The Royal Navy's claim to have had a lower incidence of psychological and mental health problems than the other armed forces because by recruiting only men who had chosen to serve in the navy it had a higher quality of recruit can certainly be challenged. Despite the claim that there had been an 'immense improvement in the health and muscular development in the young men' called up in the Second World compared to their counterparts in the Great War and that they had 'real beauty in features and appearances', not all new recruits were up to physical standard and had to be brought up to scratch.[59] The isolated nature of life at sea could also cause its own psychological problems to be dealt with by naval psychiatrists. Boredom was a major problem which faced the psychiatrists and industrial psychologists now employed for the first time to deal with mental health and individual happiness. Physical exercise and recreation were considered of value not to enhance physical fitness but to raise the spirits of the men, keep them entertained and distracted from the stresses and strains of naval life. Unlike the army and RAF, who had regular periods of leave, the navy, at all times geared for war, could enjoy leave, rest and recreation only when in port for refitting. The resultant fatigue reduced the general fitness of the navy, but little was done to remedy the problem. Sailors were meant to be hardy and able to endure whatever the challenge.

The greatest challenge in wartime was maintaining morale and it was through upholding tradition and a pride in the service that the navy was able to maintain fighting efficiency and determination to win the war. The seaman was constantly reminded that he represented the best of the British character and was encouraged to forge a sense of comradeship with his shipmates and pride in his ship and his uniform. Inevitably though he was all too aware that the ship came first and that he was a mere cog in the efficiency of that fighting machine. Any comfort in his living and working conditions was sacrificed to operational needs. Little money was spent on his needs. His life was of secondary importance to winning a naval battle, but he was proud to be part of the senior service with its conservative, hierarchical ways. Keeping up spirits did not demand great expenditure but it did call for great effort. The importance of sporting activity in naval life was not in improving levels of physical fitness but in keeping up good spirits. Good morale was essential to naval health and fitness. A healthy man was not only physically fit but psychologically strong. An optimistic outlook could aid the work of the ship's surgeon in overcoming bodily illness and infirmity.

Wartime medical statistics were neglected by the Royal Navy despite its insistence that medical officers kept detailed journals from which the annual returns of sickness were compiled, yet statistics can be used to measure the success or failure of attempts to control injuries and diseases. Unfortunately, for the Second World War only very crude statistics are available, although they do indicate trends. Sir Sheldon Dudley, Director of Naval Medical Services, described the wartime failure to compile adequate medical records which could have been used to inform and guide future policy as 'heartbreaking'.[60] The call-up of administrative staff for active duties, wartime paper salvage and attempts to reduce what was seen as unnecessary paperwork meant that good record keeping was neglected. The sinking of ships with the consequent loss of records also made it difficult for accurate statistics to be compiled. It is hard to assess accurately how effective preventative health measures were in keeping men healthy at sea in wartime conditions that showed a marked deterioration from peacetime habitability standards. However, sampling of surviving records does suggest that wartime sick list admission rates were actually lower aboard carriers, battleships and cruisers than they had been before the war. Infections and parasitic illnesses were lower aboard wartime carriers, skin diseases less prevalent on battleships, and skin diseases, injuries and generative system disorders reduced on cruisers compared with pre-war rates. Illness rates varied by ship type, with the lowest rates found aboard carriers. This would suggest that in the treatment of sickness, the Royal Navy was generally successful in meeting the wartime challenge of keeping men fit on overcrowded ships in adverse conditions.[61]

The principal infections causing illness in the Second World War navy were respiratory tract infections, venereal diseases, tropical diseases and infectious fevers, just as they had been in the First World War. Infectious diseases, however, caused fewer deaths in the Second World War compared with the First World War.[62] Rates for cases of dysentery in 1939 were a quarter of the rate in 1915 and the incidence of enteric infections, typhoid and paratyphoid continued to decline throughout the war but rose again in 1945 due to the concentration of the fleet in tropical waters.[63] Moreover, by the end of the war, the relative sickness incidence in the Tropics was more than double that in temperate waters, with three times more diseases of the skin, a reflection of the effect very different climates could have on sickness rates.[64] Malaria rates, though, fell from 5 per 1,000 in 1944 to 3 per 1,000 in 1945, despite more men being deployed in malarial areas, thanks to the success of prophylaxis once it was adopted. Pulmonary tuberculosis rates, by contrast, remained high and actually rose towards the end of the war because of the number of cases now being identified among the apparently fit by X-rays.[65] Meanwhile, average daily sick rates per thousand declined during the war until 1945 and then rose again slightly.[66] The Royal Navy could congratulate itself on a measure of success in keeping its men healthy in wartime.

So did the German navy, which generally paid attention to maintaining the health of its sailors. After the sinking of the *Scharnhorst* in 1943 it was noted that 'nearly all the German prisoners were of good physique and seemed well-nourished'.[67] Surgeon Lieutenant Mooney was impressed as a prisoner of war by 'the very good' medical facilities at the German naval camp near Bremen, with its twenty-bed sick bay, diagnostic equipment, radium heat room, dental surgery and X-ray apparatus for routine chest screening.[68] The Royal Navy, though, considered its medical services superior and it perhaps had to operate in greater climate extremes than the German navy with wars to fight in the Far East as well as in Europe.

The traditional Thursday naval toast was for 'A Bloody War or a Sickly Season'. In the Second World War, a bloody war with battle casualties could not be avoided in contrast with the Great War where the set-piece naval battles were less frequent than had been anticipated in the pre-war arms race though still destructive, but the importance given to preventative medicine helped to keep the navy healthy, in good spirits and fit to fight despite the strains brought about by modern warfare. It had been a successful war for naval health, morale and fitness. The lessons learned were to lay the basis of post-war naval health and fitness. This emphasis on keeping men healthy and fit meant that in the Second World War there was no sickly season even in the midst of a bloody war. That was no mean achievement even for a service that prided itself on recruiting and retaining the fittest of the fit.

Appendices

Appendix 1: Naval Recruitment and Rejection, 1939-1945

	1939	1940	1941	1942	1943	1944	1945
Accepted	19,527	6,107	3,412	1,912	1,840	1,826	5,659
Rejected medically	20,590	5,807	3,511	3,149	2,815	2,548	5,705
Rejected, other reasons	37,257	27,277	20,266	14,641	7,632	4,488	9,628

These figures are of candidates for continuous service engagements (boys, apprentices and marines)

Source: J L S Coulter, *The Royal Naval Medical Service* (1954), p. 33.

Appendix 2: Royal Navy Medical Personnel, 1939-1946

	Jan 1939	Jan 1946
Medical Officers RN	389	276
Medical Officers, retired, Emergency and Reserve	360	1,454
Dental Officers RN	117	60
Dental Officers, retired	42	546
Wardmaster Officers RN	22	23
Wardmaster Officers retired	19	101
Nursing Sisters RN	91	57
Nursing Sisters retired	320	924
Occupational Therapists	–	2
Physiotherapists	–	16
Pharmacists	25	115
Sick Berth Staff RN	1,500	1,000
Sick Berth Staff Pensioners and Reserve	1,800	8,500
VAD Officers and Members	500	3,590
Entomologists, RNVR	–	12

Source: TNA, WO 163/485, Committee on the Organisation of the Medical Services, 24 January 1946.

Appendix 3: Royal Navy Hospital Ships, 1939-1945

Ship	Owner	Built	Requisitioned	Derequisitioned	Tonnage	Cots	Total Patients 1939-45
Aba	Elder Dempster	1919	Sep 1929	Transferred to War Office, Mar 1940	7,937	450	–
Amarapoora	P Henderson	1920	Sep 1939	Transferred to War Office, Aug 1946	9,342	503	9,767
Cap St Jacques	French	1922	Apr 1945	April 1946	8,900	299	1,207
Empire Clyde (ex-Leonardo da Vinci)	City Line	1925	May 1945 (transferred from War Office)	Renamed *Maine* in 1948 and served as permanent naval hospital ship and scrapped in 1954	7,515	411	237
Gerusalemme	Italian	1920	Jan 1945	1946	8,052	388	464
Isle of Jersey	Southern Railway	1930	Aug 1939	Jul 1945	2,143	170	10,144
Maine	Admiralty	1902	Purchased by Admiralty from P&O 1921	Scrapped, Apr 1947	8,599	217	13,514
Ophir	Dutch	1928	Jul 1942	Apr 1946	4,115	346	12,111
Oxfordshire	Bibby	1912	Sep 1939	Dec 1945	8,646	505	22,331
Tjitjalengka	Dutch	1939	Jul 1942	Apr 1946	10,972	504	7,270
Vasna	British India	1917	August 1939	Mar 1946	4,820	279	12,412
Vita	British India	1914	May 1940	Jan 1946	4,691	240	3,685
Totals						4,312	93,142

Source: J L S Coulter, *The Royal Naval Medical Service* (1954), pp. 97–123.

Appendix 4: Royal Navy Death Rates (per thousand)

	1915	1939	1940	1941	1942	1943	1944	1945
Pneumonia	0.6	0.1	0.1	0.1	0.1			
Tuberculosis	0.3		0.1	0.1	0.1	0.1	0.1	0.1
Burns, scalds	3.2	0.2	0.1	0.3	0.5	1.0	0.3	0.4
Drowning		2.7	0.5	0.6	0.7	0.9	0.6	0.4
Injuries in action	28.2	14.3	14.3	14.3				

Source: F P Ellis and A Richards, 'Health of the Navy in Two World Wars', *Journal of Royal Naval Medical Service*, 52 (1966), 12.

Appendix 5: Royal Navy Sickness and Death Rates

	Average strength	Cases of sickness	Sick daily per 1,000	Final invaliding per 1,000	Deaths per 1,000
1936	92,245	437	19.5	11.7	2.0
1939	131,858	504	19.9	13.7	4.6
1940	270,000	473	19.3	17.9	3.2
1941	396,000	434	18.1	20.9	3.2
1942	516,000	409	17.2	16.1	2.9
1943	670,000	412	15.2	14.0	3.4
1944	792,000	361	15.1	14.5	2.8
1945	772,000	377	16.1	25.9	2.6

Source: F P Ellis and A Richards, 'Health of the Navy in Two World Wars', *Journal of Royal Naval Medical Service*, 52 (1966), 8.

Notes

Preface
1. TNA, ADM 178/317, letter from B C Harvey to R W Postgate, 8 January 1944.

Chapter One: Our Men: Finding the Fittest
1. *In Which We Serve* (Two Cities, 1942), dir. Noel Coward (DVD, Carlton Visual Entertainment 3711501663, 2003).
2. *We Dive at Dawn* (Gainsborough, 1943), dir. Anthony Asquith (DVD, ITV Studios, B0000CDUX6, 2003).
3. *Went the Day Well?* (Ealing Studios, 1943), dir. Alberto Cavalcanti (DVD, Optimum Home Entertainment, B0005XNJ, 2006).
4. TNA, ADM 116/5559, Ministerial Committee on the Work of Psychologists and Psychiatrists in the Services, 31 January 1945.
5. TNA, ADM 1/1008, memorandum, 13 October 1939.
6. TNA. INF 1/293, Home Intelligence special reports, 1943–4.
7. TNA LAB 6/150, Naval and air force recruiting preferences, 1940.
8. J L S Coulter, *The Royal Naval Medical Service* (1954), p. 26.
9. Ibid., p. 24.
10. Ibid., p. 230.
11. IWM, Documents.13249, memoir of John Somers, c. 1990s.
12. H Philip, *Two Rings and a Red* (1944), p. 9.
13. TNA, WO 163/485, Committee on the Organisation of the Medical Services, 24 January 1946.
14. TNA, Memo on reduction of medical standard of recruits, May 1943.
15. TNA, ADM 1/14002, 'One Company', film treatment by John Bains for recruitment of youth into Navy's Y Scheme, 1943.
16. J L S Coulter, *The Royal Naval Medical Service* (1954), p. 454.
17. *Instructions for the Guidance of Medical Boards under the National Service (Armed Forces) Act* MRB1 (1940).
18. TNA, ADM 1/14708, letter to R V Luce, Minister of Labour from Personnel Services, Admiralty, 5 April 1943.
19. TNA, WO 163/485, Committee on the Organisation of the Medical Services, 24 January 1946.
20. TNA, LAB 29/249, Guide for the use of local officers of the Ministry of Labour and National Service in placing in civilian employment men and women with specified service qualifications in Royal Navy, Royal Marine Forces and Army, 1945.
21. Admiralty Fleet Order 524/41, February 1942.
22. TNA, ADM 1/13702, Submarine Detector Ratings: aural selection, report and statistics, 1943.
23. TNA, ADM 1/12114, Navy Estimates, 1942.
24. J L S Coulter, *The Royal Naval Medical Service* (1954), p. 34. See also Appendix 1.
25. TNA, ADM 261/6, report on training in HMS *Bristol*, 18 May–28 December 1943.
26. Ibid.
27. TNA, ADM 1/14708, Memo on reduction of medical standard of recruits, May 1943.
28. TNA, ADM 1/11280, report of Admiralty Selection Tests Committee, 20 March 1941.
29. TNA, ADM 298/455, Progress in physiological matters relating to Coastal Force, 1943.
30. TNA, ADM 1/11280, report of Admiralty Selection Tests Committee, 20 March 1941.
31. J Davies, *Stone Frigate* (1947), p. 6.

239

32. TNA, ADM 1/11280, report of Admiralty Selection Tests Committee, 20 March 1941.
33. TNA, ADM 1/21955, history of personnel selection methods, 1950-1.
34. TNA, ADM 1/12067, 'Psychologists', 1942.
35. TNA, ADM 1/11280, report of Admiralty Selection Tests Committee, 20 March 1941.
36. TNA, ADM 1/21955, history of personnel selection methods, 1950-1.
37. TNA, ADM 1/11280, report of Admiralty Selection Tests Committee, 20 March 1941.
38. TNA, ADM 1/21955, history of personnel selection methods, 1950-1
39. TNA, ADM 1/12114, Navy Estimates, 1942.
40. TNA, ADM 1/21955, history of personnel selection methods, 1950-1.
41. TNA, ADM 1/12133, Navy Estimates, 1943.
42. TNA, ADM 1/12067, Note by Cabinet Section, 19 June 1942.
43. TNA, ADM 213/76, 'German Neuropsychiatry with special reference to the Kriegsmarine' by Surgeon Captains D Curran and MacDonald Critchley, August 1946.
44. R Ransome Wallis, *Two Red Stripes* (1973), p. 44.
45. D J Kevles, 'Testing the Nation's Intelligence: Psychologists in World War I', *Journal of American History*, 55 (1968), 565-81.
46. B Lavery, *Churchill's Navy* (2006), p. 58.
47. TNA, ADM 298/352, M Le Fanu, 'What shall We do for the Post-War Sailor?, March 1946.
48. J L S Coulter, *The Royal Naval Medical Service* (1954), pp. 35-6.
49. B Lavery, *Hostilities Only* (2004), pp. 152-4.
50. TNA, ADM 1/21955, history of personnel selection methods, 1950-1.
51. TNA, ADM 1/11280, report of Admiralty Selection Tests Committee, 20 March 1941.
52. B Lavery, *Hostilities Only* (2004), p. 155.
53. TNA, ADM 11361, report of Dr Vernon on training methods in anti-submarine schools, 1943.
54. TNA, ADM 1/14091, report of investigation into the value of an intelligence test given to borderline CW candidates, August 1943.
55. TNA, ADM 1/18698, HMS *King Alfred*: medical aspects of selection and training of RNVR officers during the war, 1945.
56. P Scott, *The Eye of the Wind* (1961), p. 280
57. A. Guinness, *Blessings in Disguise* (1985), p. 153.
58. B Lavery, *In Which They Serve* (2008), p. 177.
59. See Chapters 5 and 6.
60. V L Mathews, *Blue Tapestry* (1948), p. 81.
61. TNA, ADM 1/12680, Naval training of WRNS, 1942.
62. G. Rewcastle, 'Minor Maladies of Wrens', *Journal of the Royal Naval Medical Service*, 28 (1942), 215.
63. TNA, ADM 1/15308, memo on medical fitness of WRNS, 21 May 1943.
64. Ibid., notes concerning the medical examination of WRNS candidates, August 1941.
65. H Philip, *Two Rings and a Red* (1944), p. 21.
66. Private information, Suzanne Willson, ex-Wren.
67. TNA, ADM 1/15308, notes concerning the medical examination of WRNS candidates, August 1941.
68. TNA, ADM 1/14697, Medical examination of WRNS, 7 January 1943.
69. Ibid., memo on WRNS discharge on medical grounds, 1 March 1943.
70. V L Mathews, *Blue Tapestry* (1948), pp. 179-80.
71. M H Fletcher, *The WRNS: a History of the Women's Royal Naval Service* (1989), p. 28.
72. J L S Coulter, *The Royal Naval Medical Service* (1954), pp. 82-3.
73. G. Rewcastle, 'Minor Maladies of Wrens', *Journal of the Royal Naval Medical Service*, 28 (1942), 215.
74. C M Wilson, *Anatomy of Courage* (1945), pp. 92-3.

Chapter Two: In Which They Healed
1. B Lavery (ed), *The Royal Navy Officer's Pocket Book 1944* (2007), p. 56.
2. *In Which We Serve* (Two Cities, 1942), dir. Noel Coward (DVD,

NOTES

Carlton Visual Entertainment 3711501663, 2003).
3. B Hunt, *A Doctor's Odyssey* (1995), p. 74.
4. TNA, ADM 116/3277, note by Arthur Gaskell on shortage of naval medical officers, 15 March 1930.
5. TNA, ADM 116/4550, Report of Committee on the Medical Branches of the Defence Services, Cmd. 4394, 1933.
6. TNA, ADM 1/100062, shortage of medical officers, 25 February 1938.
7. Editorial, *Journal of Royal Navy Medical Service*, 26/1 (1940), 1.
8. TNA, WO293/3, Military Training for Medical Students, 10 December 1915.
9. Letter, *St Mary's Hospital Gazette*, 21/6 (1916), 90–1.
10. TNA, ADM 1/11336, Committee of Inquiry on Medical Personnel, 1 January 1941.
11. Ibid., response of Admiralty to Committee of Inquiry on Medical Personnel, 4 April 1941.
12. TNA, ADM 1/11336, Committee of Inquiry on Medical Personnel, 1 January 1941.
13. TNA, ADM 1/14961, note by S F Dudley, 13 August 1943.
14. TNA, WO 163/485, Committee on the Organisation of the Medical Services, 24 January 1946. Medical Personnel figures 1939–46 show the great rise in the number of doctors, nurses and other medical staff during the war: see Appendix 2.
15. TNA, ADM 1/24249, memo by S F Dudley, 1943.
16. Ibid., memo on the civil medical position and Royal Naval Medical Service, 29 April 1943.
17. Ibid., memo by S F Dudley, 1943.
18. Ibid., memorandum on manpower of the Royal Naval Medical Service, S F Dudley, 16 March 1943.
19. Ibid., note by S F Dudley, 10 December 1942.
20. R Ransome Wallis, *Two Red Stripes* (1973), pp. 10–11.
21. B Hunt, *A Doctor's Odyssey* (1995), pp. 52–3.
22. M Kater, *Doctors under Hitler* (1989), pp. 153–4.
23. K Brown, *Fighting Fit* (2008), pp. 144–5.
24. St Mary's Hospital Archives, DP5/11, letter from F M McRae to A H Buck, 30 September 1940.
25. St Mary's Hospital Archives, DP5/15, letter from F M McRae to A H Buck, 26 April 1941.
26. Obituary, James Macfarlane, *St Mary's Hospital Gazette* 49/1 (1943), 3.
27. TNA, WO 163/485, Committee on the Organisation of the Medical Services, 24 January 1946.
28. J L S Coulter, *The Royal Naval Medical Service* (1954), p. 17.
29. B Lavery (ed), *The Royal Navy Officer's Pocket Book 1944* (2007), pp. 47, 49.
30. Ibid., p. 48.
31. Ibid., p. 49.
32. Ibid., p. 46.
33. B Hunt, *A Doctor's Odyssey* (1995), p. 47.
34. Ibid., p. 53.
35. R Ransome Wallis, *Two Red Stripes* (1973), p. 11.
36. Ibid., p. 15.
37. 'Points to remember before ordering your uniform' by Hector Powe, in B Lavery (ed), *The Royal Navy Officer's Pocket Book 1944* (2007), p. 19.
38. H Philip, *Two Rings and a Red* (1944), p. 7.
39. Ibid., p. 8.
40. TNA, ADM 1/24249, memorandum on manpower of the Royal Naval Medical Service, S F Dudley, 16 March 1943.
41. B Lavery (ed), *The Royal Navy Officer's Pocket Book 1944* (2007), p. 46.
42. R Ransome Wallis, *Two Red Stripes* (1973), p. 63.
43. B Taylor, *The Battlecruiser HMS Hood* (2004), p. 125.
44. TNA, ADM 101/598, medical journal, *Prince of Wales*, 1941.
45. TNA, ADM 101/624, medical journal, *Barle*, 1943.
46. TNA, ADM 101/592, medical journal, *Indomitable*, 1941.
47. B Taylor, *The Battlecruiser HMS Hood* (2004), p. 125.
48. B Lavery (ed), *The Royal Navy Officer's Pocket Book 1944* (2007), p. 52.
49. TNA, ADM 261/6, memo by J Robertson on corvettes of 'Flower' Class, 25 March 1942.

50. TNA, ADM 101/574, medical journal, F Whitwell, *Worcester*, 1940.
51. J L S Coulter, *The Royal Naval Medical Service* (1954), pp. 19–20.
52. B Lavery (ed), *The Royal Navy Officer's Pocket Book 1944* (2007), p. 50.
53. ADM 261/11, Suggested lecture for newly entered medical officers under instruction in depot, n.d.
54. ADM 1/24249, letter from A V Alexander to Lord Cranborne, 10 May 1943.
55. B Taylor, *The Battlecruiser HMS Hood* (2004), p. 125.
56. B Lavery (ed), *The Royal Navy Officer's Pocket Book 1944* (2007), pp. 54–5.
57. Ibid., p. 55.
58. ADM 261/11, Suggested lecture for newly entered medical officers under instruction in depot, n.d.
59. B Lavery (ed), *The Royal Navy Officer's Pocket Book 1944* (2007), p. 48.
60. H Philip, *Two Rings and a Red* (1944), p. 19.
61. ADM 261/2, report on tour of RAF stations, 1941.
62. F A Henley, *Chasing the Golden Fleece* (2002), p. 11.
63. B Hunt, *A Doctor's Odyssey* (1995).
64. R Ransome Wallis, *Two Red Stripes* (1973), p. 130.
65. TNA, HS 9/971/5, D S MacPhail, SOE personnel file note, 7 December 1942.
66. Ibid., Para-Military report on D S MacPhail, 4 February 1943.
67. Ibid., letter from H A Simpson to W C V Griffiths, 11 December 1942.
68. Ibid., note on responsibilities of Surgeon Lieutenant D S MacPhail, 1943.
69. Ibid., report on accidental injury, D S MacPhail, 25 May 1943.
70. Ibid., D S MacPhail, service record, 1943–6.
71. TNA, HS 9/1594/3, P E D S Wilkinson, 1943–5.
72. TNA, ADM 261/11, Suggested lecture for newly entered medical officers under instruction in depot, n.d.
73. G Clark, *Doc: 100 Year History of the Sick Berth Branch* (1984), p. 130.
74. St Mary's Hospital Archives, DP5/19, letter from F M McRae to A H Buck, 18 August 1943.
75. St Mary's Hospital Archives, DP5/16, letter from F M McRae to A H Buck, 13 February 1943.
76. St Mary's Hospital Archives, DP5/19, letter from F M McRae to A H Buck, 18 August 1943.
77. Letter from 'Nelson Expects', *St Mary's Hospital Gazette*, 49/3 (1943), 53–4.
78. R P M Miles, 'OHMS', *St Mary's Hospital Gazette*, 49/8 (1943), 143.
79. J Rose, *Nursing Churchill* (2018), pp. 116, 128.
80. TNA, ADM 234/4, censorship, 1943.
81. J Rose, *Nursing Churchill* (2018), p. 125.
82. TNA, HS 9/971/5, note on D MacPhail, 20 July 1943.
83. Letter from 'Surgeon Lieutenant RNVR', *St Mary's Hospital Gazette*, 46/2 (1940), 36.
84. St Mary's Hospital Archives, DP5/16, letter from F M McRae to A H Buck, 13 February 1943.
85. Obituary, Christopher Congreve Henry Dent, *St Mary's Hospital Gazette* 47/6 (1941), 85.
86. Obituary, Cecil Charrington Kirby, *St Mary's Hospital Gazette* 48/5 (1942), 72.
87. *St Mary's Hospital Gazette* 48/9 (1942), 152.
88. St Mary's Hospital Archives, DP5/16, letter from F M McRae to A H Buck, 13 February 1943.
89. TNA, ADM 261/6, memo by J Robertson on corvettes of 'Flower' Class, 25 March 1942.
90. St Mary's Hospital Archives, DP5/19, letter from F M McRae to A H Buck, 18 August 1943.
91. R Ransome Wallis, *Two Red Stripes* (1973), pp. 83–4.
92. R P M Miles, 'OHMS', *St Mary's Hospital Gazette*, 49/8 (1943), 143–4.
93. TNA, ADM 1/16764, memo from Medical Officer in Charge of Royal Naval Hospital Haslar, 5 October 1943.
94. Ibid., memo from Medical Officer in Charge of Royal Naval Hospital Plymouth, 20 October 1943.
95. TNA, LAB 29/249, guide for the use of local officers of the Ministry of Labour and National Service, 1945.
96. G Clark, *Doc: 100 Year History of the Sick Berth Branch* (1984), p. 136.

NOTES

97. Ibid., p. 153.
98. TNA, LAB 29/249, guide for the use of local officers of the Ministry of Labour and National Service, 1945.
99. TNA, ADM 1/ 16764, memo from Surgeon Rear Admiral, RN Hospital Chatham on 'Depreciation in the Standard of Nursing Efficiency', 20 September 1943.
100. TNA, ADM 101/563, medical journal, *Foresight*, 1940.
101. TNA, ADM 261/ 7, mobilisation in war, 1939.
102. Ibid., memo from Surgeon Rear Admiral, RN Hospital Chatham on 'Depreciation in the Standard of Nursing Efficiency', 20 September 1943.
103. TNA, ADM 261/5, medical report on Operation 'Husky', 10 July 1943.
104. G Clark, *Doc: 100 Year History of the Sick Berth Branch* (1984), p. 140.
105. B Hunt, *A Doctor's Odyssey* (1995), p. 62.
106. TNA, ADM 261/ 6, memo by J Robertson on corvettes of 'Flower' Class, 25 March 1942.
107. TNA, ADM 1/26791, 'The post-war sick berth staff', January 1950.
108. J L S Coulter, *The Royal Naval Medical Service* (1954), pp. 48–9.
109. TNA, ADM 1/12682, letter from A V Alexander, Ministry of Labour, 26 January 1943.
110. Ibid., letter from A V Alexander to Ernest Bevin, 9 February 1943.
111. Ibid., letter from Sir Dudley Sheldon to H N de Villiers, 12 March 1943.
112. TNA, ADM 1/17778, distribution of nurses, 25 April 1945.
113. S M Sacharski, *To Be a Nurse* (1990), p. 51.
114. TNA, ADM 1/13975, memo by S F Dudley, 17 June 1943.
115. TNA, ADM 1/1697, letter from R Phipps Hornby to L W Joynson-Hicks, 29 May 1943.
116. Ibid., memo from First Lord, 26 May 1944.
117. J L S Coulter, *The Royal Naval Medical Service* (1954), p. 20.

Chapter Three: Hospitals Under Fire
1. E Birbeck, A Ryder and P Ward, *The Royal Hospital Haslar* (2009), pp. 107–8.
2. TNA, WO 163/485, Committee on the Organisation of the Medical Services, 24 January 1946.
3. TNA, ADM 261/7, mobilisation in war or an emergency, 1939.
4. A L Revell, *Haslar the Royal Hospital* (2000), p. 25.
5. H Richardson, *English Hospitals 1660-1948* (1998), p. 86.
6. TNA, ADM 261/7, mobilisation in war or an emergency, 1939.
7. K Brown, *Poxed and Scurvied* (2011), p. 73.
8. TNA, ADM 261/7, mobilisation in war or an emergency, 1939.
9. J L S Coulter, *The Royal Naval Medical Service* (1954), pp. 9-13.
10. Ibid., p. 367.
11. H Richardson, *English Hospitals 1660-1948* (1998), p. 86.
12. J L S Coulter, *The Royal Naval Medical Service* (1954), p. 343.
13. D P Gourd, 'Where the Cider Apples Grow', *Journal of the Royal Naval Medical Service*, 68 (1982), 42.
14. G Clark, *Doc: 100 Year History of the Sick Berth Branch* (1984), p. 153.
15. D P Gourd, 'Where the Cider Apples Grow', *Journal of the Royal Naval Medical Service*, 68 (1982), 40.
16. B Hunt, *A Doctor's Odyssey* (1995), pp. 75–6.
17. TNA, ADM 1/27771, annual report of Naval Health Officer, Western Approaches Command, 1942.
18. B Hunt, *A Doctor's Odyssey* (1995), pp. 75–6.
19. J L S Coulter, *The Royal Naval Medical Service* (1954), p. 331.
20. Ibid., p. 350.
21. Ibid., p. 371.
22. R Ransome Wallis, *Two Red Stripes* 1973), p. 129.
23. B F Avery (ed), *The History of the Medical Department of the United States Navy in World War II* (1953), p. 37.
24. Ibid., p. 38.
25. TNA, ADM 261/7, mobilisation in war or an emergency, 1939.
26. TNA, ADM 178/355A, letter to H T C May from R May, 1 June 1942.
27. Ibid., notes on Chief Petty Officer Arthur John Dunnett, Queen Victoria Cottage Hospital, East Grinstead, Maxillo-Facial Unit, 5 June 1942.

28. J L S Coulter, *The Royal Naval Medical Service* (1954), p. 338.
29. Ibid., p. 364.
30. TNA, ADM 1/11076, minute on procedure for invaliding and discharge of limbless men, 1941.
31. F C Hunot, 'Administrative Experiences at the Royal Naval Hospital Haslar in Connection with the Reception of Casualties, March 1942 to October 1944', *Journal of the Royal Naval Medical Service*, 32 (1946), 32.
32. J L S Coulter, *The Royal Naval Medical Service* (1954), p. 320.
33. H R Vickers, 'Royal Naval Hospital, Haslar 1940-44', *Journal of the Royal Naval Medical Service*, 70 (1984), 105.
34. TNA, ADM 179/201, memo from Commander-in-Chief, Portsmouth, 8 July 1941.
35. Ibid., protection of Royal Naval Hospital Haslar against enemy attack, 1 July 1941.
36. F C Hunot, 'Administrative Experiences at the Royal Naval Hospital Haslar in Connection with the Reception of Casualties, March 1942 to October 1944', *Journal of the Royal Naval Medical Service*, 32 (1946), 20.
37. G Clark, *Doc: 100 Year History of the Sick Berth Branch* (1984), p. 138.
38. F C Hunot, 'Administrative Experiences at the Royal Naval Hospital Haslar in Connection with the Reception of Casualties, March 1942 to October 1944', *Journal of the Royal Naval Medical Service*, 32 (1946), 20.
39. TNA, ADM 1/1006, underground operating theatre at Chatham, May 1939.
40. J L S Coulter, *The Royal Naval Medical Service* (1954), p. 336.
41. TNA, ADM 261/9, air raids on RN Hospital, Plymouth, 1941; J L S Coulter, *The Royal Naval Medical Service* (1954), pp. 328–31.
42. G Clark, *Doc: 100 Year History of the Sick Berth Branch* (1984), p. 154.
43. J L S Coulter, *The Royal Naval Medical Service* (1954), pp. 328–31.
44. TNA, ADM 1/12874, note by Medical Director General on establishment of RN Hospital Dartmouth, 8 February 1943.
45. J L S Coulter, *The Royal Naval Medical Service* (1954), p. 388.
46. G Clark, *Doc: 100 Year History of the Sick Berth Branch* (1984), p. 150.
47. B B Waterman, 'Memories of Malta 1940-42', *Journal of the Royal Naval Medical Service*, 70 (1984), 182.
48. Ibid., 183.
49. G. Clark, *Doc: 100 Year History of the Sick Berth Branch* (1984), p. 150.
50. TNA, ADM 1/16092, repair of Bighi Hospital, 30 August 1944.
51. TNA, ADM 1/29928, recommendation for decoration of Sister Edith Joyce MacDonald, 9 August 1944.
52. TNA, ADM 199/27766, medical situation in the Mediterranean Fleet, 10 December 1941.
53. Ibid., medical situation in the Mediterranean Fleet, 30 June 1941.
54. G Clark, *Doc: 100 Year History of the Sick Berth Branch* (1984), p. 145.
55. F Henley, *Chasing the Golden Fleece* (2002), p. 49.
56. TNA, ADM 199/27766, medical situation in the Mediterranean Fleet, 10 December 1941.
57. J L S Coulter, *The Royal Naval Medical Service* (1956), p. 144.
58. TNA, ADM 116/4972, note by J Eccles, 15 August 1942.
59. TNA, ADM 199/1286, report by H L Cleave, 23 October 1945.
60. Ibid.
61. TNA, ADM 1/17920, letter from H L Cleave, 20 December 1945.
62. TNA, ADM 199/1286, report by H L Cleave, 23 October 1945.
63. TNA, ADM 1/18699, report on activities and employment during period served as prisoner of war of the Imperial Japanese Army, 25 December 1941–8 September 1945, John A Pager, 11 October 1945.
64. TNA, ADM 199/1286, report by H L Cleave, 23 October 1945.
65. Ibid.
66. WO 141/101, atrocities committed by the Japanese in Hong Kong, 1942.
67. J L S Coulter, *The Royal Naval Medical Service* (1954), p. 408.

NOTES

68. TNA, ADM 1/18700, history of Royal Naval Hospital Simonstown, 1939-41.
69. J L S Coulter, *The Royal Naval Medical Service* (1954), p. 14.
70. TNA, ADM 116/5121, note by Sir Sheldon Dudley on hospitalisation facilities and requirements in the Far East, 16 December 1943.
71. B F Avery (ed), *The History of the Medical Department of the United States Navy in World War II* (1953), p. 35.
72. Ibid., p. 37.
73. J L S Coulter, *The Royal Naval Medical Service* (1954), p. 411.
74. G Clark, *Doc: 100 Year History of the Sick Berth Branch* (1984), pp. 140-3.
75. Ibid., p. 141.
76. Appendix 3.
77. J L S Coulter, *The Royal Naval Medical Service* (1954), pp. 102-3.
78. Ibid., p.105.
79. Ibid., p. 108.
80. Ibid., pp. 97-108.
81. B F Avery (ed), *The History of the Medical Department of the United States Navy in World War II* (1953), p. 34.
82. TNA, ADM 179/413, report of medical officer in charge of RN Hospital Haslar, 15 August 1944.
83. TNA, ADM 39/256, instructions concerning Naval Hospital Ships and Hospital Carriers, 1939.
84. J L S Coulter, *The Royal Naval Medical Service* (1954), p. 100.
85. Ibid., pp. 56-7.
86. TNA, ADM 116/5121, note by Sir Sheldon Dudley on hospitalisation facilities and requirements in the Far East, 16 December 1943.
87. TNA, WO 32/11697, report by R M Porter on role of British Pacific Fleet in repatriation of released allied prisoners of war and internees, 1945.
88. J L S Coulter, *The Royal Naval Medical Service* (1954), p.108.
89. Ibid., p. 106.
90. Ibid., p. 103.
91. Ibid., p. 113.
92. Ibid., p. 116.
93. Ibid., p. 58.

Chapter Four: Our Ships at Sea
1. W J Forbes Guild, 'Some Observations on the Potentialities of Air-conditioning for HM Ships on Tropical Service', *Journal of Royal Navy Medical Service*, 26 (1940), 262.
2. TNA, FD 1/7018 Minutes of RNPRC, 6th meeting, 30 March 1943.
3. TNA, ADM 261/4, seasickness, by H E Holling, 28 July 1943.
4. TNA, ADM 298/342, report on visit to USA by C E J Streatfield and G M Weddell, October 1945.
5. TNA, FD 1/7018 Minutes of RNPRC, 1st meeting, 17 November 1942.
6. TNA, ADM 261/ 6, memo by J Robertson on corvettes of 'Flower' Class, 25 March 1942.
7. Ibid., improvement of warship habitability in Tropics, nd.
8. TNA, ADM 298/316, proposals for organisation of a tropical research unit, by H C Bazett and M Critchley, 30 November 1944.
9. RRHL, 'Tropical Tales', *St Mary's Hospital Gazette* 48/10 (1942), 164.
10. M Critchley, 'Problems of Naval Warfare under Climatic Extremes', *British Medical Journal*, 2 (1945), 208.
11. TNA, ADM 298/303, RNPRC Gunnery Sub-committee, reduction of heat in ships, nd.
12. TNA, ADM 261/6, report on living and working conditions in the Tropics by Macdonald Critchley and H E Holling, 22 April 1944.
13. TNA, ADM 298/338, bacterial content of the air of HM ships under wartime conditions, by F P Ellis and W F Raymond, August 1945.
14. TNA, ADM 101/631, medical journal, *Emerald*, 1943.
15. TNA, ADM 28/1/100, habitability report on HM ships serving in the Tropics, August 1944-March 1945 by H E Holling, June 1945.
16. J B Hattendorf, R J B Knight, A W H Pearsall, N A M Rodger and G Till (eds), *British Naval Documents 1204-1960* (1993), p. 1002.
17. TNA, ADM 101/623, medical journal, *Aire*, 1943.
18. TNA, ADM 298/452, MRC notes on condensation and ventilation in MTBS, MGBs and MLs, 29 April 1943.

19. TNA, ADM 28/1/100, habitability report on HM ships serving in the Tropics, August 1944 – March 1945 by H E Holling, June 1945.
20. TNA, ADM 1/16735 Plan for investigation of effects of hot environments upon working efficiency and health of navy personnel, July 1944.
21. Ibid., note by Director of Naval Ordnance, 25 August 1944.
22. TNA, ADM 298/316, proposals for organisation of a tropical research unit, by H C Bazett and M Critchley, 30 November 1944.
23. TNA, ADM 261/6, report on living and working conditions in the Tropics by Macdonald Critchley and H E Holling, 22 April 1944.
24. Ibid., 'Living and Working Conditions among RN Personnel in the Tropics' by M Critchley and H E Holling, 1945.
25. A J Sims, 'The Habitability of Naval Ships under Wartime Conditions', *Transactions of the Royal Institute of Naval Architects*, 87 (1945), 64.
26. TNA, ADM 1/16156, HMS *Lewes* living and working conditions, 25 October 1944.
27. TNA, ADM 28/1/100, habitability report on HM ships serving in the Tropics, August 1944 – March 1945 by H E Holling, June 1945.
28. TNA, ADM 261/6, report on living and working conditions in the Tropics by Macdonald Critchley and H E Holling, 22 April 1944.
29. TNA, ADM 28/1/100, habitability report on HM ships serving in the Tropics, August 1944 – March 1945 by H E Holling, June 1945.
30. Ibid.
31. TNA, ADM 1/17236, first report of the Habitability Mission to the Eastern Fleet, 1944, by F P Ellis, July 1945.
32. Ibid. Incidences of sickness on ship and ashore were:
    Skin diseases 43 per cent in ships, 40 per cent ashore.
    Dysentery 12 per cent in ships, 13 per cent ashore.
    Common cold, 7 per cent in ships, 8 per cent ashore.
    Minor injuries, 19 per cent in ships, 15 per cent ashore.
33. TNA, ADM 298/338, bacterial content of the air of HM ships under wartime conditions, by F P Ellis and W F Raymond, August 1945.
34. TNA, ADM 1/17236, first report of the Habitability Mission to the Eastern Fleet, 1944, by F P Ellis, July 1945.
35. TNA, ADM 261/11, conditions in HMS *Devonshire*, by J W Scott, December 1945.
36. TNA, ADM 298/341, living arrangements in American warships, by C E J Streatfield and G M Weddell, October 1945.
37. TNA, ADM 298/454, visit to US naval units, by M Critchley, 12 July 1943.
38. Ibid.
39. TNA 261/1, HMS *Bellona*, medical journal, A Daunt Bateman, 1 April–31 June 1944.
40. TNA, ADM 298/352, M Le Fanu, 'What shall We do for the Post-War Sailor?', March 1946.
41. A J Sims, 'The Habitability of Naval Ships under Wartime Conditions', *Transactions of the Royal Institute of Naval Architects*, 87 (1945), 52.
42. TNA, ADM, 298/451, memorandum on medical conditions observed during passage on Northern Convoy in North Russia, by Macdonald Critchley, 17 November 1941.
43. TNA, ADM 261/11, memo on medical conditions observed during passage of Northern Convoy in North Russia and Iceland, nd.
44. TNA, ADM 1/15312, medical action report, HMS *Scylla*, J L S Coulter, 15 February – 13 March 1943.
45. R Ransome Walls, *Two Red Stripes* (1973), p. 72.
46. TNA, ADM 1/15312, medical action report, HMS *Scylla*, J L S Coulter, 15 February – 13 March 1943.
47. L J Thomas, *Through Ice and Fear* (2015), p. 79.
48. TNA, ADM 116/4972, SNBNO North Russia to Admiralty C in C Home Fleet, Naval Cypher A1, 4 August 1942.
49. Ibid., note by J Eccles, 15 August 1942.
50. TNA, ADM 298/4, observations on cold weather clothing trials by J C D Hutchinson, June 1944.

NOTES

51. TNA, ADM 261/9, report on action damage on HMS *Norfolk*, 21 January 1944.
52. TNA, ADM 261/10, report of Royal Naval Personnel Research Committee visit to Coastal Forces, 13 January 1943.
53. TNA, ADM 1/15312, medical action report, HMS *Scylla*, J L S Coulter, 15 February – 13 March 1943.
54. M Critchley, 'Problems of Naval Warfare under Climatic Extremes', *British Medical Journal*, 2 (1945), 174.
55. IWM, Documents.2130, memoir of J K Neale, 1994.
56. J L S Coulter, *The Royal Naval Medical Service* (1954), pp. 198–9.
57. TNA, ADM 261/6, report on living and working conditions in the Tropics by Macdonald Critchley and H E Holling, 22 April 1944.
58. TNA, ADM 261/11, conditions on HMS *Devonshire* en route from Devonport to Sydney, by J W Scott, December 1945.
59. J B Hattendorf, R J B Knight, A W H Pearsall, N A M Rodger and G Till (eds), *British Naval Documents 1204-1960* (1993), p. 1003.
60. J L S Coulter, *The Royal Naval Medical Service* (1954), p. 193.
61. TNA, ADM 261/6, report on living and working conditions in the Tropics by Macdonald Critchley and H E Holling, 22 April 1944.
62. TNA, ADM 261/1, action damage report on HMS *Warspite*, nd.
63. TNA, ADM 298/2, protection from flash burns by light weight fabrics, by O M Lidwell, April 1944.
64. TNA, ADM 298/3, tests of flash burn protective cream, USA NMRI-70, by R B Bourdillon and O M Lidwell, 4 May 1944.
65. J P W Mallalieu, *Very Ordinary Seaman* (1944), p. 88.
66. TNA, ADM 101/6528, medical officer's journal, *Belfast*, J H Nicolson, 1 January–31 March 1944.
67. TNA, ADM 261/5, report on medical department of HMS *Brittany* during Operation 'Husky', A M McWatt Green, 1943.
68. TNA, ADM 101/6528, medical officer's journal, *Belfast*, J H Nicolson, June 1944.
69. TNA, ADM 1/12114, Navy Estimates, 1942,
70. TNA, ADM 101/574, medical journal, *Worcester*, Surgeon Lieutenant Whitwell, 1940.
71. R Lovell, *Churchill's Doctor* (1992), p. 213.
72. TNA, ADM 261/6, report on living and working conditions in the Tropics by Macdonald Critchley and H E Holling, 22 April 1944.
73. TNA, ADM 298/454, visit to US naval units, by M Critchley, 12 July 1943.
74. TNA, ADM 219/380, systems of messing in ships and store establishments, April 1943.
75. E Hampshire (ed), *Brinestain and Biscuit* (2007), pp. 4–12.
76. TNA, ADM 298/338, bacterial content of the air of HM ships under wartime conditions, by F P Ellis and W F Raymond, August 1945.
77. TNA, ADM 219/380, systems of messing in ships and store establishments, April 1943.
78. TNA, ADM 261/11, conditions on HMS *Devonshire* en route from Devonport to Sydney, by J W Scott, December 1945.
79. J B Hattendorf, R J B Knight, A W H Pearsall, N A M Rodger and G Till (eds), *British Naval Documents 1204-1960* (1993), p. 1004.
80. E Hampshire (ed), *Brinestain and Biscuit* (2007), pp. 4–12.
81. TNA, ADM 298/454, visit to US naval units, by M Critchley, 12 July 1943.
82. TNA, ADM 1/15312, medical action report, HMS *Scylla*, J L S Coulter, 15 February – 13 March 1943.
83. J L S Coulter, *The Royal Naval Medical Service* (1956), p. 108.
84. J B Hattendorf, R J B Knight, A W H Pearsall, N A M Rodger and G Till (eds), *British Naval Documents 1204-1960* (1993), p. 864.
85. NAAFI Public Relations Branch, *The Story of NAAFI* (1944).
86. TNA, ADM 199/604, SBNO to Admiralty, 12 June 1942.
87. TNA, ADM 298/352, M Le Fanu, 'What shall We do for the Post-War Sailor?', March 1946.

Chapter Five: Sea-Room for Change
1. K Brown, *Poxed and Scurvied* (2011), p. 192.

2. K Brown, *Fighting Fit* (2008), pp. 110–38.
3. TNA, FD1/5892, blood transfusion research, 1940.
4. W M Butler, 'Blood Groups and Blood Matching', *Journal of the Royal Naval Medical Service*, 26 (1940), 148.
5. TNA, FD1/5939, memo to R E Ford re proposed co-operation between Royal Naval Blood Transfusion Service and Regional Blood Transfusion Service Ministry of Health Region 2, 24 October 1941.
6. L Whitby, 'Blood Transfusion in the Field: Organisation of Supplies' in H Letherby Tidy (ed), *Inter-Allied Conferences on War Medicine 1942–1945* (1947), pp. 123–6.
7. TNA, WO 222/1479, Army Transfusion Service, 1940; FD 1/5290, Progress Report of Blood Transfusion Emergency Depots Committee covering the period from the outbreak of war to 30 September 1940.
8. J C Watts, *Surgeon at War* (1955), p. 42.
9. TNA, FD 1/5290, progress report on Blood Transfusion Emergency Depots from the outbreak of the War to 30 September 1940.
10. Ibid., minutes of the Blood Transfusion Emergency Depots Committee, 1 May 1940.
11. Ibid., progress report on Blood Transfusion Emergency Depots from the outbreak of the War to 30 September 1940.
12. TNA, ADM 261/4, report on treatment of a number of burns, May 1943.
13. F P Ellis, 'A Description of the Blood Transfusion and Resuscitation Unit, 64th General Hospital', *Journal of the Royal Naval Medical Service*, 28 (1942), 136–44.
14. F A Henley, *Chasing the Golden Fleece* (2002), pp. 29–30.
15. TNA, FD1/5939, report on Royal Naval Transfusion Service, 5 November 1941.
16. Ibid., memo to R E Ford re proposed co-operation between Royal Naval Blood Transfusion Service and Regional Blood Transfusion Service Ministry of Health Region 2, 24 October 1941.
17. S G Rainsford, 'Royal Navy Blood Transfusion Service', *Journal of the Royal Navy Medical Service*, 35 (1949), 164.
18. A Hood, 'Army Medical Services in Action', *Journal of the Royal Army Medical Corps*, 38 (1943), 287–90.
19. J L S Coulter, *The Royal Naval Medical Service* (1954), p. 145.
20. TNA, ADM 101/6528, medical officer's journal, *Belfast*, J H Nicolson, June 1944.
21. TNA, ADM 261/5, report of medical officer on Operation 'Husky', *Scotsman*, 10 July 1943.
22. W M Butler, 'Blood Groups and Blood Matching', *Journal of the Royal Naval Medical Service*, 26 (1940), 153.
23. TNA, ADM 261/4, note by A N Drury, 26 May 1941.
24. C P G Wakeley, 'War Burns and their Treatment, *Journal of the Royal Naval Medical Service*, 27 (1941), 20.
25. TNA, ADM 261/9, account of battle of River Plate by Surgeon Lieutenant Hunter, 28 April 1942.
26. S M Cohen, 'Experience in the Treatment of War Burns', *British Medical Journal* (1940), 251–4.
27. TNA, FD1/6300, memorandum by A H McIndoe on treatment of burns in the RAF, 1942.
28. TNA, AIR 20/10269, George H Morley, 'Plastic Surgery in the Royal Air Force', May 1948.
29. Emergency Medical Service, 'The Local Treatment of War Burns', *British Medical Journal* (1940), 489.
30. J Bunyan, 'Treatment of burns and wounds by the envelope method', *British Medical Journal*, 2 (5 July 1941), 1–7.
31. C P G Wakeley, 'War Burns and their Treatment, *Journal of the Royal Naval Medical Service*, 27 (1941), 24.
32. Ibid., 26.
33. Emergency Medical Service, 'The Local Treatment of War Burns', *British Medical Journal* (1940), 489.
34. TNA, FD 1/6300, letter from L Colebrook to Dr Drury, 17 April 1942.
35. TNA, FD 1/6248 Report to the Army Council of the Army Advisory Committee on Maxillo-Facial Injuries (1940), p. 3.

36. Gillies Archive, Queen Mary's Hospital, Sidcup, file 2324, Able Seaman W Vicarage, RN, 2 August 1917–8 September 1920.
37. TNA, ADM 178/355A, notes on A J Dunnett, Queen Victoria Cottage Hospital Maxillo-Facial Unit, 5 June 1942.
38. TNA, FD1/6300, memorandum by A H McIndoe on treatment of burns in the RAF, 1942.
39. J P Bennett, 'A History of the Queen Victoria Hospital, East Grinstead', *British Journal of Plastic Surgery*, 41 (1988), 422–40.
40. Bob Marchant, who worked as McIndoe's operating theatre attendant in the 1950s has commented that McIndoe was definitely 'the boss' but was not as difficult as he has often been made out and always thanked everyone if they met his demanding standards (conversation with author, July 2007); E R Mayhew, *The Reconstruction of Warriors* (2004), pp. 62–4.
41. C P G Wakeley, 'War Burns and their Treatment', *Journal of the Royal Naval Medical Service*, 27 (1941), 26–7.
42. TNA, AIR 49/354, report on maxillo-facial and plastic injuries in the RAF, 1942.
43. TNA, AIR 20/10269, press cutting from *The Daily Sketch*, 20 October 1942.
44. Ibid., 'The Guinea Pig', Christmas number, December 1947, p. 5.
45. TNA, ADM 178/355A, letter from R B Richards to P Humphrey Davies, 30 August 1943.
46. C P G Wakeley, 'War Burns and their Treatment', *Journal of the Royal Naval Medical Service*, 27 (1941), 34.
47. TNA, INF 6/519, 'Plastic Surgery in Wartime', Realist Film Unit, 23 October 1941.
48. TNA, ADM 178/255, memo on pulmonary tuberculosis in the Royal Navy, 18 October 1938.
49. W G C Fitzpatrick, 'Mass Miniature Radiography in the Royal Navy', *Journal of the Royal Naval Medical Service*, 27 (1941), 3.
50. TNA, ADM 178/255, memo on pulmonary tuberculosis in the Royal Navy, 18 October 1938.
51. W G C Fitzpatrick, 'Mass Miniature Radiography in the Royal Navy', *Journal of the Royal Naval Medical Service*, 27 (1941), 15.
52. TNA, ADM 1/27771, annual report of Naval Health Officer, Western Approaches Command, 1942.
53. TNA, ADM 178/255, memo on pulmonary tuberculosis in the Royal Navy, 18 October 1938.
54. TNA, ADM 178/255, memo on Admiralty decision on officers with TB, 30 May 1942.
55. W G C Fitzpatrick, 'Mass Miniature Radiography in the Royal Navy', *Journal of the Royal Naval Medical Service*, 27 (1941), 16.
56. TNA, ADM 261/6, report on living and working conditions among RN personnel in the Tropics, by Macdonald Critchley and H E Hollis, 22 April 1944.
57. TNA, ADM 298/317, tropical jungle clothing, by H C Bazett and Macdonald Critchley, December 1944.
58. TNA, FD 1/6239, memorandum on malaria for use of ships' surgeons, July 1942.
59. P W Sewell (ed), *Healers in World War II* (2001), pp. 21–2.
60. TNA, WO 222/159, malaria control in mobile warfare, Italian campaign, by A W S Thompson, 15 November 1945.
61. TNA, WO 204/4945, malaria control dusting by aircraft, 23 March 1944.
62. TNA, WO 222/159, malaria control in mobile warfare, Italian campaign, by A W S Thompson, 15 November 1945.
63. E J Mockler, 'DDT', *Journal of the Royal Naval Medical Service*, 33 (1947), 20.
64. Ibid., 24.
65. C M Wilson (Lord Moran), *Winston Churchill: The Struggle for Survival, 1940-1965* (1966), pp. 163–4.
66. K Brown, *Penicillin Man* (2004).
67. R D Coghill, 'The development of penicillin strains', in *The History of Penicillin Production*, American Institute of Chemical Engineers, Chemical Engineering Progress Symposium, 66/100 (1970), 15.
68. Pfizer Records Centre, Sandwich, Kent, Kemball Bishop records, Box

96B-2E, file 7, J G Barnes, 'Early Work on Penicillin in England with Special Reference to Bromley', May 1971.
69. R W Mussen, 'The Royal Navy Medical School', *Journal of the Royal Naval Medical Service*, 33 (1947), 63.
70. Ibid., 65.
71. TNA, ADM 1/15311, memo from C A Green, 17 March 1942.
72. Ibid., memo from Medical Officer in Charge, RN Medical School, 12 April 1943.
73. Ibid., letter from H W Florey to Admiral Griffiths, 28 April 1943.
74. Ibid., letter from C A Green to Admiral Dudley, 17 May 1943.
75. R Campbell, *Clevedon, Places and Faces* (2010), pp. 67–8.
76. K Brown, *Penicillin Man* (2004), pp. 114–15.
77. R W Mussen, 'The Royal Navy Medical School', *Journal of the Royal Naval Medical Service*, 33 (1947), 65.

Chapter Six: It's in the Air
1. TNA, ADM 261/12, report on Fleet Air Arm, 1946, citing senior medical officer of *Furious*, 1917.
2. B Crowhurst Archer, 'The Emotional Factor in Service Aviation', *Journal of the Royal Naval Medical Service*, 25 (1939), 113.
3. Ibid., 115.
4. TNA, AIR 2/11/87/9528, Report of Air Board Research Committee (Medical), 25 April 1917.
5. H E Whittingham, 'Medical Research and Aviation', *Journal of the Royal Naval Medical Service*, 26 (1941), 20.
6. B Crowhurst Archer, 'The Emotional Factor in Service Aviation', *Journal of the Royal Naval Medical Service*, 25 (1939), 109.
7. J D Simpson, 'The Medicine of Flying', *Journal of the Royal Naval Medical Service*, 27 (1941), 252.
8. C McAra, *Mainly in Minesweepers* (1991), p. 3.
9. TNA, ADM 1/16644, training for pilot and observer category B recruits for Fleet Air Arm of lower educational standard, 1943.
10. C McAra, *Mainly in Minesweepers* (1991), p. 25.
11. TNA, AIR 2/11/87, J G Priestley, report on 'Flight at High Altitudes', 30 April 1917.
12. Ibid., J S Haldane, report to Air Board Research Committee (Medical), 1917.
13. B Crowhurst Archer, 'The Emotional Factor in Service Aviation', *Journal of the Royal Naval Medical Service*, 25 (1939), 109.
14. TNA, ADM 101/602, medical journal, *Blackcap*, 1942.
15. H Popham, *Sea Flight* (1954), p. 4.
16. TNA, ADM 1/10119, Fleet Air Arm Station at Hatston, 1939.
17. J L S Coulter, *The Royal Naval Medical Service* (1954), p. 287.
18. R H Smith (ed), *Articles and Extracts from the MTE Journal* (1946), p. 499.
19. TNA, ADM 261/2, report on tour of RAF stations and establishments, July and August 1941.
20. N Hanson, *Carrier Pilot* (1979), p. 146.
21. TNA, ADM 261/2, report on tour of RAF stations and establishments, July and August 1941.
22. H E Whittingham, 'Medical Research and Aviation', *Journal of the Royal Naval Medical Service*, 26 (1941), 20–1.
23. B Jones (ed), *The Fleet Air Arm in the Second World War* (2012), pp. 267-70.
24. B Crowhurst Archer, 'The Emotional Factor in Service Aviation', *Journal of the Royal Naval Medical Service*, 25 (1939), 112.
25. B Lavery, *Churchill's Navy* (2006), p. 194.
26. TNA, ADM 261/4, meeting to discuss the problems of flying stress and neuroses in the flying personnel of the Fleet Air Arm, 22 November 1940.
27. TNA, ADM 1/17883, medical care of Fleet Air Arm in Middle East, 20 October 1942.
28. J L S Coulter, *The Royal Naval Medical Service* (1954), p. 292.
29. TNA, ADM 261/2, report on tour of RAF stations and establishments, July and August 1941.
30. TNA, ADM 261/4, meeting to discuss the problems of flying stress and neuroses in the flying personnel

NOTES

of the Fleet Air Arm, 22 November 1940.
31. B Jones (ed), *The Fleet Air Arm in the Second World War* (2012), p. 268.
32. TNA, ADM 261/4, meeting to discuss the problems of flying stress and neuroses in the flying personnel of the Fleet Air Arm, 22 November 1940.
33. B Jones (ed), *The Fleet Air Arm in the Second World War* (2012), p. 268.
34. TNA, ADM 261/4, meeting to discuss the problems of flying stress and neuroses in the flying personnel of the Fleet Air Arm, 22 November 1940.
35. TNA, ADM 261/2, report on tour of RAF stations and establishments, July and August 1941.
36. TNA, AIR 2/5016, extract from War Cabinet Scientific Advisory Committee, 7 July 1944.
37. J D Simpson, 'The Medicine of Flying', *Journal of the Royal Naval Medical Service*, 27 (1941), 258.
38. TNA, AIR 2/5016, creation of RAF Institute of Aviation Medicine, 1943–4.
39. H E Whittingham, 'Aviation Medicine', in R H Smith (ed), *Articles and Extracts from the MTE Journal* (1946), p. 298.
40. T M Gibson and M H Harrison, *Into Thin Air* (1984), pp. 109–12.
41. Ibid., p. 81.
42. Ibid., p. 125.
43. TNA, ADM 261/12, report on Staff Air Medical Officers' visit to School of Air Medicine, RNAS Eastleigh, 16 March 1944.
44. TNA, ADM 261/2, report on tour of RAF stations and establishments, July and August 1941.
45. TNA, WO 309/468, Military Tribunal no. 1. case no, 1, USA v. Karl Brandt, Siegfried Handler, Paul Rostock et al., 1947.
46. TNA, ADM 213/241, review of existing arrangements for obtaining information from Germany on recent advances in medicine and physiology, F P Ellis, November 1946.
47. G Enever, 'Edgar Pask and his Physiological Research: An Unsung Hero of World War Two', *Journal of the Royal Army Medical Corps*, 157/1 (2011), 8–11.
48. T M Gibson and M H Harrison, *Into Thin Air* (1984), p. 198.
49. H E Whittingham, 'Aviation Medicine', in R H Smith (ed), *Articles and Extracts from the MTE Journal* (1946), p. 299.
50. TNA, ADM 1/17883, medical care of Fleet Air Arm in Middle East, 20 October 1942.
51. TNA, ADM 261/2, report on tour of RAF stations and establishments, July and August 1941.
52. J L S Coulter, *The Royal Naval Medical Service* (1954), p. 195.
53. R H Smith (ed), *Articles and Extracts from the MTE Journal* (1946), p. 499.
54. H E Whittingham, 'Aviation Medicine', in R H Smith (ed), *Articles and Extracts from the MTE Journal* (1946), p. 300.
55. TNA, ADM 1/14112, report on ontological problems in the Fleet Air Arm by S Gay French, 24 November 1943.
56. TNA, ADM 1/17883, medical care of Fleet Air Arm in Middle East, 20 October 1942.
57. J L S Coulter, *The Royal Naval Medical Service* (1954), p. 294.
58. TNA, ADM 261/4, meeting to discuss the problems of flying stress and neuroses in the flying personnel of the Fleet Air Arm, 22 November 1940.
59. TNA, ADM 261/2, report on tour of RAF stations and establishments, July and August 1941.
60. Ibid.
61. TNA, ADM 261/12, report on Aviation Medicine course at Pensacola, by L G Topham, September – December 1943.
62. B F Avery (ed), *The History of the Medical Department of the United States Navy in World War II* (1953), pp. 226–7.
63. TNA, ADM 261/4, meeting to discuss the problems of flying stress and neuroses in the flying personnel of the Fleet Air Arm, 22 November 1940.
64. TNA, ADM 261/2, report on tour of RAF stations and establishments, July and August 1941.

65. TNA, FD1/6061, memo on proposed Medical Research Institute for the Royal Navy, 5 November 1945.

Chapter Seven: The Waves Above
1. H Philip, *Two Rings and a Red* (1944), p. 53.
2. J Hood (ed), *Submarine* (2007), p. 99.
3. Ibid., p. 35.
4. H Philip, *Two Rings and a Red* (1944), p. 41.
5. J L S Coulter, *The Royal Naval Medical Services* (1956), p. 13.
6. B Lavery, *Churchill's Navy* (2006), p. 212.
7. H Swaffer, *What Would Nelson Do?* (1946), p. 35.
8. C W Shilling and J W Kohl, *History of Submarine Medicine* (1947), pp. 46–7.
9. C Prag, *No Ordinary War* (2009), p. 79.
10. J L S Coulter, *The Royal Naval Medical Service* (1956), p. 13.
11. B Hunt, *A Doctor's Odyssey* (1995), p. 105.
12. H Philip, *Two Rings and a Red* (1944), p. 20.
13. Ibid., p. 40.
14. B F Avery (ed), *The History of the Medical Department of the United States Navy in World War II* (1953), p. 43.
15. TNA, ADM1/17235, medical officer's report on life and conditions on board a submarine, 20 February 1945.
16. H A Warner, *Iron Coffins: A U-boat Commander's War, 1939–1945* (1969), p. 158.
17. B Lavery, *Churchill's Navy* (2006), p. 214.
18. H Philip, *Two Rings and a Red* (1944), p. 40.
19. S Palmer and S Wallis (ed), *A War in Words* (2003), p. 234.
20. TNA, ADM 105/95, 'Living and Working Conditions on HM Submarine *Andrew* Operating in Tropical Waters' by J D Walters, September 1966.
21. TNA, ADM 261/6, report on living and working conditions among RN personnel in the Tropics, MacDonald Critchley and H E Holling, 22 April 1944.
22. H Philip, *Two Rings and a Red* (1944), p. 41.
23. TNA, ADM 261/6, report on living and working conditions among RN personnel in the Tropics, MacDonald Critchley and H E Holling, 22 April 1944.
24. C W Shilling and J W Kohl, *History of Submarine Medicine* (1947), p. 102.
25. TNA, ADM 261/6, report on living and working conditions among RN personnel in the Tropics, MacDonald Critchley and H E Holling, 22 April 1944.
26. Ibid., 'Living and Working Conditions among RN Personnel in the Tropics' by M Critchley and H E Holling, 1945.
27. TNA, ADM 28/1/100, habitability report on ships serving in Tropics, August 1944–March 1945, H E Holling, June 1945.
28. TNA, ADM 261/11, medical report on patrol conditions in HMS *Surf* and HMS *Storm*, Innes F Logan, 19 April 1944.
29. H Philip, *Two Rings and a Red* (1944), p. 69.
30. TNA, ADM 298/447, report on visit to HMS *Forth*, 19 March 1943.
31. M Arthur, *Lost Voices of the Royal Navy* (2005), p. 401.
32. TNA, ADM 298/447, report on visit to HMS *Forth*, 19 March 1943.
33. M Arthur, *Lost Voices of the Royal Navy* (2005), pp. 403–4.
34. C W Shilling and J W Kohl, *History of Submarine Medicine* (1947), p. 103.
35. TNA, ADM1/17235, medical officer's report on life and conditions on board a submarine, 20 February 1945.
36. TNA, ADM 105/95, 'Living and Working Conditions on HM Submarine *Andrew* Operating in Tropical Waters' by J D Walters, September 1966.
37. TNA, ADM 298/530, report on visit to assault units and submarines at Taranto, E M Case, September 1944.
38. TNA, ADM 298/309, observations on clothing for use in submarines, J C D Hutchinson, 1944.
39. TNA, ADM 1/20399, report on victualling stores for German navy,

F Brookhouse, M O Pelton and J S Weiner, October 1945.
40. TNA, ADM 298/309, observations on clothing for use in submarines, J C D Hutchinson, 1944.
41. IWM, Documents.2432, memoir of J P Mullins, 1993.
42. TNA, ADM 1/10065, report on messing in submarines, 14 June 1939.
43. C W Shilling and J W Kohl, *History of Submarine Medicine* (1947), pp. 147, 152.
44. TNA, ADM 1/10065, report on messing in submarines, 14 June 1939.
45. TNA, ADM 116/5346, Services' manpower requirements and allocations, 1944.
46. TNA, ADM 205/28, Binney Committee Manpower Enquiry, 1943.
47. TNA, ADM 116/5771, War Manning, 1941.
48. TNA, ADM 116/4429, report on effects of high pressure, carbon dioxide and cold, E M Case and J B S Haldane, 25 July 1940.
49. H Philip, *Two Rings and a Red* (1944), p. 73.
50. TNA, ADM 298/326, Medical Research Council Visual Problems Sub-Committee, 22 March 1945.
51. A F M Barron, 'The Lookout Problem on Submarines: Defective Night Vision', *Journal of the Royal Naval Medical Service*, 29 (1943), 195.
52. TNA, ADM 261/11, medical report on patrol conditions in HMS *Surf* and HMS *Storm*, Innes F Logan, 19 April 1944.
53. TNA, ADM 298/530, report on visit to assault units and submarines at Taranto, E M Case, September 1944.
54. TNA, ADM 213/76, German Neuropsychiatry with special reference to the Kriegsmarine, D Curran and MacDonald Critchley, August 1946.
55. A P Dickison, *Crash Dive* (1999), pp. ix–x.
56. TNA, ADM 205/28, Binney Committee Manpower Enquiry, 1943.
57. TNA, ADM 116/4429, report on effects of high pressure, carbon dioxide and cold, E M Case and J B S Haldane, 25 July 1940.

58. TNA, ADM 1/10239, Davis submerged escape apparatus, 1940.
59. TNA, ADM 116/4429, report on effects of high pressure, carbon dioxide and cold, E M Case and J B S Haldane, 25 July 1940.
60. S Jenkinson, 'Submarine Sinking', *Journal of Royal Naval Medical Service*, 25 (1939), 50.
61. Ibid., 51.
62. TNA, ADM 116/4429, physiological factors concerned in escape from submarines, E M Case and J B S Haldane, 22 April 1941.
63. TNA, ADM 116/4429, Admiral Sir Dunbar-Nasmyth's Physiological Sub-Committee for Saving Lives from Sunken Submarines, 14 February 1941.
64. E Young, *One of Our Submarines* (1952), p. 63.
65. TNA, ADM 261/6, report on living and working conditions among RN personnel in the Tropics, MacDonald Critchley and H E Holling, 22 April 1944
66. Ibid.
67. TNA, ADM 261/11, medical report on patrol conditions in HMS *Surf* and HMS *Storm*, Innes F Logan, 19 April 1944.
68. *We Dive at Dawn* (Gainsborough, 1943), dir. Anthony Asquith (DVD, ITV Studios, B0000CDUX6, 2003).
69. TNA, ADM 213/76, German Neuropsychiatry with special reference to the Kriegsmarine, D Curran and MacDonald Critchley, August 1946.
70. B F Avery (ed), *The History of the Medical Department of the United States Navy in World War II* (1953), p. 56.
71. Ibid., pp. 53–4.
72. TNA, ADM1/17235, investigation of Research Institute for German U-boat medicine, Carnac, France, A J Vorwald, C L C Pratt and M Case, 5 April 1945.
73. J L S Coulter, *The Royal Naval Medical Services* (1954), p. 259.

Chapter Eight: Absent Friends: Battle Fatigue
1. *In Which We Serve* (Two Cities, 1942), dir. Noel Coward (DVD,

Carlton Visual Entertainment 3711501663, 2003).
2. TNA, ADM 1/12067, the use of psychologists and psychiatrists in the Services, 1942.
3. TNA, ADM 116/5559, Ministerial Committee on the Work of Psychologists and Psychiatrists in the Services, 31 January 1945.
4. TNA, ADM 101/565, surgeon's journal, *Icarus*, Richard P Coldrey, June 1940.
5. TNA, ADM 101/609, medical journal, *Kent*, 1942.
6. J L S Coulter, *The Royal Naval Medical Services* (1956), p. 467.
7. TNA, ADM 261/1, medical officer's journal, RS *Zaafaran*, G McBain, 5 July 1942.
8. A S McNalty and W F Mellor, *Medical Services in War* (1968), p. 43.
9. J L S Coulter, *The Royal Naval Medical Services* (1956), p. 99.
10. IWM, Documents.2112 J E N Carter, diary, 9 October 1941.
11. C M Wilson, *Anatomy of Courage* (1945), p. 75.
12. Ibid., p. 101.
13. J L S Coulter, *The Royal Naval Medical Services* (1956), p. 48.
14. Ibid., p. 89.
15. TNA, ADM 261/1, medical and other aspects of the sinking of HMS *Bonaventure*, 31 March 1941, W H Edgar, 1941.
16. E W Anderson, 'Hysteria in Wartime', *Journal of the Royal Naval Medical Service*, 27 (1941), 148.
17. H G Silvester, 'A Provocative Dose', *Journal of the Royal Naval Medical Service*, 27 (1941), 374.
18. TNA, ADM 1/15659, memo from Secretary to the Admiralty, 24 October 1944.
19. TNA, ADM 261/1, medical officer's journal, Rescue Ship *Zaafaran*, G McBain, 1942.
20. E W Anderson, 'Abnormal Mental States in Survivors, with special reference to Collective Hallucination', *Journal of the Royal Naval Medical Service*, 28 (1942), 372.
21. TNA, ADM 1/27768, morale on HMS *Valiant* June 1942–April 1943, C R G Howard, 1943.
22. TNA, ADM 1/27768, survival experience following the loss of HMS *Dunedin*, Commander A C Watson, September–November 1942.
23. TNA, ADM 261/1, medical officer's journal, Rescue Ship *Zaafaran*, G McBain, 1942.
24. N Monsarrat, *Three Corvettes* (2000), p. 31.
25. J B Hattendorf, R J B Knight, A W H Pearsall, N A M Rodger and G Till (eds), *British Naval Documents 1204-1960* (1993), pp. 841–2.
26. TNA, ADM 1/12067, advice to medical officers in ships on psychiatric cases and casualties, c. 1942.
27. Ibid.
28. G Clark, *Doc: 100 Year History of the Sick Berth Branch* (1984), p. 151.
29. TNA, ADM 1/24362, welfare services, 1949.
30. *In Which We Serve* (Two Cities, 1942), dir. Noel Coward (DVD, Carlton Visual Entertainment 3711501663, 2003).
31. TNA, ADM 101/570, surgeon's journal, *Repulse*, J R Brennan, September 1940.
32. R P M Miles, 'OHMS', *St Mary's Hospital Gazette*, 49/8 (1943), 144.
33. TNA, ADM 101/6528, medical officer's journal, *Belfast*, J H Nicolson, July–September 1944.
34. TNA, ADM 1/12067, advice to medical officers in ships on psychiatric cases and casualties, c. 1942.
35. TNA, ADM 1/15312, medical action report, HMS *Scylla*, J L S Coulter, 15 February–13 March 1943.
36. E W Anderson, 'Hysteria in Wartime', *Journal of the Royal Naval Medical Service*, 27 (1941), pp. 147–8.
37. IWM, Documents.4348, memoir, H Balfour, 1995.
38. TNA, ADM 1/12067, advice to medical officers in ships on psychiatric cases and casualties, c. 1942.
39. E W Anderson, 'Hysteria in Wartime', *Journal of the Royal Naval Medical Service*, 27 (1941), 147–8.
40. R. Ransome Wallis, *Two Red Stripes* (1973), pp. 72–3.
41. J L S Coulter, *The Royal Naval Medical Service* (1956), p. 101.
42. R Lovell, *Churchill's Doctor* (1992), pp. 234–5.

43. J G Danson, 'The Effort Syndrome', *Journal of the Royal Naval Medical Service*, 28 (1942), 109. Similar advice is given in J R Forbes, 'Effort Syndrome', Journal of the Royal Naval Medical Service, 30 (1944), 169.
44. IWM, Documents.8202, memoir, W I D Scott, 1993.
45. D Curran, 'Functional Nervous States in Relation to Service in the Royal Navy', in H L Tidy and J M Browne Kutschbach (eds), *Inter-Allied Conferences on War Medicine* (1947), p. 220.
46. D Curran, 'Operational Strain: Psychological Casualties in the Royal Navy in H L Tidy and J M Browne Kutschbach (eds), *Inter-Allied Conferences on War Medicine* (1947), pp. 233–8.
47. D Curran and G Garmany, 'Post-operational Strain in the Navy', *British Medical Journal*, 2 (1944), 144–6.
48. TNA, CAB 21/2548, neuropsychiatry, Royal Navy, 1943.
49. TNA, ADM1/12067, organisation for handling nervous and mental diseases in the Royal Navy, 1942.
50. G Garmany, 'Psychiatry under Barracks Conditions', *Journal of the Royal Naval Medical Service*, 28 (1942), 164.
51. B Crowhurst Archer, 'The Emotional Factor in Service Aviation', *Journal of the Royal Naval Medical Service*, 25 (1939), 108.
52. E Jones and N Greenberg, 'Royal Naval Psychiatry: Organization, Methods and Outcomes, 1900-1945', *Mariners Mirror*, 92 (2006), 195.
53. TNA, ADM 178/254, report on arrest and trial of Henry Edmond Smith, Grimsby, 12 November 1940.
54. J L S Coulter, *The Royal Naval Medical Services* (1956), p. 453.
55. H Scott Forbes, 'Rehabilitation of Neuropsychiatric Cases at a Royal Naval Auxiliary Hospital', *Journal of the Royal Naval Medical Service*, 30 (1944), 206-14.
56. J L S Coulter, *The Royal Naval Medical Services* (1954), p. 155.
57. J L S Coulter, *The Royal Naval Medical Services* (1956), p. 48.
58. J L S Coulter, *The Royal Naval Medical Services* (1954), p. 155.
59. F G Ward, 'Rehabilitation', *Journal of the Royal Naval Medical Service*, 30 (1944), 37.
60. J Jens, 'Retraining of the Injured in a Naval Depot', *Journal of the Royal Naval Medical Service*, 30 (1944), 93.
61. TNA, ADM 178/355A, letter to Rear Admiral H T C Walker from R May, 1 June 1942.
62. TNA, ADM 178/355A, letter from R B Richards to P Humphrey Davies, 30 August 1943.
63. TNA, ADM 178/355A, draft scheme of rehabilitation, September 1943.
64. TNA, ADM 178/355A, Notes on Queen Victoria Cottage Hospital, East Grinstead Maxillo-Facial Unit, A J Dunnett, 5 June 1942.
65. TNA, ADM 178/355A, letter from A McIndoe to R C May, 13 August 1942.
66. TNA, ADM 101/570, surgeon's journal, *Repulse*, J R Brennan, September 1940.
67. T Beaton, 'Some Observations on Mental Conditions as observed amongst the Ship's Company of a Battleship in War-time', *Journal of the Royal Naval Medical Service*, 1 (1915), 447–52.
68. E T Meagher, 'Nervous Disorders in the Fighting Forces', *Journal of the Royal Naval Medical Service*, 10 (1924), 11
69. J R Rees, 'Three Years of Military Psychiatry in the United Kingdom', *British Medical Journal*, 1 (1943), 6.
70. TNA, WO 222/158, divisional psychiatry report by P J R Davies, March 1946.
71. 'Seamen and Hardship', *The Lancet*, 2 (1943), 199.
72. T Carter, *Merchant Seamen's Health 1860-1960* (2014), p. 151
73. L Kennett, *GI: the American Soldier in World War II* (1987), pp. 34–5.
74. F Avery Bennett (ed), *The History of the Medical Department of the United States Navy in World War II*, p. 323.
75. TNA, ADM 213/76, 'German Neuropsychiatry with special reference to the Kriegsmarine' by Surgeon Captains D. Curran and MacDonald Critchley, August 1946.

76. TNA, ADM1/12067, organisation for handling nervous and mental diseases in the Royal Navy, 1942

Chapter Nine: Ourselves: Rest and Recreation
1. TNA, ADM 239/335, 'Guard book for fighting experience', 1943.
2. T Mason and E Riedi, *Sport and the Military* (2010), pp. 29–31.
3. TNA, ADM 1/8549/16, physical and recreational training of the Royal Navy, 1919.
4. TNA, ADM 1/8566/237, games and sport in the Royal Navy, 1919.
5. B Taylor, *The Battlecruiser HMS Hood* (2004), pp. 163, 180.
6. R O'Conor, *Running a Big Ship* (2017), p. 136.
7. Ibid., p. xiv.
8. TNA, ADM 101/565, medical journal, *Hood*, K A Ingleby Mackenzie, August 1940.
9. TNA, ADM 1/18968, encouragement of team games in HM ships, 26 January 1945.
10. TNA, ADM 234/9, 'Handbook of Physical and Recreational Training for the Use of the Royal Navy', 1940, p. 5.
11. Ibid.
12. TNA, ADM 1/18968, encouragement of team games in HM ships, 26 January 1945.
13. TNA, ADM 1/21034, memo on Directorate of Physical Training and Sports, 10 October 1942.
14. TNA, ADM 1/18968, encouragement of team games in HM ships, 26 January 1945.
15. Ibid., note by Director of Naval Training, 30 March 1945.
16. Ibid., encouragement of team games in HM ships, 26 January 1945.
17. TNA, ADM 1/21034, memo on Directorate of Physical Training and Sports, 10 October 1942.
18. TNA, ADM 234/9, 'Handbook of Physical and Recreational Training for the Use of the Royal Navy', 1940, p. 6.
19. TNA, ADM 1/14736, staff pay for PRT instructors, 8 November 1943.
20. *Picture Post*, 27 April 1940, pp. 38–41.
21. TNA, ADM 234/9, 'Handbook of Physical and Recreational Training for the Use of the Royal Navy', 1940, p. 5.
22. Ibid., p. 50.
23. Ibid., p. 36.
24. R O'Conor, *Running a Big Ship* (2017), p. 29.
25. TNA, ADM 234/9, 'Handbook of Physical and Recreational Training for the Use of the Royal Navy', 1940, p. 49.
26. 'The Prevention of Unnecessary Casualties in a Ship', by 'A Medical Officer, R.N.', *Journal of Royal Naval Medical Service*, 29 (1943), 114.
27. St Mary's Hospital Archives, DP5/16, letter from F M McRae to A H Buck, 13 February 1943.
28. 'The Prevention of Unnecessary Casualties in a Ship', by 'A Medical Officer, R.N.', *Journal of Royal Naval Medical Service*, 29 (1943), 113.
29. H Philip, *Two Rings and a Red* (1944), p. 30.
30. Ibid., pp. 30–1.
31. TNA, ADM 1/18968, encouragement of team games in HM ships, 26 January 1945.
32. Ibid., note by Director of Naval Training, 30 March 1945.
33. Ibid., encouragement of team games in HM ships, 26 January 1945.
34. R Ransome Wallis, *Two Red Stripes* (1973), p. 26.
35. TNA, ADM101/6528, HMS *Bellona*, medical journal, A Daunt Bateman, 1 April–30 June 1944.
36. TNA, ADM 261/5, report on medical department of HMS *Brittany* during Operation 'Husky', A M McWatt Green, 1943.
37. TNA, ADM 101/6528, medical officer's journal, *Belfast*, J H Nicolson, July–September 1944.
38. TNA, ADM 101/570, HMS *Repulse*, medical journal, J R Breman, 1 January–31 March 1940.
39. TNA, ADM 1/12615, note by Director of Naval Air Division on request from RN Air Station *Hatston* for sailing dinghies, 28 March 1942.
40. T Mason and E Riedi, *Sport and the Military* (2010), p. 180.
41. *Times*, 24 February 1940.
42. *Times*, 17 May 1943.
43. *St Mary's Hospital Gazette* 49/6 (1943), 111.

NOTES

44. *St Mary's Hospital Gazette*, 51/3 (1945), 43.
45. TNA, ADM 1/17144, letter from A V Alexander to Lord Wigram, 25 September 1944.
46. TNA, ADM 1/17115, letter from A V Alexander to J V Bank, 12 May 1944.
47. Ibid., letter from A V Alexander to J V Bank, 16 May 1944.
48. V R Cardozier, *Colleges and Universities in World War II* (1993), p. 101.
49. W D Jones, *Football! Navy! War!* (2009), p. 54.
50. V R Cardozier, *Colleges and Universities in World War II* (1993), p. 101.
51. *Holborn and Finsbury Guardian*, 27 March 1942.
52. *Tanfield Association Newsletter*, 39 (2017), 13.
53. F J Wade, *The Story of West Stanley* (2008), p. 30.
54. TNA, ADM 1/18225, letter from Sidney H George, Mayor of Aldeburgh, to F W Mottershead, 2 June 1943.
55. TNA, ADM 1/18090, letter from Mayor of Darlington to Secretary to the Admiralty, 23 November 1943.
56. Ibid., letter from Secretary to the Admiralty to Mayor of Darlington, 4 December 1943.
57. Ibid., letter from Town Clerk of South Shields to Secretary to the Admiralty, 7 April 1942.
58. J L S Coulter, *The Royal Naval Medical Service* (1956), p. 421.
59. R Ransome Wallis, *Two Red Stripes* (1973), p. 125.
60. TNA, ADM 1/18090, letter from Secretary to the Admiralty to Town Clerk of Halesowen, 14 January 1943.
61. 'Points to remember before ordering your uniform' by Hector Powe, in B Lavery (ed), *The Royal Navy Officer's Pocket Book 1944* (2007), p. 18.
62. E Musgrave, *Sharp Suits* (2009), pp. 79–80.
63. A Scrimgeour, *Scrimgeour's Small Scribbling Diary 1914-1916* (2008), p. 250.
64. TNA, ADM 1/15101, memo from Commander-in-Chief Nore, 13 August 1943.
65. Ibid., 'Uniform Wearing', NI 14155/43, 6 January 1944.
66. Ibid., minute, 27 August 1945.
67. TNA, ADM 1/19164, minutes of meeting to discuss problem of providing civilian clothing to discharged naval ratings, 9 January 1945.
68. TNA, ADM 1/15101, minute, 27 August 1945.
69. The clothing that Scott happily traded in for the less elegant attire of a naval rating was very expensive for the time. 7,000 francs would have been worth £37 in 1944 and the equivalent of £1,605 in 2018. A bespoke Savile Row suit cost 25 guineas in 1945 compared to 14 guineas before the war, P Ziegler, *London at War* (1995), p. 320.
70. IWM, A 25870, 'Manchester Survivor comes back after 2 years', 7 October 1944; TNA, ADM 1/14757, French sailors captured on HMS *Manchester*, 1943–45.
71. TNA, T 61/1163, provisional cost of entertainment for 4 weeks ended 12 August 1944.
72. TNA, T 161/1163, memo, 8 November 1941.
73. H Philip, *Two Rings and a Red* (1944), p. 32.
74. *Stage Door Canteen* (Sol Lesser Productions, 1943), dir. Frank Borzage, (DVD, Elstree Hill Entertainment, B000EGEW18, 2006).
75. J G Hughes, *The Greasepaint War* (1976), p. 45.
76. TNA, T 161/1457, Independent Entertainments Board report, March 1941.
77. TNA, ADM 1/17034, letter from A V Alexander to Ernest Bevin, 27 January 1944.
78. Ibid., report on ENSA by Sir John Fisher, 1944.
79. E Laye, *Boo to My Friends* (1958), p. 57.
80. Ibid., pp. 145–6.
81. Ibid., p. 148.
82. *Times*, 25 June 1940.
83. B Dean, *The Theatre at War* (1956), p. 63.
84. TNA, T 161/1457, Independent Entertainments Board report, March 1941.
85. I Newton, *At the Piano* (1966), p. 228.

86. TNA, ADM 1/24362, History of Welfare Services in the Royal Navy', 1945.
87. IWM, Documents.4348, memoir, H M Balfour.
88. TNA, T 161/1163, letter to F E Evans, 1 December 1941.
89. Ibid., telegram from Washington Embassy to Foreign Office, 22 December 1942.
90. H Philip, *Two Rings and a Red* (1944), p. 40.
91. R Ransome Wallis, *Two Red Stripes* (1973), p. 52.
92. Private information, Suzanne Willson.
93. TNA, ADM 199/1104, 'Northern Light', May 1943.
94. R Ransome Wallis, *Two Red Stripes* (1973), p. 108.
95. D Bret, *George Formby: A Troubled Genius* (1999), p. 92.
96. *Let George Do It* (Associated Talking Pictures, 1940), dir. Marcel Varnel (DVD, Studio Canale, B000N3T2JY, 2009).
97. *Bell Bottom George* (Columbia, 1944), dir. Marcel Varnel (DVD, Sony Pictures Home Entertainment, B00358R2R8, 2011).
98. B Lavery, *Churchill's Navy* (2006), p. 141.
99. R O'Conor, *Running a Big Ship* (2017), pp. 138–9.
100. IWM, *Documents*.13249, memoir, J W Somers.
101. G Prysor, *Citizen Sailors* (2012), p. 137.
102. J L S Coulter, *The Royal Naval Medical Service* (1956), p. 39.
103. TNA, ADM 1/24362, 'History of Welfare Services in the Royal Navy', 1948.
104. R O'Conor, *Running a Big Ship* (2017), p. 141.
105. Ibid., p. 139.
106. TNA, ADM 1/18872, Dover Command, 1 November 1944.
107. G Prysor, *Citizen Sailors* (2011), p. 393.
108. R P M Miles, 'OHMS', *St Mary's Hospital Gazette*, 49/8 (1943), 144.
109. R Ransome Wallis, *Two Red Stripes* (1973), p. 86.
110. B Taylor, *The Battlecruiser HMS Hood* (2004), p. 145.
111. R Ransome Wallis, *Two Red Stripes* (1973), p. 26.
112. J L S Coulter, *The Royal Naval Medical Service* (1956), p. 37.
113. H Philip, *Two Rings and a Red* (1944), p. 62.
114. 'Crossing the Line in Wartime', *Naval Review*, 29 (1941), 62–6.
115. R Ransome Wallis, *Two Red Stripes* (1973), pp. 19–20.
116. K Brown, *Poxed and Scurvied* (2011), p. 195.
117. Report of Central Board of Control, Cd. 8243, 1916.
118. K Brown, *Poxed and Scurvied* (2011), p. 172.
119. TNA, ADM 116/5216, annual report of Missions to Seamen in East London, 1941.
120. Ibid., annual report of Missions to Seamen in East London, 1943.
121. Ibid., annual report of Missions to Seamen in East London, 1942.
122. Ibid., annual report of British Soldiers' and Sailors' Institute of Colombo, 30 June 1944.
123. Ibid., annual report of Seamen's Home, Alexandria, Merchant Navy Club and Merchant Navy Officers' Club, 1943.
124. TNA, ADM 1/24362, 'History of Welfare Services in the Royal Navy', 1948.
125. TNA, T 161/1163, letter from C H Lefebure to Basil Dean, 17 October 1944.
126. TNA, ADM 116/5216, annual report of Barrow Sailors Home Mission, 1943–4.
127. G H and R Bennett, *Survivors* (1999), pp. 203–4.
128. TNA, ADM 199/2138, statement of Captain H M McLean, 1941.

Chapter Ten: Neither Wives nor Sweethearts

1. F A Henley, *Chasing the Golden Fleece* (2002), pp. 51–2.
2. TNA, ADM 261/4, guidelines for lectures on VD, 25 May 1944.
3. TNA, HLG 7/756, Health and Local Government, circular letter from Arthur McNalty, Chief Medical Officer, 1 September 1939.
4. Ibid., Ministry of Health Circular 1956, 26 January 1940.

NOTES

5. TNA, AIR 2/5995, memorandum of Air Council Committee on morals and discipline, 28 September 1943.
6. T Jones, *Heart of Oak* (1984), p. 19.
7. S Palmer and S Wallis (ed), *A War in Words* (2003), pp. 250-2.
8. TNA, ADM 261/4, guidelines for lectures on VD, 25 May 1944.
9. H Philip, *Two Rings and a Red* (1944), p. 25.
10. IWM, Documents. 4348, memoir of H M Balfour, 1996.
11. IWM, Documents.2222, diary of A I Hughes, 1945.
12. W L River, *The Malta Story, based on the Diary and Experiences of Flying Officer Howard M. Coffin* (1943), p. 98.
13. G Clark, *Doc: 100 Year History of the Sick Berth Branch* (1984), p. 143.
14. K Brown, *The Pox* (2006), p. 182.
15. TNA, WO 204/3015, report on VD in 15th Army by Gordon Cheyne, director of Public Health, 5 December 1943.
16. TNA, WO 204/6725, letter from B H Robertson, 13 April 1944.
17. Ibid., note by Robert Lees, 8 April 1944.
18. S Longden, *To the Victor the Spoils* (2004), p. 119.
19. F A Henley, *Chasing the Golden Fleece* (2002), pp. 55-6.
20. H Philip, *Two Rings and a Red* (1944), p. 26.
21. P Ziegler, *London at War* (1995), p. 53.
22. At the London Lock Hospital, the average annual number of new male patients was 2,000 throughout the war and rose to 3,408 only in 1946 on the return of demobilised troops. New cases of women rose from 218 in 1940 to 446 in 1943 and 594 in 1945. D I Williams, *The London Lock* (1999), p. 132.
23. TNA, MH 55/2317 notes of conference at Home Office, 16 April 1943.
24. Private information, Barbara Gammon.
25. TNA, MH 55/2317, notes on meeting held at Home Office, 29 October 1942.
26. Commission on Training Camp Activities, *Keeping Fit to Fight* (1918), p. 4.
27. TNA, ADM 261/4, guidelines for lectures on VD, 25 May 1944.
28. TNA, HLG 7/756, Health and Local Government, circular from Chief Medical Officer, 20 January 1943.
29. Wellcome Institute, RAMC 466/48, Royal Army Medical Corps collection, poster 'That's Phyllis, that was', anti-venereal disease campaign among troops in Italy, 1943-4.
30. TNA, HLG 7/756, Health and Local Government, Health circular, 16 February 1943.
31. Ibid., letter to W W Andrews, 16 February 1943.
32. *The Lancet*, 2 (1942), 18.
33. TNA, HO 45/10893/359931, Order in Council, 22 March 1918.
34. TNA, WO 32/4745, War Office Memorandum, 28 August 1918.
35. TNA, MH 55/1341, Statutory Rules and Orders, amendment by Order in Council of Defence (General) Regulations Act of 1939, 5 November 1942.
36. Ibid., Ministry of Health circular, 8 January 1943.
37. TNA, MH 55/2317, minutes of Joint Committee on Venereal Disease, 10 December 1943.
38. TNA, HO 45/10893/359931, letter from chief petty officer on active service, 2 November 1918.
39. TNA, WO 32/11404, B B Cubitt to Officers Commanding at Home, 18 March 1916.
40. TNA, WO 204/6725, notes on prophylactic treatment, 1944.
41. TNA, ADM 101/565, medical officer's journal, *Hood*, K A Ingleby Mackenzie, 1940.
42. Sulphonamide Resistant Gonorrhoea' (editorial), *Journal of the Royal Army Medical Corps*, 82 (1944), 283-5.
43. M H Salaman, A J King, D I Williams and C S Nichol, 'Prevention of Jaundice Resulting from Antisyphilitic Treatment', *The Lancet*, 1 (1944), 7-10.
44. TNA, WO 222/1302, report of Robert Lees, 28 April 1944.
45. TNA, ADM 101/565, medical journal, *Hood*, 1940.
46. G L M McElligott, 'The Prevention of Venereal Disease', in H L Tidy and

J M Browne Kutschbach (eds), *Inter-Allied Conferences on War Medicine* (1947), p. 264.
47. G O Watts and R A Wilson, 'A Study of Personality Factors among Venereal Disease Patients', *Canadian Medical Association Journal*, 53 (1945), 119–22; E D Witkower, 'The Psychological Aspects of Venereal Disease', *British Journal of Venereal Diseases*, 24 (1948), 59–67.
48. TNA, WO 222/1302, Robert Lees, 'Method of Prevention of Venereal Disease', 14 April 1942.
49. H Philip, *Two Rings and a Red* (1944), pp. 25–6.
50. Ibid., p. 26.
51. St Mary's Hospital Archives, DP5/19, letter from F M McRae to A H Buck, 18 August 1943.
52. F A Henley, *Chasing the Golden Fleece* (2002), p. 41.
53. G Prysor, *Citizen Sailors* (2012), p. 411.
54. TNA, HO 45/10893/359931, letter from chief petty officer on active service, 2 November 1918.
55. TNA, ADM 182/127, confidential fleet order, 25 April 1940.
56. TNA, ADM 101/6528, medical journal, *Berwick*, Robert Vickery Herriman, 1944.
57. TNA, ADM 261/4, guidelines for lectures on VD, 25 May 1944.
58. TNA, ADM 1/14719A, memo from S F Dudley, 12 May 1943.
59. Ibid., memo from Head of Navy, 8 May 1943.
60. Ibid., letter from G Dunn to L Harrington, 5 August 1943.
61. National Archives, College Park, Maryland, Records Group 227, Office of Scientific Research and Development, Committee on Medical Research, memorandum on use of penicillin in syphilis by Chester Keefer, 27 October 1943.
62. *New York World Telegram*, 1 May 1946.
63. J F Mahoney, R C Arnold and A Harris, 'Penicillin Treatment of Early Syphilis: a Preliminary Report', *Venereal Diseases Information*, 24 (1943), 355–7; J F Mahoney, R C Arnold, B L Sterner, A Harris and M R Zwally, 'Penicillin Treatment of Early Syphilis', *Journal of the American Medical Association*, 126/2 (1944), 63–7.
64. J E Moore, J F Mahoney, W H Schwartz, T H Sternberg and W B Wood, 'The Treatment of Early Syphilis with Penicillin: A Preliminary Report of 1,418 Cases', *Journal of the American Medical Association*, 126/2 (1944), 67–73.
65. National Archives, College Park, Maryland, Records Group 90, Public Health Service, general classified records, group 9, box 531, file 0425, memorandum from W S Bean to R C Williams, 13 July 1944.
66. TNA, ADM 261/4, penicillin in the treatment of syphilis in the Royal Navy, 26 July 1945.
67. W Franklin Mellor (ed), *Casualties and Medical Statistics* (1972), pp. 119, 192, 240, 242, 246, 264, 282 and 334.
68. H W Florey and H Cairns, 'Penicillin in Warfare', *British Journal of Surgery*, 32 (1944), 110–24.
69. J Howie, 'Gonorrhoea: A Question of Tactics', *British Medical Journal*, 2 (1979), 1631.
70. *British Medical Journal* (25 March 1944), 428–9.
71. TNA, ADM 261/4, postscript to *Lancet* article, Sir Sheldon Dudley, 24 March 1945.

Chapter Eleven: A Bloody War
1. T N Darcy, 'The Casualties of War', *Journal of the Royal Naval Medical Service*, 26 (1940), 117.
2. J L S Coulter, *The Royal Naval Medical Service* (1956), p. 20.
3. M Arthur, *Lost Voices of the Royal Navy* (2005), p. 239.
4. TNA, ADM 261/7, 'Medical aspects of damage control', 1946.
5. T C Larkworthy, 'Surgery by a Non-Surgeon, *Journal of the Royal Naval Medical Service*, 27 (1941), 284.
6. T N Darcy, 'The Casualties of War', *Journal of the Royal Naval Medical Service*, 26 (1940), 119.
7. B Lavery (ed), *The Royal Navy Officer's Pocket Book 1944* (2007), p. 58.
8. TNA, ADM 101/565, medical journal, HMS *Hotspur*, K W Donald, 10 April 1940.
9. Ibid.

NOTES

10. J L S Coulter, *The Royal Naval Medical Service* (1956), p. 14.
11. B Lavery (ed), *The Royal Navy Officer's Pocket Book 1944* (2007), pp. 58-9.
12. TNA, ADM 261/1, 'medical experience in action on HMS *Palomares*', nd.
13. ADM 101/570, surgeon's journal, *Resolution*, A W Gunn, 4 May 1940.
14. B Lavery (ed), *The Royal Navy Officer's Pocket Book 1944* (2007), p. 68.
15. T N Darcy, 'The Casualties of War', *Journal of the Royal Naval Medical Service*, 26 (1940), 118.
16. M Pearson, *Red Sky in the Morning* (2002), p. 93.
17. T N Darcy, 'The Casualties of War', *Journal of the Royal Naval Medical Service*, 26 (1940), 116.
18. J K Herman (ed), *Battle Station Sick Bay* (1997), p. 203.
19. B Lavery (ed), *The Royal Navy Officer's Pocket Book 1944* (2007), p. 65.
20. TNA, ADM 101/399, medical officer's journal, *Warspite*, W W Kerr, 31 May 1916.
21. 'The Prevention of Unnecessary Casualties in a Ship', by 'A Medical Officer, R.N.', *Journal of the Royal Naval Medical Service*, 29 (1943), 110.
22. ADM 101/570, surgeon's journal, *Resolution*, A W Gunn, 4 May 1940.
23. B Lavery (ed), *The Royal Navy Officer's Pocket Book 1944* (2007), p. 65.
24. TNA, ADM 261/8, account of Battle of River Plate by Surgeon Lieutenant Hunter, 28 April 1942.
25. TNA, ADM 76/624, proposed BBC talk by J Coulter, April 1956.
26. TNA, ADM 101/6528, medical officer's journal, *Belfast*, J H Nicolson, June 1944.
27. TNA, ADM 261/1, 'method of treatment of severe buttock and thigh wound, HMS *Palomares*, 9 July 1942', W D G Thompson, 22 September 1942.
28. R Ransome Wallis, *Two Red Stripes* (1973), p. 85.
29. Ibid., p. 100.
30. Ibid., p. 102.
31. M Arthur, *Lost Voices of the Royal Navy* (2005), p. 236.
32. H Philip, *Two Rings and a Red* (1944), pp. 108-10.
33. J L S Coulter, *The Royal Naval Medical Service* (1956), p. 339.
34. TNA, ADM 1/14479, report on services of Surgeon Lieutenant Hood to survivors of HMS *Achates*, 24 August 1943.
35. TNA, ADM 261/8, account of Battle of River Plate by Surgeon Lieutenant Hunter, 28 April 1942.
36. T N Darcy, 'The Casualties of War', *Journal of the Royal Naval Medical Service*, 26 (1940), 116-22.
37. F A Henley, *Chasing the Golden Fleece* (2002), pp. 38-9.
38. 'The Prevention of Unnecessary Casualties in a Ship', by 'A Medical Officer, R.N.', *Journal of the Royal Naval Medical Service*, 29 (1943), 112.
39. TNA, ADM 101/570, medical officer's journal, *Renown*, 1 October – 31 December 1940.
40. M Arthur, *Lost Voices of the Royal Navy* (2005), p. 221.
41. TNA, ADM 261/11, 'A suggested lecture for newly entered medical officers under instruction in depot', n.d.
42. TNA, ADM 261/1, report on sinking of HMS *Prince of Wales*, 10 December 1941.
43. Ibid., T M Adams, 6 February 1942.
44. Ibid., medical officer's journal, RS *Zaafaran*, G McBain, 5 July 1942.
45. N Monsarrat, *The Cruel Sea* (1951), p. 328.
46. E W Anderson, 'Abnormal Mental States in Survivors, with special reference to Collective Hallucination', *Journal of the Royal Naval Medical Service*, 28 (1942), 361.
47. TNA, FD 1/7025, 'A guide to the preservation of life at sea after shipwreck', 1942.
48. TNA, ADM 1/18695, prisoner of war journal of Hugh G Singer, 16 June 1945.
49. TNA, ADM 261/11, 'A suggested lecture for newly entered medical officers under instruction in depot', n.d.

50. TNA, ADM 1/18695, prisoner of war journal of Hugh G Singer, 16 June 1945.
51. N Monsarrat, *Three Corvettes* (2000), p. 60.
52. TNA, ADM 261/1, report of medical officer of HMS *Grenade*, Surgeon Lieutenant Lavelle, 17 February 1940.
53. TNA, ADM 261/1, report from W McC Scott, 12 November 1941.
54. Obituary, Ivan Jacklin, *St Mary's Hospital Gazette* 49/4 (1943), 64.
55. St Mary's Hospital Archives, DP5/40, *The Star* (1945).
56. St Mary's Hospital Archives, DP 5/26, N M Simon, HMS *Activity* to Mr Buck, 23 August 1944.
57. R D Wilkins, 'Convoy Rescue Ships', *Journal of the Royal Naval Medical Service*, 30 (1944), 65–9.
58. J W McNee, 'Convoy Rescue Ships', *Journal of the Royal Naval Medical Service*, 31 (1945), 3.
59. Ibid., 7.
60. J L S Coulter, *The Royal Naval Medical Service* (1956), pp. 462–3.
61. TNA, ADM 261/1, medical officer's journal, RS *Zaafaran*, G McBain, 5 July 1942.
62. TNA, ADM 261/9, account of battle of River Plate by Surgeon Lieutenant Hunter, 28 April 1942.
63. R Ransome Wallis, *Two Red Stripes* (1973), p. 101.
64. J L S Coulter, *The Royal Naval Medical Service* (1956), p. 56.
65. TNA, ADM 1/24249, memorandum on manpower of the Royal Naval Medical Service, S F Dudley, 16 March 1943.

Chapter Twelve: Went the Day Well?
1. TNA, WO 163/485, Committee on Organisation of Medical Services, 24 January 1946.
2. TNA, ADM 234/936, notes for medical officers attached to landing parties, 1943.
3. TNA, ADM 261/5, medical aspects of Operations 'Dynamo', 'Avalanche' and 'Husky'.
4. TNA, ADM 1/10275, report on transport and care of wounded during operations at Dover, 11 May – 5 June 1940, by Senior Medical Officer, Dover, 7 June 1940.
5. TNA, ADM 101/565, medical officer's journal, *Icarus*, Richard P Coldrey, 1 April–30 June 1940.
6. J L S Coulter, *The Royal Naval Medical Service* (1956), p. 311.
7. TNA, ADM 1/10275, report on transport and care of wounded during operations at Dover, 11 May–5 June 1940, by Senior Medical Officer, Dover, 7 June 1940.
8. TNA, ADM 101/565, medical officer's journal, *Icarus*, Richard P Coldrey, 1 April–30 June 1940.
9. TNA, ADM 1/10275, report on transport and care of wounded during operations at Dover, 11 May–5 June 1940, by Senior Medical Officer, Dover, 7 June 1940.
10. Ibid.
11. TNA, ADM 261/5, 'Avalanche, part ix, medical', 1944.
12. TNA, ADM 199/947, report on Operation 'Husky', 1943.
13. TNA, ADM 261/5, report on medical department of HMS *Brittany* during Operation 'Husky', A M McWatt Green, 1943.
14. TNA, ADM 234/936, notes for medical officers attached to landing parties, 1943.
15. TNA, ADM 261/5, medical report on Operation 'Husky', 10 July 1943.
16. Ibid., 'Avalanche, part ix, medical', 1944.
17. TNA, MT 40/99, war planning for Operation 'Overlord', 1944.
18. S A Preece, '"Performing Miracles": The Importance of Royal Naval Medical Officers in Operations Overlord and Neptune during World War II', *Journal of the Royal Naval Medical Service*, 96 (2010), 108–9.
19. F C Hunot, 'Royal Naval Hospital Haslar and Operation Overlord', *Journal of the Royal Naval Medical Service*, 80 (1994), 57.
20. TNA, ADM 1/1673, report on the medical aspects of Operation 'Neptune' as regards Force 'S', 5 July 1944.
21. M Osborne and J E Smith, 'Action Stations! 100 years of Trauma Care on Maritime and Amphibious Operations in the Royal Navy', *Journal of the Royal Naval Medical Service*, 101 (2015), 8.

22. IWM, Documents.13574, diary of G R Airth, 6 June 1944.
23. TNA, ADM 1/1673, report on the medical aspects of Operation 'Neptune' as regards Force 'S', 5 July 1944.
24. J L S Coulter, *The Royal Naval Medical Service* (1956), p. 520.
25. IWM, Documents.13574, diary of G R Airth, 12 June 1944.
26. Ibid., 3 August 1944.
27. TNA, ADM 101/6528, medical journal, *Bellona*, A Daunt Bateman, 1 April–30 June 1944.
28. TNA, WO 222/174, evacuation of casualties from beaches and from small harbours, notes from a casualty evacuation post, Normandy, 1944.
29. TNA, ADM 179/480, operation of hospital carriers, Operation 'Neptune', 1944.
30. TNA, ADM 1/1673, report on the medical aspects of Operation 'Neptune' as regards Force 'S', 5 July 1944.
31. TNA, ADM 101/6528, medical officer's journal, *Belfast*, J H Nicolson, June 1944.
32. TNA, ADM 179/413, report of medical officer in charge of RN Hospital Haslar, 15 August 1944.
33. Ibid., medical report on Operation Overlord, July–October 1944.
34. Ibid., report of medical officer in charge of RN Hospital Haslar, 15 August 1944.
35. Ibid., medical report on Operation Overlord, July–October 1944.
36. Ibid., report of medical officer in charge of RN Hospital Haslar, 15 August 1944.
37. Ibid, report on RN Hospital Portland, 14 August 1944.
38. R P M Miles, 'Pacific Letter', *St Mary's Hospital Gazette*, 51/8 (1945), 115.
39. Ibid.
40. TNA, ADM 1/13143, Director of Plans, 26 January 1943.
41. Ibid., memo, 7 February 1943.
42. Ibid., adult education in Far Eastern affairs, 5 September 1944.
43. R P M Miles, 'Pacific Letter', *St Mary's Hospital Gazette*, 51/8 (1945), 115.
44. J Rose, *Nursing Churchill* (2018), p. 237.
45. TNA, WO 32/11697, report by R Porter on role of British Fleet in repatriation of released Allied prisoners of war and internees, 1945.
46. Letter from Geoffrey Cutts, 30 September 1945, *St Mary's Hospital Gazette*, 51/3 (1945), 132.
47. TNA, WO 32/11697, report by R Porter on role of British Fleet in repatriation of released Allied prisoners of war and internees, 1945.
48. B McL Ranft (ed), *Beatty Papers* (1989), p. 141.
49. TNA, ADM 298/338, bacterial content of the air of HM ships under wartime conditions, by F P Ellis and W F Raymond, August 1945.
50. C McKee, *Sober Men and True* (2002), pp. 73-144.
51. A J Sims, 'The Habitability of Naval Ships under Wartime Conditions', *Transactions of the Institute of Naval Architects*, 87 (1945), 50-70.
52. K Brown, *Fighting Fit* (2008), pp. 110–38.
53. TNA, ADM 105/116, Institute of Naval Medicine, 1985.
54. TNA, WO 163/485, Committee on the Organisation of the Medical Services, 24 January 1946.
55. H G G Eastcott, *St Mary's Gazette*, 88/3 (1982), 9.
56. TNA, WO 183/485, committee on the organisation of the Medical Services, 24 January 1946.
57. H Parry Price, 'Service Anaesthetics: the Variation between Service and Civilian Anaesthetics', *Journal of the Royal Naval Medical Service*, 26 (1940), 134.
58. TNA, ADM 1/14708, Memo on reduction of medical standard of recruits, May 1943
59. Letter from H J Starling, *Proceedings of the Royal Society of Medicine*, 34 (1941), 542.
60. J L S Coulter, *The Royal Naval Medical Service* (1954), p. 242.
61. C G Blood, W M Pugh, E D Gauker, D M Pearsall, 'Comparisons of Wartime and Peacetime Disease and Non-Battle Injury Rates Aboard Ships of the British Royal Navy',

Military Medicine, 157/12 (1992), 641-4
62. F P Ellis and A Richards, 'Health of the Navy in Two World Wars', *Journal of Royal Naval Medical Service*, 52 (1966), 12. See Appendix 4.
63. Ibid., 11.
64. Ibid., 20
65. Ibid., 10-11.
66. Ibid., 8. See Appendix 5.
67. TNA, ADM 261/9, sinking of the *Scharnhorst*, 26 December 1943.
68. TNA, ADM 1/18696, account of experiences in a German POW camp, R Mooney, 6 July 1945.

Bibliography

Archive Sources

The National Archives, Kew
TNA, ADM, Admiralty
TNA, AIR, Air Ministry
TNA, CAB, Cabinet
TNA, FD, Medical Research Council
TNA, HLG, Local Government Office
TNA, HO, Home Office
TNA, HS, Special Operations Executive
TNA, INF, Information
TNA, LAB, Ministry of Labour
TNA, MH, Ministry of Health
TNA, MT, Ministry of Transport
TNA, T, Treasury
TNA, WO, War Office

Imperial War Museum, Department of Documents
IWM, Documents.2112, John E N Carter (92/45/1)
IWM, Documents.2130, Jack K Neale (98/1/1)
IWM, Documents.2222, Alex I Hughes (93/1/1)
IWM, Documents.2432, J Patrick Mullins (92/27/1)
IWM, Documents.4348, Harry M Balfour (95/23/1)
IWM, Documents.8202, William I D Scott (99/12/1)
IWM, Documents.13249, John W Somers (05/6/1)
IWM, Documents.13574, Graham R Airth (05/63/1)

National Archives (USA), College Park, Maryland
RG 90, Public Health Service

Pfizer Records Centre, Sandwich, Kent
Kemball Bishop records

Queen Mary's Hospital, Sidcup, Gillies Archive
Case files of Harold Gillies, 1917–25

St Mary's Hospital Archives (Imperial College Healthcare NHS Trust), London
DP 5, papers of F M (Peter) McRae

Primary Printed Sources
Anon [A Medical Officer, R.N.], 'The Prevention of Unnecessary Casualties in a Ship', *Journal of the Royal Naval Medical Service*, 29 (1943), 110–14
Anderson, E W, 'Hysteria in Wartime', *Journal of the Royal Naval Medical Service*, 27 (1941), 141–9

——, 'Abnormal Mental States in Survivors, with special reference to Collective Hallucination', *Journal of the Royal Naval Medical Service*, 28 (1942), 361–76
Arthur, Max (ed), *Lost Voices of the Royal Navy*, London, Hodder, 2007
Barron, Arthur F M, 'The Lookout Problem on Submarines: Defective Night Vision', *Journal of the Royal Naval Medical Service*, 29 (1943), 189–96
Beaton, T, 'Some Observations on Mental Conditions as observed amongst the Ship's Company of a Battleship in War-time', *Journal of the Royal Naval Medical Service*, 1 (1915), 447–52.
Bunyan, John, 'Treatment of burns and wounds by the envelope method', *British Medical Journal*, 2 (5 July 1941), 1–7
Butler, W M, 'Blood Groups and Blood Matching', *Journal of the Royal Naval Medical Service*, 26 (1940), 148–53
Cohen, S M, 'Experience in the Treatment of War Burns', *British Medical Journal* (1940), 251–4
Commission on Training Camp Activities, *Keeping Fit to Fight*, Washington DC, 1918
Critchley, Macdonald, 'Problems of Naval Warfare under Climatic Extremes', *British Medical Journal*, 2 (1945), 145–8, 173–7, 208–12
Curran, D, 'Functional Nervous States in Relation to Service in the Royal Navy', in H L Tidy and J M Browne Kutschbach (eds), *Inter-Allied Conferences on War Medicine* (1947), pp. 219–24
——, 'Operational Strain: Psychological Casualties in the Royal Navy', in H L Tidy and J M Browne Kutschbach (eds), *Inter-Allied Conferences on War Medicine* (1947), pp. 233–8
——, and Garmany, G, 'Post-operational Strain in the Navy', *British Medical Journal*, 2 (1944), 144–6
Danson, J G, 'The Effort Syndrome', *Journal of the Royal Naval Medical Service*, 28 (1942), 108–18
Darcy, T N, 'The Casualties of War', *Journal of the Royal Naval Medical Service*, 26 (1940), 116–22
Davies, John, *Stone Frigate*, London, MacMillan, 1947
Dean, Basil, *The Theatre at War*, London, Harrap, 1956
Dickison, Arthur, *Crash Dive: In Action with HMS Safari, 1942-43*, Stroud, Sutton, 1999
Dixon, Thomas Benjamin, *The Enemy Fought Splendidly: Being the 1914-1915 Diary of the Battle of the Falklands and its Aftermath by Surgeon T B Dixon of HMS Kent*, Poole, Blandford Press, 1983
Ellis, F P, 'A Description of the Blood Transfusion and Resuscitation Unit, 64th General Hospital', *Journal of the Royal Naval Medical Service*, 28 (1942), 136–44.
Emergency Medical Service, 'The Local Treatment of War Burns', *British Medical Journal* (1940), 4
Fitzpatrick, W G C, 'Mass Miniature Radiography in the Royal Navy', *Journal of the Royal Naval Medical Service*, 27 (1941), 3–20
Florey, H W and Cairns, H, 'Penicillin in Warfare', *British Journal of Surgery*, 32 (1944), 110–24
Forbes, J R, 'Effort Syndrome', *Journal of the Royal Naval Medical Service*, 30 (1944),163–70
Forbes Guild, W J, 'Some Observations on the Potentialities of Air-conditioning for HM Ships on Tropical Service', *Journal of the Royal Naval Medical Service*, 26 (1940), 262–73
Garmany, G, 'Psychiatry under Barracks Conditions', *Journal of the Royal Naval Medical Service*, 28 (1942), 160–4
Gourd, D P, 'Where the Cider Apples Grow', *Journal of the Royal Naval Medical Service*, 68 (1982), 39–45
Guinness, Alec, *Blessings in Disguise*, London, Hamish Hamilton, 1985
Henley, Francis Austin, *Chasing the Golden Fleece: The Wartime Adventures of Surgeon Lieutenant Commander Francis Austin Henley*, Lewes, The Book Guild, 2002
Hampshire, Edward (ed), *Brinestain and Biscuit: Recipes and Rules for Royal Navy Cooks*, London, National Archives, 2007
Hanson, Norman, *Carrier Pilot: An Unforgettable True Story of Wartime Flying*, Sparkford, Patrick Stephens, 1979

Hattendorf, John B, Knight, R J B, Pearsall, A W H, Rodger, N A M, and Till, Geoffrey, (eds), *British Naval Documents 1204-1960*, Aldershot, Navy Records Society, 1993

Herman, Jan K (ed), *Battle Station Sick Bay: Navy Medicine in World War II*, Annapolis, Naval Institute Press, 1997

Hood, A, 'Army Medical Services in Action', *Journal of the Royal Army Medical Corps*, 38 (1943), 287-90

Hood, Jean (ed), *Submarine: An Anthology of First-hand Accounts of the War under the Sea, 1939-1945*, London, Conway, 2007

Howie, J, 'Gonorrhoea: A Question of Tactics', *British Medical Journal*, 2 (1979), 1631

Hunot, F C, 'Administrative Experiences at the Royal Naval Hospital Haslar in Connection with the Reception of Casualties, March 1942 to October 1944', *Journal of the Royal Naval Medical Service*, 32 (1946), 19-32

——, 'Royal Naval Hospital Haslar and Operation Overlord', *Journal of the Royal Naval Medical Service*, 80 (1994), 55-61

Hunt, Bernard, *A Doctor's Odyssey: Memoirs of a Doctor*, Salisbury, Salisbury Printing Company, 1995

Jenkinson, S, 'Submarine Sinking', *Journal of Royal Naval Medical Service*, 25 (1939), 45-52

Jens, John, 'Retraining of the Injured in a Naval Depot', *Journal of the Royal Naval Medical Service*, 30 (1944), 92-5

Jones, Ben (ed), *The Fleet Air Arm in the Second World War: Norway, the Mediterranean and the Bismarck*, Farnham, Naval Records Society, 2012

Jones, Tristan, *Heart of Oak*, New York, St Martin's Press, 1984

Larkworthy, T C, 'Surgery by a Non-Surgeon', *Journal of the Royal Naval Medical Service*, 27 (1941), 281-7

Lavery, Brian (ed), *The Royal Navy Officer's Pocket Book 1944*, London, Conway, 2007

Laye, Evelyn, *Boo to My Friends*, London, Hurst and Blackett, 1958

Letherby Tidy, H, and Browne Kutschbach, J M (ed), *Inter-Allied Conferences on War Medicine 1942-1945*, London, Staples Press, 1947

Mahoney, J F, Arnold, R C, and Harris, A, 'Penicillin Treatment of Early Syphilis: a Preliminary Report', *Venereal Diseases Information*, 24 (1943), 355-7

——, Arnold, R C, Sterner, B L, Harris, A, and Zwally, M R, 'Penicillin Treatment of Early Syphilis', *Journal of the American Medical Association*, 126/2 (1944), 63-7

Mallalieu, J P W, *Very Ordinary Seaman*, London, Victor Gollancz, 1944

Mathews, Vera Laughton, *Blue Tapestry*, London, Hollis and Carter, 1948

McAra, Charles, *Mainly in Minesweepers*, London, R J Leach, 1991

McNee, J W, 'Convoy Rescue Ships', *Journal of the Royal Naval Medical Service*, 31 (1945), 1-7

Meagher, E T, 'Nervous Disorders in the Fighting Forces', *Journal of the Royal Naval Medical Service*, 10 (1924), 1-14

Miles, R P M, 'OHMS', *St Mary's Hospital Gazette*, 49/8 (1943), 142-4

——, 'Pacific Letter', *St Mary's Hospital Gazette*, 51/8 (1945), 115

Mockler, E J, 'DDT', *Journal of the Royal Naval Medical Service*, 33 (1947), 17-24

Monsarrat, Nicholas, *The Cruel Sea*, London, Burford Books, 1951

——, *Three Corvettes*, London, Cassell, 2000

Moore, J E, Mahoney, J F, Schwartz, W H, Sternberg, T H, and Wood, W B, 'The Treatment of Early Syphilis with Penicillin: A Preliminary Report of 1,418 cases', *Journal of the American Medical Association*, 126/2 (1944), 67-73

NAAFI Public Relations Branch, *The Story of NAAFI*, London, HMSO, 1944

Newton, Ivor, *At the Piano: Ivor Newton, The World of an Accompanist*, London, Hamish Hamilton, 1966

O'Conor, Rory, *Running a Big Ship: The Classic Guide to Managing a Second World War Battleship*, Oxford and Philadelphia, Casemate, 2017

Palmer, Svetlana and Wallis, Sarah (ed), *A War in Words*, London, Simon and Schuster, 2003

Parry Price, H, 'Service Anaesthetics: the Variation between Service and Civilian Anaesthetics', *Journal of the Royal Naval Medical Service*, 26 (1940), 134-8

Philip, Hugh, *Two Rings and a Red: A Naval Surgeon's Log*, London, International Publishing Company, 1944

Popham, Hugh, *Sea Flight: A Fleet Air Arm Pilot's Story*, London, Kimber, 1954
Rainsford, S G, 'Royal Navy Blood Transfusion Service', *Journal of the Royal Navy Medical Service*, 35 (1949), 155-86
Ranft, B McL (ed), *The Beatty Papers: Selections from the Private and Official Correspondence and Papers of Admiral of the Fleet Earl Beatty*, vol. 1, Aldershot, Navy Records Society, 1989
Ransome Wallis, Ralph, *Two Red Stripes: A Naval Surgeon at War*, London, Ian Allen, 1973
Rees, J R, 'Three Years of Military Psychiatry in the United Kingdom', *British Medical Journal*, 1 (1943), 1-6
Rewcastle, Genevieve, 'Minor Maladies of Wrens', *Journal of the Royal Naval Medical Service*, 28 (1942), 215-18
River, Walter Leslie, *The Malta Story, based on the Diary and Experiences of Flying Officer Howard M. Coffin*, New York, E P Dutton, 1943
Salamon, M H, King, A J, Williams, D I and Nichol, C S, 'Prevention of Jaundice Resulting from Antisyphilitic Treatment', *The Lancet*, 1 (1944), 7-10
Scott Forbes, H, 'Rehabilitation of Neuropsychiatric Cases at a Royal Naval Auxiliary Hospital', *Journal of the Royal Naval Medical Service*, 30 (1944), 206-14
Scrimgeour, Alexander, *Scrimgeour's Small Scribbling Diary 1914-1916: The Truly Astonishing Wartime Diary and Letters of an Edwardian Gentleman, Naval Officer, Boy and Son*, ed Richard Hallam and Mark Beynon, London, Conway, 2008
Scott, Peter, *The Eye of the Wind*, London, Houghton Mifflin, 1961
Shilling, C W, and Kohl, J W, *History of Submarine Medicine*, New London, Connecticut, US Naval Medical Research Laboratory, 1947
Silvester, H G, 'A Provocative Dose', *Journal of the Royal Naval Medical Service*, 27 (1941), 371-4
Simpson, J D, 'The Medicine of Flying', *Journal of the Royal Naval Medical Service*, 27 (1941), 249-58
Sims, A J, 'The Habitability of Naval Ships under Wartime Conditions', *Transactions of the Institute of Naval Architects*, 87 (1945), 50-70
Smith, R H (ed), *Articles and Extracts from the MTE Journal*, Halton, RAF Medical Training Establishment and Depot, 1946
Swaffer, Hannen, *What Would Nelson Do?*, London, Victor Gollancz, 1946
Thomas, Leona J (ed), *Through Ice and Fire: A Russian Arctic Convoy Diary, 1942*, London, Fonthill, 2015
Vickers, H R, 'Royal Naval Hospital, Haslar 1940-44', *Journal of the Royal Naval Medical Service*, 70 (1984), 103-9, 105
Wakeley, Cecil P G, 'War Burns and their Treatment, *Journal of the Royal Naval Medical Service*, 27 (1941), 20-34
Ward, F G, 'Rehabilitation', *Journal of the Royal Naval Medical Service*, 30 (1944), 37-45
Waterman, B B, 'Memories of Malta 1940-42', *Journal of the Royal Naval Medical Service*, 70 (1984), 182-5
Watts, G O and Wilson, R A, 'A Study of Personality Factors among Venereal Disease Patients', *Canadian Medical Association Journal*, 53 (1945), 119-22
Watts, J C, *Surgeon at War*, London, George Allen and Unwin, 1955
Whitby, Lionel, 'Blood Transfusion in the Field: Organisation of Supplies' in H Letherby Tidy and J M Browne Kutschbach (ed), *Inter-Allied Conferences on War Medicine 1942-1945* (1947), pp. 123-6
Whittingham, H E, 'Medical Research and Aviation', *Journal of the Royal Naval Medical Service*, 26 (1941), 15-24
——, 'Aviation Medicine', in R H Smith (ed), *Articles and Extracts from the MTE Journal* (1946), pp. 297-300
Wilkins, R D, 'Convoy Rescue Ships', *Journal of the Royal Naval Medical Service*, 30 (1944), 65-9
Wilson, Charles McMoran (Lord Moran), *Anatomy of Courage*, London, Collins, 1945
——, *Winston Churchill: The Struggle for Survival, 1940-1965*, London, Constable, 1966
Witkower, E D, 'The Psychological Aspects of Venereal Disease', *British Journal of Venereal Diseases*, 24 (1948), 59-67
Young, Edward, *One of Our Submarines*, London, Rupert Hart-Davis, 1952

BIBLIOGRAPHY

Secondary Printed Works
Avery Bennett, F (ed), *The History of the Medical Department of the United States Navy in World War II*, Washington DC, United States Government Printing House, 1953
Bennett, G H and R, *Survivors: British Merchant Seamen in the Second World War*, London, Hambledon Press, 1999
Bennett, J P, 'A History of the Queen Victoria Hospital, East Grinstead', *British Journal of Plastic Surgery*, 41 (1988), 422–40
Birbeck, Eric, Ryder, Ann, and Ward, Philip, *The Royal Hospital Haslar: A Pictorial History*, Chichester, Phillimore, 2009
Blood, Christopher G, Pugh, William M, Gauker, Eleanor D, and Pearsall, Dianna M., 'Comparisons of Wartime and Peacetime Disease and Non-Battle Injury Rates Aboard Ships of the British Royal Navy', *Military Medicine*, 157/12 (1992), 641–4
Bret, David, *George Formby: A Troubled Genius*, London, Robson Books, 1999
Brown, Kevin, *Penicillin Man: Alexander Fleming and the Antibiotic Revolution*, Stroud, Sutton, 2004
——, *The Pox: The Life and Near Death of a Very Social Disease*, Stroud, Sutton, 2006
——, *Fighting Fit: Health, Medicine and War in the Twentieth Century*, Stroud, HistoryPress, 2008
——, *Poxed and Scurvied: Health and Sickness at Sea*, Barnsley, Seaforth, 2011
Campbell, Rob, *Clevedon, Places and Faces*, Leicester, Matador, 2010
Carter, Tim, *Merchant Seamen's Health 1860-1960: Medicine, Technology, Shipowners and the State in Britain*, Woodbridge, Boydell Press, 2014
Clark, Gregory, *Doc: 100 Year History of the Sick Berth Branch*, London, HMSO, 1984
Coghill, R D, 'The Development of Penicillin Strains' in A Elder (ed), *The History of Penicillin Production*, American Institute of Engineers, Chemical Engineering Progress Symposium, 66/100 (1970), 14–15
Coulter, J L S, *The Royal Naval Medical Service: Volume 1, Administration*, London, HMSO, 1954
——, *The Royal Naval Medical Service: Volume 2, Operations*, London, HMSO, 1956
Crozier, V R, *Colleges and Universities in World War II*, Westport, Connecticut, Praeger, 1993
Elder, Albert, (ed), *The History of Penicillin Production*, New York, American Institute of Engineers, Chemical Engineering Progress Symposium, 66/100 (1970)
Ellis, F P, 'Ecological Factors affecting Efficiency and Health in Warships', *British Journal of Industrial Medicine*, 17 (1960), 318–26
————, and Richards, A, 'Health of the Navy in Two World Wars', *Journal of the Royal Naval Medical Service*, 52 (1966), 5–23
Enever, Gary, 'Edgar Pask and his Physiological Research: An Unsung Hero of World War Two', *Journal of the Royal Army Medical Corps*, 157/1 (2011), 8–11
Fletcher, Marjory H, *The WRNS: A History of the Women's Royal Naval Service*, London, Batsford, 1989
Gibson, T M, and Harrison, M H, *Into Thin Air: A History of Aviation Medicine in the RAF*, London, Robert Hale, 1984
Hughes, John Graven, *The Greasepaint War: Show Business 1939-45*, London, New English Library, 1976.
Jones, Edgar, and Greenberg, Neil, 'Royal Naval Psychiatry: Organization, Methods and Outcomes, 1900-1945', *The Mariner's Mirror*, 92 (2006), 190–203
Jones, Wilbur D., *Football! Navy! War!: How Military "Lend-Lease" Players Saved theCollege Game and Helped Win World War II*, Jefferson, North Carolina, McFarland, 2009
Kater, Michael, *Doctors under Hitler*, Chapel Hill, North Carolina, University of North Carolina Press, 1989
Kennett, Lee, *GI: the American Soldier in World War II*, New York, Charles Scribner, 1987
Kevles, Daniel J, 'Testing the Nation's Intelligence: Psychologists in World War I', *Journal of American History*, 55 (1968), 565–81
Lavery, Brian, *Hostilities Only: Training the Wartime Royal Navy*, London National Maritime Museum, 2004
——, *Churchill's Navy: The Ships, Men and Organisation 1939-45*, London, Conway, 2006

—— , *In Which They Served: The Royal Navy Officer Experience in the Second World War*, Annapolis, Naval Institute Press, 2008
Longden, Sean, *To the Victor the Spoils: D-Day to VE Day, the Reality Behind the Heroism*, Moreton in Marsh, Arris Books, 2004
Lovell, Richard, *Churchill's Doctor: A Biography of Lord Moran*, London, Royal Society of Medicine, 1992
Mayhew, E R, *The Reconstruction of Warriors: Archibald McIndoe, the Royal Air Force and the Guinea Pig Club*, London, Greenhill Books, 2004
McKee, Christopher, *Sober Men and True: Sailor Lives in the Royal Navy, 1900–1945*, Cambridge, Massachusetts, Harvard University Press, 2002
McNalty, A S, and Mellor, W F, *Medical Services in War: The Principal Medical Lessons of the Second World War*, London, HMSO, 1968
Mason, Tony, and Riedi, Eliza, *Sport and the Military: The British Armed Forces 1880-1950*, Cambridge, Cambridge University Press, 2010
Mellor, W Franklin (ed), *Casualties and Medical Statistics: History of the Second World War: United Kingdom Medical Services*, London, HMSO, 1972
Mussen, R W, 'The Royal Navy Medical School', *Journal of the Royal Naval Medical Service*, 33 (1947), 61–7
Musgrave, Eric, *Sharp Suits*, London, Pavilion, 2009
Osborne, M, and Smith, J E, 'Action Stations! 100 years of Trauma Care on Maritime and Amphibious Operations in the Royal Navy', *Journal of the Royal Naval Medical Service*, 101 (2015), 7–12
Pearson, Michael, *Red Sky in the Morning: The Battle of the Barents Sea 1942*, Marlborough, Crowood Press, 2002
Prag, Christian, *No Ordinary War: The Eventful Career of U-604*, Barnsley, Seaforth, 2009
Preece, S A, '"Performing Miracles": The Importance of Royal Naval Medical Officers in Operations Overlord and Neptune during World War II', *Journal of the Royal Naval Medical Service*, 96 (2010), 108–16
Prysor, Glynn, *Citizen Sailors: The Royal Navy in the Second World War*, London, Penguin, 2012
Revell, A L, *Haslar the Royal Hospital*, Gosport, Gosport Historical Society, 2000
Richardson, Harriet (ed), *English Hospitals 1660-1948: A Survey of their Architecture and Design*, Swindon, Royal Commission on the Historical Monuments of England, 1998
Rose, Jill, *Nursing Churchill Wartime Life from the Private Letters of Winston Churchill's Nurse*, Stroud, Amberley Publishing, 2018
Sacharski, Susan M, *To Be a Nurse*, Chicago, Northwestern Memorial Hospital, 1990
Taylor, Bruce, *The Battlecruiser HMS Hood: An Illustrated Biography 1916-1941*, Barnsley, Seaforth, 2004
Wade, Frederick J, *The Story of West Stanley*, Annfield Plain, Annfield Plain Family History Society, 2008
Williams, David Innes, *The London Lock: A Charitable Hospital for Venereal Disease 1746–1952*, London, Royal Society of Medicine Press, 1999
Ziegler, Philip, *London at War, 1939–1945*, London, Sinclair-Stevenson, 1995

Index

Aba 237
Achates 25, 167, 199, 204
Achilles 142
Adams, T M 206
Aggie Weston's Sailors' Rests 179–80
Aire 72
Airth, Graham 219–20
alcohol 179
Aldegrove 181
Alderman Wood School, West Stanley 166
Alexander, A V 164
Alexandria 64th General Hospital 56–7
Allen, Chesney 93, 172
Alliance 123
altitude flying 111–14
Alverstoke Emergency Medical Services Hospital 52
Amarapoora 64, 66, 237
Anchusa 166
Andrew 123–4
Antenor 24, 27
antibiotics 98–101, 192–5
Arctic convoys 58, 68, 76–8, 84–5, 137, 141–2, 145, 147, 174
Argonaut 205
Ark Royal 116, 147, 148, 163
Arnold, Richard 193
Arsenal FC 164
Atlantic convoys 69, 72, 84, 134, 141, 159, 210
Atrebin 97
Attenborough, Richard 136
'Avalanche', Operation 217–18

aviation medicine 102–18, 226

Bailey, Second Lieutenant 103
Balfour, Harry 145, 172–3, 184
Barfleur 167
Barle 29
Barnes, John Gray 99
Barrow Gurney Royal Naval Auxiliary Hospital 48–50
Barrow Sailors Home Mission 180–1
battle, organisation for 196–201
Beaton, Thomas 152
Beatty, David 225
Belfast 82, 89–90, 144, 147, 162–3, 201–2, 221
Bell Bottom George 175
Bellona 162, 220
Bennett, Norman 45
Berwick 76, 137, 191–2
Bighi Royal Naval Hospital 55–6
Bingham Arctic Suit 79
Blackcap 106
Blackpool FC 164
Bleeding Beauty Chorus 88
blood transfusion 52, 86–90, 227
Blum, Stoker 122
Bonaventure 139
boxing 6, 120, 156–7, 160, 162, 164
Brierly, Jimmy 171
Bristol 6–7
British Sailors' Society 171

British Soldiers' and Sailors' Institute of Colombo 180
Brittany 82, 162, 217
brothels 184–5
Bunyan, John 91
burns 31–2, 52, 81, 86, 90–4, 115, 151–2, 204, 215, 222, 226, 238
Butler, W M 90
Buttle, G E 87
Byng, Douglas 93

Cadet Nurse Force 43–4
Cairns, Hugh 194
Calcutta 92
Campanula 208
Cap St Jacques 237
Carnation 209
Carter, John 138
Chatham Royal Naval Hospital 40, 41–2, 46–8, 54, 189
Chelsea FC 163
cholera 99, 217
Cholmondley Castle Royal Naval Auxiliary Hospital 49, 148–9
Churchill, Winston 83, 97–8, 112, 138, 147, 194
cinema 174–5
Cleave, H L 60–1
clothing: 26–9, 79–81, 183; civilian 168–9; protective 79, 81, 114–15, 128, 226
Clyde Shipping Company 210
Coghill, Robert 98
Colebrook, Leonard 91
Collingwood 12, 173
concert parties 176

271

Contagious Diseases Acts 184
Contest 167
contraception 188–90
Cork and Orrery, Earl of 158
Cornwall 38
Cossack 209
Coulter, Jack 77, 135, 138–9, 144, 149, 151, 161, 176, 178, 201
courage 136, 138, 165, 199, 213
Courageous 205
Coward, Noel 136
cowardice 136, 139–40
Critchley, MacDonald 71, 75
crossing the line ceremony 178
Cunningham, Andrew 147
Curran, Desmond 148

Dachau Concentration Camp 112–13
Dauntless 175–6
Davies, John 8
Davis Submerged Escape Apparatus (DSEA) 131–3
Day, Frances 93
DDT 97
Dean, Basil 170
Deep Sea Diving School, Washington, DC 121
Defence of the Realm Act (1918) 187
Defence Regulation Act (1943) 187–8
Demetriton 221
Dent, Christopher 38
dentists 44–5
Deutschland 157
Dickens, Gerald Charles 185
Dickison, Arthur 131
diet 82–5, 129
Dinky-Doo 174–5
Directorate of Physical Training and Sports (Admiralty) 159

disease 4–5, 16, 22–3, 32, 35, 49, 74, 77, 85, 96–8, 217, 226, 231–2
distributing stations 151, 177, 196–9
Dolphin 130, 131–2
Donald, James 19
drowning 114, 238
drunkenness 179
Dudley, Sheldon 22, 43, 62, 192, 195, 231
Duke of Argyll 220
Dunedin 140–1
Dunkirk evacuation 31, 90, 137, 214–16
Dunn, Vivian 171
Dunnett, Arthur John 92, 152
Durbin, Deanna 173
Durdham Down Royal Naval Auxiliary Hospital 49
'Dynamo', Operation 214–16
dysentery 35, 66, 74, 217, 224, 232

Eagle, Harry 193
East London Missions to Seamen 180
Eastcott, Felix 228
Eclipse 137
educational standards 7–8
Ehrlich, Paul 189, 193
Elizabeth, queen consort 173–4
Ellis, F P 74
Emerald 72
Empire Clyde 237
Empress of Canada 209
entertainment 169–76
Entertainments National Service Association (ENSA) 169–74
entomologists 45
Erebus 80–1
Eskimo 41
euchre 175
Europa 50, 164
Exeter 137, 163, 197, 203

eyesight 3–5, 16, 103, 105, 114, 130–1

Family Welfare Centres 143
family worries 37, 70, 142–4, 223–4
fatigue 70, 107, 124, 136–55, 214, 230
fear 138–40, 144, 145, 146, 201, 206, 229
Ferryville Sick Quarters, Tunisia 57–8, 182, 185
Fields, Gracie 170, 185
first aid posts 198–9
Fisher Committee 20
Flack, Martin 106
Flack Test 106
Flanagan, Bud 93, 172
Fleet Air Arm 5, 6, 14, 20, 22, 33, 69, 92, 97, 102–18, 147–8, 149, 163, 183, 226, 228
Fleming, Alexander 98
Florey, Howard 98–100, 194
flying hours 108–9
Flying Personnel Research Committee 110–11
football 156–7, 160, 161, 162, 163–4, 165, 174
Football Association 164
Foresight 41
Formby, George 174–5
Franklin, Sister 59–60
French Forces of the Interior 169
funerals 212
Furious 102

Gable, Clark 93
Gallagher, Petty Officer 89
games 175–6
Ganges 183
Gaskell, Arthur 20
George VI, King 97–8, 173
Gerusalemme 237
Gilles, Marcel 169
Gillies, Harold 52, 91–2
Glasgow 83, 84, 191
Glendower 13
Gloucester 207

INDEX

Goldrich, Robert 183
good time girls 186
Graf Spee 163
Green, C A 99–100
Green, Martyn 171
Grenade 208
Grenfell, Joyce 93
Grenville 208
grog 179
Groom, Dale L 199–200
Guinness, Alec 14

habitability 68–77, 123–6, 224–6
Habitability Mission to the Eastern Fleet 74
Haldane, J G 105–6
Hall, I G 191
Hanson, Norman 107
Hare, Doris 170, 171–2
Harries, John 144
Hart, J 152
Hart, Sydney 122–3
Haslar Royal Naval Hospital 40, 41, 46–8, 52–4, 117, 119, 221–2
hearing 5, 130–1
Henley, Frank 33–4, 57–8, 88–9, 182, 185, 191, 205
Henson, Leslie 173
Herriman, Robert 191–2
Hill, John 182
homosexuality 191–2
Hong Kong Royal Naval Hospital 58–61
Hood 29–30, 38, 157, 175–7, 189–90
Hood, Maurice 190, 204
hospital ships 48, 63–6, 237
hospitals: overseas 55–63; UK 40, 41–4, 46–55; US Navy 51–2, 62–3
Hostile 198
Hotspur 197–8
Hughes, Alex 184
Hunt, Bernard 19, 24, 27, 42, 50, 121
Hunter, John 93
Hunter, Surgeon Lieutenant 201, 204, 211

'Husky', Operation 82, 162, 216–7
hysteria 215

Iago, John 29–30
Ibis 212
Icarus 137, 215
Illustrious 56
Implacable 83–4
In Which We Serve 1, 19, 136, 143, 175
Indomitable 29
Institute of Aviation Medicine 111
intelligence testing 11–14
Inverclyde, Lord 171
Ipswich 71
Isle of Jersey 220, 237

Jacklin, Ivan 25, 209
Johnson, Celia 143
Jones, Tristan 183
Juno 206
Jutland, battle of 91, 152, 173, 200

Kandahar 206
Kapok 78–9, 128, 226
Keats, J W 201
Kelly 136
Kent 137
Kilmacolm Royal Naval Auxiliary Hospital, 49, 51
King Alfred 12–14, 147
King George V Fund for Sailors 164
Kingston 138
Kirby, Cecil 38
Kriegsmarine: health of 232; medical research 112–13, 134, 227–8; psychiatry 154–5; recruitment 10–11; submarine medicine 120–2, 123, 127, 128, 133–4

Lamb, Charles 205
Lancashire, Roger 203

Landing Craft Assault (LCA) 220
Landing Craft Personnel 220
Landing Ship Infantry (LSI) 219
Landing Ship Tank (LST) 65, 218–21
Landrail 106
Largs 220–1
Laughton Mathews, Vera 14
laundries 81
Lawton, Frank 1
Laye, Evelyn 1, 170–2, 173
Le Fanu, Michael 76, 85
Leda 137
Leonardo da Vinci 237
Let George Do It 174–5
Lewes 73
libraries 176
Lillie, Beatrice 172
Liverpool Radium Institute 52
London 39, 77, 146, 174, 178
Lynn, Vera 170

MacDonald, Edith 56–7
Macfarlane, James 25, 199
MacIver, Surgeon Lieutenant 221
Macnab, R C G 84–5
MacPhail, Dugald Stewart 34–5, 37
Mahoney, John 192–4
Mahratta 36, 209–10
mail 37, 70, 144
Maine 55, 63–5, 237
malaria 95–8, 227, 232
Malaya 91
Mallalieu, J P W 82
Manchester 169
Maori 167
Markham, Henry 9–10
Maristow Royal Naval Convalescent Home 50–1, 55
Martin 39, 177, 202, 212
Mary, Queen Dowager 174
Mason, Marine 191
mass radiography 94–5, 227

273

masturbation 191
Maund, Captain 163
McAra, Charles 105
McCormack, John 172
McIndoe, Archibald 52, 92–3, 152
McNalty, Arthur 182
McRae, Peter 24–5, 36–9, 161, 209–10
Meagher, Surgeon Captain 152
medical inspections 2–3, 14–16
medical officer: role in recreation and sport 161–2; Fleet Air Arm 116–18; increasing specialisation 25, 28, 34, 116–18, 148, 226, 228–7; non-medical duties 36–7; paperwork 30–1; recruitment of 19–24; resentment of RNVR officers at lack of differentiation from conscripts 28; medical officers, routine medical duties 31–3; shortage of 20–2; tedium of life at sea 19, 36; training 25; uniform 26–9; women 17–18
medical standards for naval service 4–5, 16–17, 103, 105, 114, 130, 131
Mepacrine 97–8
Merchant Navy 11–12, 27, 58, 65, 78, 153–4, 170–1, 180–1, 210–11
Merseyside Blood Transfusion Services 52
messing 82–5, 129, 225
Miaoules 35
Middleton 145
Mihailović, Dragoljub 35
Miles, Doris 224
Miles, Roger 39, 143–4, 177, 223, 224
Mills, John 136
missions for seamen 179–80

Mobile Naval Base Defence Organization (MBDO) 34
Mollison, Clifford 171
Monsarrat, Nicholas 141, 206, 208
Mooney, Surgeon Lieutenant 232
morale: entertainment and 169–76, 181; Fleet Air Arm 147–8; for fighting in Far East 223–4; mail and 37, 70, 144; sport and 158–9, 162–3, 181; submarines 129–30, 133; tradition and 177–9; maintenance 155; mental health and 136–55, 230–1; pets and 177; royal visits and 173–4
Moran, Lord *see* Wilson, Charles McMoran
Mountbatten, Lord Louis 136
Mumby, Ann 89
Musketeer 177

Narvik, battle of 41, 197
National Sailors' Society 210
National Savings Campaign 166
National Service Act (1939) 1–2
Naval Medical Research Institute at Bethesda, Maryland 134
Naval Rugby Club 155
Navy League 170
Navy, Army and Air Force Institute (NAAFI) 85, 170, 173, 180
Neale, Jack 79
Negro 149
Neil Robertson stretcher 33, 42, 198, 199, 202, 207, 215
'Neptune', Operation 218–22
Newton Abbot Royal Naval Auxiliary Hospital 48, 55

Nicholls, Percival 22–3
Nizam 166
Northern Gem 204
nursing 38–44, 56–7, 65–6, 174

Oakley House, Chatham 51
Obdurate 204
O'Conor, Rory 157–8, 160
Ophir 66, 237
overcrowding 68–9, 71–2, 81–2, 224–5
'Overlord', Operation 65, 89, 218–22
Overseas League 85
Oxford Military Hospital for Head Injuries 52
Oxfordshire 64, 66, 237

P.44 see United
Palomares 199, 202
Paris 218
Park Prewett Emergency Medical Services Hospital 52, 151
Parry, Edward 142
Pask, Edgar 113
Paul, Vaughn 173
Pearson, Marine 137
penicillin 98–101, 192–5, 227
Peter II, King of Yugoslavia 174
pets 177
Philip, Hugh 3, 16, 27, 28, 119, 121, 161, 173–4, 178, 183, 185, 190, 203
physical training 6–7, 155–6, 160, 162–3
'Piccadilly Warriors' 185–6
plastic surgery 52, 91–4, 152, 226
Plymouth Royal Naval Hospital 22, 40, 41–2, 47–8, 50, 53–5
political discussion 176
Poppy 183
Portland Royal Naval Hospital 222
Priestly, J S 105
Prince of Wales 29, 206

INDEX

prostitution 184–6
psychiatric problems 136–7, 163, 215, 230–1
psychiatry: 4, 131–4, 139–40, 148–5, 163, 230–1; airmen 110; army 153
psychology 8–13, 25, 49, 69, 93, 102, 107, 116, 131, 145, 148–9, 152–4, 230–1
Public Morality Council 186

Quality 223
Queen Alexandra's Royal Naval Nursing Service 41–4, 56–7, 65–6, 174
Queen Victoria Hospital, East Grinstead 52, 92–3, 151–2
quinine 97

Ramillies 71
Ransome Wallis, Patrick 5
Ransome Wallis, Ralph 10–11, 23, 27, 28, 34, 39, 77, 146, 174, 178, 202–3, 212
Rascher, Sigmund 112
Rathlin 211
reading 176
recreation 155–78, 181
recruitment: 1–18, 229–30; dental standards 4–5, 16–17; Fleet Air Arm 103–5; rehabilitation of the unfit 6; visual standards 3–5, 16, 103, 105, 114, 130–1
Red Cross 210, 224
rehabilitation 149–52
religion 177
Renown 83, 205
repatriation of prisoners of war and civilian internees in Far East 65–6, 224
Repulse 143, 163
rescue ships 137, 206, 210–11
Research Institute for U-boat Medicine 134

Resolution 199
Rewcastle, Attracta Genevieve 17–18
River Plate, battle of the 90, 142, 197, 201, 203–4, 212
Robinson Committee on Visual Standards 3
Rockingham 72
Rogers, A T H 143
Roosevelt, Franklin D 185
Roxburgh, John 126–7
Royal Air Force Medical Service 103, 107, 115–16
Royal Army Medical Corps 23, 49, 56, 58, 60, 86–7, 214, 215, 217, 218
Royal Marine Commandos 34
Royal Marines Band 171, 175
Royal Marines Naval Base Defence Organization (RMNBDO) 34
Royal Naval Air Medical School 118
Royal Naval Air Station Eastleigh 118
Royal Naval Auxiliary Hospital La Maddalena, Sardinia 121
Royal Naval Blood Transfusion Service 89, 227
Royal Naval Dental Service 44–5
Royal Naval Engineering College, Heysham 164
Royal Naval Medical Branch 19–20
Royal Naval Personnel Research Committee 69, 134
Royal Navy Football League 155
Royal Navy Medical School 98–101, 227
Royal Navy Physical Training Branch 156
Royal Navy War Amenities Fund 85

Royal Victoria Military Hospital, Netley 51
rugby 24, 37, 156, 161–2, 164
Russian Navy Club, Polyarnoe 174

salvarsan 189
Scharnhorst 147
Scotsman 90
Scott, Peter 14
Scott, Walter 169
Scott, Walter McC 209
Scott, William 147
Scrimgeour, Alexander 168
Scylla 76–7, 79, 84, 144, 149, 151, 176, 212
Seaforth Royal Naval Auxiliary Hospital 50
Sebbage, R 57
sex 182–7
Shelton, Anne 170
Sherborne Royal Naval Auxiliary Hospital 49
Shipmates Ashore 171
Shipwrecked Mariner's Society 181
sick berth 29–30
sick berth attendants 38–42
sick quarters 57–8
Simpson, J D 104
Simpson, Roger 166
Singer, Hugh 207–8
sinkings 140–1, 205–12
skin diseases 4–5, 74, 77, 231
Smith, Henry 149
Smith, Wilfred 80–1
Somers, John 3, 175–6
Sparrowhawk 106
Special Operations Executive 34–5
Speedwell 79
Spiess, Johannes 123
Spitfire Fund 170
sport: 6–7, 109, 155–65, 181; community solidarity 163–4, 181; facilities 163
St Mary's Hospital Boxing Club 164

275

St Mary's Hospital Rugby Football Club 164
St Vincent 104, 117
Standard 149–51
Stanmore, William 41
Stannard, William 91
Storm 125, 130
Stott, K 72
stress 136–55
Submarine Base, New London, Connecticut 121, 134
submarine medicine 119–35, 226
Surf 133
surgery 201–4
swimming 6, 157, 158, 162, 205–6

Tijitjalengka 66, 237
tombola 175
Topham, L G 117
Tottenham Hotspur FC 163
Tracker 84
tradition 177–9
Triad 123
Trinder, Tommy 93
Trinidad 166
tropical diseases 25, 66, 224, 231–2
tuberculosis 42, 49, 66, 94–5, 224, 227, 232, 238
Tunney, James J 165

U-9 123
U-230 122
U-604 120–1
Uckers 175–6
Udine 121
Ulster Queen 77
Umpire 132–3

uniform 80–1, 26–9, 167–8, 183
United 126–7
United States Marine Hospital, Staten Island 192–4
United States Naval Station Pensacola 117
United States Navy: hospitals 51–2, 62–3; lessons for Royal Navy 75–6, 85, 225; models for ship design 75–6, 83–4, 85; psychiatry 154; recruitment 11; sport 165; submarine medicine 119–22, 125, 127, 129, 134
United States Submarine *N* 125
United States Submarine *P* 127
Ursula Suit 128

Vaenga Auxiliary Hospital 58, 78, 174
Valiant 140
Vasna 64, 66, 237
venereal disease 183–95
ventilation 70–5, 124–5
vermin 82
Vernon, P E 13
Vickarage, W 91–2
Vita 237
Voluntary Aid Detachment (VAD) 43, 61

Wallflower 30–1
Ward, V J 99
Warship Week 166–7, 181
Warspite 200

Watson, A C 140–1
Watts, J C 87
We Dive at Dawn 1, 133
welfare 142–4, 179–81
Went the Day Well? 1
Weston, Agnes 179–80
Weston, T 164–5
Whelan, Gordon 171
Whitby, Lionel 87
Whittingham, Harold E 107, 115
Whitwell, Francis 31
Wilkinson, Edward Darrell Sheldon 34–5
Willson, Suzanne 174
Wilson, Charles McMoran 18, 83, 97–8, 138, 147
Wilson, John 147
Wings for Victory 166
Women's Voluntary Service 210
Wood, Arthur 205
Worcester 31, 82–3
Worthing 218
wounds 33, 66, 78, 93, 194, 199, 203–5, 215, 216, 222
Wraxham Court Convalescent Home for Officers 51
WRNS (Wrens) 9–10, 14–18

Yarmouth Royal Naval Auxiliary Hospital 46, 48, 149
Young, Edward 132–1

Zaafaran 137, 206, 211
Zamelek 206
Zinnia 208